THE STRONG BROWN GOD

The Strong Brown God

THE STORY OF THE NIGER RIVER

Sanche de Gramont

Illustrated with
Maps and Photographs

HOUGHTON MIFFLIN COMPANY BOSTON

For information about permission to
reproduce selections from this book, write to
Permissions, Houghton Mifflin Company,
2 Park Street, Boston, Massachusetts 02108.

Library of Congress Cataloging
in Publication Data
Gramont, Sanche de
The strong brown God.
1.   Niger Valley—Discovery and exploration.
I.   Title.
DT360.G67   1976   916.6′2   75-33298
ISBN 0-395-19782-1
ISBN 0-395-56756-4 (pbk.)

Printed in the United States of America

AGM 10 9 8 7 6 5 4 3 2 1

For Amber, who was born in Africa

I do not know much about gods; but I think that the river
Is a strong brown god – sullen, untamed and intractable,
Patient to some degree, at first recognized as a frontier;
Useful, untrustworthy as a conveyor of commerce;
Then only a problem confronting the builder of bridges.
The problem once solved, the brown god is almost forgotten
By the dwellers in the cities – ever, however, implacable,
Keeping his seasons and rages, destroyer, reminder
Of what men choose to forget.

T S Eliot, *Four Quartets*

CONTENTS

LIST OF ILLUSTRATIONS

following page 176

Chief Kofe
Portuguese on the West African Coast
Niamey
Sixteenth-century map
Confluence of Niger and Chadda
Sir Joseph Banks, KB
Mungo Park
Fishermen
The Niger delta
Catalan Atlas
Prince Henry the Navigator
Ferry near Farie
Mungo Park memorial
Djenne
Portuguese map of 1468
Frederick Lugard
John Hawley Glover
Richard Lander
Sir John Barrow
Captain Hugh Clapperton
Dixon Denham
Heinrich Barth
Gordon Laing
William Balfour Baikie
Sir George Goldie
Louis Archinard
Slave-traders
Slave ship plan
Mungo Park's death
Saharan sandstorm
El Kenemy

LIST OF ILLUSTRATIONS

Farie, Niger
Timbuctu, Mali
The Tripoli Route
A King of Ibo
Riverside architecture
Lancer of Sultan of Begharmi
René Caillié
Caillié's drawing of Timbuctu
Pears' Soap poster
The *Quorra*
A slave caravan
James Richardson
Obie war canoes
Samuel Crowther
Kano, Northern Nigeria
Dr Cheetham
The *Henry Venn I*
Three iron paddle-steamers
Sampling palm-oil
David McIntosh
Port Harcourt
A King of Benin
A tribal chief
Chief Bob's canoe
Young Briggs
Will Braide
Hunting giraffes
West African slaves
United Africa Company bus
The *Pleiad*
Trophies
A medicine case

LIST OF MAPS

AUTHOR'S PREFACE

THIS book came about in a rather haphazard way. I was living in Morocco in 1972, and decided to visit Africa south of the Sahara, since I was on the right continent and the chance might not come again. My plan was simple – I would fly to Abidjan, the capital of the Ivory Coast, and make my way back to Morocco overland. Friends in Abidjan suggested that when I reached Mali I should travel part of the way on a river boat that connected the two principal ports of the Niger bend – Mopti and Gao. From Gao, I could cross the Sahara on one of the many trucks that carry sheep to Algeria and bring back dates. I was lucky enough to arrive in Mopti on the eve of the river boat's departure – it was an ancient paddlewheeler which in the days of the French had been named for a colonial hero, Colonel Archinard, but had been rechristened *Liberté* after Mali had won its independence. The trip lasted five days, with the *Liberté* stopping at half a dozen villages each day, and when it docked at Gao I felt that a privileged episode of my life was over. I had gone from amazement to amazement, and would forget neither the landscape, unchanged since the first white man had appeared on the river, nor the people, whose lives were fused with their surroundings. I admired their vibrant appreciation of simple things, a sunset, or a fish caught without bait, or a man telling a story.

I decided, partly to give myself a reason for going back, and partly following George Bernard Shaw's advice that the best way to learn about a subject is to write a book about it, to become the Niger's story-teller. I would describe the river I had seen, and tell the story of its discovery. As African rivers go, the Nile had grabbed most of the attention, while the Niger was neglected, relatively unsung, a shadowy lady with a gift for keeping secrets. The Niger's story was in a sense more fascinating than the Nile's – the Niger curled like a question-mark through West Africa, its course and termination remaining a riddle for centuries. On early maps, it evaporated into the Sahara, or drained into Lake Tchad, or emptied into the Atlantic. When Mungo Park stood on the Niger's banks in 1795, he made a major geographical discovery merely by ascertaining that the river flowed from west to east. It took twenty more years before the Niger's termination in the Gulf of Guinea became known.

The adventures of the Niger explorers, groping their way across Africa for an unmapped river, are comparatively little-known: Park, blinded by self-confidence after his initial discovery, drowning in the river during his second expedition; Lander, captured by pirates and forced to drink poison, and knowing when he saw sea-gulls from his river dug-out that he had found the termination; Clapperton and Oudney, whose failed expedition was envenomed by personal animosity and accusations of homosexuality; Gordon Laing, the romantic young officer who was murdered near Timbuctu; Barth, the great scholar-explorer, who cut open his veins and drank his own blood to keep from dying of thirst in the desert – these men, nearly all of whom died following the river's ruthless indirection, deserve their share of fame.

Once the river was discovered, it became, for England, the highway into Africa – and Empire. British traders settled the delta and the river's lower third, buying, first slaves, then palm oil. In the north, the French extended their hold over the upper Niger. The two greatest colonial powers of the nineteenth century met on the Niger, and eventually divided it. Thus the explorers, who had acted out of personal ambition and an obsession to be first, served as the scouts of Empire.

In October 1972, I bought a Land-Rover and started south from Tangier. I wanted to reach the Niger after the rainy season, but while it was still navigable. I crossed the the Sahara, as those early explorers who had taken the Tripoli route had done – but I had two considerable advantages: I knew where the Niger was, and I had my wife Nancy along. I took a banana-boat into

Guinea and saw the Niger's source, on the border of Sierra Leone. I proceeded down the river's 2600-mile course, by car, boat, dugout, train, truck, and camel. Road maps were hopeless. Sometimes we would follow a path for several days to reach a ferry service that crossed the river, only to find that no such service existed. At one point, I became so enraged that I tried to drive into the river, but my wife jumped in front of the car and stopped me. When we reached the delta, and saw the gulls flying over the mangrove forests, I felt the same intense relief that Richard Lander must have felt, and I knew why finding the place where the river ends had been worth the losses.

Sanche de Gramont

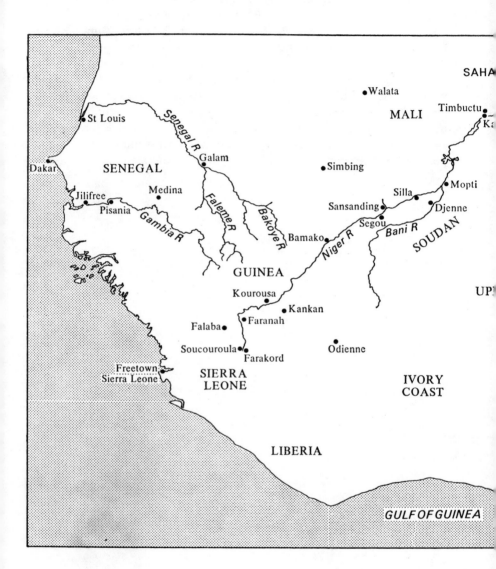

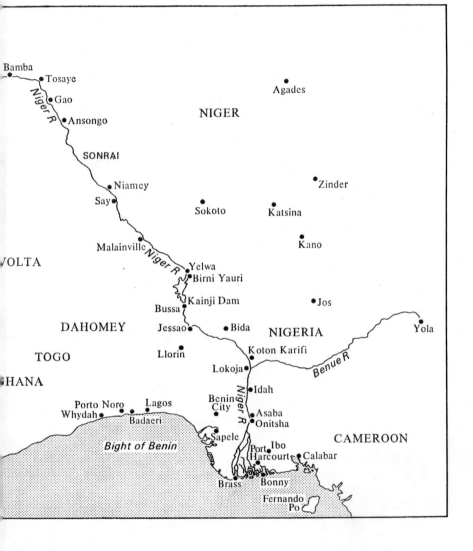

One

THE NIGER SOUGHT

On 9 June 1788 nine of the twelve members of an informal eating club, which gathered on Saturday evenings at St Albans Tavern in the Pall Mall section of London, voted on and passed the following resolution:

> That, as no species of information is more ardently desired, or more generally useful, than that which improves the science of Geography; and as the vast Continent of Africa, notwithstanding the efforts of the Ancients, and the wishes of the Moderns, is still in a great measure unexplored, the Members of this Club do form themselves into an Association for Promoting the Discovery of the Inland Parts of that Quarter of the world.

Each member subscribed five guineas a year for three years, which they could easily afford, since they were all wealthy men. A committee of five was elected to choose explorers who would be sent into the African interior. The committee promised not to disclose, except to members, 'such intelligence as they shall, from time to time, receive from the persons who shall be sent out on the business of discovery'.

The changing of the Saturday's Club into the African Association went unnoticed at the time. It was a modest event submerged in the tide of history, and later rescued from oblivion. For these twelve men, this collection of lords, members of Parliament, and landed gentry, these wealthy dilettantes, accomplished what governments and scholars could not: they solved the riddle of the Niger river. They were responsible for

17

what was perhaps the greatest epic of African exploration, in which more than thirty explorers were sent to their deaths in their search for a river no one could find.

Their enterprise was disassociated from gain or conquest. They were moved by nothing stronger than simple curiosity, except that curiosity is never simple. At the close of the eighteenth century, the Age of Enlightenment had produced a social type, the gentleman dabbler, who made curiosity his avocation. He collected insects, or grew orchids, or wondered at the blanks in the map of Africa and resolved to fill them.

Who were these twelve distinguished men, and what led them, after dining in the cloistered elegance of a private room in a London tavern, to turn their thoughts towards Africa? The prime mover was Sir Joseph Banks, heir to a large fortune and an equally large Lincolnshire estate, who was fascinated by botany and started an herbarium that became world-famous. In 1768 Banks joined Captain Cook's first expedition, and spent three years collecting plants on the coasts of Brazil, Australia, Tahiti, and New Zealand. Returning to England at the age of thirty-five, in 1778, he was elected president of the Royal Society. It was a post of great distinction – Sir Christopher Wren and Sir Isaac Newton were among his predecessors – and he kept it for forty-two years. Banks became an armchair explorer. He concentrated on the last great unknown. Africa.

Then there was Henry Beaufoy, the son of a wine merchant and a Quaker, who had joined the Society for the Abolition of Slaves in 1787. Beaufoy was credited with first proposing the plan for an African Association, and became its secretary. Another member of the Saturday's Club who was an active abolitionist was the Bishop of Llandaff. The other men were an Irish peer, the son of another Irish peer, a retired general, and six Scotsmen: three large landowners, the richest commoner in England, a lawyer, and a doctor. Six of the twelve were members of the Royal Society, which brought them into contact with Banks, and eight were members of either the House of Lords or the House of Commons. Several had written essays, and one had invented a furnace for brewers. They were men who shared a way of life founded on land and wealth, with a vision of life based on progress and the practical application of their century's scientific and geographical knowledge.

It was natural for a group seeking an outlet for its curiosity to fasten on Africa, the last unexplored continent, and the closest to Europe. Another reason was the renewed interest in Africa as a result of the abolition movement, which had gathered momentum after Lord Chief Justice Mansfield ruled in 1772 that any slave who set foot in England was automatically free. The Saturday's Club was divided over the issue. Beaufoy and the Bishop of Llandaff were abolitionists, but several members voted against abolition in Parliament, and Banks himself was not opposed to slavery, arguing that there was nothing against it in the Bible and that freed Negroes did not seem able to find useful occupations.

The members of the Saturday's Club may also have reasoned that England, having lost its American colonies, needed new sources of raw materials and new markets for its manufactured products. Unknown Africa could be seen as a timely substitute. To men of great means and a practical bent, the exploration of that *terra incognita* must have seemed a worthwhile goal. The government under thrifty Mr Pitt showed no interest in supporting expeditions, whereas the sponsorship of explorers by private groups was in keeping with the spirit of the times. In choosing the study of Africa as their hobby, these twelve establishment Englishmen were sowing the first seeds of England's land empire there. Upper-class dilettantes rushed in where governments feared to tread.

To spread the expense, the African Association sensibly decided to enlarge its membership. By 1791, there were ninety-five dues-paying members. It continued to be a resolutely élitist club, and included three dukes, twelve earls, seven other lords, two generals, and two titled ladies. In its forty-three years of existence, the African Association was to have a total of 212 members, but the years that counted were from its founding in 1788 until 1805. Thereafter, its activity and membership declined, and it was finally absorbed by the Royal Geographical Society.

The African Association did not dawdle. An explorer was on his way within a month of the memorable 9 June dinner. These early volunteers were sent out untrained and unprepared, with instructions that were impossible to follow, to lands about which the little that was known was usually inaccurate. They were like point men in a patrol, expendable, the necessary casualties of a great enterprise. They strolled defenceless into the unknown, with their paltry offerings of beads and trinkets making up for the maps and information they did not have. They were at first not even paid salaries, and went only for the fame success would bring. The venture's guiding principle was enthusiasm fed by ignorance, for if the sponsors and the explorers had known more about the conditions of travel in West Africa there might never have been a single expedition. At their best, the members of the African Association could be seen as noble, disinterested men who acted only from the highest motives. At their worst, they were a group of rich amateurs who hired men to take suicidal risks while they sat in frock-coats in their book-lined panelled dens over a glass of old port studying maps of Africa, like generals plotting strategy from behind the front lines.

The first explorer whom the African Association dispatched was John Ledyard, a thirty-seven-year-old Connecticut-born roustabout. The son of a sea captain, Ledyard had as a boy run away from home to live with Indians in the north-west. Later, he accompanied Captain Cook as a corporal of marines on his last expedition and saw Cook killed in Hawaii.

Ledyard was a romantic, unencumbered by scholarship or scientific training, whose single passion was to be always on the move. In 1786 he had the idea of crossing Europe and Russia to reach America, and Banks advanced him a small sum. The trip was a series of mishaps. His equipment and most of his money were seized at English customs, but he left anyway, with two guineas in his pocket. From Sweden he tried to cross the frozen Gulf of Bothnia on foot, but the ice was not solid. He reached St Petersburg in a desperate condition and was saved by the Portuguese ambassador, who loaned him £20. He travelled six thousand miles to Yakutz in Siberia, but was prevented by bad weather from crossing the straits. At this point he was seized by Russian soldiers, who put him on a sled to the Polish border and told him that if he returned to Russia he would be hanged. Now, two years later, he was knocking on Banks's door in Soho Square, in rags, exhausted and penniless, but ready to set out again. According to the Association proceedings, Banks 'told him, knowing his temper, that he could recommend him for an adventure almost as perilous as the one from which he had returned'.

Banks proposed Ledyard to the selection committee, who felt that his lack of education and inability to speak Arabic were balanced by his adventurous nature. They chose a man who 'from his youth had felt an invincible desire to make himself acquainted with the unknown, or imperfectly discovered regions of the globe'.

Ledyard went to see Beaufoy, who was struck by 'the manliness of his person, the breadth of his chest, the openness of his countenance, and the inquietude of his eye'. Beaufoy unrolled a map of Africa and drew a line from Cairo eastward, explaining that this was the route he should follow. He asked Ledyard when he would be ready to leave. 'Tomorrow morning,' Ledyard said. Beaufoy, surprised by such eagerness, said he did not think his instructions could be prepared in such a short time.

Ledyard's instructions were preposterous. He was to go from Cairo to Mecca, where Christians were in mortal danger, 'and from thence (unless insuperable difficulties shall occur), he shall cross the Red Sea, and taking the route of Nubia shall traverse the Continent of Africa as nearly as possible in the direction of the Niger'.

While Ledyard was crossing Africa from east to west, the African Association had recruited a second explorer who would cross it from north to south. This was Simon Lucas, whom Henry Beaufoy may have known, because he too was the son of a wine merchant. Lucas, sent to Cadiz as a youth to learn the Jerez trade, was captured by pirates and sold as a slave to the Moroccan court. He was released three years later, and was named vice-consul in the land where he had been a slave. Returning to London sixteen years later, he was appointed oriental interpreter at the Court of St James, and came to the African Association's attention. An undated note in Beaufoy's handwriting says: 'Mr Lucas, Oriental interpreter, whose salary is 80 pounds per annum, offers to proceed, by way of Gibraltar and Tripoli to Fezzan, provided his salary is continued during his absence.' Banks used his influence to have Lucas detached from his duties. He seemed a choice recruit. Not only did he speak Arabic, but at court he had become friendly with the Foreign Minister of Tripoli.

The Lucas and Ledyard expeditions were financed by an interest-free loan of £453 raised among the members. Each explorer received an advance of £100, with the possibility of drawing further sums once in the interior. The selection committee made a virtue of its stinginess, 'persuaded that in such an undertaking poverty is a better protection than wealth'. They thought that a man carrying little money was less likely to be robbed. It certainly cannot have been the prospect of financial gain that drew John Ledyard and Simon Lucas to African exploration – two more dissimilar men would in any case have been hard to find – but the failures of their missions can be seen as growing out of their different temperaments: one failed from over-impulsiveness, the other from over-caution.

Ledyard left England on 30 June and arrived in Cairo on 19 August. He found lodgings in a convent maintained by the order of Recollets. He wrote to his sponsors that Cairo in August was hot, but that he had seen it hotter in Philadelphia. Ledyard prepared his inland journey and toured the Egyptian capital, visiting the slave markets and meeting a minister of the Bey. He was all the more eager to start when he found that Christians in Cairo were insulted and molested in the street.

Ledyard communicated his impressions regularly to Beaufoy. Suddenly his letters stopped, and great was the disappointment in London when some time later news arrived from Egypt announcing the death of the Association's first explorer.

> A bilious complaint [Beaufoy wrote in the proceedings], the consequence of vexatious delays in the promised departure of the caravan, had induced him to try the effect of too powerful a dose of the acid of vitriol; and the sudden uneasiness and burning pain which followed the uncautious draught, impelled him to seek the relief of the strongest Tartar emetic. A continued discharge of blood discovered the danger of his situation . . . he was decently interred in the neighbourhood of such of the English as had ended their days in the capital of Egypt.

While Ledyard was dying in Cairo, Simon Lucas was in Tripoli looking for an escort to take him across the Libyan desert. Lucas had left England in August 1788 and reached Tripoli in mid-October. When he told the bashaw (pasha) of Tripoli, Ali Karamanli, that he wanted to visit the Fezzan, the suspicious bashaw remarked that no Christian had ever attempted such a trip. Lucas replied that his only interest was to collect plants and Roman antiquities. The bashaw told him, as he was to tell other explorers taking the Tripoli route, that personally he would be glad to help, but the moment was not well chosen, because the tribes in the south were in revolt. Lucas, looking elsewhere for help, found two sherifs from the Fezzan who offered to escort him and left with them in February 1789. He wore Turkish dress and had let his hair grow so long that, as he wrote to his sponsors, he looked 'like a London Jew in deep mourning'. Carrying presents for the King of Fezzan, including brandy, which the monarch was known to like, Lucas travelled east along the coast, past the ruins of Leptis Magna, to the seaside city of Misurata, and was about to turn inland when the governor warned him that warring tribes would bar his way. With the prudence of the civil servant he was, Lucas decided to wait until the tribes calmed down. The two Fezzan sherifs grew impatient and left him, but not before he had obtained considerable information concerning the geography of southern Lybia. Left alone, Lucas decided to return to England. On 30 June 1789 he wrote to Banks that he had arrived penniless in Marseilles and drawn a bill on his name. He apologized for not pursuing his route, and added that his journey had produced valuable information and that he was bringing back a collection of seeds. He must have known that he was destined for better things than perishing in the Fezzan, and in 1793 he was named consul to Tripoli, where he died a natural death eight years later.

The failure of its first two missions and the death of its first explorers acted as a spur rather than a deterrent to the African Association. They immediately began to look for new recruits. In all their talk of Africa, it was on the Niger that the Association's interest focused. The Niger, more than anything else, embodied the unattainable. As Beaufoy wrote, its discovery was 'made doubly interesting by the consideration of its having engaged the attention, and baffled the researches, of the most inquisitive and most powerful nations of antiquity'.

Here was the challenge: that one of the world's great rivers could have kept the secret of its course and termination for more than two thousand years. A river does not hide, it moves along its bed openly, making no secret of the direction of its current, its beginning and its end. And yet the Niger remained, among the works of nature, the mysterious object of conflicting theories, like the pyramids among the works of man. Did it flow east or west? Was it merely a branch of another major African river, the Congo or the Nile? Did it empty into the Atlantic, into a salt lake in the heart of Africa, or into the Mediterranean, after crossing the Sahara desert underground? Over the centuries historians like Herodotus and geographers like Ptolemy had puzzled over the Niger in vain. It remained for a group of English clubmen to succeed where they had failed.

The Niger was a jewel protected by multiple safety devices: the lethal climate, the physical barriers of the Sahara and the rain forest, and the human barriers of Christian-hating Moslems and rapacious blacks. But its best protection was its own shape. It did not seem possible that the 2600-mile-long Niger, the tenth longest river in the world, originating in granite hills only 150 miles from the Atlantic, was the same river that divided into hundreds of creeks in a mangrove delta 1500 miles to the east and spilled into the great continental indentation known as the Gulf of Guinea.

There seemed to be no reasonable connection between its source and its mouth, no explanation for its abrupt change of direction. For the boomerang-shaped Niger first flows north, away from the sea, gathering strength from its affluents as it prepares to meet the desert. Then, after advancing three hundred miles from west to east along the Sahara's southern fringe, it is deflected due south, from the desert to the semi-tropical Nigerian rain forest, and empties into the sea at the underside of Africa's great hump. The Niger is a geological freak, moving backwards, away from the sea. It does not behave the way rivers are meant to.

On the other side of Africa, the search for the headwaters of the Nile had caught the public fancy. The Nile, cradle of a glittering civilization, and its larger-than-life explorers, David Livingstone and Richard Burton, stole the scene from the Niger, which posed the equally fascinating but opposite problem: its source was known, but no one could locate its mouth. Dozens of books were written expounding this or that theory, like mystery stories in which the detective is led astray by decoys. The true detectives were the explorers, who followed the only real clue, the river itself. But the Niger, like the custodian of an ancient curse, claimed the lives of those who tried to find it.

THE NIGER SOUGHT

Why risk human life merely to add to geographical knowledge? It was implicit in the process of discovery that explorers would be followed by traders, missionaries, and settlers. Without the Niger as a highway of empire, the West African interior would have remained unknown. The explorers initiated the chain of events that led to the scramble for Africa.

But to see the explorers as nothing but the involuntary agents of imperialism is to belittle the men who found the Niger, for the explorer belongs to the same breed as the builder of Gothic arches: he is out to conquer nature.

Some of the men who sponsored explorers were clearly after practical advantages: opening up new trade routes, finding gold, increasing national power. Call it greed: as a Portuguese navigator put it, 'we suffer from a disease that only gold can cure'. Others were guided by a militant faith. Behind every explorer there was a missionary. God puffed the navigator's sails. Call it zeal: Irish monks, sailing in skin-covered boats called curraghs, discovered Iceland in the eighth century. Or again, like the African Association, others wanted only to extend the frontiers of human knowledge. Call it enlightenment: In the eighteenth century, navigators for the first time were asked to bring back species of marine life and coastal charts instead of gold and spices.

But for the men who were sent into Africa, the urge to explore was self-redeeming. It required no gold mines or converted natives. It had to do with a passion for fame, an aching need to be remembered in the written records of their time, to last longer than their mortal existence. It had to do with Western man the knowledge-seeker and world-eater, with the marriage of scholarship and experience: 'Tell us what is new,' the map-makers asked the sea captains. It had to do with a race of men willing to risk their lives for a point of geographical information, who defined themselves by challenging nature, for every voyage of discovery was a voyage of self-discovery. And finally, it had to do with the greatest of human dreams, to behold a land in its newness, to see it as Adam saw Eden, unspoiled, fruitful, as yet unnamed, and to find at last something commensurate with man's capacity for wonder.

Two

THE NIGER DESCRIBED

Fo r the ancient Greeks, rivers were divine, heaven-sent, the sons of oceans and the fathers of nymphs. Live bulls and horses were drowned in their waters to appease 'he river god. They could only be crossed by men who respected the rites of puri- fication and prayer. Hesiod wrote: 'Whoever crosses a river without purifying his hands of the evil that soils them invites the gods' anger, and their terrible punishment.' This warning could have applied to the European explorers who were to perish search- ing for the Niger.

The Niger is the cradle of West Africa. It is a moving path into the heart of the continent, a long, liquid magic wand, that makes fertile the soil it touches. Cattle drink its water and graze on its green banks. Its fish and game birds provide food. Its trees give wood for dugouts. The river means an end to hunger, thirst, and isolation.

Like other fertilizing powers, the river is capricious. It can provide but it can also withhold. It can irrigate, but it can also flood. It can carry a boat or capsize it. It can be used as a route for peaceful trade or for conquest and colonial expansion. The medieval empires of West Africa were founded by raiding river cities, and in the nineteenth century French and English gunboats steamed up the Niger and claimed it. Soni Ali, the mighty ruler of the fifteenth-century Songhai empire, drowned in 1492 while crossing the Niger on a raid, just as the explorers who served as scouts for Europe's colonial empires were later to perish, drowned like Mungo Park, murdered like Gordon Laing, or killed by dysentery like Hugh Clapperton.

The key to the Niger's strange shape is to be found in the struggle between river and desert. For the Niger is a geological accident, a joining of two distinct rivers which originally flowed in opposite directions. Before the Sahara dried up, between 4000 and 400 B C, it was a fertile, populated region, irrigated by rivers and teeming with wild-life. The upper Niger, which natives call the Joliba, originating in hills near the Atlantic, flowed north, 450 miles past Timbuctu, and emptied in the salt lake of Juf near the Taodenni salt mines. The lower Niger, which natives call the Quorra, flowed south into the Gulf of Guinea, and rose in the now desolate Saharan mountains of Ahaggar. The drying up of the Sahara caused these two rivers to alter their courses until one was captured by the other. The Niger bend is the elbow of capture, where the retrenched headwaters of the south-bound Quorra absorbed the deviated channel of the north-bound Joliba.

From this curious geological graft of two amputated rivers the Niger was born. There is no other way to explain why it flows so far north, to the edge of the desert, and then turns south again. The dried-up beds of both the original rivers can still be traced in the desert, past empty stone huts and the shells of fresh-water molluscs commonly found in equatorial Africa. When the Joliba was captured by the Quorra to become the Niger, the salt lake of Juf, no longer receiving river-water, dried up from evaporation. The two linked fragments formed one great looped river, 2600 miles long. It was not the longest river in the world – the Mississippi is 4200 miles long and the Amazon 4000 miles – but it became, because of its chance creation, the most secretive. On the other side of Africa, the Nile flowed straight from south to north, its mouth lying almost on the same degree of longitude as its source. The Niger by comparison was a geographical conundrum.

Only a thousand miles of the Niger are navigable. Rivers, after all, are not designed for navigation: their function is to drain to the sea the rain-water that falls into their catchment basins. Navigation requires a wide, deep channel, smooth curvatures, and low water velocity. The Niger has none of these. Its flow and its current vary, with the uneven distribution of rainfall over its course. Differences of thirty-five feet between high and low water levels have been recorded. Over most of its course, the Niger has a two-season climate: a dry season that lasts roughly from November to March, followed by five to seven months of steady rain. Rapids dangerous even for a dugout testify to the indifference of the river to navigation, as it carries out its patient task of drainage and erosion.

The Niger's journey begins in the Futa Jalon watershed, a narrow belt of high ground between the borders of Guinea and Sierra Leone, from which rivers flow in opposite directions, some heading south towards the Atlantic, others, like the Niger, unexpectedly flowing north into the African interior. The Futa Jalon uplands are granite plateaux, for West Africa is made up of ancient crystalline rocks that have been above sea level long enough to be worn to plateau surfaces, and has no true fold mountains like the Alps.

It is rough country, sparsely populated. Between the villages of Farakoro and Soucouroula, there is a ravine curtained off by cane thickets ten feet high. Climbing up the steep ravine, the traveller comes upon a pile of moss-covered boulders lying amid granite screes, under a thick dome of vegetation, flanked by fern-covered slate embankments. Half-concealed among the boulders are three hollows ten yards apart, one above the other, each four feet in diameter, like sheltered fountains, from which water trickles. Three rills join further down the embankment to form a yard-wide stream flowing slowly on a bed of fine sand.

The water mysteriously bubbling from these hollows was identified by an 1899 Anglo-French border commission as the source of the Niger, a beginning as incongruous as the acorn is to the oak. To the natives living in nearby villages, the source was sacred.

In 1822, the Scottish officer Gordon Laing, sent on a mission from his base in Sierra Leone, got as far as the town of Falaba, about sixty miles from the source.

Regarding a river of such importance as the Niger [he reported], which is looked upon in the Negro world as the largest river in the universe, there are naturally to be found among such superstitious people, many extraordinary traditions; it is said, that although not more than half a yard in diameter at its source, if anyone was to attempt to leap over it, he would fall into the spring, and be instantly swallowed up, but that a person may step over it quietly, without apprehension or danger; also that it is forbidden to take water from the spring, and that anyone who attempts it will have the calabash wrested from his hand by an invisible power and perhaps lose an arm.

Today the natives still refuse to take water from the source. They discourage visits, which they fear will provoke the spirit that inhabits the place to some form of activity. They live in the neighbourhood of the Niger's source like men living in the shadow of a volcano, respectful of a force they do not understand. European visitors, less awed, have carved their initials on the boulders.

This brook that is the Niger filters through rock formations into an eastern valley, under the shade of semi-tropical foliage and thick creepers. Picking up tiny affluents, it widens its bed and advances north, as the vegetation thins into gradations of acacias and gum trees, set in fields of yellow plum-grass. It gains strength quickly, and by the time it has reached its first city, Faranah, eighty miles from its source, it is as wide as the Thames in London.

After Faranah, the first meanders appear and the course changes from north to north-east. Meanders lengthen a river's course and slow down its flow. They provide a natural braking action to preserve the river's ground-water reserves and to keep its bed from being hollowed out. The word 'meander' comes from a river in Asia Minor famous for its winding route. Broadening its bed, the Niger begins its thousand-mile excursion to the Sahara, gathering affluents like a general recruiting troops for a campaign, swelling its volume for its passage through the desert.

Flat-bottomed boats laden with green bananas are carried on its current towards Bamako, the capital of Mali, where it rushes down shallow rapids of black rocks as smooth as glass. Potholes have been dug in the rock by whirlpools swirling pebbles. This is one of the ways the Niger has deepened its solid rock bed, the potholes merging to form ever larger cavities.

North of Bamako, the river forms an interior delta, a swampy area made up of lakes and tributaries that is flooded part of the year. It may once have been one large lake like Lake Tchad in Central Africa. Villages in the inner delta are made of sun-baked brick, and every two or three years a new coating of clay is added. The mosques are made of the same material, built into conical towers. The wooden spikes on the outside walls, which seem to be a decorative element, are there so that workers can climb up the sides after each rainy season and apply a new layer of puddled clay. The towers of the most important mosques are topped with ostrich eggs.

The brown clay villages are set in sand flats fringed with green reeds where horses hock-deep in the shallows graze on the white flowers of water lilies. The horses run free for breeding, but when the colts are a year old they are broken to the saddle. On low islands stand fishermen's huts covered with straw matting that is removed when the river is high, leaving only the empty, arced frames.

Henri Lhote, discoverer of the Sahara's Tassili paintings, went down part of the Niger in a kayak in 1942 and found three hundred different species of fish, the largest of which, the *capitaine*, can reach six feet in length. Lhote went harpoon fishing in the inner delta with two natives and asked one:

'Do you ever catch crocodiles that way?'

'He never catches crocodiles,' said the other, 'because he is not a Sorko, he is a Bozo, and the crocodile is his father. The crocodile saved the Bozos during a war by taking them across the Niger on his back. Since then, they have had a blood pact with the crocodiles. When a crocodile catches a Bozo, he lets him go.'

'It's a nice story,' Lhote said, 'but how can a crocodile tell a Sorko from a Bozo?'

'Look,' said the Bozo, 'a few years ago I was fishing in the Bani river when I was caught by a crocodile. I told him, "O my brother crocodile, can't you see I am a Bozo?" And he let me go.' The Bozo pointed to a deep scar on his thigh, like the teeth in a handsaw.

Ethnologists who have studied the Bozos believe that this tiny nation of fishermen came from Egypt five thousand years ago and settled in the Niger bend. They have not moved since, or changed their ways, which are derived from the river people of the Nile under the early dynasties, as is their language. The Bozos have maintained their spiritual independence from Islam and Christianity and kept alive traditions that originated before the fall of Memphis. Watching a Bozo religious ceremony, the dancers' heads covered with animal masks, is like watching living hieroglyphics.

The Bozo is above all a fisherman. He knows that the great river will not let him starve. He is disdainful of those who work the land. One of his oaths is: 'If I do not do such and such a thing, may I be obliged to take up the hoe.' One of his proverbs is: 'If you see a Bozo bent over, do not think he is working the earth, he is throwing up.' The Bozo is taught fishing from infancy. He is given fish bones and fish heads to play with. As he grows older, he learns to make nets and use the harpoon. The nets are made from locally grown fibre according to a technique the Bozos say they learned from ancient models left by 'the men of before'. The most common method of fishing during the rainy season, when the Niger is high, is to dam part of a river arm from one bank to the other with large braided sheets fixed to poles that are sunk in the riverbed. The trapped fish are then caught in nets. When the river is low, ancient net ballasts made of terra cotta are uncovered. They have been scientifically dated and some of them go back to the neolithic. The Bozos also hunt the hippopotamus with poisoned spears. The hunt is preceded by ceremonies to purify and protect the hunters, who wear special brown tunics and amulets, and belts made of a live snake sewn inside a goat skin. As long as the snake keeps moving, danger is warded off. The poison for the spears is tested by pricking a rooster and throwing it in the air. If it is dead when it lands, the poison is considered effective.

At Segou, where the great Scottish explorer Mungo Park first saw the Niger in 1796, the river becomes pastoral, with grassy peninsulas. Park wrote that it was 'as broad as the Thames at Westminster'. White herons and sandpipers line the banks, and the river steamer's noisy arrival sends kingfishers and cormorants rising from the millet stalks.

Past Segou, surrounded by a natural moat and a lattice of waterways, stands the amazing city of Djenne, an African Venice. When the river is high, it can only be reached by boat. Protected by water, Djenne is said to have resisted ninety-nine sieges in the course of its history. If the pharaoh awoke there today, he would think he was in ancient Egypt. The clay houses have decorated façades with trapezoidal porticos, pointed crenels, and columns in low relief. The mosque, as large as a Gothic cathedral, is awe-inspiring in its use of primitive materials on a monumental scale. The people of Djenne are fishermen and traders, attached to their city, seldom leaving it. Geography has made Djenne insular and serene, and has protected it from invasion. It has even been spared the tourist invasion because it cannot be reached by car or plane. The big canopied dugouts that supply Djenne take away dried fish. In the evening, men do as their ancestors did, sitting on mats against the walls of their clay houses, gripping the nets between one hand and their out-stretched feet, as the other hand holding the bobbin dips in and out. The trees on the river-banks near Djenne were once covered with egrets, but the hunt for feathers to ornament the hats of nineteenth-century ladies turned into a massacre.

The banks between Djenne and Mopti, the Niger bend's busiest port, are dotted with a number of Peulh villages. Peulh women wear large disc-shaped gold earrings and arrange their front hair in tiny plaits like Victorian ringlets. They are languid and delicate, aquiline-featured and light-coloured. Peulh men look like weary greyhounds, but strike heroic postures when being photographed.

The presence of the Peulh on the Niger bend is an example of trans-African migration. They are a race of herdsmen believed to have originated in the area of the Red Sea. Early converts to Islam, they practised a more austere form than other tribes. There is little dancing or singing among the Peulh, and there is no Peulh sculpted art. They are a serious, grave people, in contrast to most other West Africans, proud of their light skins and eastern origin, and, unlike the Bozo, of their pastoral vocation. 'Because of the services it renders,' they say, 'the cow is superior to any work of creation.' The German explorer Barth considered them the most intelligent of African tribes, but they are generally disliked by other West Africans because of their superior airs and Islamic zeal.

Continuing north along its inner delta, the Niger receives one of its main tributaries, the Bani. At the confluence of these two rivers the city of Mopti was built, on three islands. Its sloping cobbled embankment serves as the Niger bend's most important market.

Beyond, the river widens to four miles. Its banks are lined with thorny brake, reeds, and grass. Pied kingfishers dive at the brown water, dip their heads under, and shake them out with fish wriggling in their beaks. Partly hidden by reeds, a family of hippos can be seen, their curved black backs gleaming over the water like huge inner tubes.

At Timbuctu, the inner delta ends and the Niger begins its improbable crossing of the desert, moving almost due east for three hundred miles until its course abruptly deflects south. Timbuctu's fortune was made by its position at the juncture of river and desert. It had grown from a seasonal camp of the nomadic Tuaregs into a great city because of the prosperous trans-Saharan trade in slaves and gold and other goods. As in Italian Renaissance cities, learning developed along with wealth, and Timbuctu boasted famous scholars, holy men, and a university. The fabled city declined when Europeans landing on the west coast of Africa in the fifteenth century provided an alternative to the trans-Saharan trade route, and when it was captured by Moroccan mercenaries in 1591. Timbuctu the powerful became Timbuctu the mysterious. Its reputation, embellished beyond all measure, fired the imagination of explorers and poets. To find it became an obsession that cost the explorer Gordon Laing his life. In 1829 Tennyson won the chancellor's prize at Cambridge with the poem 'Timbuctu', which describes the Niger drying up in the desert:

> *Lo! How he passeth by*
> *And gulfs himself in sands as not enduring*
> *To carry through the world those waves, which bore*
> *The reflex of my City in their depths.*

Even today the name evokes all that is desirable and unattainable, although it has become easy to reach and its desirability is questionable. Eight months of the year, the temperature in the shade varies between 100 and 110 degrees Fahrenheit. In August and September so much rain falls that water collects in the streets more quickly than the sand can absorb it and the city looks like a lake.

It is a city of box-like clay houses, beehive ovens at street corners, neighbourhood water pumps that are unlocked one hour each morning and afternoon, minarets, sand that collects in doorways, and a tomb-like evening stillness. Its people are devout, and on Fridays its three mosques are packed. A Protestant mission was maintained there for sixteen years without making a single convert. The only monuments to the past are the cemeteries that circle the city. In a plot reserved for European soldiers, rusted metal and white wood crosses face each other across the sand and remind one of Louis Simpson's line: 'Grave by grave we civilized the ground.'

To see the Niger flowing through the desert is one of nature's wonders, as incongruous as the umbrella on the operating table made famous by the Surrealists. A great river is passing through an area which is by definition without water. Tuareg tents are pitched in the sand, camels drink from the river, and on a gently sloping rose dune indigo tunics have been stretched out to dry, like flags. In the late afternoon, the dunes throw shadows, a wind flurry scoops up sand, and wild ducks fly in formation across the lilac sky.

The Niger reaches its northernmost point at the Tosaye gorges, rust-coloured low cliffs between which it threads its narrow bed. Then, as if realizing it is in the desert where it has no business to be, it veers south, almost at a right angle. It reaches Gao, the end of the line for the river steamers, another great trading city, like Timbuctu a link between river and desert peoples.

Rolling south, the river crosses a border into the country of Niger, its bed broadening again, its banks teeming with livestock and small villages. It ripples down a series of scattered rapids, and reaches Niamey, Niger's capital, cutting it in half as the Seine does Paris. In Niamey the Niger's banks are dotted with the rusted hulks of turn-of-the-century paddlewheels which could no longer compete with trucks.

The river then makes a series of short, sharp bends in the shape of a 'W' as it crosses a large game park where the vegetation is like the jungle in Tarzan films. Here the river is dense with hippos and alligators, and monkeys screech from behind creepers, their voices merging with other animal sounds, harder to identify. Here also, the river performs the office of border between Niger and Dahomey for eighty miles, slips under the Malainville bridge, and enters the last of its host countries, Nigeria, where its banks rise steeply in a semi-arid landscape.

In this, its final section, the Niger is easily navigable all the year round and runs through a valley between four and ten miles wide. It forms a 'Y' with its principal tributary, the Benue, and drops from a two thousand-foot-high plateau of sedimentary rocks, due south to the sea 340 miles away. The landscape changes to rain forest, and soon the delta begins, with its hundreds of capillaries reaching to the sea, soft and porous, like a swollen sponge through which the Niger's waters seep out to the Gulf of Guinea. It is the largest delta of any river in the world except the Ganges, so vast that the Europeans who traded there for centuries never realized it was all part of the same river. It is also the largest mangrove swamp in the world, but no one has yet discovered what the mangrove is good for besides breeding malaria.

The delta is a vast hothouse, soured with the rank smell of rotting leaves. Its backwaters are so narrow that the mangroves lace their branches overhead to form a dark vault. At low tide – for past Port Harcourt the influence of the tide begins to be felt – the flanged roots of mangroves and cottonwoods emerge from the water, and a line on the vertical banks like a ring on a bathtub marks high-tide water level. Scattered among the mangroves are white lilies, banana trees with pale green leaves, and wild palms. The natives say that at night they can hear the crabs bubbling under the mud. Through this network of intersecting streams and creeks, the sea is reached along one of the Niger's many mouths. As one emerges from the steamy shade of the mangrove forest, the broadening river abruptly turns blindingly bright and salt spray fills the air. Directly ahead, surf is pounding a spit of yellow sand crowned by giant cottonwoods. The Niger has reached its destination.

The delta has its relics, the rotted hulks of the small-masted trading ships that changed West Africa. For the second half of the nineteenth century was the fabulous era of the palm oil ruffians. The slave trade was abolished, but the growing use of soap in England created a demand for palm oil. The delta slave centres or 'counters', as they were called, like Bonny, Brass, and Calabar, became palm oil depots. The oil was collected in the interior and brought down the delta channels in puncheons. At the depot it was boiled in copper urns. The system improved with the use of river hulks. Ships ready for the breaker's yard were sunk close to shore and roofed with thatch, and served as office and home for the company agent and as storehouse for the oil. The hulks cut the ships' loading time, but not the mortality rate among agents.

Today the delta's wealth is still oil. The slave counters turned palm oil depots have made a final conversion. Now teams of English and American technicians living in air-conditioned trailers dredge the channels, build the pipelines, and dig the underwater wells, at 'a million dollars a bang'. These crude oil ruffians are the direct descendants of the palm oil ruffians of the nineteenth century.

I like to imagine that instead of crossing four countries, the Niger river is itself a country, with a population of forty million riverine citizens who derive their livelihood from its waters: the Guinea skipper of a banana boat, the Bozo fisherman casting his nets, the Nigerian technician who operates the locks of the Kainji dam, the pastoral Peulh tapping the rumps of his long-horns to lead them to fresh pastures, the Tuareg who spends four months on the river with his camels before heading into the desert, the English head of a dredging crew in the delta, and the thousands of dark figures silently poling their dugouts up and down and across the Niger's length and breadth, the river's eternal travellers.

Three

THE NIGER REACHED

A LTHOUGH it was the closest to Europe, only a few nautical miles away across the Straits of Gibraltar, Africa was the last continent to be explored. It remained unknown long after North and South America had been discovered and settled, after the trade routes with the Far East had been established, after Australia and Tahiti had been found.

There were four main barriers to European penetration of Africa. The first was its sheer size, a land mass of 11,684,000 square miles, one-fifth of the world's land surface, more than twice the size of Europe, nearly three times the size of the United States. The shape of this land mass is such that there are points 820 miles from the sea, whereas in Europe no point is more than 370 miles away.

The second barrier was the landscape – an unindented coastline with few natural harbours, where sandbars conceal the entrances to rivers and high surf pounds the beaches. A long strip of the Guinea and Sierra Leone coast is still marked 'all approach dangerous' on Admiralty maps. There were no inland seas or navigable rivers flowing across the breadths of the continent. To the north lay the Africa that Horace described – *leonum arida mutrix* – inhospitable and dry. The desert, with its sandstorms and absence of water, was a formidable barrier.

Climate was the third, and deadliest, barrier. The African interior, with its oppressive damp heat, provides an ideal breeding ground for the insect carriers of malaria, yellow fever, bilharzia, and sleeping sickness. Until quinine was first used as a

preventive medicine in the middle of the nineteenth century the
chances of surviving in West Africa were poor. The area became
known as the white man's grave, and English sailors sang:

> *Beware and take care of the Bight of Benin,*
> *For one that comes out there are forty goes in.*

The fourth barrier was human. Africa was inhabited by a
negroid population which had been there for thousands of
years. Perhaps they were the first men on earth. Certainly they
were the first discoverers of the Niger river. When they moved
into West Africa in prehistoric times they settled along its
banks. The exact date is a matter of conjecture, but it is safe to
say that they are not recent arrivals. Tiny fragments of charcoal
found with Stone Age tools in the tin strip mines near Jos on the
Nigerian plateau have been scientifically dated as being more
than thirty-nine thousand years old.

There were two striking things about this negroid population.
They had no written tradition. The written history of West
Africa begins with the arrival of the Arabs, who brought with
them an alphabet, a book, the habit of writing, and the profession of scribe. Events prior to the Arabs were handed down
orally, as part of a tradition similar to that of the European
chanson de geste. Men were trained to commit to memory the
story of their people, and to recite for hours the accomplishments
of past rulers. No West African Rosetta stone will ever be found.

And they never travelled outside their own area. The barriers
that kept visitors out hemmed them in. They had a horror of
ocean navigation, and never built sailing ships. When they first
saw Portuguese caravels in the fifteenth century they thought
they were large birds with white wings. The irony is that these
people, who feared the sea and never showed the slightest
interest in the outside world, were forced through slavery into
the greatest migration in history.

Between fifteen and twenty million West Africans left their
native shores from the sixteenth to the nineteenth century.
Manacled, they discovered the world. There was never a black
African explorer or a black African navigator. Always the outside world came to them, first the Arabs across the Sahara, then
the Europeans by sea. They never sought to export their religion

or create trade routes. They showed a fundamental lack of interest in what lay beyond their own horizon line that the restless Western mind found baffling.

In some ways isolation was a blessing. In the fourteenth century, when epidemics ravaged Europe, there was no plague in West Africa, for the simple reason that the flea that carried the disease could not survive the crossing of the desert. But it was also because of their isolation that the blacks were misunderstood. Just as European geographers for centuries mapped the Niger incorrectly, so European scholars developed fanciful theories about the native populations. It was convenient to think that the black man was a primitive savage until the arrival of the white man, a big child who could do nothing without outside help. Such beliefs justified the scramble for Africa. Only in recent years have ethnologists discovered that these so-called barbarous, inferior, and primitive people were living in highly developed societies with sophisticated forms of social organization before the explorers arrived. The classic European view was the one expounded by the fourth Earl of Chesterfield in a letter to his son in 1774: 'The Africans are the most ignorant and unpolished people in the world, little better than the lions, tigers, and leopards, and other wild beasts, which that country produces in great numbers.' A more recent and less prejudiced point of view was expressed by another English writer, J. H. Oldham: 'The African is not clay to be cast into Western moulds, but a people which must develop in accordance with its own laws and express its own native genius.'

The African's thought process is alien to the European. It is based on different notions of nature, society, and death, and it survives to a surprising degree in modern African states, co-existing with Western-inspired technology and learning. In traditional, rural West African societies, man is in such close communion with nature, and is so dependent on natural phenomena such as rainfall, that he tends to see cause and effect as the coincidence between two completely unrelated phenomena. Just as he sees rain falling and millet growing, so, if a man crosses his path as his head begins to ache, he will think: that man is the cause of my headache. More than that, he will attach some symbolic significance to the event, as he does to natural phenomena. He will think: that man who crossed my path and gave me a headache must be a member of a tribe antagonistic to mine.

With a construction of the world based on chance phenomena, magic is required for protection, and is often based on the influence of like on like, or of opposite on opposite. To bring an end to rains, a tribal chief will put water in a tobacco box and close the lid. In the Niger delta there is a tribe that stops rain by sprinkling coal dust in the fields, fire being the opposite of water. Hundreds of magic remedies (to keep a secret, bury an egg, it has no mouth) are necessary to help order a precarious world where all actions are attributed to irrational, mystical causes. The Bambara (a Niger bend tribe) who goes hunting and sees two gazelles coupling will take it as a warning that his wife is unfaithful.

In West Africa before colonialism, political authority was unstable. One empire was rapidly replaced by another, or dissolved into tiny kingdoms that were often no more than collections of villages. The only enduring unit was the tribe, and tribal society was rigidly structured so that each member had a specific place and knew it.

In tribal society the Western notion of the individual has no place. A member of the tribe has no personal destiny, he is no more than a fragment of the collectivity. Each man has his character, his qualities, and his faults, but much of the time he finds himself absorbed by the group. If he hunts or fishes after carrying out certain rituals to make the game and fish plentiful, he is performing a collective act. If he is observing funeral rites or carving a mask or turning over his son to be circumcized, he is doing it as a member of the group. Ethnologists in the field were at first unaware that an apparently benign question could raise a conflict between individual and collective morality. Ask a Bambara how many there are in his village – as an individual he will be glad to tell you, but as a fragment of the collectivity he will wonder whether you intend to tax the village, or whether there is a taboo concerning this sort of information, and thus will give an evasive reply.

The black West African is convinced that sympathetic and hostile spirits surround him, and does what he can to attract the former and repel the latter. His life is honeycombed with prohibitions: eat not of the lion, fear cold water, do not marry into a certain tribe. His religion is part of the fabric of his daily life. When he is tilling the land or fishing he is performing at the same time a practical act and a ceremony that is part of the endless liturgy of his life.

Such were, and in many ways still are, in broad and incomplete outline, the blacks whom the first explorers found on the Niger's banks. Apart from superstitious fears, they had sound economic reasons for not wanting Europeans to go inland. The gold trade and the slave trade were handled through African middlemen who did not want to be undercut by Europeans dealing directly with the source of supply. And tribal chiefs did not want their authority challenged by the white intruder, whose technological superiority was so obvious. Also, the Christian Europeans brought with them an alien faith. On all these levels, economic, political, and religious, the policy was to keep the white man at arm's length. African chiefs were glad to trade with the men who came in the big sailing ships, but did not want them to go beyond the establishment of coastal trading counters.

The sheikh of Bornu was shrewd enough to see that what had happened in India could be repeated in West Africa, and that explorers were the forerunners of settlers. It was not an incorrect analysis, since in the half century that followed the deaths of Clapperton and so many other explorers West Africa was to be divided between two colonial powers. The sheikh of Bornu can thus be seen as an early and enlightened apostle of African nationalism.

The point, however, is that from their earliest landings on the West African coast, Europeans were discouraged from proceeding further inland, to such an extent that as late as the eighteenth century the interior of Africa was a cipher called Nigritia, with mythical monsters decorating the maps for want of accurate geographical information. These maps, which showed the Niger river in steady boil because of the heat and warned of strange animals like hyenas with disjointed backs, were lampooned in a quatrain by Jonathan Swift:

> *So Geographers in Afric-Maps*
> *With Savage-Pictures fill their Gaps:*
> *And o'er unhabitable Downs,*
> *Place Elephants for want of Towns.*

The stock picture of Africa before the era of the English explorers can be sampled in a notice accompanying the de Mornas map of 1761:

> It is true that the centre of the continent is filled with burning sands, savage beasts, and almost uninhabitable deserts. The scarcity of water forces the different animals to come together to the same place to drink. Finding themselves together at a time when they are in heat, they have intercourse with one another, without paying regard to the differences between species. Thus are produced those monsters which are to be found there in greater numbers than in any other part of the world.

Could any fair-minded man doubt the existence of monsters after being offered such a sensible explanation?

The first mention of the Niger in recorded history is probably to be found in Herodotus, although not by name. The 'Father of History', who recorded on wooden tablets whatever he learned about far-off lands, and who had travelled in Egypt and Lybia, recounted in his *Euterpe*, written in the fifth century BC, a tale he had heard from the people of Cyrene: five young members of a Berber tribe called the Nasamonians had crossed an immense sandy desert and come to a fertile region where they met a tribe of black dwarf-like creatures whose city lay alongside 'a swift and violent river, flowing from the West to the rising sun, wherein were to be seen hideous and terrible serpents called Crocodiles'. Herodotus thought this river was a branch of the Nile, which he believed divided Africa as the Danube divided Europe. It seems more likely to have been the Niger, the first river travellers crossing the West African desert would have encountered. The word Niger turned up in the first century BC in a scholarly treatise on Africa written by the Rome-educated Berber king of Numidia (roughly modern Algeria), Juba II. He described a river that flowed eastward from lower Mauretania and ran underground, surfacing to join the Nile; he called it the Niger, a term apparently derived from the Tuareg expression *n'ger-n-gereo*, which means 'river of rivers'.

The Romans, tireless colonizers of North Africa, never reached what the Arabs came to call 'the land of the blacks'. The farthest south that Roman coins have been found is near a long-established trade route to Mauretania. And Roman coins could travel without Romans. As the Gambia trader Richard Jobson remarked: 'The Romans, careful relaters of their great victories, do speak little of the interior parts of Africa.' The little they spoke concerning the Niger was wrong. Pliny the Elder (AD 23–79), whose thirty-seven-volume *Natural History* constitutes a prodigious compilation of second-hand information, told of a Roman general who, after a ten-day march from the West African coast, arrived at Mount Atlas and 'in a desert of dark-coloured sand met a river that he supposed to be the Niger'. 'The river Niger,' Pliny reasoned, 'is of the same nature as the Nile. Its banks are lined with reeds and papyrus, it breeds the same living creatures and rises or swells at the same season.'

The view that the Niger and the Nile were one was first challenged by the Hellenized Egyptian astronomer and geographer Claudius Ptolemy (AD 87–150), who, as a resident of Alexandria, the wealthiest trading city of his time, was able to glean first-hand information from merchants and travellers. In his *Guide to Geography*, the sum of all the geographical knowledge then possessed by man, he drew a map of Africa showing the Niger running along the bottom of the Sahara, from an inland lake to the Atlantic Ocean, near the Canary Islands, a map that was not improved upon until the seventeenth century.

Subsequent geographers drew heavily on Ptolemy, among them the grandson of the Emir of Malaga, Al-Idrisi, born in Ceuta in the twelfth century. Al-Idrisi settled at the court of Roger II, the Norman king of Sicily, and a patron of scholars, and wrote a geographical compilation called *The Book of Roger*, which contains one of the worst mistakes in the annals of geography, the assertion that the Niger flows west. The great river of West Africa, Al-Idrisi said, was 'the Nile of the Negroes', which rose from the same headwaters as the Nile of Egypt and flowed *west* until it emptied into the Atlantic. This mistake endured over the centuries in various versions and was laid to rest only when Mungo Park stood on the Niger's banks in 1796 and saw its waters flowing *east*. Although he had never visited the lands he described, Al-Idrisi's wealth of detail made his account convincing. Reading a Latin translation of *The Book of Roger* published in 1619, Gibbon, the eighteenth-century chronicler of Rome's demise, marvelled that the geography of

Africa 'had been less invisible to the Arabian Moors than to any other nation of the ancient or modern world'. Even so, it took the Arabs centuries to reach Africa south of the Sahara.

Arab navigators venturing down the Atlantic coast did not get very far. They could not use galleys because there was no water to be found for the crews along the Mauretanian shore. Heading back northwards against winds and currents, in summer, the only season when the waters were calm enough, each man would have required a minimum of a quart of water a day, a quantity too great to store on board and unavailable on shore. Food and wood for repairs also had to be stored, for none was to be found along the way. Arab sailing vessels, operating out of the harbour of Ceuta, navigated along the Moroccan coast, reaching Safi and a little beyond. The key factor in navigation down the Atlantic coast was the constant north–south wind blowing off the Canaries. They could get as far south as they wished, but how would they get back? The only way was to head out to sea and tack, but this was a technique perfected only in the fifteenth century, by the Portuguese.

The currents, the winds, and the groundswells, as well as legends about what lay beyond the point of no return, discouraged Atlantic navigation south of Gibraltar for centuries. The groundswell alone prohibited navigation along the West African coast from October to April. The Arab historian Ibn Khaldoun wrote in the fourteenth century that Arab dhows hugged the Moroccan coast and never ventured beyond the Dra valley, a point which today would roughly coincide with Agadir. It is not even certain whether Arab navigators reached the Canary Islands. Authorities on early navigation agree that, except by accident, they never got further south than Cape Bojador, 100 miles south of what is today the capital of the Spanish Sahara, Aaiun. The fear that beyond the cape beckoned a maelstrom populated by great sea dragons was firmly rooted in the Arab mind. Further progress along the Atlantic coast had to await the time when certain navigational problems could be solved.

Apart from the problems of navigation, the drying up of the Sahara was another major reason for the pre-Islamic isolation of black Africa. Archaeological digs have provided ample evidence for the existence of a sedentary population in the

Sahara during the neolithic era. A rich variety of prehistoric sites, among them fortified villages, have been found in places that are today either totally abandoned or just points of passage for nomads. Water must have been plentiful, for the men of the neolithic did not have the technology to dig deep wells: they could not pierce stone with their horn and stone tools.

But Herodotus, writing around 450 BC, described the Sahara as desert. In a few thousand years, between 4000 and 400 BC, an awesome ecological transformation had taken place and a fertile region had become a desert. How did it happen? It seems probable that at the end of the Ice Age, the southern limit of rainfall coming from the polar front moved northwards when the glaciers began to melt. The zone that no longer received this source of rainfall was the Sahara. At the same time north–south winds blocked the rain from the south and piled up sand in the increasingly rainless region. As water disappeared from the steppes, animals migrated south, but some caught north of the widening barrier were cut off from their natural Sudanese habitat – which explains the presence of elephants in North Africa. The vegetation could not adapt to the change in climate. The rivers dried up or were absorbed by tributaries in regions that had rain. As fertile land disappeared, the Saharan population settled in oases, which accelerated the drying-up process, for the oases used up wood and water reserves, and the wood was not replanted. Once the process was under way, it would have moved fairly fast. Even today there are points on the fringe of the Sahara, in southern Tunisia for example, where desert conditions are eroding arable land at the rate of five miles a year. Eventually the Sahara became what it is today, a region where few forms of animal life can survive and where man's survival depends on finding wells.

The desert isolated black Africa from the ferment of Mediterranean civilization. The isolation was never total, for trans-Saharan caravan routes preceding the Arab invasion have been found. Nevertheless, for many centuries the desert served as a barrier effectively separating the static, rural societies south of the Sahara from the dynamic, expansionist, mercantile societies to the north.

The negroid people who settled West Africa showed a preference for the Niger basin. Their origins and their blackness puzzled Arab scholars as well as European travellers. Like the Europeans, the Arabs made no real attempt to understand West African tribal civilization, and found it convenient to write the blacks off as savages. Thus the fourteenth-century historian Ibn Khaldoun affirmed that 'the negroes are in general characterized by levity, excitability, and great emotionalism. They are found eager to dance whenever they hear a melody. They are everywhere described as stupid.'

Despite their lack of sympathy for the blacks, it was the Arabs who brought them out of their isolation. The central fact of West African history before the arrival of the Europeans is that for at least eight centuries the area was placed in the economic, cultural, and religious orbit of the Arab world. The Arabs found a people emerging from the neolithic and introduced it to a more advanced civilization. Despite the barrier of the Sahara and the problems of navigation along the Atlantic coast, West Africa began, as early as the eighth century, to submit to the Arabs' conquering drive.

They crossed the desert from their North African bases, carried by their Berber camels, drawn by the lure of gold. It was the beginning, for black West Africa, of eight centuries of exclusive contact with the Arab world. When the Arabs pushed south, they were amazed to find, instead of a scattered and disorganized collection of quarrelling tribes, a veritable African empire, bounded by the desert to the north, and stretching from the Niger bend to the Atlantic. The Ghana empire, founded around 300 AD, was a strong monarchy, with a tax system, civil servants, and cities that conducted extensive trade. Its economy was based on gold. Pressed by the demands of commerce, Arabs settled on the Niger bend, bringing with them a way of life which the Africans began to adopt.

Conversion to Islam, which would later be imposed by the sword, began voluntarily, long before the Arab conquest of Ghana in 1076. Moslems were looked up to as people of the book. Black Africans were quick to realize the usefulness of keeping written records of goods and transactions, and came to depend on Arab accountants. Arabic became the *lingua franca* of trade. The merchants' ability to read, write, and communicate over long distances made them valuable to local rulers, and they gained political as well as economic influence. Islam came to be seen as the religion of successful men who enjoyed a high standard of living, and a convenient new cult that could be added to their existing beliefs. Not only did it represent a social advantage, but it was easy to join. All one had to do was recite 'there is but one God and his name is Allah'. There was no complicated theology or stern priesthood. Islam was suited to trading communities, since it is a religion of travellers: it is not attached, as animism is, to the tombs of ancestors. The Moslem gives up his soul to Allah, a nomadic divinity, a portable god that he can pray to in the middle of the desert, without priests or temples, while the animist is a member of a sedentary clan, who lives close to the spot where his ancestors are buried, and whose own place in the burial ground is reserved.

Moslems belonged to a great, worldwide religion, which had conquered a considerable part of the known world. An African trader converted to Islam found that it was good for business, that it gave him a safe conduct through the Arab world, and membership in a community of rich men and scholars. Islam replaced a religion that involved cannibalism and human sacrifices with one that was based on a sacred book and a written law. It brought to the Africans a way of thinking, a literature, a history, and a cultural heritage. It created an Islamic-Negro civilization durable enough to survive to this day.

But many Africans adopted Islam as they would an outer garment, keeping their traditional costume on underneath. Few were able to read or write Arabic or understand their new faith, and they continued to adhere to their animist beliefs.

When the Ghana empire declined, it was replaced by the Mali empire, which was in turn replaced by the Songhai empire. These little-known empires of the Niger bend, which controlled the area more or less steadily from the fourth to the sixteenth centuries, despite Arab incursions, all followed the same policies: they controlled the trading cities of the Niger, raised armies to keep the peace and protect themselves against invasion, and extended some form of administration over their lands. When a dynasty could no longer perform these tasks it was overthrown.

Several Arab travellers visited these obscure empires. The best-known in Europe, because he wrote in a language other than Arabic, was Leo the African. Born Al Hassan Ibn Mohammed Al Wezar Al Fasi in Granada, the last Moslem stronghold in

Spain, a year or two after its surrender to Ferdinand and Isabella in 1492, he moved to Fez with his parents, joining the growing community of Spanish Moslem exiles. Leo studied, and worked at the Moristane, the Fez hospital for aliens. He began to travel, financing his trips with legal work. In 1518, bound for Constantinople in an Arab galley, he was captured off the coast of Tunisia by Christian corsairs. Impressed with his learning, they presented the young Moslem to Pope Leo X, the son of Lorenzo the Magnificent. The Medici pope freed him, obtained his conversion, and baptized him Giovanni Leone, giving him his own name.

The pope encouraged Leo to learn Italian and write an account of his travels, for he had made two trips south of the Sahara to the western Sudan, a region still unknown to Europe, between 1510 and 1518. He had seen Timbuctu and Gao, and stood on the banks of the Niger. Writing in Italian, Leo finished his *History and Description of Africa and the Notable Things Contained Therein* in 1526. His patron never saw the finished work, having died three years before. Translated into English in 1600, it was the first eyewitness account of the interior of Africa to which Europeans had access. It was full of fascinating observations on the gold trade, on the great and prosperous city of Timbuctu, and on other fine cities that were centres of trade and learning.

It also contained a passage on the Niger confirming the mistake made four centuries earlier by Al-Idrisi:

> The Niger [wrote Leo the African], rises from a very large lake in the desert of Seu in the East, and flows *westward* into the ocean; and our cosmographers assert that it is a branch of the Nile, which flows underground and on issuing forms the lake referred to. Others assert that this river rises in some mountains in the West, flows East, and forms a lake. Such, however, is not the case, for we navigated it with the current from Timbuktoo to Guinea and Melli, which are to the West of Timbuktoo.

In the face of such irrefutable evidence, most European maps after the publication of Leo the African's book showed the Niger flowing west. It was not until Mungo Park saw the current flowing east that the error was corrected.

How could Leo, who claimed to have navigated the Niger for

several hundred miles, have mistaken the direction of its current? Perhaps he paid no attention to the river's course. Perhaps Italian geographers, familiar with the work of Al-Idrisi, confronted Leo, who changed his story to conform to the theory advanced by a respected predecessor. Leo was the sort who goes along to get along. He did not resist conversion, and wrote: 'For mine own part, when I hear the Africans ill spoken of, I will affirm myself to be one of Granada; and when I perceive the nation of Granada to be discommended, then will I profess myself to be an African.' Whatever the reason, Leo the African had a chance to solve the riddle of the Niger's direction, and missed it. Another great Arab traveller, Ibn Batuta, had accurately described the Niger as flowing east in the fourteenth century. But what was his word against the concerted evidence of the respected geographer Al-Idrisi and the learned traveller Leo the African? They remained the authorities on the geography of West Africa until the eighteenth century.

Leo, however, should not be judged on this one mistake. Usually he was accurate, and some of his descriptions would serve to this day. On his first trip south of the Sahara around 1512, he saw the Songhai empire at its height, during the rule of Askia I. He took the classic route from Morocco, from Fez to Sijilmasa to Tāghaza.

That journey is very dangerous which is of late found out by the merchants of our days [he wrote]. In the way are certain pits [wells] marked either by the hides or bones of camels. Neither do the merchants in summertime pass that way without great danger of their lives, for oftentimes it falleth out, when the South wind bloweth, that all those pits are stopped with sand. And so the merchants, when they can find neither those pits, nor any mention thereof, must perish with extreme thirst: whose carcasses are afterward found lying scattered here and there, scorched with the heat of the sun. One remedy they have in this case, which is very strange: for when they are so grievously oppressed with thirst, they kill forthwith some of their camels, out of whose bowels they wring and express some quantity of water, which they drink and carry about until they have either found some pit of water or until they pine away with thirst.

Leo added that he had heard of a rich merchant who was so thirsty he paid ten thousand ducats for a single cup of water.

Once safely across the desert, another disappointment awaited Leo, who found that 'the Negroes lead a beastly kind of life, being utterly destitute of the use of reason, of dexterity of wit, and of all the arts. They behave as if they lived in a forest among wild beasts. They have great swarms of harlots among them, whereupon a man may easily conjecture their manner of living.' Like Ibn Batuta two centuries earlier, Leo was shocked by the harshness of life in black Africa. He added, however, that the Niger 'through its inundation bringeth such fruitfulness unto all the land of the Negroes as no place in the world can be imagined more fertile'.

By his own reckoning, Leo visited fifteen African kingdoms. He seems to have been adaptable, good-humoured, open-minded, and at home everywhere. His curiosity applied itself to everything from the price of slaves (twenty ducats apiece) to the taming of a hippopotamus ('the Africans tame and manage some of these water-horses, as they prove exceeding swift; but a man must beware how he passes over deep water with them for they will suddenly dive under').

The passage in his book that more than any other fired European imaginations was the description of Timbuctu. It is on the basis of Leo's account that the legend of a fabled, romantic city arose, a city young men could dream of reaching, magical in its remoteness and tangible in its wealth. Leo saw the city at its most prosperous. European explorers reaching Timbuctu in the nineteenth century wondered whether it could be the same place.

The rich king of Tombuto [wrote Leo], hath many plates and sceptres of gold, some whereof weigh 1300 pounds. And he keeps a magnificent and well-furnished court . . . he hath always three thousand horsemen, and a great number of footmen that shoot poisoned arrows . . . they often have skirmishes with those that refuse to pay tribute, and so many as they take they sell unto the merchants of Tombuto . . . here are a great store of doctors, judges, priests, and other learned men, that are bountifully maintained at the king's expense.

And hither are brought diverse manuscripts or written books out of Barbarie, which are sold for more money than any other merchandise. The coin of Tombuto is of gold without any stamp or superscription; but in matters of small value they use certain shells brought hither out of the kingdom of Persia . . . the inhabitants are people of a gentle and cheerful disposition, and spend a great part of the night in singing and dancing through the streets of the city; they keep a great store of men and women slaves, and their town is much in danger of fire: at my second trip there one half the town almost was burned in five hours space.

A few European travellers had reached the Niger bend before Leo the African, but had not written about their travels with as much detail. They performed the same feat as English explorers three centuries later, but in a safer time, before Moslems began to persecute Christian travellers. A Genoese merchant named Antonio Malfante visited Timbuctu in 1447 and left a brief account in Latin. 'At the gates of the city,' he wrote, 'flows the great river which then crosses Egypt until it gets to Cairo.' Malfante asked Tuaregs why they were veiled and they told him: 'The mouth is an ugly thing, out of which come bad smells and wind and it must remain hidden.' He told of the Moslems' astonishment at seeing that a Christian was physically no different from themselves. A letter written by another merchant, the Florentine Benedetto Dei, in 1469, said: 'I visited Timbuctu, a place located above the kingdom of Barbary, in a very arid land. They do a brisk trade in cloth, serge, and cloth that is made in Lombardy.'

In the fifteenth century, the balance of power changed in the Mediterranean: the Portuguese gained a foothold in North Africa by capturing Ceuta in 1415, and the Arabs were expelled from Spain when their last stronghold, Granada, fell to King Ferdinand in 1492. For the first time in centuries, all of Spain was ruled by a Christian king. The Arabs reacted by closing the Saharan route to Christians. An infidel who tried to reach black West Africa from the north risked his life, as Gordon Laing and others learned. But by this time the Portuguese had navigated the west coast of Africa and discovered an alternative to the caravan routes.

This happened because they were able to solve problems of navigation that had since antiquity kept ships from advancing further south along the west coast of Africa than Safi and Agadir. While France and England exhausted their resources against one another in the Hundred Years War, and while Spain was busy fighting the Arabs on its own soil, Portugal took the lead in empire-building under kings who made maritime expansion the crown's priority.

In the capture of Ceuta in 1415, twenty-one-year-old Prince Henry, the third son of the Portuguese king, John I, distinguished himself. He was named governor of the new province, a Gibraltar-like peninsula on the Moroccan coast with a fine natural harbour, which was then perhaps the most important port in North Africa. While in Ceuta, Henry became fascinated by accounts of the gold-based trans-Saharan trade. He returned to Portugal imbued with a great purpose: to find a sea route to the gold mines of West Africa and undercut the caravan trade. In doing so, he was to become the architect of the Portuguese empire and would go down in history as Henry the Navigator.

A principal motive for maritime expansion was that by the fifteenth century Europe was already a consumer society dependent on raw materials from remote regions. The Genoese and Venetians had long been trading with the East, distributing such luxury goods as Chinese silks, Indian emeralds, and, above all, spices. Portugal, which had been elbowed out of the Italian-controlled Mediterranean sea trade, founded great expectations on the persistent accounts of West African gold in unlimited quantities. A colony of Jews on Majorca, first known as makers of clocks and astrolabes, had begun in the late fourteenth century to draw maps based on information supplied by African Jewish traders. It was on their maps that names like Gengen (Gao), Melli (Mali), and Tembuch (Timbuctu) first appeared in roughly accurate positions, and that the West African gold mines were first located. The best-known of these geographical compilations, Abraham Cresque's Catalan Atlas, which appeared around 1375, identified a Rio de Ouro leading to the gold mines of Mandingo, and showed a black monarch holding a large gold nugget. The map's intimations of great wealth were probably enough to convince the Portuguese that West Africa was a frontier of opportunity.

No less important was the crusading zeal of a Catholic monarchy. The crusades were over, but the Arab–Christian conflict found a new arena in Africa. Like Islam, Christianity is a militant creed, suited to exploration, expansion, and the subjugation of unbelievers. In his search for gold, the Portuguese captain would be competing with religious rivals, planting a Christian banner on undiscovered shores, and baptizing pagans.

The Portuguese expeditions also had a specific religious purpose that was connected to one of the most bizarre myths of the Middle Ages. Stories that may have grown out of rumours about the Coptic kingdom of Abyssinia had been spreading through Europe concerning a very rich, very powerful, very pious, and very white Christian king who lived somewhere in Africa. His name was Prester John, and his residence, in the unknown centre of the dark continent, was marked on early maps. His discovery became a cause sponsored by religious orders, who claimed to have received letters from his jungle headquarters. If found, he would be a valuable African ally against the Moslems. Natives captured on the coast were taught the rudiments of Portuguese and sent into the hinterland to look for Prester John. The natives were only too happy to join in the search, and in 1540 a black ambassador from the Niger delta kingdom of Benin presented the Portuguese with a cross which he claimed had belonged to Prester John. Portuguese kings so firmly believed in his existence that their instructions to navigators included the order to find Prester John.

Finally there was the pull of the unknown, a disease that seems to have afflicted only Western man. As one of Prince Henry's chroniclers, Zurara, noted, the reasons for exploring the world were not only 'to engage in great and noble conquests, but above all . . . to attempt the discovery of things which were hidden from other men'. This itch to be first, first to see a coastline, first to find a river, first to do almost anything, was illustrated by the Venetian adventurer Alvise Ca' da Mosto, who ate elephant meat on the Gambia river in 1456: 'I had a portion cut off, which, roasted and broiled, I ate on board ship . . . to be able to say that I had eaten of the flesh of an animal which had never been previously eaten by any of my countrymen. The flesh, actually, is not very good, seeming tough and insipid to me.' There was, among individual explorers and the governments that sponsored them, a strong element of disinterested curiosity. In the case of the eighteenth-century African Association, it could be traced to the lessons of the Enlightenment, but it already existed in fifteenth-century Portugal, hovering between the Middle Ages and the Mediterranean influences of the Renaissance. One of the instructions to Portuguese explorers was to bring back botanical specimens, a task quite separate from the profits to be made from gold and slaves.

Navigators had the backing of the crown and had inherited a long seafaring tradition, thanks to which Prince Henry could place trusted gentlemen of his own household in command of his ships. He never took part in an expedition, probably because it would not have been seemly for the son of a king to spend long months aboard an uncomfortable ship in daily contact with the crew. But under Henry's sponsorship the Portuguese developed the technology to implement their expansionist policy. Henry helped found a community of scholars devoted to geographical studies at Sagres, on the Portuguese coast. Mapmakers and mathematicians were invited there to meet sea captains. As they pursued their research on the Sagres promontory, they could, on three sides, see their old adversary, the sea.

Some of the conditions for ocean-going vessels had already been met. The steering oar had been replaced by the stern-post rudder, the oldest of which, found in Denmark, goes back to the twelfth century. Because it was located along the ship's median, the stern-post rudder made it possible to tack and get away from hugging the coast – in short, it made ocean navigation possible. The compass, at first a needle magnetized by a lodestone floating on a wooden chip in a bowl of water, had by the thirteenth century been perfected by Italian instrument-makers. The 64-point boxed compass permitted navigation in cloudy weather and long continued to be the most trustworthy instrument aboard ship.

But the main fifteenth-century Portuguese innovations lay elsewhere, first in the use of several masts and triangular sails to replace the cumbersome one-masted square-riggers. The days when Agamemnon had to sacrifice his daughter Iphigenia to obtain favourable winds were over. The ocean could now be crossed against the wind. A ship with a stern-post rudder, three masts, and triangular or lateen sails could point to within fifty-five degrees of the wind, instead of sixty-seven degrees with square sails.

The two- and three-masted ships with lateen sails that the Portuguese launched were christened caravels. They taught the Portuguese a secret that was to give them a virtual monopoly over West African navigation during the fifteenth century. They learned that they could sail down the coast of West Africa and return, not the way they had come, fighting contrary winds, but by heading westwards out to sea until they found trade winds blowing north and east to carry them home. They kept that secret for quite a while, just as centuries earlier Phoenician captains had kept their sea routes secret by purposely going off course to confuse trailing Roman ships.

Equally important were the Portuguese advances in mapping their positions. A sea captain reaching a newly discovered position on the West African coast knew that his description of it would be undependable, since the wind, the tides, and the seasons might make it unrecognizable to his successors. The only sure way of describing a position was to relate it to a fixed observable object, and the only fixed observable objects were stars. The navigators saw that the North Star's altitude dropped as their ships sailed further south.

Ca' da Mosto, as a member of a Portuguese expedition in 1454, came to the mouth of the Gambia river, where he saw the North Star 'about a third of a lance above the horizon'. Using astrolabes, navigators could measure the angle between the North Star and the horizon and calculate how far south they had gone. Conversely, if a navigator knew a position's North Star altitude, he could be reasonably sure to find it. But the Portuguese eventually sailed so far south that they saw the North Star sink out of sight and had to use other stars.

Latitudes could also be calculated by measuring the angle of the sun to the horizon line at midday. In 1484 John II of Portugal commissioned a group of mathematicians to devise a way of finding latitudes by solar observation. They drafted simplified tables, known as the Rule of the Sun, that any intelligent sailor could use with the help of an astrolabe. The manual they published, called the *Regimento do Astolabio e do Quadrante*, was the first European navigation almanac, summing up all the knowledge of the fifteenth century. Thanks to these efforts, the Portuguese became the first navigators who could not only sail down the unknown coast of West Africa and back in their caravels, but also faithfully record the positions they had discovered. They produced the first accurate maps of the West African coast.

Under John II a chart-making industry started in Lisbon. One of the cartographers the king employed was Christopher Columbus's brother Bartholomew. A 'master of charts and of navigation compasses' was named by appointment to the crown. The chart-makers specialized in portolans, beautifully drawn parchment charts of known coastal features and harbours that were specifically designed to help sea captains find their way. They were based on first-hand observation and listed known distances, principal landmarks, and navigational hazards like reefs. They gave little inland detail, as if symbolizing European inability to penetrate the African interior. Portuguese cartographers were the first to draw a meridian on their portolans, and the first to mark latitudes and give a north-south distance scale. John II tried to keep his new charts secret, but without much success. There was a trade in smuggled charts, and in 1468 a portolan produced by the Italian Grazioso Benincasa showed the West African coastline to a point south of Sierra Leone, with Portuguese place names.

Progress down the coast was slow. The navigators inched along like bloodhounds sniffing a trail, circling the great hump of West Africa and discovering that the land did not end there. The breakthrough came in 1434, when Gil Eannes, one of Prince Henry's young squires, sailed further than Cape Bojador, a promontory 200 miles past Morocco's southern border, across from the Canary Islands. Gil Eannes performed a feat which had not been recorded for two thousand years, since the time in 613 BC when the Phoenicians are said to have circled Africa. And he did not use a caravel, but a cumbersome, fifty-ton, square-sailed barca. The caravels were not operational until 1441. In Portugal Gil Eannes's feat was likened to a labour of Hercules.

The climate of opinion at the time of his voyage should be kept in mind. It was still believed that near the equator the water boiled, and that there was no passage round Africa, the continent being joined to the *terra incognita*. Cape Bojador, mariners were convinced, was the point of no return, the point where the sea became legend, the point of serpent-infested rocks and spirit-haunted islands, of water unicorns and the terrible Bishop of the Seas who drove ships to destruction. Beyond the cape, sailors said, there was a land like the Libyan desert, without water or green grass, the sea was dangerously low a league away from shore, and the current was so strong that ships could never return. No one had ever gone beyond Cape Bojador, not because they lacked courage, but because fear of the unknown was stronger than any reason for making the attempt. But Gil Eannes sailed past Cape Bojador, inspired by Prince Henry's words: 'You cannot find a peril so great that the hope of reward will not be greater.' He was able to report, when he returned to Lisbon, that the coast past Cape Bojador was no different from the coast preceding it, that the sea did not boil, that he had seen no dragons, that his ship and all its crew had not been sucked into a whirlpool. He had sailed into the unknown and returned to tell about it. And he had brought Prince Henry, instead of a water unicorn, a sprig of rosemary picked on the mainland south of Bojador.

Once the evil spirits of Cape Bojador had been exorcized, the Portuguese sent annual expeditions down the West African coast, and estabished trading posts and missions. In 1444, Nuno Tristo sailed beyond the Mauretanian desert and saw fertile land and free blacks, dispelling the double legend that the desert did not end and that the Negroes were the slaves of Arabs and nomadic Tuaregs. He discovered the mouth of the Senegal river, and, thinking it was the Niger, called it, as Herodotus had, the western branch of the Nile. Henry's coat of arms and motto, *Talent de Bien Faire*, were carved on a tree in the Senegal estuary, branding West Africa a Portuguese discovery. In 1460 Pedro da Sintra, sailing past the Guinean coast, reached the northern edge of the rain forest and saw mountains under a roaring lion-like thunderstorm, and he christened them Sierra Leone.

By 1469 the first Portuguese settlers had arrived in the Cape Verde islands, three hundred miles off the coast of present-day Dakar. The Portuguese had by this time obtained promises from the pope that their sovereignty over the lands they had discovered would be recognized. But the expeditions were costly, and King Alfonso V decided to lease the Guinea trade for five years to a merchant named Fernao Gomes, on condition that he explore 100 leagues of coast annually. Gomes showed that the trade could be profitable, and when his lease was up in 1475 Alfonso turned it over to his son, who would become John II in 1481.

Gomes kept his end of the bargain and pushed south along the Guinea coast, exploring as far as the Bight of Benin. It was also during this period that Fernando Po discovered the island across from the Niger delta that bears his name. Sailing past the many mouths of the delta, the Portuguese did not realize it was the estuary of a great river whose mainstream was less than a hundred miles inland and whose headwaters rose only two hundred miles from the Guinea coast they had already found. They thought the river rose in a chain of granite mountains north of the delta.

Fifteenth-century Benin, the Portuguese found, was a prosperous and well-organized little state. In 1486 Affonso d'Aveiro came to Benin with a small trading mission and bought the first pepper to reach Europe from West Africa. 'Samples of it were sent to Flanders,' a Portuguese writer said, 'and soon it fetched a great price and was held in high esteem.' The Portuguese were the first white men the Niger delta people had ever seen. The Benin king, or Oba, who had slaves for his own use, began to sell them to his white visitors in exchange for copper bracelets. This was the start of the greatest forced migration in history, which scattered West Africans all over the globe. Slavery in Africa had been going on for centuries. An Egyptian relief from the tomb of Horemheb (1350 BC) shows African slaves, thick-lipped, with rings in their ears, sitting on the ground as Egyptian overseers brandish rods and whips over their heads. But the Portuguese began the first systematic, large-scale effort to export slaves from Africa.

Relations between the King of Benin and the King of Portugal were cordial. The Oba sent an ambassador, 'a man of good speech and natural wisdom', to Lisbon, 'because he desired to learn more about these lands, the arrival of people from them in his country being regarded as an unusual novelty'. The ambassador returned to Benin with 'a rich present of things which he thought the Oba would greatly esteem, also holy and Catholic advice, with entreaty to embrace the faith, and great censures for the heresies and idolatries and fetichism the Negroes profess in these lands'. Portuguese priests came to the delta and told the natives to cover their nakedness and give up polygamy and cannibalism.

Going into the Oba's genealogy, the Portuguese compiled a list of seventeen Benin kings previous to the one then in power, revealing the existence of a dynasty older than their own Aviz dynasty, which only went back to 1385. They stayed long enough to teach the Oba Portuguese, for when the English trader Richard Windham visited Benin in 1554, he found that the Oba 'could speak in the Portugall tongue'. Trade soon waned, for, the chronicler of the period wrote, 'as the country was afterwards found to be very unhealthy and not so fruitful as had been expected, their commerce ceased'. It was through this Portuguese trade that the Benin obtained the firearms with which they conquered an empire reaching from Lagos to the Niger delta. But in the next century, Benin fell into economic and political chaos, and as the decline grew more pronounced the use of human sacrifices became more frequent.

The Portuguese visitors to Benin were portrayed in bronze plaques cast by the natives. The plaques can be seen in the British Museum, showing the Portuguese in sixteenth-century costume, knee breeches and boots, feathered hats, matchlocks, swords and cross-hilt daggers, accompanied by dogs. When these Benin bronze sculptures reached Europe after the British punitive expedition of 1897, no one could believe they were of African inspiration. It was decided that the Portuguese must have taught the natives casting techniques. It has since been established, however, that the Benin people had been casting bronze from the thirteenth century, long before the arrival of the Portuguese. How did an isolated people in this unhealthy corner of West Africa develop bronze-casting to such a level that their bronzes equal those of classical Greece and the Renaissance? The technique may have reached them from the East, for they used the lost wax method practised by the Egyptians. In any case, apart from their great beauty, the Benin bronzes are a remarkable chronicle of the first confrontation between Europeans and West Africans.

In 1482 the warehouse fortress of Sao Jorge de la Mina (Saint George of the Mine) was built on the coast of Guinea with cut stone shipped from Portugal. It was manned by a garrison of sixty and had gallows and a pillory to deal with undisciplined natives. The fortress traded in gold and slaves, exchanged against comparatively worthless goods such as striped cloth and copper pots. At the end of the fifteenth century, between 2500 and 5000 pounds of gold and 500 slaves were being sent annually to Portugal from Sao Jorge de la Mina. The Portuguese thought the gold came from one large mine, but in fact it was extracted from hundreds of alluvial deposits.

Prince Henry the Navigator had died in 1460, too soon to see the results of the expeditions he had launched, which culminated in the discovery of the fabled route to the Indies. In 1498 Vasco da Gama sailed around Africa and reached the capital of the Malabar coast, Calicut. Under Prince Henry's inspired leadership, and thanks to the courage and ambition of his sea captains, Portugal, a small nation with a population of about one million, extended its rule during one amazing century over a maritime empire in West Africa, India, and the East Indies, and a land empire in Brazil.

The Portuguese kept their trade monopoly on the West African coast for nearly a hundred years, but in 1530 European competitors began to arrive. In the sixteenth century the Gold Coast was dotted with Dutch, English, and French forts. The Portuguese were over-extended, unable to consolidate their discoveries. They dug into a few fortified coastal bases, but settling the interior proved impossible. Life was hard, the climate unhealthy, tribes hostile, home too distant; supplies arrived irregularly, and officials had to be frequently replaced. The Portuguese made the first sustained commercial connection on the West African coast, but never found the gold mines Prince Henry had dreamed of. The Reformation limited the influence of the papal bull granting them sovereignty over the coast, and their own interest in the area waned with political difficulties at home: in 1578 a Portuguese army of seventy-six thousand men was destroyed in Morocco, and in 1580 King Henry died childless and Portugal was annexed by Spain.

In the meantime, other maritime powers gained footholds on the coast. With the discovery of the West Indian colonies, a demand for slaves gave rise to the 'ebony trade', which would flourish for three centuries. Slaves were needed in the plantation colonies that Europeans settled, and were obtained from West Africa, where Europeans could not settle. The Dutch, the English, and the French followed the Portuguese example and built coastal fortresses.

The French, who had been trading on the Senegal coast since the middle of the sixteenth century, established a permanent post at St Louis, on the mouth of the Senegal river, in 1638.

They sailed up the Senegal looking for a passage to the Gambia below it, convinced that they were two arms of one great westward-flowing Niger river. Attempts to penetrate the interior met the usual difficulties. The report following one typical 1667 expedition stated: 'Our people . . . sent thirty men in barks, who went up near 300 leagues from our Residence, but they underwent such fatigues that but five of them returned.' The French eventually did venture three hundred miles up the Senegal and founded a post at Galam, at the junction of the Senegal and the Faleme, in the early eighteenth century. Plans for further navigation, to see whether the Senegal joined the Niger and to find Timbuctu, came to nothing. The route was considered too hazardous because of the climate and warring tribes.

The English, who took over St Louis in 1763 as part of the Treaty of Paris, sent three expeditions up the Senegal, but in all three cases the officer in command died during the trip. Prior to that, the English had occupied a small island in the mouth of the Gambia, in 1660, calling it James Island. English slavers had been running cargoes from West Africa to the West Indies since Sir John Hawkins made the first crossing in 1562. He had commanded a squadron of seven slave ships, and his flagship was called the *Jesus*. When he was knighted, he chose as his crest 'a demi-Moor in his proper colour, bound with a cord'. The English would later obtain a thirty-year monopoly on the slave trade between West Africa and the Spanish colonies. This stipulation in the Treaty of Utrecht in 1712 made England the leading slave-trading nation. More than half the slaves captured during this prosperous era of unrestricted slave traffic left from the Niger delta area between Calabar and Bonny in British ships, and were sold in the West Indies for three times what they had cost. English trade, however, was not exclusively in slaves. A Captain Welsh arrived in Benin in 1588 and brought home a cargo of 'peppers and elephants' teeth, oil of palm, cloth made of cottonwood very curiously woven, and cloth made of the bark of the palm tree'.

But, apart from the difficulties of founding West African settlements, the English were reluctant to get involved in that area of the world. Far more profitable discoveries were being made elsewhere, in North and South America, India, and the Pacific. What did the trickle of African gold matter when Sir

Francis Drake could return in 1580 with such riches after circling the world in marauding expeditions that his ship the *Pelican* was rechristened *The Golden Hind*? As Charles II put it in the seventeenth century: 'What is Cape Verde? A stinking place.'

The Portuguese had succeeded in outflanking the trans-Saharan trade routes and establishing coastal counters dealing in gold and slaves, and in the sixteenth and seventeenth centuries, these two highly profitable forms of trade came to be increasingly shared among the main European maritime powers. They took from West Africa what was negotiable, yellow metal and black men, and ignored the rest. Between the time the Portuguese first set foot on the Gold Coast in the middle of the fifteenth century, and the time Mungo Park saw the Niger 350 years later, scarcely anything was added to European knowledge of the West African hinterland, except that it contained large reserves of manpower. The traders and soldiers and sea captains in their coastal trade posts and fortresses had no knowledge of the inland empires that flourished and declined.

Four

THE NIGER EXPLORED

BY 1800 sixty per cent of the earth's land surface had been explored. Apart from the African interior, there seemed to be no corner of the earth upon which some restless European foot had not set. After the voyages of discovery and conquest there came a new kind of exploration, which had knowledge as its goal. In 1785 Louis XVI sent the Comte de La Pérouse round Cape Horn to survey and map the coastal regions of Japan and Australia, and to start a fur trade with China. The names of his ships, the *Astrolabe* and the *Compass*, were emblems of the age's preoccupation with science. The instructions La Pérouse received from the hands of the king specified benevolence towards native populations: 'Le sieur de La Pérouse . . . will prevent his crews from ever using force to take away from the inhabitants what they do not wish to give voluntarily.' With this single sentence, buried in private instructions to a French navigator, the era of humanitarian exploration began.

La Pérouse was unlucky. Last heard from a year later, the remains of his ships were eventually found sunk on reefs off islands north of the New Hebrides. But the principle of scientific exploration was now established. The trip sponsored by the French Académie des Sciences in 1793 was typical: a group of mathematicians, astronomers, and biologists was sent to the Andes to measure three degrees of a meridian close to the equator. In 1801 an English naval officer named Matthew Flinders sailed to Australia for the specific purpose of charting the south and east coasts. He was the first to establish that

Australia was not made up of several islands, but constituted a fifth continent. Two years later his suggestion that it be recognized as such was adopted, and he gave the new continent the name of the mythical southern land-mass, *Terra Australis*, or Australia.

The man who had laid to rest the ghost of *Terra Australis* was James Cook, who more than any other explorer exemplified the spirit of the age. In three voyages that took a total of ten years, from 1768 to 1778, this self-made son of a Yorkshire tenant farmer made impressive contributions to geographical knowledge, charting the north-west coast of America, the east coast of Australia, and New Zealand. When his accomplishments are listed, Cook seems to be everywhere: in Tahiti, in the Antarctic, in Australia, looking for the North-west Passage, intrigued by the stone figures on Easter Island, and, the final and tragic vignette, dying on a Hawaiian shore, stabbed by one of the native daggers he had described with such precision in his journal.

Cook possessed the balance of qualities an explorer required: he was a leader of men, but showed tact and decency towards natives. His sense of discipline did not stifle a basic cheerfulness and his natural enthusiasm did not spill over into impulsiveness. An adventurous nature was at the service of scholarly dedication. He made up for lack of scientific training with an unflagging attention to detail and great powers of deduction. The English explorers who charted the interior of West Africa all had some of these qualities to some degree, but none matched the model that Cook became.

It was in the eighteenth-century climate of scientific curiosity that the exploration of the African interior became possible. Men were moved by ideas, and ideas for the first time were widely diffused in newspapers and periodicals. Fascination with the unknown was one reason for the success of books like *Robinson Crusoe*, published in 1719. The French Benedictine writer Abbé Prévost caught the trend and published a 74-volume *History of Travels*. The *Encyclopaedia Britannica*'s first edition came out in 1768. On at least one subject, Africa, the *Britannica* confessed ignorance. It said in its second edition in 1778: 'Though the greatest part of this continent hath been in all ages unknown to the Europeans and Asiatics, its situation is more favourable than either Europe or Asia for maintaining intercourse with other nations.'

Exploration became the probing arm of the eighteenth century's pursuit of knowledge. Its focus had shifted. Instead of being told to find gold mines, explorers were now asked to find out, for example, what was at the bottom of the sea; they took microscopes, and returned with hundreds of new varieties of seashells. Men with private means devoted their lives to learning and collecting. Natural history collections became fashionable, and an international body of scientific knowledge was born as learned men throughout Europe exchanged information.

The direct if unexpected link between the spirit of the Enlightenment and the discovery of the Niger was botany. In England, the eighteenth century was not only a time of intellectual ferment, but also the great era of gardening. An eighteenth-century invention, the heated greenhouse, made it possible to grow tropical plants in northern latitudes. Landed gentlemen became famous for their orchids. So many new species were introduced that the need for classification arose, and classification is the line that separates the gardener from the botanist. The Swedish father of botany, Linnaeus, devised the binomial method of designating plants and animals. Thanks to him, botany shed the amateurish, tinkering, shears-and-sunbonnet side of gardening and became a science.

One of Linnaeus's disciples was Sir Joseph Banks, whom we met as a founder of the African Association at the beginning of this book, and to whom we now return. At the age of fourteen, while walking down an Eton lane, Banks was seized by the beauty and mystery of wild flowers. He decided that 'it is surely more natural that I should be taught to know all these productions of Nature in preference to Latin and Greek'. At Eton he studied botany. At Oxford he studied botany. While his fellow students crossed the Channel and started their Grand Tours, Banks left in the opposite direction in 1766 aboard a Fisheries Protection ship prophetically called the *Niger*, and visited Newfoundland and Labrador, bringing back plant specimens. Botany led to exploration, first when he joined Captain Cook, and then when he helped found the African Association.

After the failure of the missions, of John Ledyard and Simon Lucas in 1788, Banks was one of those who urged the immediate recruitment of more explorers. Having had no success with the northern route, the African Association was now disposed to send an explorer along the west coast and up the Gambia river, where he would find help from a few English trading posts along the way. An ideal candidate offered his services in July 1790. Daniel Houghton was a fifty-year-old Irishman, a retired army major, late of the 69th Regiment, who had in his long years of service been posted in Goree Island, off the coast of Senegal. There he had learned Mandingo and become friendly with several native kings.

The Association was impressed by his credentials, and by his zeal, which was a way of saying that he was not asking for much. He wanted only £300 in expenses, and made no demands for himself should he return, or for his wife should he not. In fact, Houghton's eagerness was due to extreme financial difficulty. He was bankrupt, creditors had seized all that he and his wife possessed, he was desperate for employment. When he sailed in October 1790, he left behind a wife and three children in great distress. The Association sent Mrs Houghton the sum of £10. Sir Joseph Banks explained that 'as an Association, they were not justified in appropriating money subscribed for the purpose of discovery to the maintenance of individuals, who happened to be connected with those whom they employ'.

Houghton's instructions were to go up the Gambia and collect information on 'the rise, the course, and the termination of the Niger, as well as of the various nations that inhabit its borders', to visit Timbuctu, and to return through the desert with a caravan. Houghton was the first English explorer to make some real headway into the African interior and the first to give the Association members in London some genuine notion of the difficulties involved in African exploration.

Houghton reached the Gambia in November, at the start of the dry season, the best time of the year to travel. Heading upriver, he stopped at Pisania, where a Scot, Dr John Laidley, had a trading station, and secured a horse and some donkeys. As he moved inland his troubles began. At one point, he had to swim across the Gambia to escape native traders who were trying to rob and kill him. He was well received by the king in the river port of Medina, but a mysterious fire ravaged the town and destroyed most of his belongings. A gun he had bought disappeared with his horse and three of his donkeys. When he left Medina in May 1791, he faced the added difficulties of quarrelling tribes and the rainy season, with its muddy tracks, overflowing river, and fevers. When he tactfully paid his respects to a local chief, the King of Bondou, he was forced to give up nearly all his trade goods for gold dust. He also found a merchant who offered to take him to Timbuctu. It was thus in reasonably good spirits that he sent his last letter to the Association from Bambuk on 24 July. It reached Beaufoy, who thought Houghton had a chance of success because of his courage and good humour, adding that 'such is the darkness of his complexion that he scarcely differs in appearance from the Moors, whose dress in travelling he intended to assume'.

After that there was one more scrawled note from Houghton to Dr Laidley in Pisania. It said he was in the village of Simbing, had been robbed of all his goods, but was in good health. Then rumours reached Pisania that he was dead, but the Association waited a year before announcing that he was missing in Africa. His wife was penniless, the Association did nothing to help her, and in 1794 she was sent to prison for debt. Eventually, she obtained a small pension and money to pay for her son's education.

Only six years later, when Mungo Park retraced his route, did Houghton's fate become known. Park reached Simbing on 18 February 1796, and was shown the spot where Houghton had been left to die by Moorish merchants who had abducted and robbed him.

Simbing was deep in the interior, about 160 miles north of present-day Bamako, which is on the Niger. Houghton had not died far from the object of his quest. He had gone further than any previously recorded European mission. The information he sent back concerning the Niger was the first solid data since Leo the African in the sixteenth century. The Niger, Houghton said, rose in mountains south of the Gambia. It was not the same river as the Senegal and the Gambia, and its course was east to west. Banks called his findings 'a real acquisition to our African geography'.

Unfortunately, Houghton was no longer alive to defend and publicize his discoveries, and they did not gain wide acceptance until Mungo Park stood on the banks of the Niger six years later.

Park's account of Houghton's death created the dismal precedent of one explorer writing his predecessor's obituary. It became one of the explorer's tasks to obtain information concerning his missing colleagues. It cannot have made their own missions any more cheerful.

In the meantime, the African Association after Houghton's trip could proudly announce:

> We now have an assurance that the Niger has its rise in a chain of mountains which bound the Eastern side of the kingdom of Bambuk, and that it takes its course in a contrary direction from that of the Senegal and the Gambia, which flow on the opposite end of the same ridge, yet the place of its final destination is still unknown; for whether it reaches the ocean; or is lost, as several of the rivers of Mount Atlas are, in the immensity of the desert; or whether, like the streams of the Caspian, it terminates in a vast inland sea, are questions on which there still hangs an impenetrable cloud.

Once again, it was botany that provided the connecting link between Sir Joseph Banks and the African Association's most renowned protégé, Mungo Park. Banks knew a London nurseryman named James Dickson, who had written several botanical monographs. Dickson's Scottish wife had a younger brother named Mungo Park who was studying medicine at Edinburgh University and who had an itch to travel. Upon finishing his studies in 1791, Park came to London job-hunting and Dickson took him to the house in Soho Square for breakfast. Banks may have seen in this young doctor eager for new horizons a reflection of himself in earlier days. He found the twenty-year-old Park a position as ship's surgeon on a Sumatra-bound East India Company ship. Park returned a year later and read a paper on eight new species of fish to a botanical society. His thirst for travel was merely whetted, and in July 1794 he offered his services to the African Association.

Mungo Park would go down in history as one of the great African explorers. He was in that line of men who turned their voyages into epics, and heard the call of Ulysses echoing across the centuries: 'Come, my friends, 'tis not too late to seek a newer world.' His life had a Greek fatality about it, for after discovering the Niger river he died in its waters. In winning his niche in the history of exploration, he joined a group of men with whom he could feel at home, for a high percentage of them were his countrymen. The number of explorers, and particularly African explorers, who were Scottish, is nothing less than amazing, and requires some explanation.

Among the best-known are Alexander Mackenzie, who followed the course of the river that bears his name to the Arctic Ocean and was the first man to cross the Rocky Mountains, in 1795; James Bruce, known as 'Abyssinian Bruce', the first great African explorer of modern times, who travelled across Ethiopia in 1770 and was credited with discovering the source of the Blue Nile (which had actually been discovered a century and a half earlier by the Portuguese Jesuit Father Paez); David Livingstone, the doctor–missionary, who discovered the Zambezi river and Victoria Falls in 1855; and, in the story of the Niger's discovery, Mungo Park, Gordon Laing, Hugh Clapperton, and Dixon Denham.

Why did a tiny nation, numbering in 1800 a mere 1,600,000 inhabitants, produce so many famous explorers?

> *Had Cain been Scot* [the saying goes], *God would have*
>   *changed his doom,*
> *Not made him wander, but confined him home.*

At the time of the African explorations Scotland was emerging from its own dark ages. Union with England went back to 1707, and the eighteenth century was a time of land reform, tree-planting, and the development of industries such as linen, whisky-distilling and coal-mining. But if Scotland was growing more prosperous, that was only by comparison with its own wretched past. It was still a land of proverbial poverty, where the peasants were as thin-ribbed as their cattle and life as pinched and grim as the weather. There were still periodic famines, a high child mortality rate, and a complicated church assessment system to support the thousands of paupers. Licensed beggars with lead tokens hanging round their necks wandered through the countryside, and stealing food was not a crime: no man could be charged with theft of as much meat as he could carry on his back. Travellers still crossed expanses of treeless waste, marshes, peatbogs, patches of broom, and unfenced stony fields. The highlands remained an immense morass, with remote glens and bleak coasts. An explorer raised in Scotland was accustomed to wilderness. The highlands, said Dr Johnson, were as unknown as the mountains of Borneo and Sumatra.

As overseas areas opened to settlers, the emigrant ship became a common sight on Scotland's western seaboard. Reasons for departure varied: some migrants were Jacobite prisoners taken at Culloden, others veterans of disbanded highland regiments. But mainly people left to escape the hardships at home. Displaced crofters, unemployed colliers, farmers ruined by a severe winter, tenant farmers disgusted by the rise in land rents, livestock-raisers affected by a fall in the price of meat: all these joined the criminals and vagrants sentenced to banishment and boarded the ships bound for Canada and the American colonies to make a new life. In one seven-year period alone, from 1768 to 1775, it is estimated that twenty thousand Scots left for America, and today they are still emigrating at a rate of twenty thousand a year.

And what is exploration but a form of migration? For men whose characters were forged in austerity and Presbyterian discipline, and who could find no outlet for their industriousness at home, exploration was a natural choice. In a country whose principal export was its own native sons, to leave home was as natural as breathing. The explorers' requirements, physical endurance and spiritual forbearance, were the Scotsman's only birthright. Like his national emblem, the thistle, the Scotsman was dry, prickly, impervious to weather, hard to destroy, and scattered like the thistle seed.

Also, in spite of poverty, there was in Scotland a tradition of erudition and a hunger for learning. Edinburgh University in 1800 was attracting students from all over Europe. Voltaire wrote in 1762: 'It is from Scotland that we receive rules of taste in all the arts – from the epic poem to gardening.' Good schools were another prerequisite for good explorers. With rare exceptions, explorers were educated men; their survival depended as much on their knowledge of geography and the natural sciences as it did on physical toughness. An uneducated man like Ledyard, we have seen, was at a disadvantage because he spoke no Arabic. The explorer had to be a man of learning and a man of action; he had to get there, understand what he saw, and report on it. The Scottish explorers generally typified that pragmatic trait in the national character that seeks a concrete application for learning.

Thus, a land of proverbial poverty and periodic calamity, derisively known as the knuckle-end of England, provided more famous African explorers than England itself, precisely because its barren soil and migratory habits were ideal for shaping adventurous and determined men.

Mungo Park was born on 10 September 1771, in a cottage four miles from Selkirk, in a region of rolling hills and sheep pastures not far from the English border. He was seventh in a family of thirteen, and his father was a small farmer. The fact that he was sent to school and later to Edinburgh University illustrates the sacrifices Scotsmen of modest condition and large families were prepared to make for the improvement of their children. He went to Selkirk grammar school and studied, among weightier subjects, the tales of border minstrelsy that Sir Walter Scott would later collect. At the age of fifteen he was placed as an apprentice to the Selkirk surgeon Dr Thomas Anderson, whose eldest daughter he would one day marry. His father was disappointed that he did not aspire to the prime ambition of the rural Scot, 'to wag his head in a pulpit'. Three years later, in 1789, Dr Anderson helped his young and industrious apprentice enter the medical school at Edinburgh University. Medicine was still in its infancy – the bond between barbers and surgeons had been severed in 1727 (blue and red barber's poles continued to symbolize arterial and venous blood) – but the medical classes at Edinburgh had attained a reputation once held by the celebrated schools of Holland. In 1750, there had been sixty medical students, in 1789 Mungo Park was one of five hundred.

What was then known about medicine did not take long to learn, and less than three years later Park was bound for Sumatra. His two strongest traits were already clearly discernible: naked ambition and Calvinistic piety. While on his trip to the East Indies he wrote to his mentor Dr Anderson: 'I have now got upon the first step of the stair of ambition . . . Macbeth's start when he beheld the dagger was a mere jest compared to mine.' But the man who could compare himself to sanguinary Macbeth could also write: 'The man whose soul has been enlightened by his Creator . . . will look upon the joys and afflictions of this life as equally the tokens of Divine Love.' Mungo Park was an odd mixture of ambitious drive and religious fatalism. He set out to conquer the world but was ready to accept whatever happened as heaven-sent.

A year after his return from the East Indies, Park offered his services to the African Association. The committee interviewed him and found that he was 'a young man of no mean talents who has been regularly educated in the medical line', and that he was 'sufficiently instructed in the use of Hadley's quadrant to make the necessary observations; geographer enough to trace his path through the wilderness, and not unacquainted with natural history'. At a meeting at the Thatched House Tavern on 23 July 1794, the committee resolved 'that Mr Mungo Park having offered his Services to the Association as a Geographical Missionary to the interior countries of Africa; and appearing to the Committee to be well qualified for the undertaking, his offer be accepted'. His instructions were to gather information 'on the rise, the course, and the termination of the Niger, as well as of the various nations that inhabit its borders'.

Although appointed in July, Park's departure was delayed because of a plan to recruit fifty men to serve as his escort. Impatient to set out, he decided to leave alone in May 1795. Park was not yet twenty-four years old, a fine-featured, high-browed young man, six feet tall, handsome in a romantic, wavy-haired, Byronic way. As he told one of his brothers, there was no doubt in his mind that he would 'acquire a greater name than any ever did'.

Park left England aboard the brig *Endeavour*, a trading ship bound for Gambia to load up with beeswax and ivory, armed with a letter of credit for £200 and an introduction to his fellow Scot, Dr John Laidley, who was still running his slave-trading counter. It took the *Endeavour* thirty days to reach Jilifree, on the northern bank of the Gambia. Park proceeded upriver to Pisania, where he was grateful for Laidley's hospitality. The first native Africans he saw were the slaves in the Pisania barracoon, 'poor wretches, while waiting shipment, kept constantly fettered two and two together, and employed in the labours of the field, and, I am sorry to add, very scantily fed, as well as horribly treated'.

Park's only further comment on the slave trade was rather startling, considering that he was a doctor, had seen the suffering of the slaves first-hand, and had been exposed to the humanitarian ideas of the age. 'If my sentiment should be required concerning the effect which a discontinuance of that commerce [the slave trade] would produce on the manners of the natives,' he wrote, 'I should have no hesitation in observing that, in the present unenlightened state of their minds, my opinion is, the effect would neither be so extensive nor beneficial as many wise and worthy persons fondly expect.' It would have been more relevant for Park to point out that three centuries of slavery were hardly conducive to furthering enlightenment among the natives, and were, on the contrary, at least partly responsible for the barbarism and disorder in West Africa. Park became an involuntary promoter of the slave trade after his book was published, for the passage on slavery was often quoted by its English advocates.

Englishmen arriving in West Africa for the first time invariably caught a fever they called 'the seasoning'. Park found himself ill with it most of August and did not leave Pisania until December, after the start of the dry season. He used the time to learn Mandingo and observe native customs. He set out with an English-speaking Mandingo guide called Johnson, a slave called Demba, a horse and two asses, food, an umbrella, a sextant, a compass, a thermometer, two fowling pieces and two pistols.

As he rode through the Gambian forest, he reflected that 'I had parted from the last Europeans I might probably behold, and perhaps quitted forever the comforts of Christian society'. He had not gone far when he was stopped by a native who said he had to pay duty to the King of Walli. This was to become the most familiar aspect of African travel. Everywhere there were native kings, some of whom controlled no more than a few villages, and one of their main sources of revenue was the duty they extracted from travellers. The white man by definition was rich, and his arrival was seen as a gift from the gods. As Park discovered, everything had to be paid for, right of way, water, wood, and information.

Park followed Houghton's route through Medina and Bondou. The King of Bondou was suspicious: he could not believe a white man would come that far unless he was a trader. Park cheered him up by giving him an umbrella. 'He was particularly delighted with the umbrella, which he repeatedly furled and

73

unfurled, to the great admiration of himself and his two attendants, who could not for some time comprehend the use of this
wonderful machine.'

Park discovered on this occasion how like greedy children these
African potentates could be. The King wanted his blue coat with
shiny buttons. 'The request of an African prince in his own
dominions,' Park commented, 'particularly when made to a
stranger, comes little short of a command. It is only a way of
obtaining by gentle means what he can, if he pleases, take by
force; and as it was against my interest to offend him by a
refusal, I very quietly took off my coat, the only good one in
my possession, and laid it at his feet.'

The king's twelve young and good-looking concubines fussed
over Park, 'particularly upon the whiteness of my skin and the
prominency of my nose. They insisted that both were artificial.
The first, they said, was produced when I was an infant, by
dipping me in milk, and they insisted that my nose had been
pinched every day till it had acquired its present unsightly and
unnatural conformation.' When Park gallantly praised the
glossy jet of their skins and the lovely width of their noses, the
ladies replied that 'honey-mouth' was not esteemed in Bondou.
Invited to watch native dancing, Park's Protestant modesty was
offended. 'The ladies,' he wrote, 'vied with each other in dis-
playing the most voluptuous movements imaginable.'

On several occasions, natives simply opened Park's bags and
took what they wanted, on the pretext that he had not paid his
duty to the king. So far, the natives had only gone after his
goods. Now that he was advancing into Islamic Africa, he would
have more serious worries. As he moved east, he found a mixture
of Islam and paganism, blacks who, 'together with the ceremonial part of the Mohammedan religion, retain all their ancient
superstitions, and even drink strong liquors'.

Park reached the town of Jarra in the Moorish kingdom of
Ludamar. The Moors there were known as bandits, cattle thieves,
and slavers. It was here, as he learned, that Houghton had died,
in circumstances that could not have cheered Park. His guide
Johnson and his other attendants, with the exception of his
young slave Demba, were so frightened by the Moors that they
deserted him.

Crossing Ludamar, Park was subjected to various forms of

abuse. In the town of Deena, which he reached on 11 March 1796, the Moors 'hissed, shouted, and abused me; they even spit in my face, with a view to irritating me, and afford them a pretext for seizing my baggage. But finding such insults had not the desired effect, they had recourse to the final and decisive argument, that I was a Christian, and that my property was lawful plunder.'

Worse was to come, for Park was seized by Moorish horsemen and taken to the residence of the Ludamar king, Ali, a collection of dirty tents on the edge of the desert. There he was kept prisoner for two and a half months and continuously threatened and humiliated. Women counted his fingers and toes to make sure he was human. They tried to make him eat wild pig, which he prudently declined. They made him take off and put on his clothes continuously, for they had never seen buttons.

Park decided that the Moors were 'a people who study mischief as a science, and exult in the miseries and misfortunes of their fellow-creatures'. On 18 March four Moors arrived with a new prisoner, Park's guide Johnson. King Ali had Park searched and took his gold, amber, and pocket compass. Ali was fascinated by the compass. He wanted to know why the needle always pointed to the Great Desert. He returned it to Park, 'manifesting that he thought there was something of magic in it, and that he was afraid of keeping so dangerous an instrument in his possession'. On 20 March a council was called in Ali's tent to decide what to do with the Christian prisoners. Messengers brought Park the good news: he would only lose his right hand, his eyes would be put out because they were like the eyes of a cat, and he would be put to death. The hazing continued. When he lay ill with fever, his blanket was pulled from him, and when he walked under shady trees on the edge of camp youths fired an unloaded pistol at him. It was pointless to escape without water in a place where, as Park wrote, 'I have often felt the wind so hot, that I could not hold my hand in the current of air which came through the crevices of my hut without feeling sensible pain'.

Some Moorish women took a kindlier interest in the handsome doctor. On 25 March a group of them came into his tent 'and gave me plainly to understand that the object of their visit was to ascertain, by actual inspection, whether the rite of circumcision extended to the Nazarenes . . . I observed that it was not customary in my country to give ocular demonstration in such cases before so many beautiful women; but that if all of them would retire, except the young lady to whom I pointed (selecting the youngest and handsomest) I would satisfy her curiosity. The ladies enjoyed the jest and went away laughing heartily; and the young damsel herself to whom I had given preference (though she did not avail herself of the privilege of inspection) seemed in no way displeased at the compliment, for she soon afterwards sent me some meal and milk for my supper.'

Eventually, it was thanks to the kindness of women that Park went free. On 30 April Ali heard that a Bambara army was approaching and struck camp to join his wife Fatima in another camp further to the north. Queen Fatima felt sorry for Park, and prevailed on Ali to let him leave with the king on a military expedition in Jarra. Park and Johnson finally left their Moorish purgatory in June, but the Moors kept the slave boy Demba. Back in Jarra, Park found himself in the middle of a war between the Moors and the Bambara. He escaped Jarra on his horse, by now 'a perfect Rosinante', but was pursued by four Moors sent by Ali to recapture him. He heard them coming after him 'whooping and brandishing their double-barrelled guns'. Knowing he could not escape, he turned to meet them, for 'when the human mind has for some time been fluctuating between hope and despair, tortured with anxiety, and hurried from one extreme to the other, it affords a sort of gloomy relief to know the worst that can possibly happen: such was my situation'. He soon realized that the Moors wanted only to rob him. They found nothing worth taking except his cloak, and then left him.

When Park found himself free at last, 'even the desert seemed pleasant'. But he had no water, and 'my thirst was by this time become insufferable; my mouth was parched and inflamed . . . and I began seriously to apprehend that I should perish of thirst'. With no watering place near, Park saw the end approaching. 'Here must the short span of my life come to an end,' he thought. As if thirst was not enough, a sandstorm engulfed him, 'driven by such force by the wind as to give a very disagreeable sensation to my face and arms'. But behind the sandstorm there was relief. Park was 'agreeably surprised by some very vivid flashes of lightning, followed by a few heavy drops of rain'. He spread out his clothes to collect the rain, and 'for more than an hour it rained plentifully, and I quenched my thirst by wringing and sucking my clothes'.

By this time Park was like one of the paupers in his homeland who roamed the straths in search of a crust of bread, empty-pocketed, with only the clothes on his back. He stopped in shepherds' huts and begged for a bowl of dates and some grain for his horse. At night he hid in thickets.

At least he was out of Moorish and into Bambara country, and the Bambara were friendly. Park had made another discovery: that within a few miles, conditions could vary from spear-waving hostility to open-handed hospitality. He joined a group of refugees from Kaarta heading east. It was with them, two weeks later, on 20 July 1796, ten months after leaving England, that Mungo Park saw the Niger. They were close to Segou.

> . . . as we approached the town, I was fortunate enough to over-take the fugitive Kaartans, to whose kindness I had been so much indebted in my journey through Bambara. They readily agreed to introduce me to the king; and we rode together through some marshy ground, where, as I was anxiously looking around for the river, one of them called out Geo affilli! ('see the water') and looking forwards, I saw with infinite pleasure the great object of my mission – the long-sought-for, majestic Niger, glittering to the morning sun, as broad as the Thames at Westminster, and flowing slowly *to the eastward*. I hastened to the brink, and having drunk of the water, I lifted up my fervent thanks in prayer to the Great Ruler of all things, for having thus far crowned my endeavours with success.

The Scottish artist who decorated the monument to Mungo Park at Selkirk with commemorative bas-reliefs chose this scene as the first of his subjects: the bearded explorer on horseback, leaning forward and craning his neck in the direction where a native is pointing. Actually, the Niger at Segou is twice as wide as the Thames at Westminster. But this was a minor point compared to Park's achievement in settling the 2000-year old controversy over the Niger's course. Park was not surprised, for every native along the way had told him that it flowed in the direction of the rising sun. The controversy was at last settled.

Simply by standing on the edge of the river, Park was able to bring back a major piece of geographical information to the civilized world.

Mansong, the King of Segou, had heard unfavourable reports about Park (news travels fast in the bush), and was all the more eager to get rid of him when he learned that he was penniless. He would not receive the explorer, and went to the unusual length of sending him a bag of five thousand cowrie shells to induce him to leave Segou. He also provided Park with a guide to take him as far as Sansanding. When Park told the guide that he had come this great distance and overcome many obstacles merely to behold the Joliba (great river), the guide sensibly asked: 'Are there no rivers in your own country, and is not one river like another?' Park found Segou a prosperous, lively city of thirty thousand, with whitewashed clay houses, mosques, and broad streets. 'It formed,' he wrote, 'a prospect of civilization and magnificence which I little expected to find in the bosom of Africa.' Three days later, he left Segou to complete his mission, see Timbuctu, and find the termination of the Niger.

In Sansanding, as everywhere he passed, there was a crowd at Park's arrival. The inhabitants jostled and squeezed 'like spectators at an execution'. The Moors insisted he go to the mosque to say his prayers and wanted him to eat raw eggs, convinced that this was the staple for Europeans. His host asked him for a saphie, or charm, and Park wrote the Lord's Prayer with a quill dipped in charcoal and gum-water on a thin board.

Continuing along the river, Park suffered from the heat and the swarms of mosquitoes. On 29 July both he and his horse collapsed. 'I sat down for some time beside this worn-out associate of my adventures,' he wrote, 'but finding him still unable to rise, I took off the saddle and bridle, and placed a quantity of grass before him. I surveyed the poor animal, as he lay panting on the ground, with sympathetic emotion; for I could not suppress the sad apprehension that I should myself, in a short time, lie down and perish in the same manner, of fatigue and hunger. With this foreboding, I left my poor horse, and with great reluctance followed my guide on foot.'

Park was worn down by sickness, exhausted by hunger and fatigue, half naked, penniless, and on foot. He did not have enough cowries left to hire a canoe, and the tropical rains had set in, obstructing travel on foot. He could not count on charity, for he was again entering the land of the Moors, and he dreaded falling into the hands of those 'merciless fanatics'. It was not in his nature to give up, but to continue was suicidal. 'I was now convinced,' he wrote, 'that the obstacles to my further progress were insurmountable.' He had gone beyond Sansanding as far as the village of Silla, when he decided to turn back. He was still nearly 400 miles from Timbuctu, and knew nothing about the termination of the Niger. The natives he asked told him that 'it runs to the world's end'.

Park by now looked so ragged that a kindly native gave him a cloth to cover himself with. He waded across miles of flooded savannah, knee-deep in water, shaky from fever. The word had spread that he was a Bambara spy. Towns closed their gates when he appeared, and natives chased him with sticks as they would have a stray dog. He had so few cowries left that for three days he lived entirely on raw grain. Passing Bamako on 25 August, he was crossing steep rocky ground when he was suddenly surrounded by armed men. One snatched his hat from his head. Another drew his knife and cut a metal button from his waistcoat. They stripped him naked, and even inspected his half-boots, the sole of one of which was fastened to his foot with a broken bit of bridle. When Park reached for his precious pocket compass on the ground one of the bandits cocked his musket. They finally left him with a shirt, a pair of trousers, and his hat, having noticed that there were bits of paper in the crown and fearing magic.

Park had reached the low point of his trip. His nerve failed him. He sat down in the wilderness, naked and alone. There seemed nothing left for him to do but lie down and die. A small moss flower of extraordinary beauty caught his eye.

> Though the whole plant [he wrote], was no larger than one of my fingers, I could not contemplate the delicate formation of its roots, leaves and capsules without admiration. Can that Being who planted, watered, and brought to perfection, in this obscure part of the world, a thing which appears of so small importance, look with unconcern upon the situation and suffering of creatures formed after his own image? Surely not.

Unexpectedly reminded of the divine scheme of things, Park decided there was no place in it for despair. He started up, 'assured that relief was at hand: and I was not disappointed'. At the next town he was received with kindness, and some of his stolen clothes were recovered.

On 16 September Park arrived in Kamalia and found a native trader sending slaves to Gambia who offered to take him along. By this time he was so wasted by illness that with his sallow complexion and long beard he was taken for an Arab. Park showed the trader his prayer book to prove he was British, and promised to reward him when they reached Pisania. Park and the slave dealer, a man named Karfa, waited out the rainy season and, after several delays, finally set out on 19 April 1797, with thirty-five slaves, who walked with ropes around their necks. On 10 June the coffle reached the point near Pisania where Park had set out eighteen months before. Villagers told him he was believed killed by the Moors, and that none of his servants had returned. Park gave the slave trader Karfa gifts of cloth worth two slaves, advanced by the Pisania trader, John Laidley. Karfa was amazed at the evidence he saw in Pisania of the white man's manufacturing skill. 'Black men are nothing,' he said, and wondered why Park had bothered to explore so miserable a country as Africa. On 15 June an American slaver, the *Charlestown*, entered the Gambia and loaded 130 slaves. Park went aboard as ship's surgeon on 17 June. The ship was bound for Carolina, but it was a leaky hulk and had to change its course to Antigua, which it reached thirty-five days later. Eleven slaves died during the crossing. From Antigua Park took the Chesterfield packet and made Falmouth on 22 December 1797.

Back in London, Park was warmly received by Banks and the other members of the African Association. He was their first successful explorer and he had solved the riddle of the Niger's course. Park was lionized, even though London hostesses thought he had 'the manner and dignities of his Niger kings'. He had no fondness for small talk, and seemed aloof and disdainful.

Banks urged him to set down at once the tale of his adventures. The notes Park had written on little bits of paper and stored in the crown of his hat prodded his memory. *Travels in the Interior of Africa* took a year to write, was published in 1799, and sold out its first edition of fifteen hundred copies in a week. It was written with verve and considerable literary skill, and was the first African travel book in English. It has seldom been out of print since. The reason for its popularity may be that it is an undramatic telling of dramatic events, like astronauts describing to mission control, in their low-keyed technical jargon, flight difficulties that may send them careening into space for all eternity. As Park said in his preface, quoting Othello, his was 'a plain, unvarnished tale'.

In the summer of 1798 Park went back to Scotland. Banks had approached him concerning an expedition to Australia, and Park had in principle agreed. Banks received a surprising letter in which Park said he had changed his mind because he felt the salary of ten shillings a day was too low. 'Pecuniary considerations,' Park wrote, 'however contemptible in themselves, serve as a good interest by which to judge the importance or utility of any office or pursuit.'

Banks called Park 'a fickle Scotsman', but got over his annoyance when he learned the real reason from Park's brother-in-law, the nurseryman Joseph Dickson. 'I have found out from his sister,' Dickson wrote to Banks, 'which is my wife, that there is some private connection, a love affair in Scotland, but no money in it. What a pity it is men should be such fools that might be of use to their country.' What Mungo Park, the intrepid explorer who had survived the dangers of Africa, did not have the courage to tell Banks was that he had fallen in love with the daughter of his mentor, the Selkirk surgeon Dr Anderson. Pretty Ailie Anderson was the magnet that for the moment kept him from further travel.

But in May 1799 Park did leave Ailie's side long enough to attend a general meeting of the African Association in London. It was a historic occasion, for Sir Joseph Banks delivered what may be the first imperialist speech ever given by an Englishman. Park's brief incursion on the Niger seemed to Banks no less than the start of a British conquest of Africa. He already saw English troops embarking on the river and easily overcoming 'the whole forces which Africa could bring against them'. He already had a grandiose vision of merchants installed in forts on the Niger's banks, collecting gold and other riches, and he warned that if England delayed 'some rival nation will take possession of the banks of the Joliba and assert by arms the right of prior possession'. With his first African success, Banks shed his enlightenment mantle to reveal the epaulets and spurs of an empire-builder. Exploration for the pursuit of knowledge and the increase of science was now enhanced by the heady fumes of conquest. Banks the botanist and cosmopolitan friend of science had become Banks the colonialist.

Such ambitious projects mattered little to Mungo Park, who returned to Scotland and married Ailie Anderson in the summer of 1799. The young couple moved to Peebles, where Park put a brass plate on his door and settled down to the quiet life of a country doctor. Amusements in the Scottish town consisted of 'a look through Mr Oman's telescope and a glass of strong beer'. One of his neighbours was Sir Walter Scott. The author of *Ivanhoe* and Park were the same age, and they struck up a friendship. One day Scott found his friend dropping stones into the Yarrow river and remarked: 'This appears but an idle amusement for one who has seen so much shining adventure.' 'Not so idle perhaps as you suppose,' Park replied. 'This was the manner in which I used to ascertain the depth of a river in Africa before I ventured to cross it, judging whether the attempt would be safe by the time the bubbles of air took to ascend.' But Africa was now a memory, Park had a family to support, and his trip had permanently affected his health. He suffered from 'an inveterate dyspepsia', and in recurring nightmares he saw himself once again a captive of the Moors.

With Park removed from the active list, the African Association turned its attention to another explorer it had sent into the field while Park was still unaccounted for in West Africa. This was a young German named Friedrich Hornemann. The son of a Lutheran pastor, Hornemann had studied theology at Göttingen University, where one of his teachers was J. F. Blumenbach, a well-known ethnologist and a friend of Banks. Blumenbach had worked out the first scientific classification of races, based on the shape of the skull, and was interested in Africa as the cradle of the black race. Hornemann's interest in Africa went back to tales of adventure he had read as a boy. Through Blumenbach, Hornemann learned about the African Association and decided to volunteer for a mission. Blumenbach gave him a letter of introduction to Banks and praised his student's robust constitution and good mind.

In 1797 the twenty-five-year-old Hornemann went to London and made a good impression on the selection committee, who offered him a salary of £200 a year plus expenses. For the first time, the Association made provisions for the next of kin in the event of the explorer's death. His widowed mother would receive an annuity starting six months from the date of his last letter. Hornemann's instructions were to reach the Fezzan from Cairo, spend some time in the desert capital of Murzuk, and continue south to the Hausa kingdom of Katsina, in what would today be northern Nigeria. It was the Association's third attempt to conquer the northern route to the Niger, after the failures of Ledyard and Lucas.

War then raged between England and France, and the French navy controlled the Mediterranean. But Hornemann was a neutral and left London for Paris in June 1797. He then sailed from Marseilles to Cyprus and from Cyprus to Alexandria. Proceeding to Cairo, he met Joseph Frendenburgh, a countryman from Cologne who had adopted the Moslem way of life. He had been to Mecca three times and spoke fluent Arabic. Perhaps it was Frendenburgh's example, or perhaps his London conversations with specialists on Egypt, that inspired Hornemann's scheme of passing himself off as a Moslem. This was not as ridiculous as it may sound, for a robe and a turban made an effective disguise, and within the Islamic community there were many Arab dialects and many shades of complexion. A light-skinned Moslem who spoke peculiar Arabic could claim that he came from some far-off eastern land. The possibility of exposure was in any case offset by the enormous advantage of disguise. It would protect Hornemann from the threats and harassment that Mungo Park was at that very moment being subjected to. A Christian in the Fezzan would be like a woodcock in open season. Whereas posing as a Moslem Hornemann would be able to join a caravan, and his desert cloak would shield him, not only from sandstorms, but from the cruel malice of the Moors. After Hornemann, it became common practice for explorers using the northern route to adopt Moslem disguise, but he was the first to try it.

Hornemann hired Frendenburgh as his servant and began to study Arabic with a Greek Catholic priest. His departure was delayed, first by a plague epidemic, which confined him to the

Catholic convent where he was staying, and then by the invasion
of Egypt by a French army. Its commander, General Bonaparte,
had seized Alexandria on 2 July 1798, and destroyed the army
of Mamelukes, as the Turkish–Egyptian slave-soldiers were
called, at the Battle of the Pyramids three weeks later. The
French occupation of Cairo upset Hornemann's plans. His
arrangements for obtaining funds from England were disrupted,
travel from the city was restricted by the occupiers, and the
streets became unsafe for Europeans. But Hornemann was a
determined and resourceful man, with a knack for making
friends. Bonaparte had come to Egypt with a formidable team
of scientists, to whom Hornemann introduced himself. Through
the chemist Berthollet and the mathematician Monge, he met the
commander-in-chief himself. Bonaparte, the greatest adventurer
of his day, could not fail to admire a man who was venturing
alone into the land of ferocious tribesmen who were then
giving his army such trouble. Thanks to Bonaparte, Hornemann
obtained a passport and the funds he needed. The future emperor
of France even offered to forward Hornemann's mail to the
African Association in London. It was a cosmopolitan age.
Thanks to a Corsican general serving France who sent to
London the reports of a German working for the British, Hornemann's journal was preserved.

In September 1798 Hornemann and Frendenburgh set out for
the Fezzan in a caravan. They were posing as Mameluke merchants and had a train of camels. Hornemann called himself
Yusuf. Almost at once they aroused suspicion. On the first
evening an elderly Arab, seeing that Hornemann was not helping
in the preparation of his meal, told him: 'Thou art young, and
yet dost not assist in preparing the meal in which thou art to
partake; such, perhaps, may be the custom in the land of infidels, but it is not so with us, especially on a journey . . . otherwise, thou wilt be less esteemed, as being of less value than a mere
woman; and many will think they may justly deprive thee of
everything in thy possession, as being unworthy to possess
anything – perhaps thou art carrying a large sum of money and
payest thine men well.'

Despite this warning, Hornemann continued to give himself
away. When the caravan reached the oasis of Siwa, in the middle
of the Libyan desert, Hornemann was amazed to find the ruins

of a temple, and began to sketch it, which no Moslem would have done. 'You are unquestionably still a Christian,' he was told, 'or why else would you come so often to visit these works of infidels?' A few days later the caravan was joined by a hundred armed nomads on donkeys. Frendenburgh overheard their conversation and went to Hornemann in a panic, saying: 'Cursed be the moment when I determined upon this journey; we are both of us unavoidably lost men; they take us for Christians and spies and will assuredly put us to death.' Hornemann met the danger head on. He approached and greeted the nomads, who exclaimed: 'You are one of the new Christians from Cairo, and come to explore our country.'

Hornemann, turning to an influential chief who had often visited his tent, played on the Moslem law of hospitality. 'Tell me, brother,' he said, 'hast thou ever before known armed men to take a journey of three days, in pursuit of two men, who dwelt in their midst for ten days, who had eaten and drunk with them as friends, and whose tents were open to them all? Thyself hast found us reading and praying the Koran; and now thou sayest we are infidels from Cairo; that is, one of those from whom we fly! Dost thou not know that it is a great sin to tell one of the Faithful that he is a Pagan?'

'What about the papers,' the Arabs wanted to know, 'the papers the infidels have written?' Hornemann, realizing it was useless to deny that he had a French passport, went to his tent and returned with the passport and a Koran. 'We did not understand what it contained,' Hornemann said of the passport, 'but were told it would allow us to quit Cairo without being molested.' Frendenburgh then took the Koran and said, 'but this book I understand', and began reading from it. His reading convinced the chiefs, and their prestige as learned men who knew the holy book was established. They were never again accused of being infidels.

The caravan reached the Fezzan capital of Murzuk on 17 November, and Hornemann stayed there seven months, collecting information on the various tribes and the geography of the place. Murzuk was a hot and pestilential hole. Fever struck down Frendenburgh, who died there. Hornemann was ill, and by the time he had recovered there were no caravans going south, so he decided to head north for Tripoli. The English consul in

Tripoli was the unsuccessful explorer Simon Lucas. Having done what Lucas had failed to do, Hornemann had a low opinion of him. From Tripoli he wrote to Banks about his disguise and its success: 'Pray, Sir, do not look on me as a European but as a real African . . . it is a new plan to travel as a Mohammedan in these countries, dangerous because of superstitious people guided by fanaticism and intolerancy, but dangerous only for the beginning, afterwards it is safer and better.' Hornemann told Banks he was off again, this time bound for Bornu, Katsina, and Timbuctu, and that he expected to be back in England in two years. He was back in Murzuk in April 1800, and from there he wrote Banks his last letter. He had seen the eyes of children suffering from smallpox treated with tamarind, he said, and venereal disease was treated with salt and colocynth. He was certain there was no communication between the Niger and the Nile, and he had heard it told that in Bornu a richly dressed girl had been thrown into the Niger.

Hornemann left in the direction of Bornu with a caravan and was never heard from again. The Association published his journal in 1802 and presented a copy to General Bonaparte. Since there was no news of his death, Banks long continued to hope that he was still alive.

It was only in 1819 that two other explorers, the surgeon Joseph Ritchie and the naval officer George Lyon, reached Murzuk and collected evidence about Hornemann's death. They met a man who had been on the same caravan to Bornu. Hornemann had gone as far as Katsina and the Nupe kingdom on the lower Niger, north of its confluence with the Benue. According to his companion, he had died of dysentery in a town called Bakkance. 'The people became greatly attached to Hornemann,' Lyon was told, 'on account of his amiable deportment and skill in medicine, and he was generally considered a Marabout [a holy man].'

What higher compliment could have been paid to Hornemann's skill in impersonation than being mistaken for a Moslem holy man? After his early blunders, this young German Lutheran became so steeped in his role, so successfully adopted the external attitudes of a Moslem, and spent so much time among them, that he became accepted by other Moslems, just as the French *coureurs des bois* in Canada became assimilated Indians.

Hornemann lived through an adventure that was equal to Mungo Park's. From all accounts, he had more of a knack than Park for getting on with the natives. Park, who was a doctor, never used his professional skills to make friends with the natives; Hornemann, who was not a doctor, became known on his last expedition for his knowledge of medicine. Hornemann also came closer than Park to discovering the termination of the Niger, since he reached the kingdom of Nupe, only 300 miles from the Niger delta. And yet Hornemann is as little-known as Park is famous. For the condition of fame is a written record, and Hornemann did not live to write the story of his adventures. The journal of his trip to Murzuk, moreover, shows none of the gift for picturesque detail that enlivens Park's narrative. Hornemann often seems insensitive to what he saw, as though completely absorbed by the daily difficulties of travel. And yet there is a great nobility in Hornemann, in his courage, his resolution, and his lonely death in the West African savannah, while still not thirty years old.

At about the same time that Hornemann was dying in Nupe, the young Peebles general practitioner Mungo Park was suffering an attack which could have been diagnosed as a form of African fever called wanderlust. Two years of married life and country doctoring made him long to be on the move again, and he wrote to Sir Joseph Banks: 'On my arrival in Scotland, it was my wish to occupy a farm; but the high price of cattle and the enormous rents made it rather a dangerous speculation . . . at this juncture, a surgeon of considerable eminence died at Peebles; and as I was tired of a life of indolence, I resolved to succeed him . . . a country surgeon is at best but a laborious employment; and I will gladly hang up the lancet and plaister ladle whenever I can obtain a more eligible situation.'

Banks replied that the Association was trying to enlist government support for another African expedition and would certainly recommend Park. It was another four years, however, before he started on his second African journey. The government had other matters on its hands, being almost continuously at war with France. A plan for Park's mission would be adopted by one cabinet, only to be scuttled by the cabinet that replaced it. The Colonial Office toyed with a number of schemes that came to nothing. At one point, it wanted a mission of conquest rather than exploration. Park was to lead three hundred soldiers up the Gambia and take a French post.

In the autumn of 1802 Park was summoned to London to meet the Colonial Secretary, Lord Hobart, who asked him to head another mission to discover the termination of the Niger, this time with a military escort. Park thought it over. He had a wife and three children, a growing medical practice, and physical and mental scars from his first journey. But ambition pulled more strongly, and he yielded to 'the demon of unrest'. He told his friend Walter Scott that 'he would rather brave Africa and all its horrors than wear out his life in long and toilsome rides over the hills of Scotland, for which the remuneration was hardly enough to keep body and soul together'.

Park's motives seemed churlish to the Victorian mind. His chief censor, John Ruskin, long after his death accused him of being an unkind husband and judged him guilty of 'an absolute want of interest in his profession, of a sense of natural beauty, and of compassion for the noblest poor of his native land. And with these absences there is the clearest evidence of the fatalest of vices, Avarice – in the exact form in which it was the ruin of Scott himself, the love of money for the sake of worldly position.'

Ruskin's judgment seems painfully unfair, for it can hardly have been the ten shillings a day in expenses and £200 a year offered by the government that made Park leave for Africa again. How could Ruskin the aesthete, who experienced his strongest emotions visiting Venice and Gothic cathedrals, understand Park's strange addiction? His African experience had been so vivid that everything that followed it seemed colourless. He had left the social and geographic confinement of Scotland and found a world without limits. In retrospect, the jeopardy and hardships of that world seemed more satisfying than the humdrum provincial life he had returned to. He was like a war veteran who keeps his gun and bullet-marked helmet as trophies and remembers with fond pride the worst moments of his campaigns. Park knew what it was to live urgently. Not only was there further glory to be won, there was the urgency to recapture.

As the government malingered, Park waited in Scotland, champing at the bit and learning Arabic. In 1804 Pitt was named

Prime Minister and Lord Camden went to the Colonial Office. Park left for London in September and presented his plan to Camden. It was based on 'the extension of British commerce and the enlargement of our Geographical knowledge'. He wanted to recruit an escort of thirty soldiers from the English garrison on the island of Goree, 'men of good physique, power of endurance, high character, and skill in arms'. In England he would hire carpenters to build the boats he would need to travel down the Niger from Segou. Park at this time believed that the Niger communicated with the Congo river. He proposed to find this juncture, follow the Congo to its mouth, and embark from there to the West Indies. This, he concluded, 'was certainly the greatest discovery that remains to be made in the world'.

Park took his brother-in-law, Alexander Anderson, as second-in-command, and hired his Selkirk friend George Scott as draughtsman. This was the first African exploration to be sponsored by the British government. The king gave Park a commission as brevet captain in Africa, and made Anderson a lieutenant. In addition, Park was authorized to draw up to £5000 from the Treasury, and arranged that his wife should receive £4000 in case of his death.

A ship had to be found, and provisions and equipment bought. The necessary arrangements for an expedition of this size took longer than expected. Ideally Park should have landed in Goree in November, at the start of the dry season. As it was, he and his party did not sail from Portsmouth until 31 January 1805, and the voyage took two months. Banks and Camden considered putting off the expedition until the following year, but decided Park could reach the Niger before the heavy July rains. And, although he had first-hand experience of the rainy season, Park was primed to go and would not hear of putting off his expedition. This lack of judgment concerning the realities of West African travel was to have disastrous results. He should have known better. But Park was a different man on his second trip. His mistreatment at the hands of the Moors still rankled, and he was determined to meet their hostility with his own. As for the natives, they were 'all thieves'. This time he came as a conqueror, imperious and blinded by a self-confidence that reached manic proportions.

Park and his party left England aboard the troop-ship

Crescent. The only carpenters he had been able to find were five navy convicts jailed aboard a hulk in the Portsmouth dockyard, who were pardoned in exchange for volunteering. The *Crescent* dropped anchor off Goree on 28 March, and Park set about recruiting his military escort from the Royal Africa Corps garrison there. Nearly all the men were convicts and deserters whose punishment in England had been commuted 'on expressing the desire to serve His Majesty abroad'. Having experienced the ghastly conditions on the hulks and in English prisons, they were often already broken in body and spirit. Life in a West African garrison was not much of an improvement, and was certainly no healthier. Out of a garrison of 332, seventy-eight had died of illness the year before Park arrived. This service record of one of the men who accompanied Park was typical: 'Thirty-one years a soldier, twelve times a corporal, nine times a sergeant; but an unfortunate attachment to the bottle always returned him into the ranks.'

And yet when Park saw them he wrote home: 'They are the most dashing men I ever saw.' He showed the garrison commander, Major Lloyd, Lord Camden's letter allowing him to take 'such measures as may be necessary for inducing such soldiers of your Garrison and such black artificers as shall appear most adapted to the service, to enlist under Mr Park's command, so as to complete his complement'.

The inducement was double pay during the trip and a discharge from the corps when they returned. This sounded so good that almost every man in the garrison volunteered, as did an officer, Lieutenant John Martyn. Park recruited thirty-three soldiers and two sailors from the crew of a frigate. With his five carpenters, plus Anderson, Scott, Martyn, and himself, the total party numbered forty-four. Park mistook the men's eagerness for relief from the tedium of garrison life and eventual freedom for genuine enthusiasm. He wrote to his wife on 4 April 1805: 'I have chosen a guard of the best men in the place. So lightly do the people here think of the danger attending the undertaking that I have been under the necessity of refusing several military and naval officers who volunteered to accompany me.'

But there was a more ominous sentence in the letter he wrote a few days later to Edward Cooke, the Under-secretary of State for

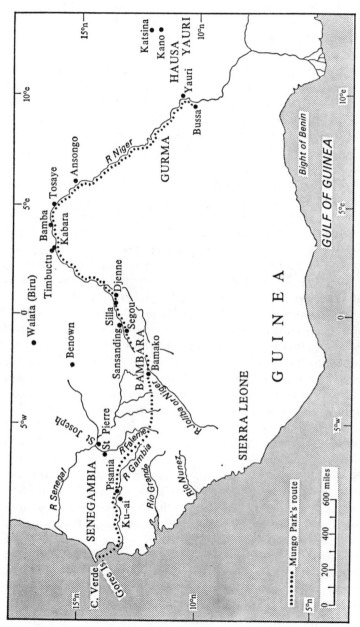

Map 1 Mungo Park's Route to Bussa

the Colonies: 'No inducement could prevail on a single Negro to accompany me.' This meant that his military escort would also have to do the heavy work usually left to natives, such as driving and loading the pack animals. But Park was full of confidence. 'I have little doubt,' he wrote, 'but that I shall be able, with presents and fair words, to pass through the country to the Niger; and if once we are fairly afloat, the day is won ... I have 40 men and 42 asses to look after, besides the constant trouble of packing and weighing bundles, palavering with the Negroes, and laying plans for our future success. I never was so busy in my life.'

In reality, nothing could have been less promising than Park's departure from Goree in April. Soon the rains would start and the country would turn into a swamp. Tropical heat would weaken his men and fever would strike. The alternative would have been a seven-month postponement until November, which would have annoyed the Colonial Office and was not in keeping with Park's ebullient temperament. They sailed up the Gambia in the *Crescent* on 6 April and reached Kayee, where Park hired an English-speaking Mandingo guide named Isaaco before they began their overland route. On the first day, Park learned that an expedition of more than forty presented an entirely different set of problems from travelling alone. Donkeys got stuck in a swamp, some of his men fell behind, others lost their way. In Pisania six days were lost redistributing the material – tents, tools, wood to build boats, food and fodder, beads and other presents, firearms – and buying more donkeys, who were marked with red paint against theft. Park had never commanded troops and was unable to enforce a discipline of march. His dashing soldiers had to be prodded like the donkeys. Straggling was the rule, and each day Park had to double back to look for lost men and animals.

On 15 May the party suffered its first casualty. A soldier named John Walters had an epileptic fit and died. Park wrote to his wife on 29 May: 'We are half through our journey without the smallest accident or circumstance.' By this time two others had dysentery, the guide Isaaco had been kidnapped by natives and rescued, and the party had been attacked by a swarm of bees which killed six donkeys and a horse.

On 8 June a carpenter died of dysentery, and on 10 June the first rain fell, an announcement of doom that shook Park's optimism for the first time, for they were still travelling overland, and were only half-way to Segou. 'The tornado which took place on our arrival,' Park wrote, 'had an instant effect on the health of the soldiers and proved to be the beginning of sorrow. I had proudly flattered myself that we would reach the Niger with a very moderate loss . . . but now the rain had set in and I trembled to think that we were only half way through our journey. The rain had not commenced three minutes before many of the soldiers were affected with vomiting, while others fell asleep as if half intoxicated.'

Park had written to Banks that he had 'high hopes' of reaching the Niger by 27 June. In fact, the ragged remnants of his column did not reach it until 19 August. By that time three-quarters of his men had died and all his pack animals were either dead or stolen. Park, like a tragic Tom Thumb, crossed the waterlogged African wilderness, leaving behind corpses instead of pebbles. Fever and dysentery proved a far greater danger than the Moors. Sick men dropped in the bush, swore they would move no further, and begged to be left in peace. When he could, Park left them in the care of a village chief. At other times they were abandoned where they fell, to be stripped naked by scavenging natives as soon as the column was out of sight. Humane standards of conduct were forgotten and survival became the only rule. By 18 June Park was no longer burying the dead. A note in his diary for that day says: 'Did not stop to bury him, the sun being very high.' Several times, he expressed regret at abandoning sick men. On 2 July he wrote: 'I regretted much being under the necessity of leaving in the hour of sickness and distress a man who had grown old in the service of his country.' The news spread from village to village that the white men were sick and could not defend their goods. Thieves who had at first worked only at night now appeared in broad daylight. On 14 July, as one native asked for snuff, another snatched a musket out of Park's hands. The thieves grew so bold that not even warning shots stopped them from making off with loaded donkeys.

In adversity Park became a figure of heroic stature. The other officers were too ill to help. He had to assume all the burdens of the expedition. His own stamina and resistance to fever were amazing. In addition to treating his sick, he had to find food, deal with village chiefs, keep the men and animals moving, and fight off thieves. In addition to illness, there were accidents. On 27 June one of his men drowned when a canoe overturned as he was crossing the river.

On 4 July the guide Isaaco was attacked by a crocodile as he was leading donkeys into the river. He had the presence of mind to jab his fingers into the animal's eyes and escaped with teeth wounds on both thighs, which Park dressed with strips of adhesive plaster. Park had to work harder as more men fell ill. 'So very much weakened were the men,' he wrote, 'that when their loads fell off, they could not lift them on again. I assisted in loading thirteen asses in the course of the march.' He had to leave one man behind after trying to keep him on a horse for six miles. He had to leave his Selkirk friend George Scott behind. Another time, he found his brother-in-law Alexander Anderson under a bush, 'apparently dying. I took him on my back and carried over the load of the ass which I drove, got over the ass, Mr Anderson's horse etc. Found myself much fatigued, having crossed the stream sixteen times.' Anderson could go no further and had to be carried on a litter.

On 19 August Park once again felt the excitement of seeing the Niger. As the discoverer of its course, he must have felt a proprietary interest in the river. 'Coming to the brow of a hill,' he wrote, 'I once more saw the Niger rolling its immense stream along the plain.' By now, he had only ten men left, and most of them were ill, and all his carpenters were dead. Perhaps Park was by this time a bit crazed by fever himself. He refused to recognize the seriousness of his situation. Continuing had become an obsession, and he deluded himself into further optimism. 'I reflected,' he wrote, 'that in conducting a party of Europeans, with immense baggage, through an extent of more than 500 miles, I had always been able to preserve the most friendly terms with the natives.' This was less than candid, for on one occasion Park had personally chased a thief who had made off with his greatcoat and shot him through the leg. 'In fact,' Park cheerfully continued, 'this journey plainly demonstrated 1st that with common prudence any quantity of merchandise may be transported from the Gambia to the Niger without danger of being robbed by the natives, 2dly that if this journey be performed in the dry season, one may calculate on losing not more than three or at the most four men out of fifty.'

It even more plainly demonstrated something that Park did not stress, the lethal effects on Europeans of the West African climate during the rainy season. His own health began to fail on 26 August, and he wrote: 'I have been subject to attacks of dysentery, and as I found that my strength was failing fast . . . I took calomel till it affected my mouth to such a degree that I could not speak or sleep for six days.' Upon reaching Bamako, Park and what was left of his column hired canoes to take them downriver. On 19 September they stopped outside Segou where emissaries of King Mansong, the same king who had given Park five thousand cowrie shells to get him out of town on his first trip, came to meet him. What Park told them seemed tactful and appropriate, but probably contributed to his downfall.

I am the white man who nine years ago came into Bambara [Park said]. I then came to Segou and requested Mansong's permission to pass to the Eastwards; he not only permitted me to pass, but presented me with 5000 cowries to purchase provisions on the road; for you all know that the Moors had robbed me of my goods. This generous conduct has made Mansong's name much respected in the land of the white people . . . You all know that the white people are a trading people and that all the articles of value . . . are made by us. If you speak of a good gun, who made it? The white people . . . we sell them to the Moors, who bring them to Timbuktoo where they sell them at a higher rate . . . now, the king of the white people wishes to find out a way by which we may bring our own merchandise to you and sell everything at a much cheaper rate . . . For this purpose, if Mansong will permit me to pass, I propose sailing down the Joliba to the place where it mixes with the salt water, and if I find no rocks or danger in the way, the white man's small vessels will come up to trade . . . what I have now spoken I hope and trust you will not mention . . . for if the Moors should hear of it, I shall certainly be murdered before I reach the salt water.

In telling King Mansong's emissaries that he planned to undercut the Moorish middlemen, Park was unnecessarily exposing himself to their retaliation. It was naïve to believe that the king's five emissaries would keep his secret in a trading city like Segou where Moorish merchants were on excellent terms with local authorities and where the passage of the white men was sure to excite curiosity. The Moors, upon learning Park's true motives, would do their utmost to block his way and protect their centuries-old caravan trade. In the light of what happened, Park's rash summary of his intentions may have been his biggest blunder.

Park sent King Mansong some silver-embossed guns and pistols, a sabre, bales of cloth, and a silver-plated tureen, and two days later he received the promise of a canoe and safe passage. But the king was as reluctant to meet him as he had been nine years before. Bypassing Segou, Park waited in Sansanding for the promised canoe. It was a long wait, and he decided to put the time to profitable use by trading his surplus goods for cowrie shells in the open market. This was simply putting into practice what he had told King Mansong's emissaries. His delight with his success made him unaware that he was infuriating the Moorish traders. 'Such was my run of business that I was sometimes forced to employ three tellers at once to count my cash,' he wrote. In one day he took in 25,756 cowries. He had started a price war with the Arabs with bargains such as six thousand cowries for a musket and twenty thousand for a span of scarlet cloth. In the meantime, two more men died on 2 October, and hyenas dragged away one of the corpses and devoured it. On 28 October Park was particularly affected by the death of his brother-in-law. 'No event which took place during the journey,' he wrote, 'ever threw the smallest gloom over my mind till I laid Mr Anderson in the grave. I then felt myself as if left a second time, lonely and friendless, amidst the wilds of Africa.'

Park had no time to dwell on his misery, for two half-rotten canoes arrived from King Mansong, and he set about converting them into a single river-worthy vessel to carry his few remaining men down the Niger. 'With the assistance of Abraham Bolton (private),' he recorded, 'took out all the rotten pieces; and repaired all the holes, and sewed places; and with eighteen days hard labour, changed the Bambara canoes into His Majesty's Schooner Joliba; the length forty feet, breadth six feet; being flat bottomed, draws only one foot water when loaded.'

Two weeks later a message arrived from King Mansong urging Park to get started before the Moors learned of his plans. This may have been a tactful way of telling him that they were already known. Park seems to have considered the possibility of ambush, for he bought bullock skins to protect his boat from spears and arrows. On 16 November Park wrote: 'All ready and we sail tomorrow morning, or evening.' The last entry in his journal, a scrap of botanical information, is dated on the same day and reads: 'There are no shea trees in Kong or Gotto, and very few in Baedoo.' The Mandingo guide Isaaco was heading back to Pisania with Park's journal and letters. Park informed Sir Joseph Banks of his intention 'to keep the middle of the river, and make the best use I can of winds and currents till I reach the termination of this mysterious stream'. In his letter to his wife, he was able to manage a tone of rather forced optimism after breaking the news that her brother was dead. 'You may be led to consider my situation as a great deal worse than it really is,' he wrote. '. . . the healthy season has commenced, so that there is no danger of sickness . . . I think it is not unlikely but I shall be in England before you receive this . . . the sails are now hoisting for our departure to the coast.'

Park was in a do-or-die frame of mind. He was taking a makeshift boat pieced together from two rotten Bambara canoes down an uncharted river whose banks were occupied by Christian-hating Tuaregs and rapacious blacks. His escort was down to three soldiers, Lieutenant Martyn, three slaves to paddle the boat, and a guide named Ahmadi Fatouma, who claimed to know the river and told Park that the only dangerous spot would be Timbuctu. One of the soldiers was already out of his mind, and Lieutenant Martyn was a brutal, hard-drinking man, to judge from a letter he sent a friend via Isaaco: 'My head is a little sore this morning – was up late last night drinking Ale in company with a Moor who has been at Gibraltar and speaks English – got a little tipsy – finished the scene by giving the Moor a damned good thrashing.'

On 20 November 1805 Park and his pathetic band embarked on the 'Schooner *Joliba*', pushed off from the Sansanding shore, and disappeared down the Niger into the troubled waters of historical conjecture. Not another word was ever heard from him. When explorers disappeared in Africa it took years for accurate information to filter out, and even today the Mungo Park puzzle is missing a few pieces.

Nearly a year later, on 21 September 1806, the British consul in the Moroccan city of Mogador, James Grey Jackson, who kept up a regular correspondence with the Cadi of Timbuctu, wrote to Banks that Park was said to have reached that city. Another mention of Park was made, astonishingly, in a Bombay newspaper, which in 1809 reported his violent death, based on the account of an Abyssinian pilgrim who had been to Mecca. Obviously these far-flung rumours were useless: the only way to find out anything certain was to send someone in Park's tracks. The Mandingo guide Isaaco, who had forwarded Park's journal and mail to London, volunteered to go into the interior in 1810. Isaaco proved an enterprising reporter, for near Sansanding he found the only man who could tell the story of Park's death, the guide Ahmadi Fatouma.

Upon seeing Isaaco, Fatouma burst into tears and said, 'They are all dead.' He then proceeded to tell his story. Park, expecting trouble, had taken fifteen muskets and plenty of ammunition on board, and enough provisions to last them, so they would not have to land. He knew he would be passing through territory controlled by Moorish tribes, whose cruelty towards Christians was still vivid in his mind from his first trip. He decided that the only way to escape capture was to remain on the river, heavily armed, and fight off attacks.

He must have realized that he was violating local custom, which required that travellers ask each local chief for permission to pass and pay a toll. By refusing to stop and pay, and by firing at everyone who got in his way, Park made enemies everywhere he went. The 'Schooner *Joliba*' came under more or less constant attack. Hostile natives prevented Park from going up the canal leading to Kabara, the river port five miles from Timbuctu. Beyond Kabara, one of the three soldiers died. 'On passing Timbuctu,' Ahmadi Fatouma told Isaaco, 'we were again attacked by three canoes, which we beat off, killing one of the natives . . . seeing so many men killed and our superiority over them, I took hold of Martyn's hand, saying "Martyn, let us cease firing, for we have killed too many already," upon which Martyn wanted to kill me, had not Mr Park interfered.' Martyn's bloodthirsty behaviour seems to have frightened the river people, for Park's boat twice passed large armies camped on the river bank and was not attacked. When he needed fresh food he sent Ahmadi on shore, and on at least one occasion the guide was seized and Park had to rescue him. Gordon Laing, who would reach Timbuctu via the northern route twenty years later, met a Tuareg who had been wounded by Park. 'How imprudent, how unthinking!' Laing wrote. 'I may even say how selfish it was in Park to attempt to make discoveries in this country at the expense of the blood of the inhabitants, and to the exclusion of all other communication: How unjustifiable was his conduct.' But what else could Park have done? The alternative was capture by the Moors, and probably murder, as Gordon Laing found out. It is probably true, however, that Park made things difficult for his successors. Fifty years later the German explorer Barth met a Tuareg 'who had had some dealings with Mungo Park, whose policy it was to fire at anyone who approached him in a threatening attitude', so that they supposed all Europeans to be *Tanakast*, or wild beasts.

Ahmadi's account was vague on dates, but eventually Park and his men got through the Moorish-held lands on the Niger bend, apparently without further incident, except for meeting families of hippos that almost capsized their flat-bottomed craft. Park had by now passed Gao and started on the Niger's southward section. He may have realized from the abrupt change in the river's direction that it was not a branch of the Congo or the Nile, but emptied into the Gulf of Guinea. He passed the rapids at Ansongo, and headed into Hausa country in present-day Nigeria. When in March or April 1806 he reached the small kingdom of Yauri on the Niger's left bank, he had travelled about 1500 miles of the river's total course of 2600 miles and was only about 600 miles from the sea. It was an impressive achievement.

Ahmadi's contract ended in Yauri, and Park, contrary to his own rules, accompanied him ashore with gifts for the king, including five silver rings, powder, and flints. The chief, according to Ahmadi, accepted the presents and asked Park whether he intended to come back the same way. Park said he did not and took his leave. The king was displeased with his presents and put Ahmadi in irons. The next morning, he sent troops downstream to intercept Park at the Bussa rapids, where a rock shelf spanned the river, broken only by a narrow gate-like opening.*

---

* Today, the spot has vanished, and in its place stand the huge cement locks of Africa's third biggest dam, the Kainji.

It was a perfect spot for an ambush, particularly since in the spring the river was low. According to Ahmadi's account,

> this army went and took possession of the top of this opening. Mr Park came there after the army had posted itself; he nevertheless attempted to pass. The people began to attack him, throwing lances, pikes, arrows, and stones. Mr Park defended himself for a long time; two of his slaves at the stern of the canoe were killed; they threw everything they had in the canoe into the river, and kept firing; but being overpowered by numbers and fatigue, and unable to keep up the canoe against the current, and no probability of escaping, Mr Park took hold of one of the white men and jumped into the water; Martyn did the same, and they were drowned in the stream in attempting to escape.

The irony is that on the one occasion when Park decided to behave in a civil manner towards a local potentate he aroused his wrath. Ahmadi's story, if it was true, confirmed that Park's strategy of staying on the river and firing when approached was the right one.

It is unfortunate that in piecing together Mungo Park's fate we have to rely on the testimony of a single native guide who may have had good reasons for distorting the truth and whose account is in several ways implausible. Park's death remains enigmatic, Ahmadi's account uncorroborated. The very fact that Ahmadi was the party's only survivor places him under suspicion. His main concern was to absolve himself of blame. What if Ahmadi had kept the presents intended for the king? There is no proof one way or the other.

There are, however, three major implausibilities in his version. First, the distance from Yauri to Bussa is forty miles. How could the troops the King of Yauri sent to Bussa on the day after Park left have caught up with him? In fact, Bussa was a separate state with its own army and its own king, who would normally not have allowed the passage of Yauri troops through his territory. Second, Ahmadi's version, in saying that Park took hold of one of the white men, jumped into the water, and was drowned, gives the impression that he did not know how to swim. But Park, in his book on his first expeditions, wrote on 3 May, when he was returning to Pisania with the slave trader: 'I went and bathed myself. Very few people here can swim, for they came in numbers to dissuade me from venturing into a pool where they said the water would come over my head.' Third, when the Lander brothers were in Bussa in 1830 on the trip that would finish what Park had begun, they were shown a book that had belonged to Park. It was an eighteenth-century nautical manual, consisting chiefly of logarithm tables. It was unmistakably Park's, for inserted among its pages was an invitation that said: 'Mr and Mrs Watson would be happy to have the pleasure of Mr Park's company at dinner on Tuesday next, at half-past five o'clock. An answer is requested. Strand, 9th Nov. 1804.' This book was obtained in 1857 by another English traveller to Bussa, Lieutenant John Glover, who exchanged it for a knife. Glover gave the book to the Royal Geographic Society, in whose museum it can be examined today. It shows no sign of water damage. And yet Ahmadi said: 'They threw everything they had in the canoe into the river', and gave the impression that Park's boat capsized into the rapids.

Clearly Park did not meet his death in the way that Ahmadi described. A little more light was shed when the explorer Hugh Clapperton visited Bussa in 1825. He found that the people were very friendly and glad to give him whatever information he wanted, with one exception. When he asked about Mungo Park's death, 'everyone appeared uneasy and said it happened before their remembrance, or that they did not see it. They pointed out the place where the boat struck, and the unfortunate crew perished. Even this was done with caution, and as if by stealth.' It seemed to Clapperton an admission of guilt, and he was left with the impression that the people of Bussa had ambushed Park in the rapids near their village. Perhaps the King of Yauri got word to them that a boat worth plundering was coming their way. Perhaps Park tried to force his way through without paying tribute to the Bussa king. He thought the river protected him from the land and its people, and it was finally the river that trapped him.

Hope long continued to flicker that Park was alive, and it was not until 1819 that the London *Times*, in its 3 May edition, wrote: 'The death of this intrepid traveller is now placed beyond any doubt. Many accounts of it have been received.'

Park's mysterious death added to his legend. He was compared to England's greatest heroes, Sir Walter Raleigh, Captain Cook and

Lord Nelson. In West Africa he became a part of oral history. The German explorer Barth, visiting Timbuctu fifty years later, found that people were still talking about Park's passage on the Niger.

In fact his second journey added nothing to geographical knowledge. The journal of his long excursion down the Niger to Bussa disappeared with most of his other belongings. Park's principal achievement was establishing beyond doubt the Niger's course. He was the archetypal explorer, to whom what Tennyson wrote about Ulysses was perfectly suited:

> *Yet all experience is an arch where thro'*
> *Gleams that untravell'd world, whose margin fades*
> *For ever and for ever when I move.*

The African Association and the Colonial Office sent him into Africa to bring back information and find a new trade route. But Park, with his semi-crazed commitment to reaching his destination, and his readiness to 'die on the Niger', was clearly engaged in a personal challenge that had little to do with his instructions. After his first trip alone into the interior, when he was mistreated by the Moors and almost died of thirst, he had every reason not to return to Africa. When he reached the Niger on his second trip with most of his men dead and hardly a chance of getting through in the improvised boat he so grandly called 'His Majesty's Schooner Joliba', he had every reason to turn back. Park's greatness lies in the force of his obsession. He had looked death in the face and survived, and whatever happened to him after that was in the nature of a reprieve.

That Park was able to get as far as he did seems even more impressive when his journey is compared to several missions that were sent out with the same aim but failed completely. Sir Joseph Banks had thus far tried three approaches to the Niger: from Tripoli with Lucas, from Cairo with Ledyard and Hornemann, and from the Gambia with Houghton and Park. He now decided that another approach should be tried, from the south. In 1804, when Park was preparing his own second journey, the African Association recruited an explorer named Henry Nicholls to start from one of the trading stations on the Gulf of Guinea and head north to find the Niger. It was of course not yet suspected that the Niger emptied into the Gulf of Guinea, so that Nicholls's

starting-point was in fact his destination. He was sent to Liverpool to talk to the men who traded on the West African coast,
but found that they knew almost nothing about the interior.

After buying equipment and presents for chiefs, Nicholls
sailed from Liverpool on 1 November 1804, aboard a ship bound
for Calabar, an important slave trading station on the estuary
of the Cross river, immediately to the east of the Niger delta.
His instructions were to spend a year there gathering information
before heading into the interior. Nicholls arrived on 14 January
1805, and died of the fever in April. All that remained of his
mission was a description of the trading station in a February
letter to the Association, which ended: 'My health is very good,
and I am in good spirits, no obstacle appearing to prevent me
from eventually accomplishing my mission.'

With Nicholls dead, the African Association's militant period
came to an end. Between 1805 and 1831, when it was absorbed
by the Royal Geographical Society, it sent out only two more
explorers. Its membership and financial resources dwindled, and
its prime mover, Sir Joseph Banks, found his health failing at
the same time that his official duties outside the Association were
multiplying. By 1804 he had lost the use of his legs and had to
be pushed around in a wheelchair. In addition to being president
of the Royal Society, he was by this time a privy councillor and a
member of the Board of Trade and of countless committees. No
one else with his energy and curiosity appeared in the Association
to take his place. The torch of African exploration, which the
Saturday's Club had lit single-handed in 1788, was passed on
to a new sponsor – the British government.

After a ten-year interruption owing to the Napoleonic agi-
tation on the Continent, two government expeditions to find
the Niger were planned in 1815, one by the Colonial Office and
one by the Admiralty. Both were dismal failures with high
casualty rates, and neither led to any increase in knowledge. They
simply confirmed that the combination of lethal fevers and
hostile tribesmen made a formidable barrier.

The leader of the Colonial Office expedition was Major John
Peddie of the 12th Foot. His aim was 'the discovery of the mouths
of the Niger', by whatever route he chose. Once in Africa, he
was to enroll a hundred volunteers from the Royal Africa Corps.
The Colonial Office did not seem to feel that volunteers might be

harder to find after Park's second expedition. Peddie reached the Senegal in November 1815 and promptly died of fever. The mission was taken over by Captain William Gray and Staff-Surgeon Dochard. They set out with one hundred men and two hundred pack animals, armed with light artillery. It was a repetition of Park's second journey, with all the attendant horror. The column was decimated by fever, men lost their minds and begged to be left behind. The natives, by now convinced that the missions were for the purpose of establishing a river trade route, were more hostile and grasping than ever. When they reached the upper Senegal, Dochard went ahead on reconnaissance with a sergeant and seven men and reached the Niger between Segou and Bamako. But the King of Segou would not give him permission to continue, and so they gave up and went back to the coast. The mission, with three times as many men as Park had, got one-third as far.

At the Admiralty there was a man whose enthusiasm to promote African exploration was second only to Banks's, John Barrow, who served as Second Secretary from 1805 to 1845. Barrow, the only child of a Lancashire farmer, was a self-made man who as a youth went to sea aboard a Greenland-bound whaler and later travelled extensively in China and Africa. He was by nature an imperialist. His colleague at the Colonial Office, Lord Bathurst, said of him: 'Barrow is a great authority, but it has often been said that if coveting islands or Foreign Settlements is a breach of the 10th Commandment, he is the greatest violator of the decalogue in the kingdom.' His passion for exploration was usually carried out behind the scenes, for Africa was the responsibility of the Colonial Office. Barrow mulishly held to the theory that the Niger was a branch of the Nile, and it is ironic that he devoted so much energy to sponsoring explorers who would one day prove him wrong. After the decline of the African Association, however, no one did more to spur reluctant ministers and tight-fisted Parliaments to finance missions to Africa. If two non-explorers should be singled out for solving the Niger's riddle, they are Banks and Barrow.

It was Barrow who sponsored the Admiralty expedition under Captain James Kingston Tuckey, who had surveyed Sydney harbour and written four technical books on maritime geography, but who had never been to Africa. His mission was to discover whether the mouth of the Niger and the Congo were one and the same (the mouth of the Congo was in fact about 900 miles south of the Niger delta). Barrow's instructions read:

> That a river of such magnitude as the Zair (Congo) should not be known with any degree of certainty beyond 200 miles from its mouth is incompatible with the present advanced state of geographical science . . . if in your progress it will be found that the general trending of its course is from the North-East, it will strengthen the conjecture of that branch and the Niger being one and the same river . . . in all your proceedings you are to be particularly mindful of the health of the officers and men under your orders.

Tuckey had six officers, a crew of forty-two, and a staff of five scientists, including a Norwegian botanist and a gardener from Kew. They set out in February 1816, aboard a sloop called the *Congo*, accompanied by a transport, the *Dorothy*, and reached the mouth of the Congo at the end of June. But the current was too strong, and both ships had to be abandoned. Thirty Europeans continued upstream in small boats but were stopped by the falls of Yallala. They trudged on overland, but were so weakened by fever that on 9 September the carriers staged a sitdown strike. They had gone 280 miles, and were now, wrote Tuckey, 'under the necessity of turning our back on the river, which we did with great regret, but with the consciousness of having done all that we possibly could'. Three of the five scientists were dead by this time, and Tuckey and a fourth scientist died after reaching their boats on 17 September. Out of fifty-four men who set out, thirty-five were buried in Africa.

Five

THE TRIPOLI ROUTE

In the spring of 1817, a letter strongly recommending Tripoli as 'an open gate into the interior of Africa' came to the attention of John Barrow, the Second Secretary of the Admiralty who had backed the disastrous Peddie and Tuckey missions. The letter had been sent by a young naval officer, W. H. Smyth, to his admiral, Sir Charles Penrose. Smyth had sailed to Tripoli to retrieve the few broken columns then above ground and twenty cases of statues from the Roman temple at Leptis Magna, which the local ruler or bashaw (pasha) had presented to the Duke of York. Smyth was impressed by the cordial relations between Bashaw Yusuf Karamanli and the English consul in Tripoli, and gained an exaggerated idea of Yusuf's influence in the interior. His letter said that 'by striking due South of Tripoli, a traveller will reach Bornu before he is out of Yusuf's influence; and wherever his power reaches, the protecting virtues of the British flag are well known. In fact, looking to the unavoidable causes of death along the malarious banks of the rivers of the Western coast, I think this ought to be the chosen route, because practicable into the very heart of the most benighted quarter of the globe.'

Smyth's letter could not have been more timely, for Barrow, discouraged by the failures of the missions originating from the West coast, was ready to be persuaded of the northern route's advantages. That same year, the first government-sponsored mission to the Niger via Tripoli was sent out. All the other important missions would use this route until 1829, when the

Lander brothers discovered the Niger's mouth by starting from the Gulf of Guinea.

A combination of factors made Tripoli seem attractive. There was the presence of a Falstaffian English consul, Hanmer Warrington, whose qualities and faults were larger than life, and who pushed the cause of the explorers with all his disorganized but considerable energy. There was also the bashaw, on whom Warrington exerted some influence, and who was well-disposed towards explorers travelling through his lands. Then there was the relative advantage of a desert climate over the fever-ridden West African coastal regions, which struck down some explorers before they could begin.

Finally, there was the cosmopolitan atmosphere of Tripoli itself, with its odd mixture of refinement and barbarism. It was a prosperous Mediterranean trading port, one of the few in North Africa where a Christian was a common sight. The major seafaring powers posted consuls there, and their ships lay at anchor in the small bay fringed with date palms, waiting to transport goods and slaves that arrived from the African interior. Tripoli was an open city. The bashaw permitted any profitable activity as long as his share was not forgotten, and corsairs used the harbour to bring in their prizes. It was a city where two civilizations coexisted and sometimes collided, with a many-hued population of sailors on leave, rum-swilling corsairs, blue-turbanned Jews, sharp-trading Maltese, Italian missionaries, Berber camel-drivers from the Fezzan, and fettered slaves in the stinking holds of ships, all mixing uneasily with the city's Moslem majority.

Tripoli had been the gateway to the African interior across the Sahara ever since the pre-Christian Garamantes tribesmen sold carbuncles to the Carthaginians. The way through the Fezzan to Murzuk and on to Bornu was the shortest, safest, and oldest of the caravan routes, used by the Romans and later by the Arabs. Tripoli itself had had many masters; the Sultan of Morocco, the Bey of Tunis, the Spanish, and the Knights of Malta among them. Whoever ruled tried to keep the caravan route open. But the nomads could not be brought under control, and as a result of their raids and the collapse of the oases the importance of the caravans declined, and in the sixteenth century Tripoli fell to the Turks. It was governed by Turkish officials and garrisoned by Janissaries, a corps of mercenaries made up of abducted Christian children in countries under Turkish rule who were trained as soldiers and brought up as Moslems. They intermarried with Arab and Berber women and their sons were called Cologhis. These Cologhis became a powerful group, until the day in 1711 when one of them, Ali Karamanli, invited the officers of the Turkish garrison to a banquet and had them murdered as they ate. Calling himself the bashaw and continuing to give allegiance to the Sublime Porte, he founded a dynasty that ruled for 125 years. Tripoli became the most civilized of the Barbary states.

At the time when English explorers began using Tripoli as a point of departure, the ruler was the bashaw Yusuf Karamanli. Yusuf was the youngest of three brothers, and in order to become bashaw he had had to murder his oldest brother, depose his father, and exile his remaining brother. He ruled Tripoli for the next thirty-seven years, extending his authority southwards with bloody campaigns against nomadic tribes. One explorer who saw his army returning after a campaign in the hinterland counted two thousand human heads on the tips of spears. They belonged to rebellious tribesmen whose beheaded bodies had been burned in caves. But although Yusuf did exercise some authority over the caravan route, his claim that he could guarantee the safety of any traveller bound for Bornu was unfounded.

There was among the European consuls in Tripoli a constant vying for influence, particularly between the British and the French. With the arrival of Hanmer Warrington in 1814, England's fortunes rose. Yusuf found in the new consul a character as extravagant as his own.

Warrington was the son of a country parson, born in 1778; he grew up in Denbighshire, where he earned a reputation as a horseman. He wanted to be a soldier, joined the First Dragoon Guards at sixteen, and saw action in Spain. In 1812 he retired from the army a colonel and married Jane Eliza Price, who was rumoured to be the natural daughter of George IV. No substantiating evidence was ever found, but Warrington did in later years seem to be under some mysterious umbrella of protection held by the royal family, which may have been the reason he was kept so long in Tripoli in spite of his excesses. In any case, court patronage did not extend to financial assistance, for by 1813 Warrington had left England and was in Gibraltar, being sued for collection of a £500 debt. He found a haven on the other side of the Mediterranean, arriving in Tripoli as consul in 1814 and remaining in that post for thirty-two years.

Warrington's influence at the bashaw's court was largely the result of his ability to negotiate a £40,000 loan from the Colonial Office. It was also connected with Lord Exmouth's shelling of Algiers in 1816 as a reprisal against the enslavement of Christians by Barbary corsairs. Yusuf freed the Christian slaves in Tripoli before Lord Exmouth's fleet arrived and always kept thereafter a healthy respect for British naval power. Warrington became a sort of eminence grise, and English explorers were certain to be well received.

Warrington was a fanatical patriot, convinced of English superiority, blustering and insensitive. Whitehall was aware of his shortcomings, but these were in a sense the right shortcomings for the job, which was to defend British interests in a city where corsairs and slavers still counted for a substantial percentage of the bashaw's revenue and where a thousand Maltese were among the British subjects in the consul's care. The bashaw, who had reached the throne through intrigue, could appreciate Warrington, who was constantly interfering in the affairs of other consuls and dispersing his energy in futile quarrels. He ended one report describing a quarrel with another consul with the words: 'I am an Englishman, (thank God). He is not.'

Warrington's favour could also be attributed partly to his toadying before the bashaw. James Richardson, an English explorer who visited Tripoli in 1845 before spending nine months with the Tuaregs in the Sahara, described Warrington at the bashaw's castle, watching troops manoeuvre on the beach below.

'Tell the bashaw I never saw such splendid manoeuvring in all the course of my life,' Warrington informed the interpreter.

'Tell the bashaw that as long as he has such troops as these, he will be invincible.'

'Tell the bashaw I myself should not like to command English troops against these fine fellows.'

Richardson smiled inwardly, for the troops' manoeuvring was, he wrote, in the style of 'the awckward squad'.

Warrington was eager to communicate the dramatic quality of Tripoli life. As he led Richardson through the mildewed corridors of the dungeon-like castle, he said: 'Well, Richardson, what do you think of this? Capital place this for young ladies to dance in, so light and airy. Many a poor wretch has entered here, with promises of fortune and royal favour, and has met his doom at the hand of an assassin! ... I'm a great reader of Shakespeare. It's the next book after the Bible. But a thousand Shakespeares, with all their tragic genius, could never describe the passions which have worked, and the horrors which have been perpetrated in this place.'

Warrington's influence with the bashaw can be seen in one typical Tripoli incident. One morning a corsair and its prize arrived in Tripoli harbour, with the flag of the captured ship flying on the corsair's forestay – and Warrington saw 'with horror and amazement', that it was a British flag. He hastened to the bashaw and demanded justice for this insult to the British flag. Within half an hour the prisoners had been freed, the flag delivered to Warrington, and the corsair captain hung from the very rope it had been on, in spite of appeals from members of the bashaw's entourage to spare the captain in case Tripoli's reputation as a haven for corsairs should suffer.

One of Warrington's occupations was to assist English explorers in their missions to the African interior. In October 1817 a fair and slender twenty-seven-year-old surgeon named Joseph Ritchie arrived in Tripoli with a twenty-three-year-old naval officer named George Lyon and a shipwright named John Belford. (Belford gave a nautical flavour to this desert mission: it would be his job to build a boat if and when they reached the Niger.) Ritchie was a Scotsman and a doctor like Mungo Park, but there the resemblance ended, for he was as bookish and introspective as Park was outgoing and resolute. A friend of a promising young poet named John Keats, Ritchie promised to fling a copy of his poem *Endymion* in the middle of the Sahara. Ritchie's instructions from Lord Bathurst were to 'proceed under proper protection to Timbuktoo . . . and collect all possible information as to the further course of the Niger, and of the probability of your being able to trace the stream of that river with safety to its termination or to any given distance towards that point'. For the first time, a concern for the explorers' safety was expressed in the instructions, as a result of the casualties on previous missions. Warrington, whose jingoism was kindled by the prospect of seeing the Union Jack hoisted on the Niger, promised the Colonial Office that 'when Mr Ritchie arrives everything shall be done for the best – the full extent of this Regency is within our grasp . . . I should suppose overtures of a specific nature must be made, and accompanied by presents.'

One can only wonder how the Colonial Office came to choose Joseph Ritchie to lead an African mission. He was by constitution and temperament totally unsuited to exploration. He fell ill almost at once and never recovered, he was introverted and morose, he took no interest in the country or the people, he did not record his observations, and he caused the mission's failure through a ridiculous oversight – he left Tripoli on a journey that might easily take over a year with only $300. He illustrated perfectly the importance of an explorer's character in the success of his mission. The Colonial Office had given him £2000 in London, and he had squandered it on largely useless equipment, such as a load of corks to preserve insects on, two large chests of arsenic bottles, brown paper for keeping plants, and six hundred pounds of lead.

What we know about the mission is thanks to George Lyon. 'He [Ritchie] relied too much on a singularly retentive memory,' Lyon graciously said. They stayed in Warrington's sumptuous villa outside Tripoli and prepared their Arab disguises, shaving their heads, growing beards, and buying caftans, turbans, and Morocco leather riding boots. While Ritchie stayed indoors studying mathematics, Lyon attended secret Marabout immolation dances to test his Arab costume. He saw Marabouts in trances with nails through their faces and blood gushing from their bitten tongues whirling half-naked until they fell exhausted.

On 18 March 1818 they were received by the bashaw at an audience and told they would be able to join the Bey of Fezzan, Mohammed el Mukni, who was leaving on a slave-raiding expedition in the south. They bought twenty-two camels and some *gerbas* (water-skins) and left four days later as part of a caravan made up of two hundred men and as many camels. Ritchie had exhausted his funds and borrowed $300 from Lyon. They also had beads and other goods to trade, but why Ritchie did not ask Warrington for more money is a mystery. Their

destination was the Fezzan capital of Murzuk, which Hornemann had already reached twenty years before, and where
Ritchie was to adopt the title of English vice-consul.

Like Hornemann, Lyon found that it was difficult to conform
to his Moorish disguise. 'As I sat in our tent writing a letter,'
he said, 'some Arabs came in and seemed to find much amusement
in seeing me write from left to right; but when I told them my
letter was addressed to a female, their astonishment knew no
bounds; and they laughed heartily at the idea that a woman was
capable of reading.' Lyon was shocked to see that for the Arabs
slavery was a normal practice.

Thirty-nine days after leaving Tripoli, the caravan reached
Murzuk, a walled date palm oasis of 2500 inhabitants, with seven
guarded gates. The houses were built of mud, since it never
rained, and were all small, one storey dwellings with courtyards,
except for the sultan's large castle. The population was black,
and Tuaregs came regularly to trade. Water for the vegetable
gardens in the shade of the date palms was brought from shallow
wells where mosquitoes bred.

Murzuk was reputed for its unhealthy climate, and within two
weeks of their arrival Lyon was ill with dysentery, Belford had
caught a mysterious ailment that made him stone deaf, and
Ritchie was struck down 'with an attack of bilious fever accompanied with delirium, and great pain in his back and kidneys,
for which he required constant cupping'.

The next six months, until Ritchie's death, were a nightmare.
They soon exhausted their funds, but Ritchie, with maniacal
stubbornness, would not let Lyon sell any of their goods, 'lest it
should lower us in the eyes of the natives'. Ritchie fell into a
state of apathy, 'almost constantly remained secluded in his
own apartment, silent, unoccupied, and averse to any kind of
society'.

They were reduced to pauperism, and lived for six weeks on
grain and dates. When, in extremity, Lyon did try to sell some
goods, he discovered that the sultan, the same friendly Mohammed el Mukni whose caravan they had joined, had forbidden the
people of Murzuk to trade with them. One young Moor who
befriended the helpless explorers told Lyon: 'Mukni hopes you
may die so that he may secure to himself all your goods.'

Mukni outwardly continued to pretend great friendship. When

Lyon tried to borrow money from him, he apologized profusely for not having any on hand, and finally said he could let him have eight dollars. Their fortunes rose a bit when Belford made a carriage for the sultan. But as the months passed, and Ritchie showed little sign of improvement, their time was absorbed by the task of day-to-day survival.

In September, Lyon took advantage of a departure for Tripoli to send Warrington a request for funds, and in the meantime sold one of their horses. But Ritchie, although bedridden and weaker, continued to oppose selling any of their goods. 'Mr Ritchie being attacked again by illness,' Lyon wrote, 'I much wished him to allow of my selling some of our powder to procure him a few comforts; but to this he would not consent.'

Ritchie's unwillingness to take obvious measures to improve their situation and assure the success of his mission verged on the pathological. Perhaps by this time he was delirious. He could eat no food and drank quantities of vinegar and water. On 17 November he felt better and drank some coffee. He looked at himself in the mirror and told Lyon: 'I was frightened at the blackness of my tongue, but now recollect I have been drinking coffee; had I observed that appearance without knowing the cause, I should have said I had bilious fever, and should bid you goodbye.'

Three days later Ritchie died: 'His respiration appeared entirely to cease; and on examination I found that he had actually expired, without a pang or groan, in the same position in which he had fallen asleep.' Belford's skills as a carpenter could finally be of service to the mission. He made the coffin Ritchie was buried in, and the first chapter of the Koran was read over his grave. That night, Lyon secretly returned to the grave and read the Protestant burial service.

Within an hour of the funeral, a letter had arrived to say that the government would allow Ritchie a credit of another £1000. But the mission was over, for Lyon could not obtain cash from the sultan and had to return to Tripoli after a short trip to the interior. In exchange for £2000 and the life of its leader, the mission produced no new information. The most important data collected by Lyon from traders in Murzuk proved to be wrong. He came to the conclusion that the Niger 'runs into a lake called the Tsaad . . . thus far are we able to trace the Nil [as he called

113

it] and all other accounts are merely conjectural. All agree, however, that by one route or another, these waters join the great Nile of Egypt.' John Barrow at the Admiralty was delighted with Lyon's report, which supported his own theory. As a result of Lyon's hearsay, the next expedition was sent to Lake Tchad to find the Niger's termination. Lyon left Murzuk in February 1819 and brought back to England a Mehari camel to present to King George IV. With the exception of the camel and Lyon's subsequent book, the mission produced nothing except misinformation and needless frustration.

Now that Lyon had convinced the civil servants who sponsored explorers that the Niger ran into Lake Tchad, their new destination became the old African kingdom of Bornu, south of Lake Tchad. Warrington, with his usual bombastic optimism, wrote to the Colonial Office that it was as easy to get from Tripoli to Bornu as from London to Edinburgh and that 'I should not hesitate to go, knowing as I do there is neither danger nor difficulty attending it'.

John Barrow, not realizing that this was pure rhetoric, began to look for someone to accompany Warrington. In 1820 he recruited Walter Oudney, like Mungo Park a lowland Scot and a doctor. Oudney, aged thirty-one, was practising in Edinburgh after some years as a naval surgeon. A character reference said of him: 'He is abstemious to a degree . . . a good active little walker; as to Horsemanship, I cannot say, but a few falls at the Edinburgh riding school may be of service to him.' Oudney's character revealed itself in the course of the mission as rather self-effacing. He was a small man with a pale grave face better suited to Edinburgh sick-beds than the African wilderness, and he was suffering from tuberculosis, which eventually killed him. It soon became clear that Warrington had no intention of turning explorer, and Oudney recruited his friend and Edinburgh neighbour, Hugh Clapperton, aged thirty-three, the tenth son of a Dumfriesshire doctor. 'My friend Lieutenant Clapperton is a gentleman of excellent disposition, strong constitution, and most temperate habits,' wrote Oudney to Barrow, 'who is exceedingly desirous of accompanying the expedition. He wishes no salary, his sole object being love of knowledge.'

Clapperton, the nonpareil who would not take money, had first gone to sea on a merchant ship as a cabin boy, and had shown his independence of mind by refusing to shine the captain's shoes. He then served in the navy, reaching the rank of lieutenant. Sent to the East Indies, he was first in the breach at the battle for Mauritius in 1814 and hauled down the French flag. He next served on the great lakes and commanded a block-house on Lake Huron. He lost half a thumb carrying an exhausted youth across the frozen lake while escaping the attack of an American schooner. He was said to have become engaged to a Huron princess, but in 1817 he was sent home on half-pay, a victim of peace. Clapperton, with his experience of far-off places, his robust constitution, and his proven military courage, seemed a welcome addition to the mission. He also looked the part. He was six feet tall in an age of short men, with a high brow, piercing eyes, and well-modelled features.

At the same time that Clapperton volunteered, the Colonial Office received a request to join the mission from a thirty-five-year-old instructor at Sandhurst, Lieutenant Dixon Denham. He had no qualifications for African exploration, but he was a brave soldier who at the Battle of Toulouse had carried his wounded commander out of the line of fire. Denham, the officer gentleman, equally poised on battlefields and in drawing rooms, was drawn to African travel on an impulse, as he might have swum the Thames in winter on a dare. He also had friends in high circles – including perhaps the Duke of Wellington himself, with whom he corresponded – and this seems to have been the key factor in securing his appointment.

If the Ritchie–Lyon expedition had been an example of a man defeating himself through a strange inability to cope with practical problems, the Denham–Clapperton–Oudney mission became a classic of personality conflict. The enmity that built up between Denham and his two associates overshadowed the whole voyage, which turned into a study of the deterioration of civilized values under the strain of travelling in the wilderness.

Considering the tensions involved, it is surprising that they accomplished as much as they did. They failed to find the termination of the Niger, but they were the first Europeans to reach the kingdom of Bornu and stand on the shores of Lake Tchad. They helped chart a large area of the African interior about which almost nothing had been written since Leo the African in the sixteenth century. They stayed in the interior for four years, showed that the Tripoli route to Bornu was practicable for Europeans travelling in Christian dress, and pushed deep into the Sudan.

Much of the trouble on the mission was due to Denham's peremptory nature. He was the sort of man who had to build himself up constantly at the expense of others. Like a child on a seesaw, he could not be up unless someone else was down. From the start he denigrated his companions and made paranoid accusations against them. The most innocent matters were turned into intrigues hatched against him. It seemed that his only focus was through the tinted lens of personal rivalry.

Although both Oudney and Clapperton had been recruited before him, and although Clapperton was his senior in service record, Denham manoeuvred to establish himself as leader of the mission. In this aim he was abetted by the vagueness of Lord Bathurst's instructions. Oudney was to assume the duties of vice-consul in Bornu, 'with a view to the successful prosecution of the discoveries now attempting in the Interior of Africa and the extension of our commerce to the interior of that Continent'. Clapperton's and Denham's goal was 'that of tracing the Niger, which is understood to flow through Bornu to its termination. The one destined for this service is Lieut. Denham, who will be directed to proceed from Bornu easterly . . . but you are not to consider him as subject to your orders, as he proceeds on a special service under my direction.' Denham was to give the most liberal interpretation to that last sentence.

In September 1821 Oudney and Clapperton sailed from Falmouth to Malta without seeing their instructions. Denham was not ready and would follow later. When the instructions were forwarded to Malta, Oudney was unhappy to learn that instead of exploring he would be tied up in Bornu doing paperwork. They arrived a month later in Tripoli aboard a Sicilian fishing boat and were warmly greeted by Warrington. Denham soon joined them with a shipwright named William Hillman whom he had hired in Malta. He lost no time in forming a low opinion of his partners, whom he had only met once previously at the Colonial Office in London, and wrote to his brother Charles: 'They are both Scotchmen and friends . . . and to push me off the stage altogether would be exactly what they wish.' Of Clapperton he wrote, 'so vulgar, conceited and quarrelsome a person I scarcely ever met with', and of Oudney he said, 'this son of war or rather of bluster completely rules, therefore any proposition from me is generally negatived by a majority'.

The next step was to obtain permission to proceed from the bashaw. The three explorers were uncertain whether to adopt Moorish costumes like their predecessors. Receiving Denham, the bashaw told him: 'Do what you will, no living creature will take you for a Mohammedan.' It had by now dawned on the bashaw that easy profits could be made by guaranteeing the safety of the explorers, a guarantee that was meaningless south of Murzuk. He offered to provide an escort of a thousand armed men to Bornu and back in exchange for £5000. Warrington forwarded this proposal to the Colonial Office with enthusiasm, as if he had negotiated a clever deal. But, apart from the expense, dependence on the bashaw meant interminable delays, while an armed escort was a dubious blessing, since, as Oudney pointed out, it would make them seem to be on a mission of conquest, and undisciplined troops were likely to make trouble everywhere they went.

After waiting four months for the bashaw to make good his promise, the explorers set out on their own in February 1822, and reached Murzuk without incident. The new Bey of Fezzan, succeeding the one who had refused to help Ritchie, was a renegade named Mustafa the Red, who had married one of the bashaw's daughters. It was Mustafa the Red who was supposed to escort them to Bornu with a thousand troops.

When they arrived in Murzuk, Mustafa the Red was about to leave, but for Tripoli, not Bornu. In his absence, the three explorers and the shipwright Hillman were left virtual prisoners in the Fezzan capital, unable to buy the camels and provisions they needed to continue south. Denham, seeing no reason to wait in Murzuk, and fearful of the climate that had killed Ritchie, doubled back to Tripoli to obtain permission to proceed from the bashaw and more funds from Warrington.

In Denham's absence, Oudney and Clapperton made short trips into the desert. They visited the Roman mausoleum of Garama, the ancient capital of the Garamantes, which looms abruptly over the desert. They saw dunes 400 feet high. They discovered in the heart of the mountain a forgotten community able to survive in the desert on next to nothing, a few hundred wretched natives settled on the shores of little salt lakes, who lived on tiny shrimp-like creatures that bred there, catching them with closely woven nets. They visited the headquarters of the Ajjer Tuaregs, the oasis of Ghat. The Tuaregs' friendly welcome seemed further proof that a military escort was not needed.

In the meantime, Denham in Tripoli found the bashaw still insisting that they should not leave Murzuk without Mustafa the Red and his men, which meant a delay of another six months. Warrington had paid the bashaw two thousand of the promised £5000, and, to ensure that he collected the rest, the bashaw was intent on maintaining the conditions of the deal. Denham, who liked to be constantly on the move, boarded a Marseilles-bound ship to force the bashaw's hand. He intended to go to London, report the missions' problems to Lord Bathurst, and ask for formal command and the rank of lieutenant-colonel. His departure had the desired effect of prodding the bashaw into a change of heart. He told Warrington the explorers could leave for Bornu with the well-known merchant Bu Khullum and an escort of two hundred armed men, against payment of a total of £2500. News of this arrangement intercepted Denham in Marseilles and sent him hurrying back to Tripoli, but not before he had written a letter to Lord Bathurst complaining about Oudney:

> Never was a man so ill-qualified for such a duty [leading the mission]. Except by water, I think, he has never travelled 30 miles from Edinbro'. Still everything would he arrange and on we went, blundering in misery, although at a considerable expense. Not one word of any language could he speak except his own, yet he did undauntedly harangue those around him who bowed, walked off, and of course cheated him.

Oudney was no more kindly disposed towards Denham, particularly when he learned from Warrington that he had deserted the mission and left for England.

> What has taken Denham to England [he wrote to Warrington]? I do not know how he can exculpate himself, or look us in the face, for leaving the Mission at a time when its objects were so near being accomplished . . . My countrymen are famed for caution, but he far surpasses them. And I am sure he would take nothing

on his shoulders . . . I really believe he would not go his body's
length without it was insured. His conduct has been all along what
has tended to alienate affection . . . for my part, I have never
borne as much from any man as from him . . . Had I known the
man, I would have refused my appointment . . . destroy this, it
may be considered spleen, Envy, or some of the evil passions
proceeding from a weakened mind.

But Warrington kept the letter, and Denham apparently saw it
as he was passing through Tripoli, which further soured relations.

Bu Khullum's trade caravan left Murzuk in November 1822.
The British mission consisted of four Europeans, five servants,
and four camel drivers. With the escort of two hundred men, the
caravan was three hundred strong. They would head due south
nine hundred miles through a great sand sea before reaching Lake
Tchad. The few wells were often choked with sand, which took
hours to dig out. They were leaving in force and with an experienced leader, so that they had a good chance of not getting
lost or being attacked. On the other hand, as the first explorers
to reach black Africa via the northern route, they were advancing
into a country as unknown and as menacing as outer space.

Previous missions had done little to dispel the ignorance
concerning the realities of African travel. They did not use
mosquito nets or boil their water or take quinine as a preventive
medicine. Having a doctor along was of little use, for medical
knowledge was limited to cupping, and taking calomel or
vinegar and water. Their equipment and means of transportation
were, with the exception of firearms, largely the same as those
the caravans had been using for more than a thousand years.
Survival depended not on medicines and purified water, but on
their two feet and the variable human qualities of courage,
stamina, and determination. The understated, matter-of-fact
accounts of their adventures would chill the spines of armchair
explorers sitting in front of warm fires in their dens. But those
accounts gave no hint of the human drama of four Englishmen,
alone in a hostile land, and dependent on close co-operation
for the success of their mission, gradually becoming bitter
enemies. Warrington in Tripoli was aware of the danger, and
wrote to the Colonial Office in November of the 'hostile disposition existing in the Southern Mission'. He believed that it
would be impossible to reconcile the partners.

The desert they crossed was lined with human skeletons, many of which were to be found near dried-up wells. Around one well, Denham saw 'more than one hundred skeletons, some of them with the skin still remaining attached to the bones – not even a little sand thrown over them. The Arabs laughed heartily at my expression of horror and said, "They are only blacks, nam boo!" (Damn their fathers!) and began knocking about the limbs with the butt ends of their firelocks, saying, "This was a woman! This was a youngster!" '

The dreariness of the crossing, with its endless billows of sand, and camels dying of exhaustion, was broken by the first open quarrel between Clapperton and Denham, in December, somewhere between Murzuk and Bilma. Denham ordered Clapperton to give him the latitudes of various points, and Clapperton refused, saying he was not to be subjected to the whim of any man. Clapperton vowed to keep from Denham all the observations he made during the mission. He wrote that Denham 'has quarrelled with and browbeat every person belonging to the mission or who has ever been attached to it'. Soon they were not on speaking terms and communicated by letter, like an estranged couple still sharing the same house, except that this was the middle of the Libyan desert. In a note dated 'Tents, Jan. 1, 1823', Clapperton informed Denham that 'you take upon yourself a great deal to issue such orders which could not be more imperative were they from the Horse Guards or Admiralty, you must not introduce a Martial system into what is civil and scientific, neither must you expect from me what it is your duty to execute'.

They both forwarded copies of their ill-tempered correspondence to the Colonial Office, via a messenger service consisting of two Tiboo tribesmen (they travelled in pairs because only one was expected to survive) who left for Tripoli with the mail pouch, a sack of grain, a skin of water, and small bags tied to their camels' tails to catch the dung which they used as fuel. The messengers risked their lives to convey the explorers' malicious gossip. Denham wrote to Lord Bathurst that Clapperton had 'an overbearing, boasting, and consequential deportment, which has made him so disliked by all the Arab sheiks ... on account of Hillman taking the part of Bu Khullum, against whom Mr Clapperton was levelling his worst abuse, such as I cannot repeat to your Lordship, he threatened to knock him down if he was not silent.'

On 5 February 1823, after ninety days in the desert, the caravan reached Lake Tchad. Its banks were lined with reeds ten feet high that hid the water. By this time, Oudney had chest pains and a bad cough, and Hillman was ill with fever. But their sickness and quarrels must have been momentarily forgotten at the sight of the great lake which no other European had seen, with its succession of gulfs, peninsulas and floating islands that surfaced and vanished according to the winds and variations in water level, and the biblical profusion of its wild-life. 'By sunrise I was on the border of the lake,' wrote Denham, 'and very quietly sat down to observe the scene before me. Pelicans, cranes four and five feet in height were scarcely so many yards from my side; immense spoonbills of a snowy whiteness, widgeon, teal, yellow-legged plover, and a hundred species of (to me at least) unknown water fowl.'

At the time of the English explorers' arrival, the kingdom of Bornu had become the most powerful state between the Niger and the Nile. It controlled Lake Tchad and one of the main caravan routes to Tripoli, as well as major cities like Kano and its capital of Kukawa, less than fifteen miles south of the lake. To the west, between Bornu and the Niger, lay the Sokoto Caliphate, ruled by a Moslem reformer, Sultan Bello. The capital of Sokoto, on the edge of the desert, had once been a hunters' camp at the foot of a tamarind tree. Sultan Bello made the Caliphate into a confederation of states held together by mutual interests and a religious bond, which lasted late into the nineteenth century. For the first time in history the Hausa states were united. The Caliphate became the largest political unit in nineteenth-century West Africa, surpassing even Bornu, with its fifteen major emirates totalling 180,000 square miles, about half the size of present-day Nigeria.

While Sultan Bello was forging the Caliphate, Bornu was ruled by another remarkable African leader, Sheikh Mohammed el Kanemi, also a religious prophet and a man of learning who spread Islam through his territory. It was Clapperton's good fortune to meet both these African leaders, who were largely responsible for the political shape of the Sudan in the nineteenth century.

On 16 February 1823 the caravan reached the Bornu capital of Kukawa, twelve miles west of the lake shore, and a few days later the English mission was received by Sheikh el Kanemi. The scene marked the passing of an age. It was the first meeting between the white men who would one day colonize Africa and a ruler deep in the impenetrable hinterland which no European in history had previously been able to reach. Now the soldier, the sailor, the surgeon and the shipwright, in English uniforms set off by turbans and Turkish boots, stood in a dark room before an African sheikh in a blue robe, who sat cross-legged on a rug, flanked by two armed guards. They were the official emissaries of a European government, the first of a long line of civil servants sent on African duty. On that day the last barrier to the inaccessible West African heartland was crossed.

They told him that they had come: 'to see the country merely, and to give an account of its inhabitants, produce, and appearance; as our sultan was desirous of knowing every part of the globe.' The explorers made Kukawa their base for nearly a year, setting out on several side trips during that time. They exchanged presents with the skeikh, giving him a double-barrelled shotgun and a pair of pistols. Clapperton amazed the local population by firing three Congreve rockets tied to the tips of spears. El Kanemi was delighted with their company and insisted on keeping them close to hand. He told them it was not safe to leave Bornu, and claimed that if anything happened to them the bashaw would invade his country.

Oudney was by this time so ill that he spent most of the time in bed. Denham, however, seemed bursting with health and enjoyed the attentions of pretty black women, who gave him what he called 'shampoos', body massages with oil. These 'shampoos' were thorough enough to make him write after one session: 'Verily I began to think that I not only deserved to be a sultan, but that I had already commenced my reign.' Denham's romps with the local girls, however, left him time to aggravate his quarrel with Clapperton. On 11 April, in a letter to Clapperton, he made an insinuation which permanently poisoned the atmosphere of the mission.

> I should neglect my duty [he wrote], were I any longer to delay setting before you in the strongest light I am able the continued extreme impropriety of your conduct both public and private . . .

when the line of conduct you pursue had the effect of injuring our respectability and National Character in the eyes of those people on whom we are but too dependent for aid in prosecuting the orders of the British government, it becomes necessary to obviate the consequences . . . the servant of the mess has now complained to me of your having beaten him here, of your having drawn a pistol on him while on the road, threatening to shoot him . . . the expression I myself heard you use toward this unfortunate person was 'You B——R, I'll pick your teeth for rings in my ears.' I have thought it right to state the foregoing facts for your serious consideration and as far as I know myself without the slightest feeling of ill will.

The outraged Clapperton asked Oudney to support his protest to the Colonial Office with a written opinion. Oudney, who had often been the butt of Denham's high-handed malice, was happy to comply. 'I cannot express my indignation at the vileness . . . of the accusations and the way in which they were arranged,' he wrote. 'It indicates a mind void of every drop of human kindness, a mind that hoards its venom to sting when it may find an opportunity – a man that takes memoranda on the conduct of others is one that ought to be expelled from society, he is a nuisance, he is a curse.'

On 16 April 1823 Clapperton and Oudney confronted Denham and asked him to clarify what he had said about Clapperton's conduct 'both public and private'. Denham replied: 'Oh you must have heard it surely . . . it was the conversation of everyone, our own servants were talking about it every night over the fire.' Oudney said he knew nothing about it. Denham then announced that it was common knowledge among the Arabs of the caravan that Clapperton had homosexual relations with one of his Arab servants. To make such a charge in pre-Victorian England, in front of a witness, could have been enough to ruin a man's career and, if proved, to send him to jail. It was the worst sort of slander, particularly since Denham must have realized it would reach the ears of the Colonial Office.

Clapperton recounted the incident in a letter to Warrington: 'When we were encamped at Achenouma, an Arab . . . came into his (Denham's) tent and told him that I had wanted to commit the foulest crime in nature with an Arab named Abdullahi who was in my service and that the Arab had gone to complain of me.' When Clapperton asked that the Arab be questioned, he was not to be found. Clapperton asked for a full investigation 'to clear my name from the most horrid stigma'.

In the meantime, Oudney investigated and wrote to Warrington that 'Abdullahi is a man above forty and very ugly'. Oudney wanted to show the implausibility of Denham's accusation, but in doing so he unwittingly left the implication that had the Arab been younger and less ugly it would have been harder to disprove. Abdullahi had been hired by Clapperton but discharged after the carcass of a young camel was stolen in the night. The accusation was in all likelihood the invention of a disgruntled Arab, but Denham dignified it, and stored it away to use when the need arose, in order to discredit Clapperton. Warrington, who was more strait-laced in matters of propriety than property, wrote to the Colonial Office: 'A more infamous, vile, diabolical insinuation to blast the reputation of a man was never before resorted to . . . as to any attempt to reconcile, it would now indeed be fruitless.'

Lord Bathurst himself wrote that Denham must either substantiate the charges or return at once to England. Denham, realizing his scheme had backfired, at once wrote that he was sure of Clapperton's innocence. 'I ever believed the report to be a very malicious falsehood,' he said. And yet he would not apologize to Clapperton, and the mission proceeded with its members hopelessly at odds. Without excusing Denham's conduct, it should be said that there was probably some truth in his description of Clapperton's short-tempered treatment of servants. Clapperton was quick to take offence, and as Warrington once wrote: 'I never sat down to table with Mr Clapperton without feeling a dread that something disagreeable would happen before we separated.'

Perhaps to get away from the growing controversy over his accusation, Denham decided in May to accompany a large slave raid heading two hundred miles south-east into Mandara country. The English government was by now abolitionist and Denham had been expressly forbidden to take part in or otherwise sanction slave raids. But he could not resist the call to action, and would on this occasion reap his full quota, barely escaping with his life. Under the guise of a pacification mission to help the Sultan of Mandara put down invading Fulani tribesmen, two thousand horsemen left Kukawa under the command of Sheikh el Kanemi's top general, a Hausa warrior named Barca Gana. Denham rode in the front ranks with Bu Khullum, the trader who had led their caravan across the desert. One of the soldiers asked Bu Khullum whether Denham was a Moslem. 'No,' said Bu Khullum, 'he is a Miskin [wretched]: they do not believe in the book; they do not pray five times a day; they are not circumcized . . . but they will see their errors and die Moslem, for they are beautiful people.'

Through his telescope Denham could see the natives fleeing into the mountains as the column approached. Others too slow to run brought gifts of leopard skins and honey, prostrated themselves, and threw sand over their heads in a gesture of obeisance. The Bornu and Arab horsemen were soon joined by two thousand Mandara horsemen led by their sultan. The column continued to the town of Musfeia where the Fulanis were entrenched in a strong position, on high ground behind a stream, that could only be approached through a narrow defile between two hills, across which a fence of pointed stakes had been stretched. The Arab horsemen rode into the defile, and the Fulanis let fly a stream of arrows, some of them poisoned. They had, as Denham put it:

> *the dreadful art*
> *To taint with deadly drugs the barbed dart.*

Barca Gana had two horses shot from under him and Bu Khullum was hit in the foot and later died from his wound. A thick burnous protected Denham from the arrows, but one, fortunately not poisoned, grazed his face, and his horse was wounded. When the Bornu and Mandara troops saw the Arab horsemen stalled before the shower of arrows and spears, they fell back, and soon the triumphant slave raid became a rout. Denham followed the others into a wood, with Fulani horsemen in pursuit. His wounded horse buckled and three Fulani warriors came at him with spears, but a show of pistols drove them off. He got back on his horse but was soon thrown, and found himself on foot, unarmed and helpless, or so he claimed in his subsequent account.

Surrounded by Fulanis, he was surprised to find that instead of killing him they stripped him. He was wounded in both hands as he tried to hang on to his trousers. And soon Lieutenant Dixon

Denham, late of His Majesty's 17th Regiment of Foot, was as naked as the natives who surrounded him. He was saved from his predicament when the natives became so absorbed in quarrelling over his clothes that he managed to crawl away. He came to a stream at the bottom of a deep ravine and took hold of a branch to let himself down, but the branch gave way. He tumbled down the ravine and found himself facing a large boa constrictor. He swam to the other side and ran naked and bleeding through the wood until he came upon some stragglers from his army who covered him with a burnous and put him on a horse.

Thus, in a rather ragged state, a little less the peacock than usual, his flesh wounds irritated by the rough wool burnous and the bony horse he rode bareback, his skin crawling with vermin, Denham returned to Kukawa. 'I suffered much,' he wrote, 'both in mind and body, but complained not.' Never so dispirited as to lose interest in the gentle sex, he took the trouble to note that Mandara women were 'singularly gifted with the Hottentot protuberance'.

While Denham was being chased by Fulani tribesmen, Clapperton and Oudney explored the southern end of Lake Tchad to see whether any of the rivers running out of it could be the Niger. The thin streams they found did not qualify, and they came to the conclusion that the Niger terminated in some other lake south of Lake Tchad.

In June the rains began to fall, and the mission waited out the wet season in Kukawa. For the next three months it would be impossible to travel. With the rains came fever. Clapperton and Hillman were bedridden with malaria, and Oudney coughed incessantly, and took nothing but a little sour milk three times a day. Only Denham withstood the debilitating climate, and, as he said, 'ate with cheerfulness'. The rains stopped, but it took Clapperton and Oudney several months to recover, and it was not until mid-December 1823 that they headed west on the 400-mile trip to Kano. Oudney would never see Kano. In his last dispatch to Lord Bathurst, dated 10 December 1823, he announced that he and Clapperton were leaving on their search for the Niger and that 'I am a great invalid and hope the present journey will recruit me a little. I am perfectly convinced the prospect of it is what alone has kept me up.' Ill as he was, it never occurred to Oudney to give up.

On 14 December they left Kukawa with a caravan of Arab
and Bornu merchants. From Kano, they intended to reach the
capital of the Sokoto Caliphate and meet its ruler Sultan Bello,
for whom they had a letter of introduction from the Sheikh of
Bornu, for the two African leaders were at that time on friendly
terms. Moving west across the Tchadian flatland in December,
they came across an unexpected hazard, the cold. Clapperton was
astonished that it could freeze at so low a latitude, and wrote to
Warrington on 27 December that 'we had such an intense cold
that the water was frozen and the dishes and the water skins as
hard as boards'. Barrow was incredulous when the news reached
England. But anyone who has travelled in the desert in winter
knows the raw cold of morning, the sun that provides no warmth,
the insinuating chill. It was enough to finish Oudney, in his
weak, consumptive state. He collapsed in the town of Murdur,
about two-thirds of the way to Kano, and coughed out his lungs.
On 12 January 1824, wrote Clapperton, 'before he could be lifted
on the camel, I observed the ghastliness of death in his countenance, and had him immediately replaced in the tent. I sat down
by his side, and, with unspeakable grief, witnessed his last breath,
which was without a struggle or groan.' Clapperton buried his
friend at the foot of a mimosa tree and enclosed the grave with a
clay wall to keep off hyenas. The grave was soon destroyed by
Arabs because Oudney was a Kafir or infidel whose bones were
believed to pollute the earth.

Oudney died at the age of thirty-two, after slightly more than
two years in Africa, a victim of the consumption which, as a
doctor, he must have known he was suffering from when he left
his native Scotland. He had successfully reached black Africa
via the northern route and visited lands that no European had
seen before. But the price had been high. For Clapperton, 'the
loss was severe and affecting in the extreme'. He mourned a
friend and Edinburgh neighbour, 'a man of unassuming deportment, pleasing manners, steadfast perseverance, and undaunted
enterprise'. The Colonial Office, always niggling when it came to
expenses, outdid itself in Oudney's case. His mother and sister
were almost entirely dependent on him. In its remembrance of a
man who had given his life in its service, the Colonial Office gave
Oudney's mother £100.

Disheartened and ill himself, Clapperton none the less pushed on to Kano, the great trading city of the central Sudan, whose goods were famous in the markets of the Barbary coast. He entered the city on 20 January 1824, resplendent in his naval uniform, but: 'I had no sooner passed the gates than I felt grievously disappointed; for from the flourishing description of it given by Arabs, I expected to see a city of surprising grandeur: I found, on the contrary, the houses nearly a quarter of a mile from the walls, and in many parts scattered into detached groups, between large stagnant pools of water.'

Clapperton spent a month inspecting the city, whose population he estimated at between thirty and forty thousand. It was surrounded by a thirty-foot-high clay wall with fifteen gates of wood covered with sheet iron, which were closed at sunset. The stench from pools of stagnant water and open gutters was overpowering. Kano was a major slave trade centre, and Clapperton visited the long sheds where the slaves were kept, and saw buyers inspecting them 'somewhat in the same manner as a voluntary seaman is examined by a surgeon on entering the navy: he looks at the tongue, eyes, and limbs, and endeavours to detect rupture by a forced cough'. Clapperton came to the conclusion that 'slavery is here so common, or the minds of the slaves are so constituted, that they always appeared much happier than their masters; the women, especially, singing with the greatest glee all the time they are at work'. On the subject of the Niger, Clapperton was told that the great river ran south into the Atlantic at the Gulf of Guinea, but, still convinced that it emptied into a lake in the African heartland, he wrote: 'I place little dependence on such accounts.'

He pushed on towards Sokoto, 250 miles north-west of Kano, and was able to cross a Hausa state still hostile to the Caliphate thanks to an escort that Sultan Bello had sent to meet him. Clapperton always tried to look his best, and entered Sokoto on 16 March 1824 wearing 'my lieutenant's coat, trimmed with gold lace, white trousers, and silk stockings, and to complete my finery, I wore Turkish slippers and a turban'. Sokoto was a walled city with two mosques and flat-roofed houses whose long water-spouts of baked clay, projecting from the eaves, resembled at first sight a tier of guns.

Clapperton found Sultan Bello sitting on a carpet in a thatch-roofed cottage, dressed in a light blue cotton robe, with a white

muslin turban worn Tuareg fashion concealing the lower part
of his face. The sultan was a youthful forty-four, noble-looking,
a little under six feet tall, with a short curling black beard, a
small mouth, a Grecian nose, and large black eyes. A man of
learning, he at once began a theological discussion with Clapperton, who cut it short by saying that he was 'a Protestant . . .
who having protested more than two centuries ago against the
suggestions, absurdities and abuses practised in those days, we
had ever since professed to follow simply what was written in
the book of our lord Jesus'. The sultan then returned to Clapperton books belonging to Denham that had been retrieved in
Mandara during the slave raid, including Bacon's essays and
Denham's journal. The sultan ingenuously wondered why his
old friend the Sheikh of Bornu had sent an army into his territory and why an English explorer had joined it. Clapperton
lamely replied that Denham had merely been touring the
country. To change this embarrassing subject, the sultan asked
what each book was about, wanted to be read aloud to, and
professed to find the sound of the English language very beautiful.

That afternoon, at a second audience, Clapperton presented
the sultan with presents from King George IV, including orna-
mented pistols, razors, gunpowder, a spyglass, a silver tea tray,
and a compass. Clapperton explained that with the compass the
sultan could always find east to pray. 'Everything is wonderful,'
the sultan said, 'But you are the greatest curiosity of all.' Then
he asked: 'What can I give that is most acceptable to the King
of England?'

'The most acceptable service you can render to the King of
England,' replied Clapperton, 'is to co-operate with His Majesty
in putting a stop to the slave trade.'

'What,' asked the sultan, 'have you no slaves in England?'

'No. Whenever a slave sets foot in England, he is from that
moment free.'

'What do you do then for servants?'

'We hire them for a stated period, and give them regular
wages.'

'God is great! You are a beautiful people.'

The sultan surprised Clapperton with his grasp of international
affairs. He knew that the English navy had sunk the Algerian

fleet in 1816 and that England had begun to colonize India. 'You were at war with Algiers,' he told Clapperton, 'and you killed a number of the Algerines.' Clapperton replied that they were a ferocious race, who made slaves of the Europeans. 'You are the strongest of Christian nations,' the sultan said, 'you have subjugated all of India.' Clapperton replied that England had simply given India good laws and protection.

Even though he knew that the English conquered other people, the sultan was tempted by the prospect of trade. He seemed willing to run the risk of an English presence in his dominion for the sake of the firearms which would give him military superiority in the Sudan. He asked Clapperton whether 'the King of England would give him a couple of guns, with ammunition and some rockets. I assured him of His Majesty's compliance with his wishes, if he would consent to put down the slave trade on the coast.' Clapperton, like a good salesman, made trade with England seem irresistible. The sultan, he said, would become one of the greatest princes in Africa. If he built a trade port on the coast he would have his own navy, the English would show him how to build ships, and once he had ships he would be able to trade with the rest of the world and send pilgrims to Mecca by the safer sea route. The sultan promised to let the English build a town on the coast. It was an empty promise, for the Sokoto Caliphate was landlocked and the sultan's influence did not extend to the coast.

At the same time, the powerful Arab lobby in Sokoto realized that Clapperton's proposals would be disastrous for the caravan trade. Slaves were their main product, and the trans-Saharan route would remain profitable only as long as there was no direct competition from the sea. Now here was a man who was asking for the abolition of slavery and the establishment of a river trade route to the sea. Clapperton's proposals horrified the sultan's Arab advisers and their influential trader friends.

Sultan Bello's final position was ambiguous. He said he welcomed trade with England, but put pressure on Clapperton to interrupt his trip and return to Bornu. Clapperton was told of the great dangers involved if he tried to continue south from Sokoto in search of the Niger. 'Think of it with prudence,' Bello told him. Bello's men told Clapperton's servants how useless it would be to risk their lives by trying to pass through regions full of warring tribes. Clapperton could not find a guide who would take him. He sensed the reasons behind the pressures.

Clapperton's and Sultan Bello's discussion of the course of the Niger provides the best example of the sultan's conflicting interests. The sultan 'drew on the sand the course of the river Quorra (Niger) which he also informed me entered the sea at Fundah.* By his account the river ran parallel to the sea coast for several days' journey, being in some places only a few hours, in others a day's journey from it. Two or three years ago, the sea, he said, closed up the mouth of the river and its mouth was at present a day or two further South; but during the rains, when the river was high, it still ran into the sea by the old channel.' Clapperton's belief that the river terminated in a lake was finally shaken, and he asked Bello to have a map drawn that he could show in England. But the map, when he got it, contradicted what Bello had told him and showed the Niger flowing east towards the Nile. Somewhere along the chain of command from the sultan to the person who drew the map, the river's direction had been diverted in an obvious attempt to mislead Clapperton.

To proceed in defiance of the sultan's wishes, ill and weary, with mutinous servants, into hostile territory, was more than Clapperton could manage. After nearly two months in Sokoto, he started back on the road to Bornu on 4 May 1824. The sultan, still of two minds, asked him to return, and promised to send an escort to fetch him at any point along the coast. He gave Clapperton a letter for George IV and bade him an affectionate farewell. Bello's letter agreed to put a stop to the slave trade 'on account of the good which will result from it, both to you and to us', in exchange for English weapons.

Ten weeks later Clapperton was back in Kukawa, looking wasted, according to Denham, who returned at about the same time from his travels in Hausa country. 'It was nearly eight months since we had separated,' Denham wrote, 'and although it was mid-day I went immediately to the hut where he was lodged; but so satisfied was I that the sun-burnt sickly person that lay extended on the floor, rolled in a dark blue shirt, was

---

* Fundah was twenty miles north of the Niger-Benue confluence, and quite a distance from the sea.

not my companion, that I was about to leave the place, when he convinced me of my error, by calling me by name: the alteration was certainly in him most striking.'

Denham had in the meantime borne his share of disappointments. When Clapperton and Oudney left for Kano in December 1823, Denham stayed behind in Kukawa still trying to determine whether the Niger ran into Lake Tchad. Soon a caravan from Tripoli arrived, bringing him an assistant in the form of a twenty-one-year-old Maltese ensign named Ernest Toole. Denham and Toole left to explore Lake Tchad, but Toole was so sick that he had to be strapped to his camel. Toole was one of those young and eager volunteers whose sole achievement was to join the growing list of casualties in the cause of African exploration. He died in Ngala, off the southern tip of Lake Tchad, on 26 February 1824. 'A cold shivering had seized him,' Denham wrote, 'and his extremities were like ice. I gave him both tea and rice-water; and there was but little alteration in him, until just before noon, when, without a struggle, he expired, completely worn out and exhausted.' Denham returned to Kukawa and in May another assistant arrived, this time a protégé of Warrington's named John Tyrwhitt, a good-natured young man who played the flute. He was to take the post of vice-consul in Kukawa at £300 a year.

Denham heard from Tyrwhitt that Warrington had called him 'unpopular', and on 25 June he wrote to his brother Charles in his most vitriolic style, railing against 'these insinuations by a man 1500 miles off who knows no more of the interior of Africa than you do of the inside of the Lying In Hospital, who gets drunk every night, and harasses the minds of those he is bound to support with his influence, that is the English influence, for he has none in Tripoli, and when they have nothing but bad water to drink is rather unkind and ungenerous'.

Denham took Tyrwhitt on another excursion along the southern tip of Lake Tchad and returned in July to find that Clapperton was back. The two explorers continued to live apart and to communicate by letter. The one thing they agreed on was that it was time to head north to Tripoli and from there to England. Tyrwhitt was given the choice of going back with them. Although the examples of Oudney and Toole must have been vivid in his mind, and the sight of malaria-stricken Clapperton cannot have been reassuring, Tyrwhitt decided it was his duty to remain. He followed Oudney and Toole to the grave several months after Denham and Clapperton had gone north. Clapperton was determined to return to the Sudan and follow up his pledge from Sultan Bello as soon as he had reported to London and recovered his health.

On 14 September 1824, Clapperton, Denham and Hillman set out across the desert on the same route they had taken twenty months before. The way back seemed a longer, harder march, with nothing but dates to eat, and the camels bruising their hooves on pointed rocks in the stony track. Clapperton, weakened by malaria, suffered terribly. The death of their partner, the common suffering, the African experience shared, all these contributed to an improvement in relations between Clapperton and Denham. Once more they spoke, and were sociable, and Clapperton later referred to Denham's kindness on the journey.

Ten miles outside Tripoli the parched explorers saw a tent that had been set up by Warrington to greet them, and soon they were washing down anchovy toasts with tumblers of Marsala wine, and experiencing the particularly intense sensation that comes from going from a threshold of pain to a threshold of pleasure. It was by now January 1825, and Clapperton's first priority in Tripoli was to write a formal letter to Warrington demanding an official inquiry into Denham's accusations. Warrington persuaded him to let the matter drop, and Clapperton then learned of a far more serious threat than Denham's malice. Lord Bathurst had sent another explorer, Captain Gordon Laing, on a Niger mission, and Captain Laing was expected shortly in Tripoli. This was a blow to Clapperton, who in Sokoto had felt the Niger within his grasp, and who now risked having the prize snatched from his hands. Clapperton's misfortunes – his malaria, his quarrel with Denham, and his friend's death – instead of making him lose heart, had in some curious way strengthened his resolve to find the Niger, like a man who refuses to stop riding a horse that has thrown him. As Mungo Park before him, Clapperton became obsessed, but in a different way. Park had been involved in a struggle against the forces that had defeated him on his first trip; he was shaking his fist at Africa, defying all its dark forces to do their worst. But Clapperton now threw himself into a frenzied race with another explorer, whom he considered a poacher on what had become, because of the hardships already invested, his private preserve. Who would reach the mouth of the Niger first? As it turned out, that particular race had no winner.

The Colonial Office, unaware of the resentment its new explorer had aroused, ordered Clapperton to 'commit to paper whatever part of that important information you are in possession of which must tend considerably to assist the operations and labours of Captain Laing'. Clapperton at first refused, but was later ordered to supply Laing with written information.

Clapperton and Denham returned to England in June 1825, after an absence of three and a half years, to a hero's welcome. They were promoted, Clapperton to captain and Denham to major, they were presented to King George IV, and they were compared to Marco Polo in the press. Clapperton was impatient to leave so that he could overtake Laing, which left Denham to write an account of the mission. Published in 1826, the wealth of new material on the African interior made it a classic of exploration, but a flawed classic, for Denham systematically belittled the contributions of his partners while magnifying his own part. Most of the book, called *Narrative of Travels and other Discoveries in Northern and Central Africa* and co-authored by Oudney and Clapperton, sounds as if he was travelling alone.

The real narrative of the Bornu mission that has come out through journals and correspondence is a Gothic tale of personal animosity, but also of courage and endurance. The explorers overcame both human and geographical obstacles, and the survivors brought back a mass of information that shed the first new light on Bornu since the sixteenth century. Yet in its main goal the mission was a costly failure. The question of the Niger's termination remained open. Each of the explorers had his own theory. Oudney had died convinced that the Niger emptied into a non-existent lake south of Lake Tchad. Denham, who had explored more of Lake Tchad than the other two, still believed the Niger was somehow connected to the lake. Clapperton, on the basis of his talks with Sultan Bello, was converted to the idea that the Niger flowed into the Bight of Benin. Only five years later would one of the three be proved right.

Ironically, Denham died before the answer became known. After capturing the warm rays of popular admiration with his book, he was elected a Fellow of the Royal Society and became a familiar guest at Lord Bathurst's table. He piled up honours and was appointed governor of Sierra Leone in 1828. Return to West Africa proved to be his undoing, and he died of fever the same year, at the age of forty-three. Perhaps the strains of the mission had permanently affected him, making him less resistant to the African climate, just as they affect present-day space explorers, who have suffered debilitating accidents, heart attacks, and nervous breakdowns back on earth.

When Hugh Clapperton and Dixon Denham sailed back to England in the spring of 1825, their ship must have crossed the path of the ship that Clapperton's rival Gordon Laing had boarded in Falmouth in February to take him to Malta, and from there to Tripoli and the quest for the Niger. Major Alexander Gordon Laing, like Clapperton and so many other explorers whose paths we have crossed, was a Scotsman, born in Edinburgh on 27 December 1793, the son of a schoolmaster. Precociously clever, he was teaching at Bruce's Classical Academy by the time he was fifteen. Restless and immoderate, at seventeen he joined the army, being 'disgusted with the people' of his birth-place and 'having contrived to get a good deal into debt'. He served in the West Indies and went to Honduras 'to cure a violent liver complaint'. He was then posted to the Royal Africa Corps in West Africa and in 1822 was named aide-de-camp to Major-General Sir Charles Macarthy, first crown governor of Sierra Leone. Upon his arrival in West Africa he had written to a friend: 'I have had for many years a strong desire to penetrate into the interior of Africa.'

Laing immediately began pulling strings. On 15 March 1821 he wrote to his superior Captain Chisolm that he wanted to find Timbuctu and the Niger's termination. With characteristic recklessness, he said that all he wanted from the government was 'a good gun on which I may depend, a barometer for measuring heights, a pocket sextant, an azimuth for taking angles, and a pocket chronometer, which instruments I would like to be sent out from home and of a good description'. This letter was forwarded to the Colonial Secretary Lord Bathurst with a flattering covering letter from the acting governor of Sierra Leone, A. Grant: 'His motives are no less disinterested than honourable, and as far as human foresight can divine, he is from his physical strength and acquirements well calculated to succeed.' But by that time John Barrow was in the process of recruiting Walter Oudney for just the mission that Laing wanted, and Lord Bathurst coolly replied: 'There does not appear at present to be any opening for the employing of Lt. Laing.'

Laing was the sort who, when the front door shuts in his face, comes in through a side door. In 1822, while serving in Sierra Leone, he led a patrol into Mandingo country, reaching Falaba, in the mountainous Futa Jalon area of present-day Guinea, about sixty miles north-west of the Niger's source. Learning that he was only three days' march from the source, he wrote, 'I was anxious to make my way to it, that, by ascertaining its height above the level of the sea, I might be satisfied if it had elevation enough to carry its waters to the Mediterranean through the Channel of the Nile.'

But those last sixty miles were controlled by a tribe hostile to King Assana of Falaba, who kept delaying Laing's departure. The king did not want to admit that he was powerless so close to home, and raised all sorts of other objections. 'How will you cross the large rivers without a canoe?' he asked.

'I suppose I must swim across them upon gourds,' Laing said.

'Allah ackbar [God is great]!' The king said. 'There are deep swamps on the way, in which you will sink to the neck; how will you pass over them?'

'I must fell trees, and laying them across, scramble over the branches, but I tell you, once and for all, that even a river of fire shall not deter me, if you are kind enough to give me your passport.'

'God is powerful! Go.'

But a day later a messenger caught up with Laing and said the king had had a bad dream about him and that he had to come back. In this way, he made two or three false starts, and there was always a new reason for detaining him. Laing showed his annoyance, and the king said: 'These white men are extraordinary people; here is one leaves me disappointed because I save his life, by preventing him from going to a set of savages, among whom I could not venture with half of Falaba at my heels.' The best Laing could do was climb the highest hill in Falaba, from which he could see that 'the point from which the

Niger issues, now shown to me, appeared to be about the level on which I stood, viz 1600 feet above the level of the Atlantic'.* He did not consider this elevation sufficient to carry the Niger's water as far as Lake Tchad.

Laing's near discovery of the Niger's source made him yearn for another mission. He wrote letters to influential persons, repeating that 'I am anxious to discover the termination of the Niger and am willing to undertake the enterprise . . . without regard to emolument or expectation of reward'. In 1823 the English became involved in a war with the Ashanti tribesmen on the Gold Coast and Laing was sent to organize and command a native force. He distinguished himself, and was chosen to report on the war in England. But like Dixon Denham, Laing's bravery was flawed by an over-impulsive nature. In England, he went over the head of his commanding officer and petitioned the Duke of York for a promotion and leave of absence (he wanted to write a book on his Mandingo expedition), an unheard-of blunder for a British regular army officer to commit.

At the same time, he continued to lobby for an African mission and met Lord Bathurst. His timing was right this time, for the Colonial Secretary had by now realized that the Bornu mission would make no headway on the Niger question and was ready to send another explorer in its wake. Laing wanted to start from the West African coast he already knew, but the one thing the Bornu mission had shown was the practicability of the Tripoli route. Laing was appointed, again over the head of his superior in Sierra Leone. His commanding officer there, General Turner, sent Lord Bathurst a letter on 9 April 1825 so spiteful that it must have reflected a long-standing enmity.

> I would not fulfill my duty either to your Lordship or to the service, were I not to characterize as unwise, unofficerlike and unmanly, the conduct of Captain Gordon Laing in this country . . . his time was occupied in editing a contemptible newspaper . . . His military exploits were worse than his poetry . . . I humbly beg your Lordship, in the name of the Regiment, that he may be removed from it – and that we may not be subject to the mortification of his calling us Brother Officers.

---

* Laing was about one-third off. The Niger's source is 2250 feet above sea level.

Despite this character assassination, Laing's persistence was rewarded and he obtained leave of absence from his regiment for 'scientific researches into the interior of Africa'. Asked to prepare a budget, he came up with a detailed list of items, with their cost down to the last penny. Laing was industrious and enterprising, naturally inquisitive, and blessed with almost miraculous qualities of endurance. At the same time he was swaggering and self-important, and criticized in others what he was about to do himself.

Laing sailed for Malta on 6 February 1825 with a West Indian servant named Jack le Bore, and two West African carpenters, Rogers and Harris. He left England convinced that the mouth of the Niger was in the Bight of Benin and determined to prove it, although he foresaw the difficulty of shaking John Barrow's faith that the Niger was the Nile.

When Laing arrived in Tripoli in May, Warrington's star had slightly faded. He still boasted 'of being able to do anything and everything in Tripoli', but it was no longer true. The bashaw now ruled by playing off the consuls against one another. The new French consul, Joseph-Louis Rousseau, was a distinguished Arabist, who could converse with the bashaw without an interpreter. Warrington, who held open house in his villa 'The Garden', two miles outside town, disliked his studious, constrained French colleague, who snubbed his invitations. To further envenom their relationship, Warrington's delicate, flower-like daughter Emma was being courted by the French consul's son, Timoleon Rousseau. To Warrington, the lover of Shakespeare, the situation may have seemed like a Tripolitan version of Romeo and Juliet.*

Laing's arrival was providential for Warrington, who lost no time in nudging his daughter in the explorer's direction, with such success that two and a half months later they were married, and Emma was saved from a shameful misalliance with a Frenchman. The thirty-two-year-old Laing had an ardent nature. While still in his teens, he had written that 'passionately fond of the fair sex, I had always in my eye some Dulcinea, on whom I used

---

* This love affair between the consuls' offspring is recounted in *Annales tripolitaines*, a history by a former French consul there named Charles Feraud, who mixes gossip with material from government archives and had an anti-Warrington axe to grind, and so must be read with caution.

to dote, make verses, and squander away money'. He was clearly smitten, while Emma was not living in an age when young girls went against their fathers' wishes. In June Laing asked his London friend James Bandinel to buy him 'a handsome little cabinet of mineralogical specimens, such a one as will suit a lady of taste and refinement . . . you must not be forming any strange conclusions from this extraordinary request . . . I am no more than interested, much interested, in the young lady in question.'

Laing's days in Tripoli were not exclusively spent in courting Emma, however, for he also had to court the bashaw in order to leave under his protection. The bashaw could only wonder at the bizarre English penchant for African exploration, but at the same time he profited from it. With each explorer, the price of protection rose. Not only did money have to be paid, but it had to be offered in roundabout subtle ways, as part of a complicated ritual. The bashaw kept finding excuses for not meeting Laing. Warrington told his minister that 'sooner than suffer Major Laing to be detained for about four months I should not hesitate to give his highness a small sum to enable him to meet his expenses'. The bashaw would not think of accepting money, the minister replied, acknowledging 'the folly of His Highness, who would not express his wants, and in consequence of those wants not being complied with would detain Major Laing, thereby defeating the views of England'.

Warrington said he could give up to £500. The answer from the bashaw came: 'Tell the consul whatever he does I shall be satisfied with.' This lukewarm response meant that Warrington could do better, and the consul finally promised a total of £2500 to be paid in stages as Laing progressed. In addition, Warrington gave Laing a letter of credit, signed by himself and 'the slave of Allah', Yusuf Bashaw Karamanli, 'authorizing the bearer Major Laing to draw on us for any money which he may require during his journey into the Interior of Africa'.

Laing saw the bashaw thirteen days after his arrival and wrote to Lord Bathurst: 'I plainly could observe from the cool and hesitating manner of His Highness . . . that without some pecuniary douceur . . . he would continue to detain me in Tripoli for months upon the most frivolous excuses.' Bathurst was furious at the mission's mounting cost, however, and sent Warrington a chastening letter, to which the consul replied with an act of contrition: 'My dilemma was great, and my situation this morning when I received your lordship's dispatch most unpleasant.'

It was arranged that Laing would leave with a Ghadames merchant named Babani. He would not follow the Garamantian way to Bornu that Clapperton and the others had taken, but head south-west through Ghadames and In Salah to Timbuctu, where Babani had good connections. It made more sense to start from Timbuctu, which Mungo Park had reached but not seen, and proceed from there down the Niger, than to grope blindly in the central Sudan for a river that might not be there. Laing now had to wait until Sheikh Babani and his caravan were ready to leave, which left Warrington enough time to give away his daughter.

On 14 July 1825 Gordon Laing married Emma Warrington. He was like a serviceman about to go overseas who marries a girl he has just met and may never see again. Not only did Laing never see Emma again after his departure two days later, but he was not even allowed to consummate the marriage. Warrington's blend of oriental intrigue and Victorian hypocrisy came out in a letter to Lord Bathurst:

> I have the honour to inform your Lordship that Major Laing was this morning married to my second daughter [Warrington wrote]. Although I am aware that Major Laing is a very gentlemanly, honourable, and good man, still I must allow a more wild, enthusiastic, and romantic attachment never before existed and consequently every remonstrance, every argument, and every feeling of disapprobation was resorted to by me to prevent even an engagement under the existing circumstances, the disadvantages so evidently appearing to attach to my daughter . . . both for the public good, as well as their mutual happiness I was obliged to consent to perform the ceremony, under the most sacred, and most solemn obligation that they are not to cohabit till the marriage is duly performed by a clergyman of the established Church of England . . . as long as doubts may arise as to the power and legality invested in me as His Majesty's Consul General to unite two of His Majesty's subjects, as man and wife, and till that doubt is completely removed, I will take good care my daughter remains as pure and chaste as snow.

In the past, Warrington had taken pride in marrying British subjects, but when it came to his daughter he had second thoughts.

Laing and Emma never did get benefit of clergy, for on 18 July he left, after a farewell visit to the bashaw, who advised him that on the route he was taking 'you must open the door with a silver key', and gave him an escort of 150 horsemen out of Tripoli. We know very little about his state of mind on the eve of his departure, for after his death his journal was lost. The only information concerning his trip came from the letters he wrote his wife, his father-in-law, and two friends, the Arctic explorer Edward Sabine, and James Bandinel, a clerk in the Foreign Office. As he left with Sheikh Babani's caravan on the road to Ghadames, he must have felt a mixture of disappointment at leaving behind his virgin bride and exhilaration at starting on a route that had not been visited by Europeans since Roman times.

To reach Timbuctu, the fabled golden city of the Sudan, he would have to cross two thousand miles of some of the worst desert in Africa, where the bashaw's jurisdiction did not extend. Conditions were harsh and life held cheaply; lawless Tuareg bands lived off the plunder of caravans. It would take Laing more than a year to reach Timbuctu, and the difficulties he met make his journey one of the great feats of endurance in a field where there are many. As he set out, unaware of the hardships ahead, Laing was guided by a mystical belief that he was destined to discover 'the far-famed capital of central Africa'. One of his letters to a friend in August had a jaunty, optimistic tone: 'I am at length thus far on my way to the Niger, and its far-famed marginal desideratum, which latter I expect to reach in November at furthest.' Among the supplies carried on eleven camels for himself, his servant Jack le Bore, and the two shipbuilders, he took plumb-lines for sounding the Niger. He was eager to reach the river before Clapperton, whom he feared would 'snatch the cup from my lips'. Before leaving, he had received via the Colonial Office the letter of advice Clapperton had been ordered to write. Its patronizing tone annoyed him. Clapperton told him to be kind and patient with the natives, to take plenty of presents, and not to meddle with local women. Laing told Warrington: 'We need not ghosts to rise from their graves to tell us this.'

It was a hard, two-month trip to Ghadames. To avoid bandits, Sheikh Babani took a circuitous route that doubled the distance from five hundred to a thousand miles. The bashaw had paid Babani $4000 to see Laing safely to Timbuctu, but the sheikh pretended he was doing it for nothing and constantly dunned Laing for more money. Laing found that every Arab he dealt with from Babani onwards was intent on cheating him. 'I never met with such a set of greedy vagabonds,' he wrote to Warrington. The caravan reached Ghadames in September; the desert city suddenly rose before Laing like an island in the ocean, under a green mantle of date palms. In the narrow alleyways of the walled town, the people of the oasis welcomed him warmly. 'Every person vies with his neighbour in the performance of kind and hospitable acts', Laing wrote.

The heat in Ghadames was fierce, reaching 120 degrees Fahrenheit, and rendering some of Laing's equipment useless. The ether in his hygrometers evaporated, his chronometers stopped, 'and a camel having unfortunately placed his great gouty foot upon my rifle one night as I lay with it by my side in the ground, snapped the stock in two'. The camels were suffering too, for there was 'as little herbage for them as in the bottom of a tin mine in Cornwall'. These and other logistical problems kept the caravan in Ghadames until 3 November. Laing wrote a love letter to Emma, in reply to which he received a reassuring note from Warrington that 'your dear wife Emma you may believe me is well and happy as it is her duty to be', and a letter that showed he had become obsessive about his mission: 'Clapperton may as well have stayed at home, if the termination of the Niger is his object – it is destined for me – it is due to me.' He remained in cheerful frame of mind and joked that 'I have attained great celebrity as a medico . . . I shall, like the apothecary who had only two drawers in his shop, one for magnesia and the other for money, do little harm.'

Before leaving for In Salah, in present-day Algeria, Laing saw a comet crossing the heavens southwards, and thought of it as a happy omen. 'It beckons me on,' he wrote, 'and binds me to the termination of the Niger.' With him were his servant Jack le Bore, the shipbuilders Rogers ('a good-humoured rough fellow, picking up Arabic fast') and Harris ('a quiet, nobody disturbing sort of Jack Tom'), and a Jewish interpreter named Abraham Nahun, of whom Laing said, 'he tries to make himself useful but is rarely successful, he is a complete Jack-a-Lent'.*

---

* A Jack-a-Lent was a figure set up at Lent to be pelted.

Moving south-west along the edge of the great eastern sand sea of southern Tunisia, they reached In Salah on 3 December. Laing was the object of great curiosity. 'Yesterday,' he wrote to Warrington, 'upwards of a thousand people of both sexes came out to meet me, and so surrounded my camel that I had much difficulty in proceeding. I have been in the habit of late of covering my face à la mode Tuareg, as a convenient protection against the sun, and as nothing but my eyes were yesterday visible, the curiosity of the multitude was not gratified and my poor attendants were beleaguered by a thousand questions – is he white? Is his hair like a Turk's? Has he a beard? Can he fire a gun without a flint?' 'My courtyard,' he added, 'was packed as close as the pit of Covent Garden on a benefit night.'

At In Salah, Laing met merchants who had been waiting as long as ten months to go south. These experienced desert travellers, familiar with local conditions, knew that Tuareg bands were in the area and had attacked caravans. The merchants' fears fed on rumours, and after a month in In Salah Laing's escort Babani still showed no sign of leaving. For Laing, racing against Clapperton to reach the Niger first, waiting was out of the question. He decided to set out alone, across the dreaded Tanezrouft, the desert of thirst, 1500 miles of barren rock and sand, without a blade of grass, or scarcely a living thing, except for crows and roving bands of thieves. Once again, his ignorance concerning his route kept him going. He wrote that he was 'determined upon setting out solus in four days more, come what will, come what may'. The merchants, seeing that a lone Christian who did not know the way showed less fear than they did, were shamed into joining him. 'The merchants having become acquainted with our determination plucked up courage,' Laing wrote, and the caravan left on 9 January 1826 with 300 camels and 150 armed men. Laing described the Tanezrouft as 'a desert of sand as flat as a bowling green and as destitute as Melville island [in the Arctic Circle] in the depth of winter'. The merchants were still so frightened, he wrote, 'that every acacia tree in the distance became magnified . . . into troops of armed foes'. To Laing, their fears seemed laughable.

On 26 January Laing wrote to the Colonial Office that the caravan had come under the protection of some friendly Tuaregs, and 'Timbuktoo began to appear within our reach, the merchant began to calculate his gains, and apprehension having entirely subsided, animadversion gave place to a profusion of thanks and benedictions. I have little time at present to say more, than that my prospects are bright and expectations sanguine.'

At about the same time that he was sending off this sunny report, twenty heavily armed Ahaggar Tuaregs joined the caravan. They were greeted with distrust, but no one wanted to start trouble by trying to turn them away. One evening a few days later Laing fired at a crow. Sheikh Babani told him not to reload his rifle, and suggested that since they were out of danger Laing should turn his gunpowder over to him. Laing foolishly agreed. The following day the caravan stopped by a well at a place called Wadi Ahnet to water the camels. That night, the Ahaggar Tuaregs surrounded the tent where Laing slept and fired into it. They then cut the tent ropes and rushed Laing before he could reach his sword. They hacked at him with swords and daggers as he stumbled bloody and unarmed through the folds of his dark tent. When he fell to the ground, the Tuaregs continued to cut at his motionless body, particularly his neck and head, and finally left him for dead. They went after his helpers, killing the shipbuilder Rogers and the Jewish interpreter Nahun with their swords, and shooting the other shipbuilder Harris in the leg, while the servant Jack le Bore ran off and hid in the dunes. After stealing what they found in Laing's tent the marauders fled.

But he was not dead: the Tuareg swords must have had very dull blades. It was clear that he had been betrayed by Sheikh Babani, who had been either frightened or bribed into helping murder the man he had been paid so handsomely to protect.

Laing was unable to travel, and the rest of the caravan left without him. The survivors of his group, Jack le Bore, Harris, a wounded camel driver named Mohammed, and a slave named Bongola, whom Laing had freed and recruited, stayed with him. So, against all expectations, did Sheikh Babani, who suddenly seemed to remember that he was responsible for Laing's safety and that the bashaw's wrath was terrible. Laing's powers of recovery were superhuman, for although covered with wounds from head to foot he soon continued four hundred miles further across the Tanezrouft desert, marching for nineteen days until he reached the camp of a friendly Arab chief called Muktar, where he spent three months convalescing.

In September Emma Laing received an undated letter from her husband telling her that 'I write with only a thumb and finger, having a severe cut on my forefinger'. This was the first news of Laing that had been received in Tripoli in five months, and it barely hinted at what he had suffered. In November the camel driver Mohammed, who had deserted Laing, reached Tripoli and gave Warrington an eyewitness account of the Tuareg attack. Laing had written Warrington a full report in May, but the letter was delayed and did not reach the consul until two years later. 'I have suffered much,' Laing wrote, 'but the detail must be reserved till another period, when I shall "a tale unfold" of base treachery and war that will surprise you . . . I shall detail precisely how I was betrayed and nearly murdered in my sleep.' He then gave Warrington an inventory of the damage: ten cuts on his head and face had fractured his jaw and separated his left ear from his temple; a musket ball had entered his hip and gone out of his back, grazing his spine; a bad gash on the back of his neck had scratched his spine; five cuts on his right arm and hand had cut the hand three-quarters across and broken three fingers; one cut on a wrist had broken the bones; three cuts on the left arm had broken it; in addition, there was a cut across his left hand, one wound in his right leg and two in his left, making a total of twenty-four wounds. The letter was written with his left hand.

One can only wonder what permanent damage had been done to Laing. He complained in a letter dated 10 July that 'I am subject to dreadful pain in my head arising from the severity of my wounds'. There are signs that his mind may have snapped, for the tone of his letters began to verge on the irrational. He now believed that he was a man of genius ordained to discover Timbuctu. On 1 July 1826 he wrote to Warrington that unless he reached the city, 'the world will ever remain in ignorance of the place, as I make no vain glorious assertion when I say, that it will never be visited by Christian man after me!' And he wrote to a relative: 'I shall do more than has ever been done before and shall show myself to be what I have ever considered myself, a man of enterprise and genius.' Clearly unsettled by his trials, Laing had made the object of his mission a mania.

Bad luck continued to pursue him, and as he recovered in Muktar's camp an epidemic of 'something similar to yellow fever' broke out and swept away half the population, including Muktar himself, Sheikh Babani, Laing's servant Jack, and the second shipbuilder. Laing was sick with it for nine days, but despite his severe loss of blood and weakened state he survived, and 'my fever yielded at length to the effects of blistering and calomel'. 'I am now the only surviving member of the mission and my situation is far from being agreeable', Laing informed Warrington on 1 July 1826.

By July Laing felt strong enough to continue, but Muktar's son, who now ruled the camp, tried to persuade him to go back to Tripoli – which was as futile as trying to change the course of a fired cannonball. Laing suspected more treachery in what was only the disinterested goodwill of someone who knew the dangers that lay ahead: the bigotry of the tribes, the uncertainty of a route lined with quarrelling bands, the helplessness of a lone Christian who still had goods worth plundering. Laing swept aside these arguments and in August Muktar's son had no choice but to let him leave, providing him with a strong escort led by a member of his family.

After spending more than a year in the desert, Laing reached his destination on 13 August 1826. He entered Timbuctu, the great caravan terminal, the city that was on both desert and river, the mysterious trading metropolis whose prosperity was said to be based on gold. He did not discover Timbuctu, for it had been visited by the Florentines in the fifteenth century and the Portuguese in the sixteenth, but he did rediscover it. However, he arrived during a time of political upheaval that made his stay precarious. A Fulani zealot named Seku Hamadu, a disciple of Sultan Bello of Sokoto, was in the process of wresting Timbuctu from Tuareg control as part of a holy war. When Laing arrived the Tuaregs had fled, but the city was not yet occupied by Seku Hamadu. It was a no man's land under the nominal control of a sheikh named Othman who took orders from the most powerful faction, in this case the Fulani.

Laing arrived with a letter to Othman from Muktar's son, thanks to which he was warmly welcomed and provided with a two-storey mud house which still stands today. He stayed in Timbuctu five weeks, gathering research on the city, studying

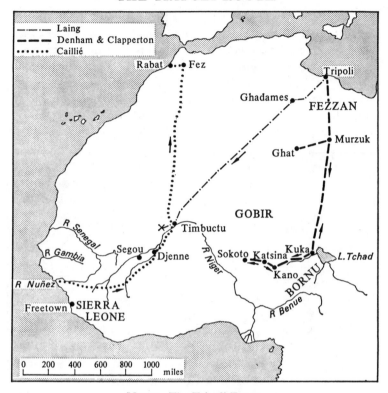

Map 2   The Tripoli Route

Arab manuscripts, copying city records, and talking to scholars.
That he was able to do this much shows that he was well received by the cosmopolitan merchant community. But soon
news arrived that interrupted his study and forced his departure.
In Sokoto Sultan Bello, who had received Hugh Clapperton in so
friendly a manner in March 1824, had now undergone a complete
change of heart concerning European penetration of the interior.
He wrote to his vassal Seku Hamadu that, as a matter of
principle, Europeans were to be prevented from visiting any
Moslem lands of the Sudan. Seku Hamadu received Sultan
Bello's orders when Laing was already in Timbuctu. He advised
Sheikh Othman that Bello's change of heart was due to 'a letter
he received from Egypt, in which the abuses and corruptions
the Christians have committed in that country are mentioned,
as well as in Andalusia and other countries in former times'. It

is ironic that events in Egypt and Spain should have affected the destiny of an English explorer who had reached a part of the world that was always considered closed to outside influences.

Seku Hamadu, passing on Bello's orders, told Sheikh Othman: 'You are to endeavour to prevent his [Laing's] entry, if not already come, and if he is come, endeavour to send him away, and take from him all hope of returning into our dominion.' Othman personally had no objection to Laing, but he could not

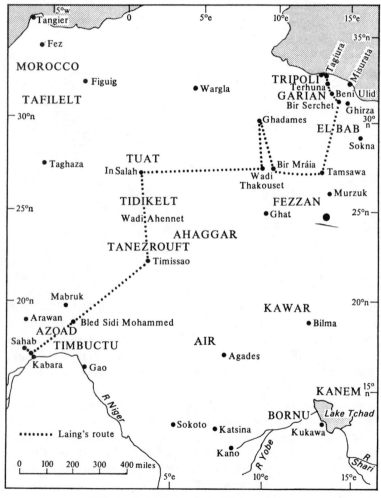

Map 3   Laing's Route to Timbuctu

disobey the powerful Fulani leader. He therefore warned Laing that if he did not leave at once Fulani warriors would be sent to kill him. Laing got his things together, taking time to send one final letter to Warrington on 21 September 1826, the last word that was ever heard from him. He described his difficulties and announced his plan of heading west towards Segou. Always optimistic, he said he hoped to get there in fifteen days, although 'I regret to say the road is a vile one and my perils are not yet at an end'. He said almost nothing about Timbuctu, since he was pressed for time and wanted to save his information until he could publish his journal.

> I have no time to give you my account of Timbuktoo [he said], but shall briefly state that in every respect except in size (which does not exceed four miles in circumference) it has completely met my expectations – Kabara is only five miles distant, and is a neat town, situated on the very margin of the river – I have been busily employed during my stay, searching the records of the town, which are abundant, and in acquiring information of every kind, nor is it with any common degree of satisfaction that I say, my perseverance has been amply rewarded – I am now convinced that my hypothesis concerning the termination of the Niger is correct.*

To reach Segou, Laing could not travel on the river or close to its banks, which were overrun with Fulanis. He had to detour north into the desert and then west, and he accepted the offer of a sheikh named Labeida to take him part of the way, not knowing that the man was a fanatical Christian-hater. Laing ended his letter to Warrington with tender words for the wife he scarcely knew: 'My dear Emma must excuse my writing. I have begun a hundred letters to her, but have been unable to get through. She is ever uppermost in my thoughts, and I look forward with delight to the hour of our meeting, which, please God, is now at no great distance.'

The next day, 22 September 1826, Laing left with his freed slave Bongola and an Arab boy, under the protection of Sheikh Labeida. They reached a spot in the desert called Sahab, thirty miles north of Timbuctu, where Sheikh Labeida, either in the pay of the Fulani or acting out of religious zeal, turned on Laing

---

* Presumably, that it emptied into the Bight of Benin.

and told him to renounce his faith and turn Moslem. When Laing refused Labeida ordered his two servants to kill him. They would not, so Labeida himself killed Laing and cut off his head.

It took many months for news of Laing's death to reach Tripoli, and on 10 November Emma wrote her husband a touching letter, full of hope for his safe return.

> Oh my beloved dearest Laing, alas alas what have you been exposed to, what danger, what suffering, to have saved you one pang I would with joy have shed every drop of blood that warms this heart – and had I been with you in that fearful moment my arms which would have encircled you might for some time have shielded you from the swords of those Demons – and at least we might have fallen pierced by the same weapons, our souls might have taken their flight together to that land where sorrow can never come. Adieu my best beloved, may heaven soon restore you to the arms of your ever adoring wife.

The first version of Laing's death was communicated to the bashaw by Muktar's son. Another version, stating that Laing had been killed at night, came out when the slave Bongola, having reached Tripoli, was questioned by Warrington on 1 September 1828:

'Did you accompany Major Laing to Timbuctu?'

'Yes.'

'How was Major Laing received by the natives of Timbuctu?'

'He was received well.'

'How long did he remain in Timbuctu?'

'About two months.'

'Was Major Laing obliged to leave Timbuctu?'

'He wished to go.'

'Who went with you?'

'A koffle of Arabs.'

'In which direction did you go?'

'The sun was on my right cheek.'

'Did you see any water, and did you proceed without molestation?'

'We saw no water, we passed unmolested during the day, but on the night of the third day, the Arabs of the country attacked and killed my master.'

'How many wounds had your master?'

'I cannot say, but all with swords, and in the morning I saw the head had been cut off.'

'Did the person who had charge of your master commit the murder?'

'The Sheikh who was the person who accompanied my master killed him, being assisted by his black servants by many cuts of the sword.'

It was not until December 1910 that the details of Laing's death were confirmed. By that time the Niger bend, including Timbuctu, had become a French colony, whose lieutenant-governor dispatched an army officer named A. Bonnel de Mézières to look into Laing's death. Bonnel de Mézières found an eighty-two-year-old Timbuctu notable named Mohammed Ould Muktar, who was the nephew of Sheikh Labeida, the man credited with killing Laing. The nephew said that Sheikh Labeida often boasted of the feat, and liked to tell the story of how he had killed the Christian, plunging a spear into his chest as his two servants held Laing's arms. After that, Labeida had told his nephew, 'we buried his cases and burned them, because he had come to poison the land, and we held our noses as we burned them.' Labeida kept only a little gold rooster which in 1910 was still in his family's possession. Bonnel de Mézières also found two Arab manuscripts describing Laing's death, and dated 1341, which is 1826 in the Western calendar. Taken to the spot where the murder was supposed to have been committed, Bonnel de Mézières began digging at the base of a tree and found bones four feet down. The bones, mainly pieces of skull and backbone, were shown to an army doctor, who said that two men had been buried there, a European adult and an adolescent, presumably the Arab boy Laing had taken along. Labeida had bragged that he had left Laing unburied to be devoured by vultures. A passing Tuareg must have seen the bodies and buried them at the base of the tree, not knowing that one was a Christian.

Thus was the death of an English explorer on the Niger investigated by a French explorer eighty-four years later. There was another mystery surrounding Laing's death that Bonnel de Mézières also helped clear up, although not as conclusively, for in this case the evidence was negative. Laing had kept a detailed journal of his trip, which was never recovered. Warrington suspected that the journal had found its way into the hands of his arch-enemy, the French consul Rousseau. In May 1827, a year before Warrington himself was able to obtain conclusive evidence of Laing's death from his servant, a letter was published in the Paris newspaper *l'Etoile* giving a detailed account of Laing's death. The letter was unsigned but was dated 5 April, Sukhara, Tripoli. Sukhara was the name of the country house occupied by Rousseau. There was a strong inference that Rousseau had obtained information from Laing's papers. Rousseau was an Arab-speaking expert on Levantine affairs with literary aspirations, who had already once been accused of plagiarism in connection with a book he had written on the Rechabites, the ascetic clan of the Old Testament. It was rumoured in France that he was about to write something momentous concerning the African interior, in a periodical he was planning to publish called *The African Investigator*. Rousseau was also a close friend of the bashaw's French-educated francophile minister, Hassuna D'Ghies. When in 1828 Laing's freed slave Bongola turned up at the British consulate, Warrington learned that Bongola had already been in contact with D'Ghies.

It was Warrington's nature to believe in plots, perhaps partly as a result of having remained so long in Tripoli, where conspiracy was always in the air. Because of the loose ends around Laing's death and the disappearance of his journal, Warrington concluded that he had been the victim of a plot hatched by Rousseau and D'Ghies, perhaps with the bashaw's complicity. An official protest was made to the bashaw, who professed ignorance and promised to send messengers into the interior to investigate. In 1829 Warrington lowered the consular flag and boycotted the bashaw's castle. The Colonial Office sent Major James Frazer of the Royal Navy to investigate, and he accepted Warrington's plot version. A sensational development soon seemed to confirm Warrington's suspicions. Hassuna D'Ghies confessed his part to the bashaw and fled Tripoli. Warrington wrote to the Colonial Office on 10 August 1829:

> I trust you will excuse me not writing you officially by this opportunity as time will not allow to make up the documents necessary to prove where the papers of Major Laing are – Suffice it to say they were brought down last March twelve months, sold by Hassuna D'Ghies to the French consul for a deduction of 40 per cent on a large claim he had of say 6000 fr. against Hassuna.

The night before last D'Ghies was smuggled from the American consulate on board an American corvette dressed as an officer . . . at 10 o'clock at night. Mohammed D'Ghies* has made a full confession to the Bashaw and he has taken the protection of the French flag.

It is possible that the bashaw, seeing the Laing affair growing into a *casus belli*, with the English fleet anchored in nearby Malta, preferred to put an end to it by forcing a confession from his former minister, which said: 'I hereby attest that the papers brought down by the people of Ghadames to my brother were those of the Major and that he told me he gave them to the French consul.' On 12 August the bashaw sent for Warrington, the Dutch consul Van Breugel, and a European employee of the English consulate, and had them sign the following document: 'We the undersigned declare that when in the presence of the Bashaw, His Highness said, "now I think that Hassuna D'Ghies and the French consul were the cause of the murder of Major Laing." '

Warrington rehoisted the consulate flag. Rousseau, directly accused by the bashaw, lost no time in returning to France, where his vindication became a matter of national honour under the jingoistic government of Premier Jules de Polignac. With the approval of King Charles X, a French naval squadron was sent to Tripoli in August 1830 under Admiral Rosamel to obtain a retraction of the charges against Rousseau, and also to obtain the settlement of a long-standing debt and other advantages. With French ships in Tripoli harbour ready to bomb the city, the bashaw signed a treaty agreeing to all the French demands. At the same time, England withdrew its support of the bashaw as a result of Laing's death. Without the help of the two major European powers and their protecting navies, the bashaw could not long survive. In 1835 he was overthrown, and Tripoli once again fell under Turkish rule. The death of an English explorer in a remote corner of the African interior had had international repercussions and ended the rule of the Karamanli dynasty. It also temporarily closed the Tripoli route to explorers, when the permissive bashaw was replaced by security-conscious Turks.

---

* Mohammed D'Ghies, Hassuna's brother, had been Foreign Minister, but had retired in 1822 due to an eye ailment.

Warrington survived the change of regime, and continued carrying out his consular duties until 1846, when his bad temper led to his resignation. He was now sixty-eight, but age had not mellowed him. He quarrelled with the Neapolitan consul Morelli over a box of cigars, and the next time he saw Morelli in the street he started to cane him. A letter arrived on 7 April 1846 from the Foreign Secretary, Lord Aberdeen:

> I regret to perceive in the Despatches now under my consideration that your conduct towards the Chevalier Morelli, the Consul of a friendly power of Her Majesty's, has been and continues to be most unjustifiable and incomprehensible . . . Considering all the circumstances of these unbecoming altercations in which you have suffered your feelings to involve you I regret to be compelled to observe that it appears to me that it would be no less for your own future comfort than for the benefit of HM service that you should make up your mind to retire.

After thirty-two years in Tripoli, Warrington's consular career came to a close. He was a choleric bumbler, a jingoistic trouble-maker, an *opéra bouffe* figure, but he had a passion for the cause of exploration and served it well. He was granted a pension of £900 a year and left for the Greek port of Patras, to visit his son-in-law Thomas Wood, the husband of his eldest daughter Jane, who was consul there. He was not the sort who could long survive the reflective inactivity of retirement, however, and he died a year later. His daughter Emma had died long before. On 14 April 1829 she had married her father's vice-consul in Benghazi, the same Thomas Wood who later married her sister Jane, once again bowing to paternal choice. She was not destined to know her second husband much longer than her first, and died of consumption six months after they were married, in Italy, where they had gone for her health. Warrington attributed her broken health to anxiety over Laing, 'watchful days and sleepless nights . . . and the subsequent tragical events'.

D'Ghies's confession and the bashaw's own admission seemed to prove conclusively that Laing's journal had been stolen by Rousseau. But the two Arabic accounts of Laing's death found by Bonnel de Mézières in 1910 both specified that all his property and papers had been burned. No trace of the journal ever turned up, either in France or England. What really happened to it will have to remain a minor historical mystery. As it was, Laing left only snatches of correspondence, and added very little to geographical knowledge. Laing died with his personal ambition unrealized, for, as he wrote in a letter: 'I have not travelled for the sake of any other reward than that which I shall derive from the consciousness of having achieved an enterprise which will rescue my name from oblivion.'

The irony is that two years after Laing's death an obscure French traveller succeeded in reaching Timbuctu, which had by then acquired a reputation as the city from which no European returned, stayed there two weeks, and got safely back to France. Fame is capricious, however, and René Caillié is even less known than Gordon Laing. This uneducated son of a Breton baker travelled entirely on his own, without backing from either the government or any private association, and without any scientific purpose. He was an example of the pure traveller one sees in great numbers in Africa today, disaffected young people of modest means who find any kind of aim or ambition spurious, and who stay on the move for the sheer sensation of movement. If they only knew it, they have a forerunner in René Caillié. He went to Timbuctu and back as one might undertake any other feat, such as flagpole-sitting, or eating goldfish – though his trip was a good deal more dangerous.

Having read *Robinson Crusoe* at an impressionable age, he left for West Africa in 1815, when he was sixteen. He had sixty francs, a pair of new shoes, a passport for La Rochelle, and a healthy dose of self-confidence. Travel, after all, requires no special experience – all one has to do is place one foot in front of the other.

Caillié got to Dakar, took a side trip to the West Indies, and while there read Mungo Park's *Travels*, which rekindled his African passion. Falling ill, he returned to France and went to work for a Bordeaux wine-merchant, leaving for West Africa in 1824, the year the French Geographical Society offered a 2000-franc prize to the first man to reach Timbuctu. He decided to pose as a Moor and spent seven months learning Arabic. His story was that he had been born in Alexandria of Arab parents, had been captured and taken to France by Bonaparte's troops in Egypt, and wanted to return to his country and find his family.

In March 1827 Caillié left Freetown, the capital of Sierra Leone, and joined a caravan heading towards Kankan and the Niger. They reached the river in June and Caillié was told that during the rainy season its water flooded the plain as far as three miles. Black Africans laughed at his long nose but showed him no malice, unlike the Moors. In a place north of Kankan called Time, Caillié was laid up for six weeks with scurvy, and lived on boiled rice and water. An old crone, a witch doctor, gave him some red wood boiled in water, and he slowly improved and joined a caravan bound for Djenne to sell kola nuts. Reaching Djenne in March 1828, Caillié learned from a merchant that a white man – undoubtedly Laing – had visited Timbuctu and been killed. 'Why did he go there?' asked Caillié. '*Iektoub torab* [to write the earth]', the merchant replied. Caillié sold his goods in Djenne for thirty thousand cowries and took a boat to Timbuctu. They were intercepted by Tuareg pirates, to whom they gave Djenne water (water and honey), a bag of rice, and some food. At each Tuareg camp along the river tribute had to be paid. They finally reached Timbuctu's river port, Kabara, on 20 April, and the Timbuctu merchants arrived on horseback to get their merchandise.

Coming into Timbuctu, Caillié's first feeling was intense disappointment. Could this mudball village be the pearl of the Sudan, the many-turreted, gold-strewn, magnificent object of his dreams? 'The idea I had formed of the city's greatness and wealth,' he wrote, 'hardly corresponded to what I saw, a cluster of dirt houses, surrounded by arid plains of yellow-white sand.' He found the city less lively than Djenne and the heat intolerable. One reason for the inactivity was the harassment of the Tuaregs, who could cut off communications with the city's lifeline, Kabara, at will. The city had no protective wall, and its streets were broad enough for three horsemen to pass abreast. He met Sheikh Othman, the same governor who had advised Laing to leave the city. He inquired about Laing and 'in the morning, a little before sunrise, the Moors showed me the spot where Major Laing was murdered. I observed there the site of a camp. I averted my eyes from this scene of horror and secretly dropped a tear – the only tribute of regret I could render to the ill-fated traveller to whose memory no monument will ever be reared on the spot where he perished'.

Caillié was given a house close to the one that Laing had occupied, but he only stayed in Timbuctu two weeks. He had no research project, no sponsor to answer to. He made drawings of some of the seven mosques, folding a blanket around him and holding a Koran to his bosom so convincingly that passers-by praised his religious zeal. He seized the first opportunity to leave Timbuctu, and joined a caravan of 1400 camels, taking gold, slaves, and ivory to Morocco. He was impressed by the way the guides could find their way without a compass. 'A dune, a rock, a difference in the colour of the sand, a few tufts of grass,' he wrote, 'are for them infallible signs.' It was 2000 miles across the desert, and Caillié suffered from thirst, bad food, and the daily insults of the Moors, 'Do you see that slave?' one Moor asked him? 'I prefer him to you. Judge by that how much I esteem you.'

Nevertheless, Caillié survived, and reached Tangier, where the French consul smuggled him aboard a sloop bound for Toulon. His arrival in Toulon excited the mild interest of the French Geographical Society, which sent him 500 francs ($80) so that he could come to Paris and be interviewed. His trip caused little stir. The French either did not believe him or were not aware that he was the first European to see Timbuctu and live to tell about it. It was only when the British press began to doubt Caillié's existence that he was brought into the limelight. As an element in Anglo-French rivalry, Caillié was made a chevalier of the Legion of Honour and given a gold medal and a pension of 3000 francs a year. When he published a book in 1830, it was better received in England than in France. The French were still suspicious that he was a fraud, and his pension was discontinued in 1833. Caillié died in 1838 at the age of thirty-nine, penniless, prematurely aged by his hardships, and dejected by the suspicions his trip had aroused. It was only years later, when another explorer was shown the house in Timbuctu where he had stayed, that he was vindicated.

Six

THE NIGER CONQUERED

CLAPPERTON had left Sultan Bello in Sokoto in May 1824 with the understanding that he would return by the sea route to the Gulf of Guinea. 'Let me know the precise time,' the sultan had told him, 'and my messengers shall be down at any part of the coast you may appoint, to forward letters to me from the mission, on reception of which I will send an escort to conduct it to Sudan.' From the Bornu capital of Kukawa, Clapperton had written to Bello to confirm that he planned to be back on the coast in July 1825. He said he would land at Whydah, a harbour close to the present-day Dahomeyan capital of Cotonou, and hoped that Bello's messengers would be there as agreed.

Back in London, in June 1825, after three and a half years' absence, Clapperton was impatient to be off again, in spite of recurring attacks of what he called 'the ague', or malaria. He wanted to catch up with Gordon Laing, who was already in Tripoli, waiting to start into the interior. It was too late for his planned July rendezvous in Whydah with Bello's messengers, but he wanted to reach the coast in time to make the 450-mile overland trip to Sokoto during the dry season. He stayed in England less than three months, just long enough to prepare his second expedition and receive new instructions from Lord Bathurst.

The instructions, dated 30 July 1825, deserve some comment, for Clapperton was asked to 'endeavour by every means . . . to impress on his [Sultan Bello's] mind the very great advantages he will derive by putting a total stop to the sale of slaves to

Christian merchants . . . and by preventing other powers of Africa from marching Koffilas [caravans] of slaves through his dominions. You will inform him of the anxious desire which the King your Master feels for the total abolition of this inhuman and unnatural traffic.' It was the first time that the abolition of slavery had been the principal goal of an African explorer's mission. From this moment, African exploration was not only commercial, scientific, and geographic, but abolitionist. The explorer became the advance man not only for the trader, but for the missionary.

The Colonial Office instructions reflected a turnabout in British policy on slavery that can be credited to successful lobbying by the abolitionist movement. The Quakers had launched the campaign in 1783, after the rebellion of the American colonies in 1776 had weakened the vested pro-slavery interests. But these interests were still formidable, including as they did the Liverpool and Bristol merchants, the West Indian plantation owners, many men in government, and the lion's share of the British establishment. The slave trade was not only approved by public opinion: it was encouraged by Parliament and enforced by treaty. There were strict prohibitions from home authorities to the governors of West Indian islands who wanted to limit the trade because of over-supply.

Within a quarter of a century, a small band of ardent reformists had succeeded in changing the attitude of a nation. In the House of Commons William Wilberforce, 'the nightingale of the House', led a lifelong crusade against slavery. The abolitionists spread the humanitarian gospel of the age: the rights of man, and the absolute immorality of ownership of human beings. They gathered evidence on the inhuman treatment of slaves, organized a nationwide boycott of West Indian sugar, and drew up hundreds of petitions to Parliament. At the same time, the economic underpinnings of slavery were being shaken loose. Britain was changing from a mercantile to an industrial economy, and the great trading companies themselves found that their interests lay in opening new markets for industrial goods rather than in keeping up the slave trade. Before abolition, Liverpool was already diverting ships from the slave trade to cotton, and Britain began to need palm oil to make soap – which meant the preservation of native manpower at home. One can take with a pinch of salt the view of the great historian of eighteenth-century England, William Edward Hartpole Lecky, in his *History of European Morals*: 'The unweary, unostentatious, and inglorious crusade of England against slavery may probably be regarded as among the three or four perfectly virtuous pages comprised in the history of nations.' It also made sound business sense.

The Danes, who had small slave-trading counters on the West African coast, declared the slave trade illegal in 1802. The English, who were the chief carriers of West African slaves, abolished the trade in 1807. The last English slaver, *Kitty's Amelia*, sailed out of Liverpool on 27 July 1807. Parliament passed an historic bill saying that 'all manner of dealing and trading' in slaves in Africa was to be 'utterly abolished, prohibited and declared to be unlawful'. An 1811 bill made it a felony for any British subject to engage in 'the carrying trade'.

Voting for abolition was one thing, but persuading other slave-trading powers to do the same was another. From having been the nation most actively engaged in the trade, England became the most zealous enforcer of its suppression. The trade continued to flourish well into the second half of the nineteenth century, as long as traders made money, and as long as North and South America continued to absorb all the slaves the coast traders and their middlemen in the interior could capture. Long after the United States prohibited the importation of slaves in 1808, and after the European powers agreed to abolition at the Congress of Vienna in 1815, the trade survived illegally. England, the poacher turned gamekeeper, formed a Blockade Squadron, which became known as the Coffin Squadron, to intercept slavers in the hundreds of coves and hidden harbours of the West African coast. English sloops lay off the mouths of rivers like motorcycle cops behind road signs waiting for Brazilian or Portuguese slavers to make their run across the Atlantic. Squadron ships received a bounty incentive of £60 per rescued male slave, which was reduced to £10 in 1824 and £5 in 1830. In a speech before Parliament, Lord John Russell, who was twice Prime Minister, called the mission of the Blockade Squadron 'high and holy work'. It was also the first demonstration of English sea power in West Africa. By the 1840s an important part of the English fleet was committed to the anti-slavery patrol.

It was in this context that Clapperton received instructions to persuade Sultan Bello to give up slavery. The English government, now vigorously engaged in the suppression of the slave trade, found a new use for explorers, who could spread the message of abolition deep into the African interior, at the very source of supply. Abolition, as much as any other single factor, led to direct English involvement in West Africa. Clapperton was also told to pursue commercial and geographical goals. He was to tell Sultan Bello that once the road was open from the coast to Sokoto, 'he will receive whatever articles of merchandise he may require at a much cheaper rate than he now pays for those which are brought across the long desert'. And, finally, he was 'to trace the course of the river which is known with certainty to flow past Kabara, or the port of Timbuktoo, and which has been known in modern times by the name of Niger'.

The Colonial Office had high hopes that Clapperton would meet Gordon Laing in the African heartland, unaware that Laing would be dead within thirteen months of Clapperton's departure, and that in any case Clapperton had no desire to meet the man he considered his arch-rival in the search for the Niger's termination. Transportation for Clapperton and his party was provided by the Admiralty aboard the sloop *Brazen*, which was leaving for the West African coast to join the anti-slavery patrol. The logbook for the *Brazen* on 28 August 1825 reads: 'Came on board Captains Clapperton and Pearce & Messrs Morison and Dickson and 4 Domestics on a Mission to the interior of Africa.' Accompanying Clapperton, who had been promoted to commander for the occasion, were Captain Robert Pearce, a naval officer who was second-in-command, Dr Thomas Dickson, a Scottish surgeon, and Dr Robert Morison, a naval surgeon who was also a naturalist.

It was now the practice on African missions to take along a doctor, although precedent showed that, far from guaranteeing the health of the missions, doctors were often the climate's first victims. Oudney and Ritchie had both been doctors. Despite the number of missions sent to find the Niger between 1796 and 1830, and the number of men who died of malaria and dysentery, no progress had been made in the treatment of tropical diseases. The pathology of the age was miasmatic. Fevers were believed to come from putrid air. No one connected malaria with mosquitoes. All fevers were treated alike, with bleeding, calomel, and emetics. Quinine was known as 'a strengthening agent after fever or dysentery', but the simple idea of using it preventively had as yet occurred to no one. Having one, or even two doctors along, as this particular expedition was again to show, provided as much insurance against fever as the fetishes the blacks believed would protect them from death in battle.

In the logbook's casual mention of four domestics was concealed the identity of one of the greatest of the Niger's explorers, Richard Lander, who had signed on as Clapperton's personal servant. With the exception of the American roustabout John Ledyard, the explorers who went searching for the Niger were army or navy officers like Clapperton and Laing, or surgeons like Mungo Park, or highly educated men like Hornemann and Simon Lucas. Lander, who would succeed where they had failed, was a man of the people, an explorer by accident who had risen from working-class origins and the humble station of domestic.

Richard Lander was born on 8 February 1804 in the Cornish town of Truro, the fourth of six children. His father kept a pub called The Fighting Cock and his grandfather had been a well-known wrestler at Land's End in Cornwall. Despite these humble origins, Lander claimed ancient lineage. His mother was a Penrose, and he liked to quote the saying: 'By Tre, Pol, Lan, and Pen, you may know most Cornishmen.' He was born with the nomadic instinct, which served him in lieu of schooling. 'I was never easy a great while together in one place,' he wrote, 'and I used to be delighted to play truant and stroll from town to town.'

He left home at the age of nine, for family reasons over which he draws a modest veil, and two years later became the servant of a merchant who took him to the West Indies, giving him his first taste of travel. He later went to South Africa as the servant of a colonial commissioner. In 1823 he returned to England, but the African bug had bitten him.

> There was a charm in the very sound of Africa [he wrote], that always made my heart flutter: whilst its boundless deserts of sand; the awful obscurity in which many of the interior regions were enveloped; the strange and wild aspects of countries that had never been trodden by the foot of a European, and even the very failure of all former undertakings to explore its hidden wonders, united to strengthen the determination I had come to.

When he heard that Commander Clapperton was setting out on a second mission, he resolved to volunteer. Friends tried to dissuade him, mentioning the dangers and diseases, but Lander believed that 'all men think all men are mortal but themselves'. He went to see Clapperton, who seemed to him 'the very soul of enterprise and adventure', and was engaged as his confidential servant. Lander was twenty-one years old when he left with Clapperton, for whom he felt open hero worship. The servant–master relationship soon wore down amid the hardships of African travel, and the experienced explorer and his devoted young disciple formed a strong bond of friendship. As Lander perceptively observed, 'It would not have been well for any haughtiness or reserve to be manifested toward me under such circumstances, merely because accident had thrown me into a lower rank of life than my master . . . such, happily, was not the disposition of Captain Clapperton; the differences in our respective conditions were willingly levelled . . . and for my part I may justly say . . . that I would willingly have laid down my life for the preservation of his.'

Leaving Spithead on 28 August, the *Brazen* reached Whydah on 23 November, after pursuing and capturing several Spanish slavers along the coast and sending their cargoes to Sierra Leone, where the slaves were freed. Dr Dickson was dropped off in Whydah to explore the interior of Dahomey. He was so bad-tempered that Clapperton warned him: 'The conquest of the people to you will be guided solely by your behaviour toward them. Set a guard over your temper, my dear Dickson, and never let it lead you into error.' It was advice that Dickson failed to heed, for news later reached Clapperton that he had reached a village called Shar, where 'he had a serious misunderstanding with a party of natives, and his life being threatened by its chief, he was so violently exasperated that he attempted to throttle the individual; which, being observed by his followers, they fell upon the unfortunate doctor, overcame and slew him'.

After dropping off Dickson, the *Brazen* landed the rest of the mission at the nearby slave-trading station of Badagri, picking up a British trader named Houtson in Porto Novo, who would guide them part of the way. Leaving the *Brazen*, Lander felt that the heartiness of their farewell with the crew was a way of covering up the deeper emotions of men convinced they would never meet again. Heading ashore in a native canoe that spanked over huge rollers, Lander put his bugle to his lips and played 'Over the Hills and Far Away', as sailors on the *Brazen*'s decks cheered.

They left Badagri in December for the long overland trip to Sokoto. There was no sign of Sultan Bello's messengers, but then Clapperton was three months late. Houtson would take them to Katunga, about 150 miles north of Badagri, through friendly Yoruba country. Soon fever struck, and Clapperton became so ill he had to be carried in a hammock. When they reached the town of Jannah, about two weeks out of Badagri, Lander was so sick 'I was bled in the temple; but the doctor, who was himself suffering from fever, being unable to hold the instruments steadily, inadvertently thrust it into my skull. This accident occasioned the most excruciating agony and made me shriek with pain.' Lander became delirious and had a violent fit, during which he attacked Clapperton and had to be forcibly held down. By this time, wrote Lander, Dr Morison and Captain Pierce 'looked more like walking spectres than living human beings'. Pierce was a slight, fair man, 'whose frame was much too delicate for the arduous task that he had undertaken'. Dr Morison was finally persuaded to return to the ship in Badagri, in the belief that his health would improve by the sea. He died of fever before he could reach it. With the mission hardly under way, both its doctors had already succumbed.

Morison's servant, an English seaman named George Dawson, stayed with Clapperton, but was delirious, and kept repeating that he had deserted his family to perish in a strange land. Dawson died in a particularly unpleasant manner, as a result of his delirium. It was night, and they were all sleeping. As Lander told it, 'the medicine-chest lying open by Dawson's side, he perceived it, and pointing to a phial, desired a black attendant to fill him a glass of its contents; which being promptly done, he eagerly swallowed it . . . about a quarter of an hour afterwards, not hearing Dawson's groans, I asked how he did; but receiving no answer, I went to his bed-side, and found him a cold and stiffened corpse.' Pierce awoke and said: 'What? Is Dawson dead? Well, poor fellow, his sufferings are over; I cannot long survive him.' The next morning, the bottle Dawson had swallowed was identi-

fied as ether. Pierce also became delirious, and had long conversations with his mother, asking her questions that he answered
himself, until he fell into a stupor and died in a village named
Engwa on 27 December, at the age of twenty-eight. Clapperton
read the burial service with a trembling voice.

It was a pathetically small band consisting of Clapperton,
Lander, Houtson, and their servants who reached the Yoruba
capital of Katunga on 23 January 1826. Clapperton, though
seriously ill, was as stalwart and uncompromising as ever, and
refused to prostrate himself before the king. They stayed six
weeks in Katunga recovering, with the exception of Houtson,
who returned to the coast, where he died a few weeks later. 'Like
the characters in Mozart's "Farewell",' wrote Lander, 'they
had dropped off one by one.' Now only Clapperton and Lander
were left, both ill and weakened. Proceeding in the African interior
astride lean, bony horses, the tall, burning-eyed Clapperton and
the short, round Lander must have seemed like Don Quixote and
Sancho Panza, somehow strayed from the Estremadura into the
rain forest of West Africa.

They headed for Yauri, the village on the Niger where Mungo
Park had gone ashore to give presents to the king before he was
ambushed and killed. Clapperton decided to stop at Bussa, where
Park had died, and it was there, on 31 March 1826, that he saw
the Niger for the first time. The object of his quest did not inspire
him, for all he wrote in his journal was: 'At 3.30 arrived at a
branch of the Quorra.' Clapperton questioned the natives in
Bussa about Park's death, and met with an evasiveness that he
considered evidence of guilt. He and Lander visited the rapids
where Park's 'schooner' had sunk. The water foaming over rock
outcroppings sounded like a forest of tall trees shaken by a strong
wind.

Clapperton's health had by then improved, for in the village
of Kiama, when the chief offered his daughter, he accepted. He
stayed with her six days, although at twenty-five, he wrote, 'she
was past the meridian in this country . . . I went to the house
of the daughter, which consists of several coozies separate from
those of the father, and I was shown into a very clean one; a mat
was spread; I sat down; and the lady coming in and kneeling
down, I asked her if she would live in my house, or I should come
and live with her: she said, whatever way I wished; very well, I

said, I would come and live with her, as she had the best house.' The Africans were surprised that the explorers travelled without women. This did not mean that they were celibate.

Clapperton and Lander scored their greatest romantic success in the village of Wawa, where a rich widow named Zuma (the Arab word for honey), whom Clapperton described as a walking water-butt, pursued them relentlessly. She first devoted her attention to the cherubic, fresh-faced Lander, appearing daily in his hut in her seductive finery, all henna and coral and indigo and gold beads. The effect was lost on Lander, who saw her as 'a moving world of flesh, puffing and blowing like a blacksmith's bellows'. When he refused to visit her hut, her passion shifted to Clapperton, who accepted her invitation, wanting to see the inside of her house. He found her comfortably installed amid pillows and carpets, holding a grass fan in one hand, and with a whip by the other, attended by a hunchbacked female dwarf, and daintily picking kola nuts from a mug of English pewter. Zuma at once declared her love and proposed marriage. When she saw the consternation on Clapperton's face, she reassured him that the difference in their ages was no obstacle. 'This was too much,' wrote Clapperton, 'and I made my retreat as soon as I could, determined never to come to such close quarters with her again.' But the lovesick widow kept hounding him, and 'I could only get rid of her by telling her that I prayed and looked at the stars all night . . . she always departed in a flood of tears.' But Clapperton must have been flattered by her attentions, for when the mission left Wawa in April he no longer considered her a walking water-butt, but viewed her with a grudging admiration, and wrote that 'had she been somewhat younger and less corpulent, there might have been great temptation to head her party, for she has certainly been a very handsome woman, and such as would have been thought a beauty in any country in Europe'.

On 10 April Clapperton and Lander crossed the Niger on a raft ferry at a place called Komie. Clapperton now heard from all sides that the river flowed south into the sea, but his instructions were to head north and find Sultan Bello in Sokoto. The main road to Sokoto was via Kano, which they reached on 20 July 1826. Clapperton stayed five weeks in Kano, too sick to proceed. He and Lander learned that war had broken out between the Sokoto Caliphate and the kingdom of Bornu. The story Lander picked up was that a famine had broken out in Bornu, and the sheikh, El Kanemi, had sent some handsome horses to Kano and the principal Fulani towns, as an oblique way of calling attention, through ambassadors that accompanied the horses, to their predicament, and asking for help. Instead of helping, the governor of Kano had the Bornu ambassadors bound hand and foot and publicly butchered on the market square. The other cities sent the horses back with bundles of spears, as a way of saying that if the sheikh wanted grain he would have to fight for it. El Kanemi at once assembled an army and marched on the Caliphate, and war had raged ever since.

With Clapperton prostrate, Lander was raised from the station of servant to that of co-explorer. He toured Kano until Clapperton's health improved. Clapperton then decided that he would go alone to Sokoto, leaving Lander behind with their Hausa servant Pasko. Clapperton reached Sokoto on 20 October and occupied the same house as on his first visit. He was cordially received by the sultan, whom he found reading an Arabic copy of Euclid's *Elements*. 'Bello's appearance was very little altered from what it was when I saw him last,' wrote Clapperton, 'except that he had got a little lustier, and dressed somewhat better.' But Clapperton soon discovered that if Bello's appearance had not altered, his attitude towards English explorers had. Clapperton had left the Sudan with high hopes of opening a trade route to the coast, building a shipyard for the Caliphate, and persuading Bello to give up slavery in return for trade advantages. The sultan had welcomed the project, as a way of obtaining firearms. But in the interval Bello had become convinced that the explorers were on a mission of conquest, and that they represented a power that would eventually seize his country and dispossess him, as it had done elsewhere. Bello saw that the explorers were the first imperialists, the thin end of the wedge, the vanguard of the scramble for Africa. He was right. Although he died before he could be dispossessed, the Sokoto Caliphate eventually did become part of the English colony of Nigeria.

Bello was also annoyed that Clapperton planned to visit his enemy El Kanemi in Kukawa when he left Sokoto. Clapperton would be crossing enemy lines and had presents for El Kanemi that might help his military effort. He might give the Bornu leader information. Bello felt that Clapperton was interfering in a local conflict, and relations between the two men soured.

Sultan Bello told Clapperton that 'when I was here two years ago, the Sheikh of Bornu had written to him, advising him to put me to death; as, if the English should meet with too great encouragement, they would come into Sudan, one after another, until they got strong enough to seize on the country, and dispossess him, as they had done with regard to India, which they had wrested from the hands of the Mahometans.' Clapperton replied that he could not believe that the Sheikh of Bornu, who had shown him such kindness in Kukawa two years earlier, had ever written such a letter. When he asked to see it, Bello said he had lent it to a relative.

In December Clapperton, although suffering from an enlarged spleen, visited Bello in his camp outside town. This time Bello told him flatly that he would not let him continue to Bornu. 'He was desired to say that I was a spy,' Clapperton wrote, 'and that he would not allow me to go beyond Sokoto; hinting, at the same time, that it would be better I should die, as the English had taken possession of India by first going there by ones and twos, until we got strong enough to seize upon the whole country.'

In the meantime, Lander in Kano received a letter from Clapperton dated 7 November 1826, informing him that the sultan did not want him to go to Bornu. In words that applied as much to himself as to his servant, he advised Lander to keep his spirits up whatever their difficulties. 'Think of your friends in England,' he wrote, 'and fancy yourself in their little circle; never permit hope to sink so far within you as to say to yourself, "I shall never see my country again." '

Lander next received a message from Sokoto that Clapperton was ill and needed him, and that he should leave at once, with all their baggage. At first he was suspicious, but he finally decided to go to his master's side. In fact, the summons came from Sultan Bello, who wanted to see the gifts Clapperton had for the Sheikh of Bornu. En route to Sokoto, Lander was given another letter from Clapperton dated 13 December. 'Their cursed Bornu war has overturned all my plans and intentions,' Clapperton wrote, 'and set the minds of the people generally against me, as it is pretty well understood by both rich and poor that I have presents for their enemy the Sheikh.' Lander reached Sokoto on 23 December. Outraged at the deception, Clapperton said 'that my business with the sultan was now finished, and I would have no more to say'.

Two days later it was Christmas, and Clapperton wrote: 'I gave my servant Richard one sovereign out of six I have left, as a Christmas gift; for he is well deserving, and has never once shown a want of courage or enterprise unworthy of an Englishman.'

His problems with Bello were not over. The sultan now insisted on seeing King George IV's letter to the Sheikh of Bornu. Clapperton showed him the letter in its tin case, but refused to open it, saying: 'To give up this letter is more than my head is worth.' Bello said he would open it himself and send a letter of explanation to the king. 'The King of England would never even look at such a letter from you,' Clapperton replied, 'after his subjects had received such treatment.' Clapperton was so high-handed with the sultan that one of the courtiers remarked: 'With truth, do you hear how that man talks before the prince of the faithful?' As stubborn as he was fearless, Clapperton stood up to a man who could have had him put to death as easily as he could order the slaughtering of a sheep. Fear of England, however, made the sultan put up with Clapperton's outspokenness. Next, the Gidado (vizier) and his brother came to Clapperton's hut and demanded the presents for the Sheikh of Bornu. Clapperton lay ill on his mat, but rose to protest that 'they were acting like robbers towards me, in defiance of all good faith; that no people in the world would act the same, and they had far better have my head cut off than done such an act; but I supposed they would do that also when they had taken everything from me'. The Gidado warned him that he could lose his head if he talked that way. 'If I lose my head,' Lander reported Clapperton as replying, 'it will be for no other crime than that of speaking for the just rights of my king and country; I repeat, you are a nation of scoundrels and robbers.'

News arrived that the Sheikh of Bornu had been defeated, with the loss of all his baggage, camels and tents, 209 horses, and a number of slaves. Bello showed Clapperton the sheikh's copper water jug, which had three sword cuts in it. The victory put him in a more cheerful frame of mind. He became more friendly, sought out Clapperton's company, and no longer treated him as a spy. On one occasion he asked Clapperton whether he ate pork, and the explorer replied that it was better than dog, which he had seen sold in the open market at Tripoli. 'The sultan said, it was strange what people would eat,' wrote Clapperton. 'In the districts of Umburm, belonging to Jacoba, they eat human flesh . . . I said I did not think any people existed on the face of the earth that eat their own kind as food . . . the sultan said he had seen them eat human flesh, they said it was better than any other; that the heart and breasts of a woman were the best part of her body.'

Clapperton's health seemed to have improved, and he went hunting almost daily. Dressed in a flowing robe and a white muslin turban, with a beard that had grown to patriarchal length, he excited considerable admiration among the locals. He and Lander occupied a beehive-shaped hut, windowless and stifling, with a door so low they had to stoop to enter. In the evening they smoked cigars, their only remaining luxury, read aloud, and laughed at jokes they knew by heart. They thought of home and wondered whether Bello would ever let them leave Sokoto. Clapperton was moved to tears when Lander sang:

> *Then gang wi' me to Scotland dear,*
> *We ne'er again will roam;*
> *And with thy smile, so bonny, cheer*
> *My native Highland home.*

Lander was discouraged, and wrote that 'like the beautiful apple said to grow on the borders of the Red Sea, our hopes wore a fair and promising outside, but produced only bitter ashes'. News now came, in March 1827, that the Sheikh of Bornu had laid siege to Kano and was about to march on Sokoto. The situation was considered serious enough for Bello to evacuate Sokoto, and he took Clapperton and Lander with him. They returned on 12 March, to a furnace-like heat of 109 degrees Fahrenheit, which further weakened Clapperton, who was again suffering from dysentery. He was too weak to keep up his journal. The last entry, dated 11 March, begins: 'Nothing worth noting down.' He then wrote of the sultan's decision to let them leave Sokoto. But Clapperton was in no condition to leave. He had nightmares and complained of a burning in his stomach.

Lander treated him with laudanum, Seidlitz powder, and Epsom salts. Clapperton knew that he was finished, and told Lander: 'Richard, I shall shortly be no more, I feel myself dying.' Lander reassured him: 'God forbid my dear master, you will live many years yet.' He lingered on another month, hollow-eyed and skeletal, and gave his last instructions, which Lander reported in a letter that shows great stress in its absence of punctuation:

What my master said to me at Sakatoo April 1827 Richard i am going to die i cannot help shedding tears as he had behaved like a father to me since i had been with him we went into the hut he was then laying in a shade outside he said Richard come here my dear boy its the will of God it cant be helped bear yourself up under all troubles like a man and an english man do not be affraid and no one will hurt you i do not fear that sir its for the loss of you who has been a father to me since when i have ben with you my dear boy i will tell you what to do take great care of my journals and when you arrive in London go to my agents and tell them to send directly for my uncul and tell him it was my wish that he would go with me to the colonoal office and delever the journals that they might not say their were anything missing my little money my close and everything i have belongs to you Bello will lend you money to buy cammels and provisions and send you home over the desert with the gaffle [Koffle or caravan] and when you arrive at Tripoli Mr Warrington will give you what money you want and send you home the first opportunity . . . writ down the names of the towns you go throw and all purticulars and if you get safe home with the journals i have no doubt of your being well rewarded for your truble.

On 13 April 1827 Lander heard the death rattle in Clapperton's throat and cradled him as he gave his last breath. Lander carried the corpse by camel to the edge of a pit five miles outside Sokoto and had it buried as he read the Church of England service, his voice drowned out by the racket made by a group of quarrelling slaves. Clapperton died without having been able to carry out any of his instructions. He did not find the Niger's end, nor did he reach an agreement with Bello to end slavery. He died without even the satisfaction of knowing that his rival Laing had come no closer to the Niger's mouth than he had. His journal, retrieved by Lander, was dry and colourless. Clapperton, wrote Lander, was 'never highly elated . . . nor

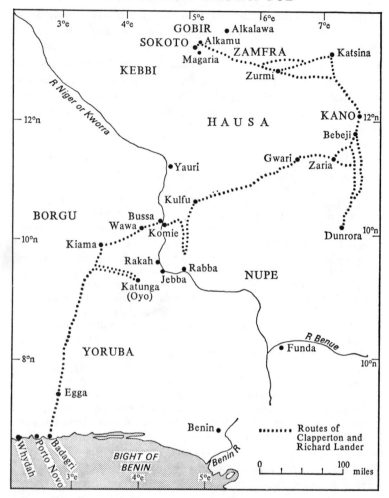

Map 4   Routes of Clapperton and Richard Lander

deeply depressed', and one result of this even disposition was
flat writing. Denham, who had published his rather florid and
self-serving account of their first expedition, won most of the
attention; wrongly so, for through his qualities of courage and
leadership, and the way he stuck to his instructions at the peril
of his life, Clapperton remains one of the most memorable of the
Niger explorers.

Hired as a servant, Lander now found himself alone in the African interior, surrounded by enemies and exhausted by illness. He too had malaria, and lay on his mat, alternately sweating and shivering, for two weeks after Clapperton's death. Bello's men searched his hut for arms and made it clear that he was unwelcome. But Lander had an instinct for dealing with natives and making the right decision. Intent at first upon carrying out Clapperton's last wishes and returning via the northern route to Tripoli, he obtained permission to leave from Sultan Bello. But when he reached Kano he saw that he was too short of money to buy the camels and equipment he needed to cross the desert. He resolved to return the way he had come, to the coast at Badagri. It was a route he had already travelled, and he was glad not to have to join unfriendly Arabs for the long desert crossing. Also, he had caught from Clapperton the urge to discover, and wanted, if the chance arose, to follow the Niger in a canoe.

Crossing Yoruba country with the faithful Pasko, Lander survived the trials by now familiar to Niger explorers: he was almost drowned crossing a river, he was almost speared by a drunken Yoruba, he had to give presents wherever he went. When asked for a charm to cure barrenness he did not scoff but offered cinnamon oil. He was happy to dispense charms wherever he passed, writing out scraps of English ballads against a variety of ailments. One good turn deserving another, the Emir of Zaria offered Lander a young female slave for a wife, and he 'accepted her with gratitude, as I knew she would be serviceable to me on my journey'. She washed his feet, bathed his temples with lime juice, and fanned him to sleep.

Lander reached Badagri on 21 November 1827, and he must have thought when he saw the bay fringed with palms and cocoa trees that his troubles were over. He had run the gauntlet of the African interior and was now only a ship's journey from England. In fact, the most serious threat to his life took place in Badagri and was plotted by white men. Badagri in 1827 was a centre for the illegal slave trade, run by a gang of ruffians, half-caste Portuguese from Brazil. Since the English were the most active in policing the illegal trade, the traders were afraid that Lander's presence announced a raid from the Blockade Squadron.

Three of the traders went to the King of Badagri and told him that Lander was a spy, and that if he was allowed to leave he would return with an army. The gullible king took the traders at their word, and soon Lander was summoned to the fetish hut, in front of hundreds of over-excited, spear-brandishing, natives, and told: 'You are accused, white man, of designs against our king and his government, and are therefore desired to drink the contents of this vessel, which if the reports to your prejudice be true, will surely destroy you; whereas, if they be without foundation, you need not fear, Christian; the fetish will do you no injury, for the fetish will do that which is right.'

Lander was given a bowl a quarter full of clear liquid, probably a concoction made from an extract of the poisonous bark of the red water tree, and told to drink it. From the resolute expressions of the armed natives who surrounded him, he saw that there was no alternative. 'I took the bowl in my trembling hands,' he wrote, 'and gazed for a moment at the sable countenances of my judges; but not a single look of compassion shone upon any of them; a dead silence prevailed in the gloomy sanctuary of skulls; every eye was intently fixed upon me; and seeing no possibility of escape, I offered up internally a short prayer to the Throne of Mercy – the God of Christians – and hastily swallowed the fetish, dashing the poison chalice to the ground.'

Lander returned at once to his hut, where he forced himself to vomit and evacuated the poison. Since it was almost always fatal, the natives were amazed to see him alive, and decided that he was under divine protection. The king befriended him, and warned him never to go out unarmed, for the Portuguese would murder him at the first opportunity.

Waiting for a ship, Lander spent several months in Badagri, and had occasion to see some of the human sacrifices that were then prevalent on the slave coast. He saw prisoners of war taken to the fetish tree and given flasks of rum to drink as they were bludgeoned from the back. 'The head is severed from the trunk with an axe,' he wrote, 'and the smoking blood gurgles into a calabash. While this is in hand, other wretches furnished with knives cut and mangle the body in order to extract the heart entire from the breast, which being done, although it be yet warm and quivering with life, it is presented to the king . . . and his majesty and suite make an incision in it with their teeth, and partaking of the foamy blood, the heart is . . . affixed to the point of a tall spear and . . . paraded through town.'

In February 1828 the captain of the English brig *Maria*, who had heard that an Englishman was stranded in Badagri, came to rescue Lander from the town's customs and inhabitants. He sailed to the island of Fernando Po, where he found an explorer from an earlier mission waiting to interview him. It was Dixon Denham, now governor of Sierra Leone, who would die that same year of the fever. Denham heard from Lander that his old enemy and mission partner Hugh Clapperton had died in Sokoto. Forgetting old quarrels, Denham 'expressed infinite concern to hear of the fate of his coadjutor in the previous expedition', Lander wrote.

Lander, who had left home in 1825 a servant, returned to London three years later a hero. But a hero of peculiar appearance, for, as he wrote, 'on arriving in London, I was met in the streets by a Jew, who ran forth and cordially embraced me, asking how I had left our Hebrew brethren in Jerusalem. The fellow, by my beard, and singular appearance, had taken it into his head that I belonged to his own fraternity, and was just returning from visiting the holy city.'

It may seem curious that the course of a river should arouse such passion, but between Mungo Park's 1796 mission and the Landers' mission in 1830 English geographical journals published a stream of articles from fierce advocates of this or that theory about the Niger. Battle was joined in the letters columns of newspapers and quarterlies. James Grey Jackson, an English merchant who at one time served as consul in the Moroccan city of Mogador, revived the time-honoured theory that the Niger was a branch of the Nile. In 1820 Jackson wrote that 'this junction is founded on the universal and concurrent testimony of all the most intelligent and well-informed native African travellers'. Jackson claimed to have irrefutable evidence in the accounts of travellers he had personally met who had travelled over water from Cairo to Timbuctu. He described those who disagreed with him as men 'who raised splendid fabrics on pillars of ice'.

Less far-fetched was the theory of Major James Rennell, the

leading English geographer of his day and a consultant for the African Association. Rennell had earned his reputation making maps of India, after spending ten years there, but in later life he turned to Africa. He rejected the Nile-Niger theory on the grounds that the difference in levels between the two rivers made it impossible for them to join. Instead, he argued, the Niger ended in a great lake in the central Sudan. In a memoir on the Niger's termination, Rennell wrote: 'On the whole, it can scarcely be doubted that the Niger terminates in a lake, in the Eastern quarter of Africa.' Rennell's maps showed the Niger stretching across West Africa in an almost straight line, blocked to the south by a range of non-existent mountains, and emptying into a non-existent lake.

There were some who hit on the truth about the Niger before it was fully explored, but their voices were drowned by the clamour of Rennell and Jackson. In 1808 the German geographer C. G. Reichard proposed that the Niger entered the Gulf of Guinea through a delta in the Bight of Benin. From the accounts of travellers he had studied, it seemed to Reichard that the area in the Bight had the appearance of a great river delta, like that of the Nile or the Ganges. It seemed reasonable to him that the Niger, after reaching a desert it could not cross, should make a great bend to the south-west and empty into the sea. A West Indian plantation manager whose hobby was geography, James McQueen, reached the same conclusion independently. Many of his slaves were West Africans who had lived on the Niger's banks. He cross-examined each one who had seen the river and pieced the puzzle together. But he was not taken seriously because he had never set foot in Africa. In 1821 he published a book describing the Niger's course with as much precision as if he had explored its length. But who were Reichard and McQueen compared to an authority like Rennell?

Ironically, the controversy was finally resolved by the man who most stubbornly clung to the theory that the Niger was the Nile. John Barrow, second secretary of the Admiralty and founder of the Royal Geographical Society, who showered unbelievers with heavy sarcasm in the pages of the *Yearly Journal,* sponsored the mission that was to close the argument.

Delta potentates such as Chief Kofe kept their power thanks to the slave trade. *UAC International*

The first Europeans to land on the West African coast were the Portuguese, at the end of the fifteenth century. Drawn by the promise of gold, they set up tracking stations. *UAC International*

The Niger at Niamey serves as a community laundry. *Beryl Goldberg, New York*

Leo the African, a Moslem born in Granada at the end of the fourteenth century, was captured by Corsicans in 1518 and was offered as a gift to Pope Leo X. He wrote an account of his travels in West Africa, including an eyewitness description of the Niger. For some reason, he got the course wrong. *Trustees of the British Museum*

Confluence of Niger and Chadda. From Allen's 'Descriptive Views of the Niger'. The London Library

Sir Joseph Banks, KB, President of the Royal Society. Drawing by George Dance, 1803. It was Banks who founded the African Association, which sponsored Mungo Park's first expedition. By kind permission of The Royal Society of London

Mungo Park, the Scottish doctor and explorer, discovered the Niger's course in 1796, laying to rest a 2000-year-old controversy. The London Library

The Bozos are the Niger's great fishermen. They learn from infancy how to cast nets. The biggest and best-tasting fish in the Niger is the Capitaine, which reaches a length of more than four feet. *Illustration from Captain W Allen's 'Expedition to the Niger', Vol I*

In the delta, the Niger winds through mangrove forests, swamps, black mud islands, and giant cotton woods.
Werner Forman Archive

The famous Catalan Atlas of 1375, drawn by the Majorcan geographer Abraham Crepques, based on reports from traders. It has a wealth of picturesque detail, including the Emperor of Mali, shown on his throne, holding a gold nugget.
Bibliothéque National, Paris

Prince Henry the Navigator, third son of the Portuguese king, John I, was fascinated by accounts of the trans-Saharan gold trade, and became determined to find a sea route to the gold mines of West Africa. In 1434 one of his ships successfully sailed around West Africa's hump and back. *Bibliothéque National, Paris*

Ferry crossing the Niger near Farie. *Beryl Goldberg, New York*

This bronze bas-relief from Mungo Park's memorial statue in Selkirk shows the exhausted explorer being fed by native women. *Royal Commission on Ancient and Historical Monuments, Scotland*

Djenne is huddled around its mosque like a feudal village around its castle. *Beryl Goldberg, New York*

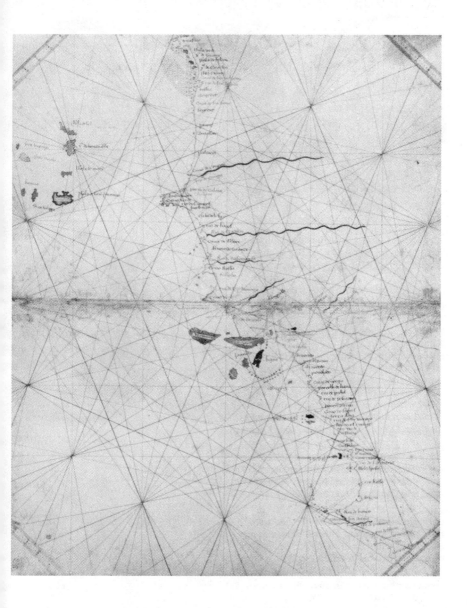

The Portuguese portolan maps, such as this one of 1468, defined known coastal features and harbours, and were specifically designed to help the sea captains find their way. *Trustees of the British Museum*

1   2   3

1 Frederick Lugard, a professional soldier
   who had made his name in the pacification of
   Uganda, took a commercial company on the
   Niger and made it into a colony called
   Nigeria. *National Portrait Gallery*

2 John Hawley Glover, *Frontispiece of Glover's
   'Voyage'. UAC International*

3 Richard Lander first went to West Africa as
   Hugh Clapperton's manservant. He returned
   in 1830 with his brother John and discovered
   the Niger's mouth. He made a third trip in
   1832 with the Liverpool trader Macgregor
   Laird and died on the Niger, ambushed by
   natives. *National Portrait Gallery, London*

7

4 Sir John Barrow, Secretary of the Admiralty,
   was convinced that the Niger joined the Nile,
   and sponsored several missions to prove his
   theory. *The Royal Society of London*

5 Captain Hugh Clapperton, the Scottish
   explorer who died in West Africa, was a
   much-travelled naval officer of proven
   courage and resourcefulness. *From engraving
   by Lupton, after a portrait by Gildon Manton.
   National Maritime Museum*

6 Dixon Denham, a gentleman officer with a
   peremptory nature, was largely responsible
   for the personal guards that plagued the
   mission he shared with Hugh Clapperton and
   Oudney. *Portrait by T Philips. National
   Portrait Gallery*

7 The German explorer-geographer Heinrich
   Barth, who accompanied James Richardson
   in his 1849 mission, has been called 'perhaps
   the greatest traveller there has ever been in
   Africa'. *The Royal Geographical Society*

8 Gordon Laing, another restless Scotsman, reached Timbuctu over the Tripoli route in 1826, and was murdered thirty miles north of the city, on his way home. *Engraving by S Freeman. The Royal Geographical Society*

9 William Balfour Baikie, a Scottish doctor like Mungo Park, led the first mission up the Niger to survive the peril of malaria, in 1854, thanks to the preventive use of quinine. *The Royal Geographical Society*

10 Sir George Goldie, founder of the Royal Niger Company, made his company the vehicle for British government involvement in the Niger. *National Portrait Gallery*

11 Louis Archinard, named commander of the upper Niger in 1888, carried out campaigns of conquest against dissident African chiefs, reaching as far as the city of Djenne, on the Niger bend. *Radio Times Hulton, Picture Library*

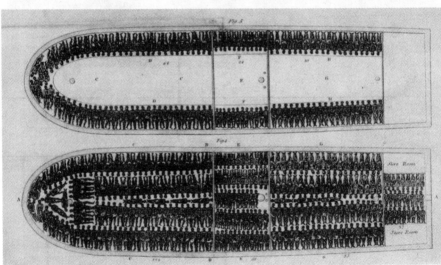

Above Arab slave-traders throwing slaves overboard to avoid capture. *National Maritime Museum*

Below The loading principle aboard a slave ship was a simple one—cram the greatest number of slaves in the least possible space. *Trustees of the British Museum*

Mungo Park's death remains mysterious. All that can be
said with certainty is that he was the victim of his own
obsession to reach the Niger's mouth. *Drawing by H Corbould.*
Trustees of the British Museum

Sandstorms, which closed wells, were one of the perils of Saharan travel. '*A Sand wind on the Desert*', *from G F Lyon's 'Narrative of Travels', 1821. The London Library*

When Hugh Clapperton, the English explorer, was received by El Kenemy, the Sheikh of Bornu, on 16 February 1823, in his capital of Kukawa, the era of the impenetrable West African hinterland came to an end. *The London Library*

Farie, Niger—site of Ferry
crossing the Niger. *Beryl
Goldberg, New York*

Timbuctu, Mali. *Beryl
Goldberg, New York*

Above After Mungo Park's death, explorers tried to reach the Niger overland via the Tripoli route. *National Maritime Museum*

Below The Obie, a king of Ibo, wearing his sugar-loaf hat and surrounded by wives, held the Landers for ransom in 1830, on their first journey down the Niger. *From Allen's 'Expedition to the Niger', Vol I. UAC International*

There is a natural elegance in the architecture of the Niger river, and in its people. *Beryl Goldberg, New York*

Lancers of the Sultan of Begharmi. *From 'Travels in Northern Africa' 1828, by Denham, Clapperton & Oudney. The London Library*

René Caillié, a French traveller, reached Timbuctu in 1828, and, after many ordeals, returned safely to his homeland. *From 'Travels through Central Africa to Timbuktu', 1830. The London Library*

Caillié secretly made drawings of Timbuctu, and wrote that 'the idea I had formed of the city's greatness and wealth hardly corresponded to what I saw, a cluster of dirt houses, surrounded by arid plains of yellow-white sand.' *UAC International*

When the British started
to take baths regularly,
palm-oil, an important
ingredient in the
manufacture of soap,
became the principal West
African export item.
Pears' Soap

The *Quorra*, a paddle-
steamer built by Macgregor
Laird, went up the Niger in
1832, but ran aground on a
sand bar, and remained
stuck for five months, until
the waters rose. *From
Laird & Oldfield's
'Narrative', Vol I. UAC
International*

Top left From Masena, seventy miles southwest of Lake Tchad, Barth joined a slave caravan and observed the slavers' brutality first-hand during the return of the Sultan of Masena in July 1852 after the slave raid. *From Vol III, Barth's 'Travels'.* *UAC International*

Above In 1849, the anti-slavery explorer James Richardson organized yet another mission to the Niger over the Tripoli route. *The Royal Geographical Society*

Left In the Niger delta, the Obie's large war canoes, flying tribal flags on bamboo masts, captured the Lander brothers. *From Captain William Allen's 'Descriptive Views of the Niger'.* *The London Library*

Samuel Crowther, a freed slave, returned to West Africa to settle a mission at the Benue confluence and became the first Bishop of the Niger. *Church Missionary Society*

The Rt. Rev. S. Crowther
The slave who became a Bishop

Kano today is a great trading city in Northern Nigeria, still devoutly Moslem. *Werner Forman Archive*

Above Dr Cheetham, a Sierra Leone bishop travelling in his diocese in 1870, showed that abolitionist views did not exclude the occasional use of slave labour. *Church Missionary Society*

Below The '*Henry Venn I*' steamer—1878–85. *Church Missionary Society*

Above These three iron paddle-steamers, *The Albert*, *Wilberforce* and *Soudan*, went up the Niger in 1871 on a mission to negotiate anti-slavery treaties with tribal chiefs. *From the voyage of H Dundas Trotter, William and Bird Allen. National Maritime Museum*

Below Sampling palm-oil in Bakana, 1896. From a large cask known as 'a Regular Liverpooler', three samples were extracted by hollow dipstick to test for free fatty acid content, impurities and moisture. *UAC International*

David McIntosh, sometime Chief Agent for the Royal Niger Company, Constabulary, Benue—later vice-consul for the Niger area. *Photograph taken after he had left the service, possibly 1907–8 when he was prospecting areas in the Benue.* UAC International

Port Harcourt, the Niger delta's busiest city, was an Ibo stronghold in the Biafran war. *UAC International*

The Oba, a king of Benin, with Consul General Moore, after his capture in 1897. The Oba was deported to Calaban and died in 1914. *UAC International*

One of the many tribal chiefs in the Niger delta, who kept in power thanks to Lugard's policy of indirect rule. *UAC International*

The elaborate canoe of
another small potentate,
Chief Bob. *UAC International*

Another delta chief, Young
Briggs, in his bathchair in
1902. *UAC International*

Chief Will Braide and soldiers, Bakana, 1899. *UAC International*

On the road from Gao to Niamey, giraffes, now protected from hunters, placidly munch the leaves on trees. *Trustees of the British Museum*

West Africans, who never willingly travelled far from their homes, saw the world in chains. *'Scene of the Coast of West Africa' painting by A F Biard. Hull Museums*

A United African company bus. *UAC International*

The *Pleiad*, a 260-ton iron screw steamer rigged as a schooner, was the ship Baikie took up the Niger in 1854 without a single casualty due to malaria. *From 'Narrative of an exploring voyage up the rivers Kwora and Binue', by William Balfour Baikie. The London Library*

TROPHIES.

The following approximate prices are published for Members' guidance. It will be well, however, to avoid any misunderstanding, that Members should have an official estimate given before any trophy is proceeded with, as variation in sizes, &c., of hoofs are liable to cause difference in cost. Members will oblige, when giving orders for hoofs to be mounted as inkstands, by stating whether they require them with or without pen-rack. Mounted specimens can be seen in the Department.

HOOFS AS TROPHIES.

		Nickel.	Brass.
No. 1.	About	37/6	35/0
„ 3.	„	40/0	40/0

No. 7. As Match stand in electro-plate and chased 50/0

		Electro.		
No. 3.	About	55/0		
„ 4.	„	42/0		

No. 9. As a Trinket Box, electro-plated and chased 50/0

		Electro.	Brass.
No. 3.	Nickel.	55/0	45/0
	45/0	42/0	35/0
No. 4.	40/0		

		Electro.		
No. 2.	About	42/6		
„	„	50/0		

No. 8. As Candlesticks, in iron and copper .... each 36/0

Engraving inscriptions on Hoofs, &c., 1/6 per dozen letters extra.

NOTE.—In addition to the prices given for mounting Hoofs, Pads, Slots, &c., there is a preliminary and extra charge for curing, viz.:—

Hoofs and Slots, 2/6 each; Pads, 1/6 each.

No definite time can be given for completion of mounting hoofs, as they must be thoroughly dry before mounts can be fixed, and this takes

The rage for trophies was a by-product of Britain's West African empire. *Taken from an Army & Navy price list of 1913. Army and Navy Stores*

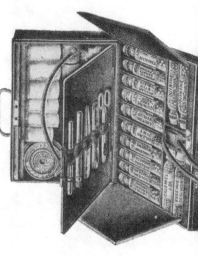

An Empire medicine case. *Army and Navy Stores*

It was to Barrow that Lander handed over Clapperton's journal, as well as his own notes, which were later published as an appendix to Clapperton's narrative. Although a hero to the public, Lander was still a manservant to the Colonial Office, and was paid the £80 intended for a mulatto interpreter who had died at the start of the mission.

Lander returned to Truro after an absence of thirteen years, married, and settled down to family life and a humdrum job with the excise department. It was outdoor work, and since he suffered from malaria attacks and rheumatism he petitioned the Colonial Office for a job 'where I may not be exposed to the inclemency of the weather'. He was transferred to the customs house as a weighing porter at a salary of £50 a year. But, like Mungo Park, he could not adapt to sedentary, small-town life. His wife Harriet gave birth to a daughter, an additional reason to keep him home. Instead, he thought of Africa and volunteered for another mission. In September 1829 Barrow wrote to the Under-Secretary at the Colonial Office, R. W. Hay: 'Would not Lander be the fittest person to send? No one in my opinion would make their way so well and with a bundle of beads and bafts and other trinkets, we could land him somewhere about Bonny and let him find his way.'

It cannot have escaped the attention of the Colonial Office that Richard Lander was willing to undertake the mission for very little money. His only condition was that he be allowed to take along his younger brother John, who was better educated, having gone to school until the age of fifteen, and become an apprentice printer with the *Royal Cornwall Gazette*. Like Richard, he was straight-nosed and curly-haired. Unlike the cheerful, extroverted Richard, John was a serious, rather dour young man, of whom it was said that as a child he never smiled. He did not seem to have the explorer's temperament, and was so fastidious that upon reaching Africa he was revolted by the sight of blacks, and confessed 'a very considerable share of aversion towards their jetty countenances'. He was studious and bookish, with literary aspirations, having written verse and essays. It was in the capacity of scribe that he complemented his more rough-hewn brother, and it is to John that the Landers' journal owes its stylistic flourishes.

In December 1829 Richard Lander received his instructions

from Hay, drafted in the formal, rather stilted style of the Colonial Office:

> Sir, I am directed by Secretary Sir George Murray to acquaint you, that he has deemed it expedient to accept the offer which you have made, to proceed to Africa, accompanied by your brother, for the purpose of ascertaining the course of the Great River which was crossed by the late Captain Clapperton on his journey to Sokoto . . . if the river should be found to turn off toward the south, you are to follow it, as before, down to the sea. In short, having once gained the banks of the Quorra, either from Katunga, or lower down, you are to follow its course, if possible to its termination, wherever that may be . . . For the performance of this service, you are furnished with all the articles which you have required for your personal convenience, during your journey, together with a sum of two hundred dollars in coin, and in case, upon your arrival at Badagri, you should find it absolutely necessary to provide yourself with a further supply of dollars, you will be at liberty to draw upon this department for any sum not exceeding three hundred dollars. During the ensuing years, the sum of one hundred pounds will be paid to your wife, in quarterly payments, and upon your return a gratuity of one hundred pounds will be paid to yourself.

These were hardly generous terms, for no mention of any payment to John Lander was made. Still, it was more than Richard Lander was earning at his customs job. The equipment included presents and goods for trading, such as 110 mirrors, 100 combs, 50,000 needles, 100 Dutch pipes, and 50 yards of scarlet cloth. Their food consisted of tinned soup, six pounds of tea, ten of coffee, and twenty of sugar. Their medicine chest contained various purgatives and emetics, two pints of opium, citric acid against scurvy, carbonate of soda for dysentery, and four ounces of sulphate of quinine. It was worthless against the West African climate.

Richard Lander the manservant, who had waited on and nursed his master Clapperton up to the moment of his death, was now Richard Lander the mission leader, who was on his way to solving the two-thousand-year-old riddle of the Niger's termination. Lander was a seasoned twenty-six and an African veteran, who had kept the mission a family affair by choosing his twenty-three-year-old brother as partner. They left Portsmouth aboard the brig *Alert* on 9 January 1830, and reached the West African

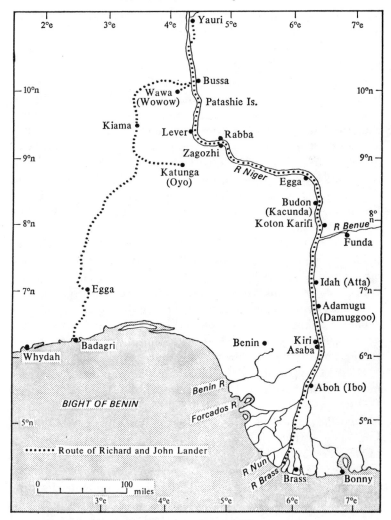

Map 5   Route of Richard and John Lander

coast on 22 February. Among the servants they hired was the Hausa Pasko, who had been on the first expedition. The anti-slavery patrol ship *Clinker* took them to Badagri, and from there the Landers planned to head north until they met the river. Had they known it, in Badagri they were only two hundred miles west of the Niger delta. They could have reached it by sailing down the coast. Instead, they had to make the hard overland

179

trek to the river, and then follow it downstream to prove that the network of creeks and rivers long known to traders was the estuary of the great river that roamed so unpredictably through the West African heartland.

Lander cannot have been pleased at the prospect of returning to Badagri, where he had been put to the poison test and lived among a people who relished human sacrifices. Badagri had not changed. The king had no time for them and scarcely looked at his presents: he was too busy preparing for the execution of three hundred prisoners. He permitted the Landers to leave for the interior on 31 March after they had paid him a tribute of sixty-two ounces of gold dust. Extortion was still the rule, the Landers found, and 'turnpikes are as common as on any public road in England'. John caught his 'seasoning' in April; his thirst was unquenchable, and in the evening he was delirious. He had to be carried in a hammock. Richard bled him and applied a blister to his stomach. John sweated the fever out. They advanced slowly, sometimes covering no more than four miles a day. Each kept a separate journal, writing the day's events every evening. Taking the same route that Lander had taken three years earlier, they reached Katunga, the half-way point between Badagri and the Niger, on 13 May, and stayed there a week.

Unlike Clapperton, Richard Lander did not disclose the real purpose of his mission. He told Mansolah, the King of Katunga, that he was back because the King of England wanted to recover Mungo Park's papers. This seemed inoffensive enough, and the king allowed them to proceed. But Lander noticed that the sense of wonder the blacks had felt upon seeing their first white men had worn off. 'The eager curiosity of the natives has been glutted by satiety,' he wrote – 'a European is shamefully considered no more than a man!'

In June John had another bad attack of fever, and Richard wrote: 'I expected every moment to be his last. During the few intervals he had from delirium he seemed to be aware of his danger and entered into arrangements respecting his family concerns.' They reached Bussa, which Richard Lander had already visited, on 17 June, firing their rifles to announce their arrival. The next day an old friend of Richard Lander's came to visit them, the widow Zuma, who complained that she had lost half her slaves and most of her wealth, but who, 'in spite of all her losses and misfortunes, has gained so much in corpulency, that it was with the utmost difficulty she could squeeze herself into the doorway of our hut, although it is by no means small'.

That same day, 'we visited the far-famed Niger or Quorra which flows by the city, and were greatly disappointed at the appearance of this celebrated river. Black, rugged rocks rose abruptly from the centre of the stream. The Niger here, in its widest part, is not more than a stone's throw across at present. The rock on which we sat overlooks the spot where Mr Park and his associates met their unhappy fate.'

They asked the King of Bussa whether he had any of Park's books, papers, or belongings, and the king replied that he had been a very young child when Park was killed, and that all traces of the white man had been lost with him. They then heard from the king's drummer, in whose hut they were staying, that one book of Park's had been retrieved. The drummer advised them that 'if but one application were made to the king on any subject whatever, very little was thought of it; but if a second were made, the matter would be considered of sufficient importance to demand his whole attention'. Next day the king showed them an eighteenth-century nautical publication that had belonged to Park, and contained a few loose papers, including an invitation to dinner. The Landers were not interested in the book and gave it back to its owner, who venerated it as a fetish. It was later exchanged for a spear-pointed knife by another explorer, and is now in the museum of the Royal Geographic Society.

The Landers could have begun their river trip to the delta, except that their instructions specified that they should try to visit the Sultan of Yauri, forty miles upriver from Bussa, and determine whether he had any of Park's papers. Probably remembering the trouble Clapperton's bluntness with Bello had caused, Richard Lander enlisted the King of Bussa's support by lying about the nature of his mission. 'We imagined that it would have been bad policy to have stated the true reason for our visiting this country,' he wrote, 'knowing the jealousy of most of the people with regard to the Niger; and, therefore, in answer to the king's inquiries, I was obliged to deceive him with the assertion that our object was to go to Bornu by way of Yauri, requesting at the same time a safe conveyance through his territories.' The king let them have a canoe, clumsily made from two blocks of wood sewn together with rope, and they headed upstream on 25 June and soon reached the Niger's main branch, which 'gradually widened to two miles, and continued so as far as the eye could reach. It looked very much like an artificial canal; the banks having the appearance of a dwarf wall, with vegetation beyond. In most places the water was extremely shallow, but in others it was deep enough to float a frigate . . . Fine trees, bending under the weight of their dark and impenetrable foliage, everywhere relieved the eye from the glare of the sun's rays.'

They came to rapids where their canoes had to be portaged to calmer waters. Reaching Yauri on 27 June, they were shown a cutlass and a double-barrelled gun that had been part of Park's present to the sultan, and they exchanged the gun for their own fowling-piece. They met the fat and jolly sultan, sitting alone in a square that looked like a clean farmyard, and asked him whether he had any of Park's papers. He laughed and replied: 'How do you think that I could have the books of a person that was lost at Bussa?' They stayed in Yauri until 2 August, for the sultan kept finding reasons to keep them, the most outlandish of which was that

> he has made us a present of a quantity of worthless feathers which he had caused to be plucked from the body of a live ostrich; and because he entertained an opinion that if others were added to them they would altogether form a very acceptable present to our gracious sovereign, he informed us that it would be necessary we should wait till such time as the ostrich should regain its plumage, in order for that part of its body which had not previously been plucked to undergo a similar operation; for the weather, he asserted, was much too cold for the bird to lose all its feathers at one and the same time. And further, to encourage their growth, he would order that 2000 cowries worth of butter should be diligently rubbed into the skin of the animal. This money has actually been deducted by the sultan, for this express purpose, from the sum which he was indebted to us [for goods the Landers had sold], because he said he did not approve of paying for the butter from his own pocket.

They were finally given permission to leave on 2 August 1830. Starting only a few miles from the place where Mungo Park had been ambushed a quarter of a century before, the Landers headed down the river's last unexplored stretch on the six hundred mile voyage to the sea. Reaching Wawa two days later, the usual problem had to be faced, for the king did not want his guests to leave, and sat in silent wonder as they told of England's power and wealth. 'Is this all true?' he asked Pasko. 'It is true,' Pasko replied, 'for I have seen it.' 'Wonderful people,' said the king. He showed Lander his collection of charms, among which was a hymn-book inscribed 'Alexander Anderson, Royal Military Hospital, Gosport, 1804'. Anderson, it will be remembered, was Mungo Park's brother-in-law, who had died of illness during Park's second expedition.

The Landers' chief problem now was to find a canoe to replace the badly stitched one the King of Bussa had given them. It seemed to them that 'there is infinitely more difficulty, and greater bustle and discussion in simply purchasing a canoe here, than there would be in Europe in drawing up a treaty of peace, or in determining the boundaries of an empire'. They were sent to a river island where the promised canoes were supposedly waiting, but found that they had been 'cajoled and out-manoeuvred very prettily'. They detained two canoes they had been loaned by the island chief and continued down the river, hiring and discharging local crews every few miles. Reaching the town of Rabba, they sold some of their needles for ten thousand cowries (the market price of a healthy lad, by comparison, was forty thousand cowries) and negotiated with a chief called the King of Dark Water for one large, river-worthy canoe. They exchanged their two canoes and ten thousand cowries for a fifteen-foot-long canoe that looked like an English punt, straight and flat-bottomed, made from a single log. On closer inspection it proved to be leaky and patched up. No one would give them paddles; they had to send men out at night to steal some. No white men had ever visited Rabba, and the Landers reported that 'the people stand gazing at us with visible emotions of amazement and terror; we are regarded, in fact, in just the same light as the fiercest tigers in England'. They paddled on, through storms and gales, their canoe tossing like a coconut shell. Hippos and crocodiles approached them, no more than a gun-butt away.

On 22 October they saw the first evidence that they were not far from the coast when a seagull flew over their heads, 'a most gratifying sight that reminded us forcibly of the object we had in view, and we fondly allowed it to confirm our hopes that we were drawing very near to our journey's end. We likewise beheld, for the first time, about half a dozen large white pelicans, which were sailing gracefully on the water.'

On 25 October they came to an important river crossroads, and took the widest channel, only realizing that they had left the Niger itself when they saw that the current was against them and they were swept back. They were the first European explorers to reach the Niger's mightiest tributary, the Benue or 'mother of waters', which flows west from the region of Lake Tchad across Nigeria for more than a thousand miles until it joins the Niger 250 miles from the sea. Heading back into the main channel, they passed a large white rock and narrowly avoided being sucked into a whirlpool. They stopped to rest on a cleared patch of ground on the river's right bank, perhaps a former market.

They were reclining on their mats when they saw a large party of almost naked men running towards them, armed with muskets, spears, and cutlasses. Instead of following Mungo Park's method of firing at hostile natives, the Landers with admirable sang-froid threw down their pistols and walked calmly towards the chief of the attackers. As they came near, making friendly waves, they saw an arrow in his bent bow. They were now only yards apart, wrote Lander, and 'just as the chief was about to pull the fatal cord, a man that was nearest him rushed forward and stayed his arm'. Through a Hausa interpreter, the chief explained:

A few minutes after you first landed, one of my people came to me and said, that a number of people had arrived at the market-place. Not doubting that it was your intention to attack my village at night and carry off my people, I desired them to get ready to fight. We were all prepared and eager to kill you, and came down breathing vengeance and slaughter, supposing you were my enemies and had landed from the opposite side of the river. But when you came to us unarmed, and we saw your white faces, we were all so frightened that we could not pull our bows, nor move hand or foot; and when you drew near me, and extended your hand towards me, I felt my heart faint within me, and believed that you were 'Children of Heaven and had dropped from the skies'.

Pushing off again, they could momentarily appreciate the serenity of river travel: 'Everything was silent and solitary; no sound could be distinguished save our own voices and the plashing of the paddles with their echoes, the song of birds was not heard, nor could any animal whatever be seen; the banks seemed to be entirely deserted, and the magnificent Niger to be slumbering in its own grandeur.' They had reached the forest belt where European influence had penetrated, and met natives partly dressed in Western clothing, who had picked up a few words of English in Bonny or Brass. At Damuggoo, about a hundred miles south of the Benue junction, they met a squinty-eyed little fellow wearing an English soldier's jacket who kept crying out 'Holloa, you Englishmen! You come here.' The open-handed Damuggoo chief gave the Landers a new canoe, food, and a bottle of rum.

The Landers were now in the domain of Ibo river pirates who plundered peaceful travellers. One day out of Damuggoo, on 5 November 1830, they were attacked by a pirate fleet and taken prisoner. They saw fifty large war canoes coming upriver towards them full of men wearing European shirts, flying flags on bamboo masts. When Richard Lander saw that among the flags was the Union Jack he was overjoyed, but when at close quarters he saw that the men in the canoes were armed with muskets trained on him he realized he was a prisoner. His square, flat-bottomed punt was no match for the big war canoes, and he watched helplessly as it was emptied of its luggage.

John Lander, following in the Damuggoo canoe, also found his way blocked by the pirate fleet, and marvelled at the huge canoes, with six-pounders lashed to their bows, each one paddled by forty men. He tried to run the blockade, but the swifter war canoes rammed him three times, capsizing and sinking his canoe. Lander was fished out of the river, but in the confusion his journal was lost. The pirates took their loot and prisoners to the river village of Kirree, the present-day Nigerian city of Asaba, which today is linked to the city of Onitsha on the other bank by the Niger's mightiest bridge.

A palaver was held in Kirree while the Landers sat in the sun, naked and destitute, without even a shirt to protect them. Kindly women brought them plantains and coconuts. They had lost almost everything they had brought down the river, including Mungo Park's double-barrelled gun, and the ivory tusks they had been given by the King of Bussa. The palaver's judgment was that they should be taken to the Obi or king of Ibo, who would decide what to do with them. They travelled for three days down the Nun, the delta's main branch, until one of the Ibos pointed to a clump of high trees and said: 'There is my country.'

In Ibo-town they met the Obi, a sprightly, intelligent-looking man who wore a cap shaped like a sugar loaf covered with strings of coral, thirteen or fourteen bracelets on each wrist, coral necklaces, and bells on his trousers. Again there was a lengthy palaver, and the Landers learned that they would be held for ransom. The next day, 10 November, they were introduced to another delta dignitary, the Brass chief King Boy, who was the Obi's son-in-law. King Boy gave a speech concerning his greatness and dignity, and produced a book full of references from traders. One of these he proudly showed the Landers. Dated Brass First River, September 1830, it was signed by James Dow, master of the brig *Susan*, and said: 'Captain Dow states that he never met with a greater set of scoundrels than the natives generally and the pilots in particular.' He went on to say that King Boy and his men had tried to steer his ship into the bar at the river's mouth so they could wreck and plunder it.

Now the Landers suffered the misery of captivity. 'In most African towns and villages we have been regarded as demi-gods,' they wrote, 'and treated in consequence with universal kindness, civility, and veneration; but here, alas! what a contrast – we are classed with the most degraded and despicable of mankind, and are become slaves in a land of ignorance and barbarism.' The next day they learned that the Obi had sold them to the vainglorious King Boy, who would take them to Brass, where an English brig was lying, whose captain would presumably pay for their freedom. The Landers had nothing of value left except their own bodies.

It was on 14 November, three days out of Ibo-town, on their way towards Brass in King Boy's canoe, that the Landers knew that, however dismal their personal situation, they had at least succeeded in their mission. They might be prisoners, subjected to the whims of a delta chief, but when they saw the canoe being rocked by the tide they felt a great sense of elation, because they knew they were near the sea. They saw foam on the brackish water, and passed under the vaults of mangroves, so thick they let no light through, down dark and narrow creeks, and their canoe became entangled in brambles and hanging mangrove shoots. The Landers were overcome by the 'peculiarly offensive odour' of swamp decay.

On 15 November they met the canoes of King Boy's father, King Forday, who was monarch of the entire area. He and King Boy performed some ju'ju to appease the water spirits, since the Landers were the first white men ever to come down the delta from the north. King Boy was rubbed with chalk from head to foot and wore a cap decorated with buzzard feathers. He stood in the bow of a canoe and held two spears, which he darted into the canoe at intervals, as if killing a wild beast. King Forday decided to hold John Lander hostage in Brass-town while Richard went with King Boy to fetch the ransom from the Liverpool ship. They were still sixty miles from the sea, and at each bend in the river the captain of the canoe called out. When there was an echo, they threw half a glass of rum, and some fish and yams, into the water. King Boy told Lander: 'Did you not hear the fetish? That is for the fetish. If we do not feed him, and do good for him, he will kill us, or make us poor and sick.' At 7.30 that evening on 17 November, Richard Lander 'heard the welcome sound of surf on the beach'.

The next morning, Lander and King Boy paddled to the side of the English brig, the *Thomas* of Liverpool. Boarding, Lander found that four of the crew had just died of fever, and four others lay sick in their hammocks. The captain, a man called Lake, 'appeared to be in the very last stage of illness'. Lander, delighted to see a countryman, and convinced that his problems were over, explained that if Captain Lake paid the ransom he would certainly be repaid by the British government.

Captain Lake responded as though he was addressing a native beggar rather than a countryman. 'If you think you have a —— fool to deal with, you are mistaken; I'll not give a b—y flint for your bill, I would not give a —— for it.' In all his African travels, Lander had not been treated so brutally as by his fellow Englishman, Captain Lake. Numbed with disappointment, he did not even press the issue, but returned to the canoe to tell King Boy the news. It was a serious loss of face before the

187

African chief, who saw that there was even less solidarity between white men than black. Lander suggested they go to Bonny, where they would find other English ships, but King Boy's faith was shattered, and he said: 'Dis captain no pay, Bonny captain no pay, I won't take you any further.' There was nothing for Lander to do but face Captain Lake's violent temper once again. 'I have a brother and eight people at Brass-town,' Lander explained, 'and if you do not intend to pay King Boy, at least persuade him to bring them here, or else he will poison or starve my brother before I can get any assistance from a man of war, and sell all my people.' This argument touched Captain Lake, for he was short-handed, and Lander's eight people could help him get his brig out. 'If you can get them on board,' he said, 'I will take them away, but as I have told you before, you do not get a flint from me.'

Lander persuaded King Boy to go back to Brass and get his brother. He left that afternoon, grumbling that he had received nothing on account. Captain Lake warned Lander that if he was not back within three days he would leave. On 22 November he told Lander that his brother must be dead or he would have arrived, and said he was leaving, but the sea breeze raised such surf on the bar that he could not weigh anchor. That evening, several large canoes camped under mangrove clumps on the river's west bank. Captain Lake's plan was to get John Lander and the others safely aboard and leave without paying King Boy. Lander had no alternative but to become an accomplice to the double-cross, although he wrote that 'I could not help feeling otherwise than distressed and ashamed of leaving the Brass people in this manner'. Lake cheerfully told Lander: 'Now we shall have a little fighting tomorrow; go you and load seventeen muskets and put five buck shot into each. I will take care that the cannon shall be loaded to the muzzle with balls and flints, and if there is any row, I will give them such a scouring as they never had.'

King Boy had left Brass with John Lander on 23 November. In his ornate, over-blown style, John described seeing the ocean that night:

> We could perceive, in the distance, the long-wished-for Atlantic, with the moon-beams reposing in peaceful beauty upon its surface, and could also hear the sea breaking and roaring over

the sandy bar which stretches across the mouth of the river. The solemn voice of ocean never sounded more melodiously in my ear than it did at that moment; O! It was enchanting as the harp of David.

The situation was less enchanting the next morning, when King Boy brought John Lander aboard the *Thomas*. Boy soon realized that Captain Lake had no intention of paying him. 'His habitual haughtiness had entirely forsaken him, and given place to a humble and cringing demeanour,' wrote Lander. Boy went up to Captain Lake, who pretended to be busy writing and asked him to wait. Lake was stalling for time, trying to avoid an open conflict and in the meantime getting the ship under way. Lander described the scene: 'Give me my bars, Boy insisted. I no will, Lake shouted, in a voice of thunder, which one could hardly have expected from so emaciated a frame as his. I no will, I tell you. I won't give up a bloody flint.'

Boy retreated, frightened by the captain's tone, and seeing sailors unfurling sails he quickly went ashore. After difficulties crossing the bar, during which the *Thomas* was nearly shattered by breakers, Captain Lake got the brig into the open sea and put the Landers ashore on Fernando Po. Lake was a typical Gold Coast captain, brutal and unscrupulous. Men like him had become a legend in England. It was said that their blood was half brine, and that when their crews had fever they whitewashed them from head to foot, sometimes blinding them. One of them in the eighteenth century had been introduced to the author of the *Dunciad* and exclaimed: 'Is this the great Mr Pope? Zounds! I have bought better men, body and soul, in the Bight of Benin for 15 pieces of eight.'

The Landers were eager to part company with Captain Lake, and waited seven weeks in Fernando Po for another ship, finally taking one bound for Rio de Janeiro, where they found passage on a ship bound for England and arrived in Portsmouth on 9 June 1831.

If the Landers succeeded where so many others had failed, it was in part thanks to the progress made by their predecessors. When they arrived in Badagri in 1830, most of the Niger's course was already known, thanks to Park, Clapperton, and others. Only the termination remained to be found. Also, the natives were by then accustomed to seeing white men. The same Bussa tribes who ambushed and killed Mungo Park welcomed the Landers warmly. The Landers put the final brick to a monument of exploration already begun and partly built. It was a joint effort, a search that had continued, despite interruption, from the foundation of the African Association in 1788 to the Landers' return in 1831. This collaboration in no way diminishes their personal achievement, for they showed great qualities of courage and resourcefulness. They were also fortunate in that most of their journey was over water, which protected them to some extent from fever.

Upon returning to England, they won their share of glory. Their narrative was bought by the publisher John Murray for one thousand guineas. It was published in 1832 and translated into half a dozen languages. Richard Lander became the first recipient of the Royal Geographical Society's gold medal. His native town of Truro erected a statue to him on Lemon Street. John Barrow, who had so inflexibly believed that the Niger joined the Nile, had to admit he was wrong. In a review of the Landers' journal that appeared in the *Yearly Journal* in 1832, he wrote:

> The long-sought-for termination of the Niger has now been discovered, and by a very humble but intelligent individual, who, without having any theory to support, or prepossession to gratify, set about the task in a straight forward manner, and accomplished, not without difficulty and danger, an undertaking in which all former travellers had failed.

The Colonial Office, the Landers' employer, treated the brothers with niggardly aloofness. It gave John no reward at all, and when Richard, suffering from the after-effects of fever, petitioned for a pension, he was refused.

The most far-reaching aspect of the Landers' success, however, was that they had proved the feasibility of a sea and river route into the West African interior. The news fired the imaginations of Liverpool merchants. Lander wrote of 'ivory, indigo, and other valuable produce' that could be 'collected in any quantity at trifling expense'. He foresaw that 'the steam engine, the grandest invention of the human mind, will be a fit means of conveying civilization among these uninformed Africans, who, incapable of understanding such a thing, will view its arrival with astonishment and terror, but will gradually learn to appreciate the benefits they will derive, and to hail its arrival with joy'.

There were men for whom those words were a marching song. With the Landers' triumph, the exploration of the Niger ended its heroic period and became profitable. The transition between the two forms of exploration was provided by Richard Lander himself, who was soon to leave on a third and final African expedition.

Seven

TRADERS AND MISSIONARIES

O N C E discovered, the Niger became the portal to West Africa. It drained the Western Sudan, gave access to the Sahara's Southern rim, and made it possible to reach the Bornu and Lake Tchad area. After the discoverer came the consolidator, a different kind of man suited to a new mission. The explorers were restless, footloose men, working out personal obsessions. Their nature was quixotic; they lived to the fullest in their moments of greatest self-denial. Their principal aim, in the words of Blake, was 'not to be another derelict wailing along the margins of existence'. They obeyed voices that commanded them to abandon home, family, and comfort, often to die in some nameless spot which they had done no more than identify.

On the explorers' heels came the do-gooders, imbued with a Victorian certainty that England's role in Africa was, as one writer put it, 'to stamp chaos underfoot and to plant wholesome cabbage'. These men were no less courageous than the explorers. Like them, they suffered great hardships and died in Africa. But their reasons were not the same. They had not come to discover, but to transplant the values of Victorian England on heathen soil. As emissaries of the world's most powerful nation, backed by a mighty navy and a spreading empire, they believed it was their God-given duty to bring civilization to less-favoured people. The way to do this was by developing trade. The beauty of it was that doing good was profitable. As Palmerston said in 1852, 'commerce may go truly forth, leading civilization with one hand and peace with the other, to render mankind happier, wiser, better'.

TRADERS AND MISSIONARIES

Victorian England believed absolutely in the obligation of a superior society to help inferior peoples. This ideology, couched in terms of progress and civilizing influence, was in fact necessary to justify the expansion required by the industrial revolution in its search for new markets. There has seldom been such a conjunction between what was expedient and what was right. The Niger delta natives who traded Manchester cloth for the raw materials of the rain forest were receiving civilization as well as contributing to England's booming economy. Hand in hand, the trader and the missionary arrived to convert African savages into Bible-thumping producers of palm oil. They sailed up the Niger and signed treaties with dozens of African kinglets in the name of Queen Victoria, extracting meaningless promises concerning the suppression of slavery and the end of human sacrifice. It was only after years of reversals that they realized that the Niger was not the Thames, and that the Africans were not potential English gentlemen who had not gone to the right schools.

The first trading missions to the Niger tied profitable commerce to the suppression of slavery. If the English traders could convince the African chiefs that it was in their interests to conserve their manpower to collect palm oil, the traffic in men would end. Palm oil was in demand as an ingredient in soap. The main ingredient was tallow, but for the soap to lather it had to be mixed with vegetable oils, and of these the best was palm oil. Thus the destiny of West Africa in the nineteenth century was joined to the rising demand for soap in Victorian England, where cleanliness was next to Godliness. A growing middle class had begun to wear cotton underwear, take daily baths, and wash with soap. Thanks to palm oil, Liverpool chemists developed a light, foamy soap. By 1850, Liverpool was producing thirty thousand tons of soap a year, one-third of the total English production. The growing need for nocturnal illumination created a secondary market for palm oil, to make candles. One company summed up the mixture of commerce and morality in its advertising: 'Buy our palm-oil candles to contribute to the abolition of the slave trade.' The use of metal machinery and the development of railroads created a third market for palm oil, as a lubricant, and the squeeze of the oil can was heard in the land.

The Niger delta's rivers became known as the Oil Rivers,

and the era of the palm oil ruffian dawned. The coastal traders used the same network of African middlemen who had previously collected slaves. They vanished into the interior and came back down the Niger in canoes loaded with puncheons of palm oil, which the trader tested for texture by feeling it between finger and thumb. In the depots like Bonny, Brass, and Calabar, an almost tangible smell of palm oil hung in the air and clung to clothes. The ships arrived in March, at the height of the season, lurching through the breakers, often scraping the bar, firing their guns to announce their coming. They sometimes had to stay in port ten months before they were loaded. Canoes stacked with oil puncheons paddled out to the ships, and the oil was poured down long canvas hoses through little hatches in the deck, and the canoes paddled back into the delta and disappeared into the mangroves. The system improved with river hulks, old ships that were sunk in shallow water, roofed with thatch, and converted to offices for the agents and storehouses for the oil, so that ships could have a quick turn-around, loading the oil in days instead of months. The bilge water at the bottom of the hulks was a perfect breeding ground for mosquitoes, and many agents died of malaria.

The suppression of slavery provided another instance of the Victorian belief that doing the right thing brought material rewards. Again it was Palmerston who, as Prime Minister, in 1858, pointed out the advantages of moral behaviour. 'It is a curious coincidence,' he said, 'though there may be no real connection between the two – that from the time when this country first began to abolish the slave trade, from that period this country has prospered in a degree which it had never experienced before.'

England, as we have seen, was the nation most actively engaged in policing the West African shore against slavers. But, humanitarian considerations apart, the Blockade Squadron was engaged in a trade war with the smugglers. The palm oil trade could not coexist with the slave trade, for it depended on plentiful manpower. Also, when the slavers were in port, all legitimate trade came to a halt. Every energy was diverted to supplying the smuggler. Once again, moral and economic reasons coincided. The development of the palm oil trade depended on the extinction of the debasing, immoral slave trade.

England's commitment to suppress slavery did not end with the Blockade Squadron. Other methods were employed, which eventually led to the occupation of African territory. The first foothold of England's vast West African empire was secured unintentionally, as a way of carrying out its moral obligations. This was done in two ways. In 1851, to seal off part of the coast where slaves were still being sold, the notorious smuggler's haunt of Lagos was attacked, occupied, and turned over to a puppet king. Ten years later, Lagos was annexed when the Foreign Office became convinced 'that the permanent occupation of this important point in the Bight of Benin is indispensable to the complete suppression of the slave trade'. The Foreign Office suffered from the illusion that it could limit British presence to Lagos. But once Lagos had been annexed, it had to be protected, and quarrelling tribes in the interior had to be pacified. England found its responsibilities, and its jurisdiction, growing like the ripples a pebble dropped into a river makes. Two companies of the West India Regiment and two gunboats were sent to Lagos to provide a necessary military force. A *de facto* protectorate was created, which might be called an example of accidental imperialism.

The second way in which England became involved in West Africa was by sending missions up the Niger to sign treaties with chiefs, who promised to abolish the slave trade in exchange for a regular trade in other goods. To implement the treaties and make sure the chiefs were carrying out their end of the bargain, trading stations had to be established, consuls had to be named in important towns, and again a British presence was established in the African interior. The British government found itself increasingly committed in a part of the world where it originally had not had the slightest intention of occupying even one square inch.

The first trading mission to be set up after the Lander brothers' discovery of the mouth of the Niger was a completely private one, however, the brainchild of a Liverpool trader who had no government support. Macgregor Laird, born in Greenock, Scotland, in 1808, was the son of one of England's most famous shipbuilders, William Laird, who founded the firm of Birkenhead. An enthusiastic, enterprising young man, he left his father's firm to found his own engineering business, and in 1832 he became the first man to follow up the discovery of the Lander brothers. There was a happy coincidence in the fact that access to the African interior via the Niger was not known until steam power was available to exploit it. Macgregor Laird's imagination was nourished by the Landers' accounts of wealth in the hinterland. His Victorian trader's mind saw the chance for profit, adventure, and doing good. In the flowery style of the period, he wrote:

> The information obtained directly from English travellers, and indirectly from captured slaves, describing that country as one on which nature had profusely bestowed her choicest treasures, with the fact that immense territory, comprising one eighth part of the surface of the globe, had been for ages excluded from all direct communication with the civilized world, seemed to hold out the most flattering prospects of success to those fortunate individuals who should be the first to break into its secluded vales.

There were also nobler motives:

> By introducing legitimate commerce with all its attendant blessings into the centre of the country, they [the Landers] knew that they were striking a mortal blow to that debasing and demoralizing traffic which has for centuries cursed that unhappy land, and rendered some of the loveliest tracts on the face of the globe the habitations of wild beasts and noxious reptiles, or of man in a condition more disgusting and degraded than either.

Within a year of the Landers' return, Laird had fitted out an expedition to the Niger that was unlike any of its predecessors. The day of the unprepared, ill-equipped, badly financed explorer, sent alone to muddle through, was over. For this maiden voyage up the Niger Laird built the first ocean-going iron ship, despite the ridicule of experts who said tropical heat would bake the crew as in an oven. His paddle-steamers were the first 'liners', for they could travel on a regular route whatever the weather was like.

The main drawback of the early steamships, before the invention of the tubular boiler, was that they consumed a great deal of wood, but Laird was sure he would find plenty on the riverbanks. The mission was made up of three ships, a large paddle-steamer called the *Quorra* (one of the native names for the Niger), a smaller, flat-bottomed, wrought-iron ship called the

Alburkah (the Hausa word for blessing), and a sailing vessel called the *Columbine*, to be used as a storeship.

Laird hired the acknowledged expert on the Niger, Richard Lander, to command the *Alburkah*, and decided to join the expedition himself. John Lander stayed behind, having been appointed tide-waiter at the Truro customs house. Lieutenant William Allen came along as an Admiralty observer. Laird would be leaving with a man who knew the area, in ships that were not dependent on the whims of the weather. The *Quorra* and the *Alburkah* both had swivel guns to keep off natives. The mission had every chance of success.

The three ships left Milford Haven on 25 July 1832. Laird was aboard the *Quorra*, commanded by Captain Harries. They stopped in Sierra Leone and filled out their crew with Kroomen, members of a tribe known for their loyalty, hard work, and seamanship, and widely used by the English. They next put in at Cape Coast Castle, west of present-day Accra, where the African Company had its headquarters. When they reached the mouth of the Nun, the main gateway up the Niger, they suffered their first casualty. Captain Harries complained of a stiff neck, which he attributed to sleeping with the cabin window open. He refused medicine and advice, and soon died. Aboard the *Alburkah*, the second engineer and the boatswain were dead.

Entering the delta in October, Laird found that 'the country on both sides of the river appeared to be one extensive swamp, covered with mangrove, cabbage, and palm trees . . . the fendamp rose in the mornings cold and clammy to the skin, in appearance like the smoke of a damp wood fire'. In the narrow Nun they met King Boy, who had ransomed the Landers but failed to collect the money. Still smarting at the white man's treachery, he greeted them coolly and followed their ships in his canoe. He was astonished to see Lander again and told him he was not a man but a devil. Laird left the *Columbine* behind under the command of Surgeon Oldfield, to receive produce brought down by the two steamers, which continued upstream.

Reaching Ibo country, they paid a call on the Obi, whose town of Ibo was situated at the junction of three delta rivers, the Benin, the Bonny, and the Nun. The Obi, wrote Laird, 'wore a cap made of pipe coral, much the same shape as the fool's cap of our schools', and bracelets and necklaces of coral – 'I should say he had nearly 100 pounds worth of coral on him.' The Ibo were traders in palm oil and slaves, and Laird was pessimistic about their giving up the latter for the former.

> The collection of palm-oil is lazily and indolently followed [he wrote]. The trouble of catching a man is trifling – that of manufacturing a ton of oil somewhat more – the price of both is about the same: can it be wondered at that the production of oil does not increase more rapidly? . . . The capture of a man partakes of the exhilarating nature of a hunt, while the collection of palm-oil is devoid of excitement, and becomes the sober tedium of business.

They had by now crossed thirty miles of delta and entered the main branch of the Niger, a thousand yards wide. The mangroves and the damp had given way to a forested zone. The river would continue to broaden until Idah, two hundred miles from the sea, where it was two miles wide. Once they left Ibo-town the fever struck again. On 18 November, aboard the *Quorra*, an eighteen-year-old volunteer named Andrew Clark 'expired with the utmost calmness'. The same day one of the firemen died, and on the 19th the chief mate and the sail-maker died. On the 20th the supervisor of cargo, the carpenter, and the chief engineer died. Laird and Lieutenant Allen, the Admiralty observer, were laid low. Only Lander seemed to resist, and was, Laird wrote, 'indefatigable in his attention to the sick, and bled and blistered the men as if he had been a regular licentiate . . . after this is done, I do not think medical skill can go further – the question becomes a pitched battle between the fever and the constitution of the person attacked with it; and medicine, after the first necessary emetics and purgatives, does more harm than good.'

Taking the toll, they found that the *Quorra* had lost thirteen men and the *Alburkah* ten. The mortality was attributed to miasma rising up from the swamps, although the worst fever had struck since they had left the swamp. Laird's remedies were to triple the brandy and rum allowance and to play music on board. He described the crew as 'crawling about the decks more like spectres than men. A mother had not known her sons, amid the skeletons of that gaunt crew.' Laird himself was 'like a scarecrow, with long beard and razor face'. He had a seizure that took fifty drops of laudanum to subdue.

By this time they had passed the red sandstone cliffs of Idah, which rose 120 feet from the river and were covered with giant creepers. The forest had turned to savannah. North of Idah, where the mythical Kong mountains were supposed to rise, they saw basalt sugar-loaf hills and flat-topped plateaux. In December, after two months on the river, they reached the confluence of the Niger and the Benue. They had only collected half a ton of ivory. Laird built a warehouse at the junction of the two rivers. The *Quorra* ran aground on a sandbar and was stuck for five months, until the waters rose. Efforts to get her afloat by carrying her cargo ashore failed. Lander took the *Alburkah* up the Niger as far as the market town of Rabba, 150 miles northwest of the Benue confluence. Laird whiled away the long inactive days aboard the *Quorra* playing chess with his friend Dr Thomas Briggs, but then Briggs died.

Although he was so ill that he could hardly walk, Laird decided to explore the Benue, and reached the village of Fundah, thirty miles from the confluence, by longboat, canoe, and hammock. He had by now, besides fever, caught a bad form of scabies called craw-craw. The inhabitants of Fundah had never seen a white man and the king kept him a virtual prisoner, taunting him, refusing to trade, and threatening to poison him. Laird was warned that the king had frequently enticed and poisoned traders to obtain their goods. The king's favourite occupation, he wrote, 'was to ridicule my weakness and mimic my attempts to walk . . . to my repeated applications to remove myself, he only replied that his gods would not allow him to part with me.' Laird sent a messenger back to the *Quorra*, who returned with some Congreve rockets. 'Everything being ready,' wrote Laird, 'I fired my pistol, and up flew four beautiful rockets, the discharge of which was immediately followed by the blaze of blue lights, throwing a ghastly glare over the whole scene. The effect was electric, the natives fled in all directions, and the king, throwing himself to the ground, and placing one of my feet on his head, entreated me to preserve him from harm . . . I then took from my pocket a little compass and explained that if the needle pointed towards me when placed on the ground I was to go, if towards him I was to stay.' It was the old compass game that had saved other explorers on the Niger.

Laird returned to the confluence to find that Lander was back.

But more men had died, and what was left of the crew lay in torpor and dejection, their eyes filled with the dread of seeing their companions die for unknown reasons. Laird himself was in such a wretched state that his hip and elbow bones had broken through his skin.

Laird had had enough. His own declining health, the crew's high mortality rate, and the disappointment of finding so little profitable trade along the river, decided him to take the *Quorra* downstream. He started down the Niger on 10 July 1833, rested two months on the British-held island of Fernando Po, and returned to England in the *Columbine*, reaching Liverpool on 1 January 1834. His health was permanently impaired, and he never returned to Africa. The mission's high cost had depleted his personal fortune. His interest in the Niger trade continued, however, and in 1849 he founded the African Steamship Company, and was the first to provide a regular service between England and Africa. He died in 1861, not realizing that his efforts to establish trade on the banks of the Niger had helped give birth to an empire.

In the meantime, the tireless Lander, who was bent on proving the trade possibilities he had described in his journal, went back to Rabba with Dr Oldfield in the *Alburkah*, but was prevented from going further by cylinder trouble. They were also out of cowries, and Lander went to Cape Coast Castle for some, leaving Dr Oldfield in the delta with the little iron steamer. He promised to be back in six weeks, but Oldfield never saw him again.

Oldfield's own situation seemed desperate. The *Alburkah*'s stern anchor had been lost and it was constantly running aground. The last white engineer had died and the mate was having hallucinations. Oldfield, recruited as a doctor, was now captain, mate, and engineer. He stubbornly decided to go up the Niger once more. Reaching Idah, he concluded a commercial treaty with its king, who thanked him for his presents and said: 'Thank God I have seen a white man! And it affords me the greatest pleasure; for my father and his father before him, never saw a white man in all their lives.' In March 1834 Oldfield was handed a letter that Richard Lander had written on 22 January:

> I was coming up to you with a cargo of cowries and dry goods worth 450 pounds, when I was attacked by the natives of Hyammah [Angiama, about 100 miles from the Niger's mouth]

. . . the shot were very numerous both from inland and shore . . .
we had three men shot dead . . . I am wounded, I hope not
dangerously, the ball having entered close to the anus and struck
the thigh-bone. It is not extracted yet . . . I lost all my papers,
and everything belonging to me, the boat and one canoe, having
escaped in one of the canoes barely with a coat to our backs, they
chasing us in their war-canoes and all our cartridges being wet, so
that we could not keep them off. We are now under weigh for
Fernando Po. I remain your most affectionate friend, R. L.
Lander.

Lander had fallen into a well-planned ambush on 20 January at
a point where the river narrowed and was divided by an island.
The current was strong and his boat grounded, and he was met
with a musket volley that killed three of his men and wounded
him and six others. He was able to escape downriver in one of the
canoes and paddled all night to escape his pursuers. The ambush
was clearly intended to put a stop to the white man's inroads.

Oldfield was relieved to hear that Lander had escaped with
a thigh wound. It was not until he was heading downstream and
had reached the delta, on 29 June, that he was handed a letter
dated 24 April 1834 and addressed to 'Surgeon Oldfield, or the
officer in charge of the African Inland Company's affairs in the
River Niger'. The letter, from the governor of Fernando Po,
Colonel Edward Nichols, said: 'Dear Sir, you no doubt will be
much annoyed at hearing that Mr Lander died of the wounds he
received in an attack that was made upon him in a most treacherous manner by the natives of Hyammah.'

Richard Lander, who had buried Hugh Clapperton on his
first mission to Africa, and who had found the mouth of the Niger
on his second mission, was claimed by Africa when he returned a
third time. He was thirty years old. Like Mungo Park, discoverer
of the upper Niger, Lander, discoverer of the lower Niger, was
killed in an ambush on the river, by its inhabitants. 'Poor
Lander,' Oldfield observed, 'he fell a victim to his too great
confidence in the natives. Had his generous heart allowed him
to be more suspicious and better prepared against their treachery,
he would have escaped their murderous design.'

After another inconclusive attempt to trade upriver, Oldfield
had decided to turn back, before he and the three other survivors
aboard the *Alburkah* all died on the river. He returned to

Fernando Po and moored his ship alongside the *Quorra* in Clarence Bay. Both steamers were abandoned there and were found rotting years later by subsequent expeditions. Oldfield left for England on 11 August and reached London on 18 November 1834, 'in a very infirm state of health, having suffered much in my constitution from exposure to climate and all kinds of privation'. He was one of nine survivors out of a total English crew of forty-eight. Trade prospects had proved disappointing, and the problems of undercutting the coastal middlemen and dealing directly with the chiefs were greater than expected. All the mission succeeded in doing was firmly establishing the Niger delta's reputation as the white man's grave.

The real barrier to inland progress was not tribesmen with poison arrows but mosquitoes. It was not until 1900 that yellow fever and malaria were identified as separate diseases carried by the female of the anopheles mosquito. Until then, fighting the fever was a guessing game the English were not very good at. Nearly every Niger mission since Mungo Park had been defeated by fever, but the Englishman still believed that, just as he brought civilization to the savage, he could impose his will on a treacherous climate. He insisted on behaving in the tropics just as he behaved at home. He exposed himself to the dangers of 'miasma', as if it was no greater menace than the first frost in Yorkshire, without a clue as to its real nature. He expected to be taken sick but believed the first attack would season him. He did not think of preventing the fever, but of contracting and conquering it. Even though the ships that sailed up the Niger soon turned into floating hospitals, with fever laying low the entire crew, the notion of contagion was not firmly established. Ships' captains did not wish to believe in contagion, the spread of which would lower the crew's morale.

A typical story concerns surgeon McKinnel of the Blockade Squadron ship *Sybille*. In 1830 yellow fever, then known as black vomit, struck the ship. To show the crew that it was not contagious, McKinnel collected a wine-glass of black vomit from the lips of a dying seaman and drank it, toasting the officer on watch. He survived, proving the supremacy of an Englishman's will against African microbes. In a sense, the large number of Englishmen who lost their lives in the early missions up the Niger may be said to have died of stubbornness.

TRADERS AND MISSIONARIES

For ten years after Laird's fiasco, there were no more Niger missions. The loss of life and the expense did not seem worth it.

Renewed interest in the Niger was the result of abolition rather than trade. The Blockade Squadron was not a sufficient deterrent to illegal slaving. It was not only a question of naval might, but of complicated international treaties for the right of search. The squadron was in the position of a man using his ten fingers to plug a hundred leaks. Commander Broadhead, giving evidence in 1841 before the commission of inquiry on the western coast of Africa, said: 'I have seen some 13 vessels laying in Lagos at one time. To give some idea of the traffic of the latter, I will mention that I blockaded it closely in the months of January, February, and March, 1840, chasing one vessel off eight times . . . I have blockaded Lagos on one occasion for 100 days without quitting it, and at two other intervals for upwards of 90.'

Even if the entire British fleet were committed to the blockade, the slavers would find secret coves to slip into under cover of darkness. There had to be another way, and it was promoted by the successor of the abolitionists, Sir Thomas Fowell Buxton, a retired member of Parliament who had devoted his final years to the suppression of the trade. In 1840 he wrote an influential book, *The African Slave Trade and its Remedy*. At the same time he founded the Society for the Extinction of the Slave Trade and the Civilization of Africa. Buxton's society was supported by the cream of the Victorian establishment. Its president was the prince consort, Albert, and among its members could be found a generous sprinkling of lords, bishops, and MPs. Buxton's idea was a simple one, borrowed from Laird: that the Africans themselves had to be persuaded to give up the slave trade. This could be done, Buxton proposed, by bringing them 'the Bible and the Plough'. Honest toil, requiring willing arms, would replace the barbaric practice of selling their brethren. Missionaries would instruct them in the first lesson of Christianity, that owning other human beings is condemned by God. The Africans would discover that their own material and spiritual interests lay in giving up slavery and becoming farmers and good Christians.

Buxton proposed that a large expedition be sent up the Niger with a three-fold mission: to show the natives the advantages of legitimate trade; to sign treaties with the chiefs in which they promised to give up slaving; and to set up a model farm at the Benue–Niger confluence which could teach the Africans the merits of agriculture and the blessings of Christianity. The reason that Buxton could propose such a utopian programme was that he had never been to Africa and knew nothing about local conditions. The underlying assumption of his plan was that beneath the skin the Africans were no different from the English and would respond to the same arguments and incentives.

The Africans were in fact baffled by the changing European attitude towards slavery. They saw the English, who had once been the leading purchasers of slaves, suddenly become the leading suppressors of the trade. The English now told them that slavery was terrible, whereas the French and Portuguese continued to tell them that it was ordained by God and must be maintained. Who were they to believe? When the mission sponsored by Buxton was on the Niger in 1841, the King of Ibo told them: 'Hitherto we thought it was God's wish that black people should be slaves to white people. White people first told us we should sell slaves to them and we sold them, and white people are now telling us not to sell slaves. If white people give up buying, black people will give up selling.'

Human sacrifices provided a good example of how the English judged Africans through Western eyes. It was easy to be shocked, but they did not consider that such practices were part of a complicated religion based on exorcizing evil spirits. From the African point of view, to tamper with their religious practices was as much of a sacrilege as it would be to tamper with a Catholic mass. Surgeon Oldfield, during the Laird expedition, saw a woman in the delta chained to a log of wood, waiting for the tide to come in 'to become the unhappy prey of voracious sharks'. She was the widow of a chief whose death she was accused of having wished for. When Oldfield interceded, the new chief quite sensibly said: 'White man's fash no be black man's fash.'

The triumph of Victorian optimism, however, was in the signing of treaties with African chiefs who had no concept of legally binding written agreements and whose own laws were based on custom orally handed down. The treaties were drafted as if the 'High Consenting Parties' were fully versed with the rights of man and English common law. It gave a comic flavour to the expedition that was eventually sent out, with queen's commissioners solemnly asking African kinglets to obey the articles of a treaty they had only signed because of the presents they received in exchange, and which they had no intention of carrying out.

Buxton was convinced that the African chiefs would eagerly sign treaties promising to abolish their principal means of livelihood, give up deep-rooted religious practices, and welcome meddling settlers and missionaries on their lands. His head was full of schemes as unrealistic as they were grandiose. He already saw the model farm growing into 'the great internal citadel of Africa, and the great emporium of her commerce'. It is a tribute to the energy generated by the missionary conscience that, instead of being ignored as a crackpot, Buxton actually persuaded the British government to sponsor an expedition with the specific aim of 'reclaiming the savages'. Through inspired lobbying, he won the backing of the Treasury, the Admiralty, and the Colonial Office. The Colonial Secretary, Sir John Russell, and the First Lord of the Admiralty, Lord Minto, promised to provide three steam vessels. The only note of reticence came from the Colonial Office, which declined Buxton's suggestion that his model farm should be given the status of a crown colony.

Never had the government, in the past so stingy with explorers' expenses, devoted such lavish attention to detail. John Laird, Macgregor's brother, built three iron paddle-steamers, all that the most advanced shipbuilding techniques could devise. They burned coal as well as wood. They were flat-bottomed; fitted with retractable keels and rudders; divided by iron bulkheads into four watertight compartments as protection against the Niger's rocky outcroppings; and equipped with newly designed contrivances such as lifeboats that also served as the covers for paddleboxes. Two of the ships, the *Albert* and the *Wilberforce*, were identical in weight (457 tons) and length (139 feet). The third, the *Soudan*, was lighter and shorter.

The ships' real novelty, however, was a ventilating system that promised to protect the crews from the fever that had wiped out the Laird mission. It had been devised by Dr Reid, whose reputation in ventilation was based on the success of the system he had installed in both Houses of Parliament. It consisted of engine-driven fans that drove fresh air through tubes to every part of the ship. The air passed through a large iron chest filled with chemicals such as chloride of lime, called a purifying chamber, which was intended to filter it. The miasma, it was hoped, would be caught in the purifying chamber, bringing clean air below decks.

No expense was spared. Supplies included tinned goods from a well-known caterer, pickled cabbage, cranberries, wine, and beer. The men were issued with straw hats against the sun. There was coffee every morning. Men and officers were on double pay. There were more surgeons than ships, five in all. The surgeon of the *Wilberforce*, W. M. Pritchett, did not believe in the miasmic theory; he was convinced that the 'Febris Africanus' came from solar exposure, which he treated with castor oil and calomel. J. O. McWilliams, surgeon of the *Albert*, who wrote a medical history of the expedition, attributed the fever to 'miasmatous poison'. The best treatment, he said, was to remove the sick from the river, where the fever seemed to be concentrated. McWilliams did not believe in contagion. 'No fact came under my observation,' he wrote, 'affording the slightest evidence that the disease was communicable from one person to another.'

Thomson, the surgeon of the *Soudan*, believed that the fever came from 'a certain peculiarity of atmosphere – call it miasma, malaria, or any other name – which though inappreciable by chemical agency, operates most powerfully on Europeans'. Thomson, however, also believed in the virtue of quinine, and took six to eight grains each day, which preserved him from the fever. He did nothing to enforce its usage among the crew, however, for the miasma theory still held sway.

They set out inflated with optimism, convinced that every possible measure for their health and safety had been taken. The captains were appointed: Commander (later Admiral) William Allen, who had already been up the Niger with Macgregor Laird as an Admiralty observer, for the *Wilberforce*; Captain (later Admiral) D. H. Trotter for the *Albert*, and Commander Bird Allen for the *Soudan*. In addition to commanding the ships, they were named queen's commissioners, with full powers to make official treaties with native chiefs. A fourth queen's commissioner was William Cook, a member of Buxton's abolitionist society. Seconding the commissioners were three chaplains: Theodore Muller, who spoke Arabic; J. F. Schön, of the Church of England Missionary Society, a leading African linguist; and Samuel Crowther, a former Yoruba slave who had been brought up in Sierra Leone. He was so bright that he was sent to school in Liverpool and was ordained, becoming the first African clergyman of modern times. He eventually became the first bishop of the Niger river. A black West Indian, Mr Carr, was to be in charge of the model farm and took along ploughs and harrows that were better suited to rural England than West Africa. Last but not least there was a bevy of scientists, including a botanist, a geologist, and a naturalist. It was, without a doubt, the most ambitious expedition that had ever set out for the Niger, and a far cry from Mungo Park's lonely venture. It was also the most expensive. The total bill, footed by the Treasury, was £80,000.

The mission appealed to Victorian sensibilities. It was a perfect example of the imperial hand reaching out wearing a philanthropic glove. How comforting it must have been to believe that increasing England's might and wealth was beneficial to less favoured peoples. At a send-off rally, the twenty-two-year-old prince consort made his first public speech since his marriage to Victoria on 10 February 1840. Prince Albert also went to Woolwich on 23 March 1841 to inspect the ships. His visit seemed a good omen. 'We were in the confusion of preparation,' wrote Captain Trotter in the mission's narrative, 'with caulkers and other artificers on board, which was explained to His Royal Highness, who, however, with his usual gracious condescension, expressed his intention of visiting all the vessels. The officers had the honour of being presented to His Royal Highness by Captain Trotter on the quarter-deck of his ship. As another proof of the sympathy of this truly amiable prince, we may here mention that he presented a handsome gold chronometer, by the best maker, to each of the three captains.'

Thus equipped with royal time-pieces, they sailed in May, but without Fowell Buxton, who was too ill to join them. After recruiting 133 Africans on the west coast to fill out their crews, they entered the Niger on 13 August, steaming over the bar despite a considerable surf. The same day their instrument-maker died, as if announcing that they were in lethal waters.

They intended to stop in the major villages on the Niger's banks. There, the commissioners would negotiate, the missionaries would preach, and the surgeons would vaccinate. Steaming up the delta, they passed villages alarmed at the 'smoke-canoes', and reached Ibo. The Obi came aboard the *Albert*, dressed in a scarlet coat, with white cotton trousers, and a conical black velvet hat. Captain Trotter, in the name of the queen, told the Obi they had been sent to sign a treaty with him to end the slave trade, and pointed out the injurious effects of slavery in terms of population loss.

Although he was one of the busiest slavers in the delta, the Obi readily agreed to do away with the trade if a better trade could be found. The commissioners questioned him through his 'mouth' or interpreter. The dialogue was reported in Captain Trotter's narrative of the expedition:

Commissioners: 'Does Obi sell slaves from his own dominions?'

Obi: 'No, they come from countries far away.'

Commissioners: 'Does Obi make war to procure slaves?'

Obi: 'When other chiefs quarrel with me and make war, I take all I can as slaves.'

Commissioners: 'The Queen of England's subjects would be glad to trade for raw cotton, indigo, ivory, gums, camwood. Now have your people these things to offer in return for English trade-goods?'

Obi: 'Yes.'

Commissioners: 'Englishmen will bring everything to trade but rum or spirits, which are injurious. If you induce your subjects to cultivate the ground, you will all become rich; but if you sell slaves the land will not be cultivated and you will become poorer by the traffic.'

Obi: 'I will agree to discontinue the slave trade, but I expect the English to bring goods for traffic.'

Commissioners: 'Have you power to make an agreement with the Commissioners in the name of all your subjects?'

Obi: 'I am the king. What I say is law. Are there two kings in England? There is only one here.'

Commissioners: 'Understanding you have sovereign power, can you seize slaves on the river?'

Obi: 'Yes.'

Commissioners: 'You must set them free.'

Obi: 'Yes' (snapping his fingers several times).

Commissioners: 'The boats must be destroyed.'

Obi: 'I will break the canoe, but kill no one.'

Commissioners: 'People may come here, and follow their own religion without annoyance? Our countrymen will be happy to teach our religion, without which blessing we should not be so prosperous as a nation as we now are.'

Obi: 'Yes, let them come, we shall be glad to hear them.'

The Reverend Schön then tried to inculcate a few sound Christian precepts.

Schön: 'There is but one God.'

Obi: 'I always understood there were two.'

Schön summed up the leading truths of the Christian faith and asked the Obi if this was not a fine religion. 'Yes, very good,' the Obi replied, but, finally growing impatient, he added: 'I want this palaver to be settled. I am tired of so much talking, I wish to go home.'

On the Obi's second visit aboard the *Albert*, the commissioners took pains to make sure he understood each of the seventeen articles of the treaty he was about to sign. In exchange, the Obi received a long list of presents, and when the commissioners knelt to say prayers he knelt with them. There was almost a diplomatic incident when one of the officers, seeing a native kneel before the Obi, pushed him away, saying that 'he could not suffer kneeling on a Christian quarter-deck to any but the King of Kings'. The interpreter explained that this native custom should be indulged.

They passed through the dreaded delta without further illness, and thought they had escaped the fever, not realizing that the mosquito that carries malaria is equally at home in savannah and rain forest. Their next stop was Idah, to negotiate with the Attah. A delegation was sent ashore to invite him on board to hear the Queen's message. But the Attah proved to be an expert at gamesmanship.

I do not like to come out in the rain [he said], but the white men were resolved to see me and I imagined from that they could stop it; but it rains as much as ever. The river belongs to me, a long way up and down, on both sides, and I am king. The queen of white men has sent a friend to see me. I have also just now seen a present, which is not worthy to be offered to me – it is only fit for a servant . . . You ask me to go on board a ship. A king in this country never goes on board ship. He never sets foot in a canoe . . . if anyone desires to see me, he must come to me.

On 4 September the commissioners went ashore with a landing party of marines that was met by a native band. Natives shook their fists at them, which in Idah was a great compliment. Palm wine and kola nuts were served – princes tasted them first to show they were not poisoned. The Attah arrived in full regalia: a brocaded gold cloak, red leather boots with bells that jingled as he walked, a feathered cap, brass rings around his neck, and ivory discs in his ears. When he laughed or smiled, fan-bearers hid his face, for it was considered beneath his dignity to show any expression.

The commissioners asked the Attah to abolish the slave trade within forty-eight hours, and he promised to do so. Although he agreed to everything, he did not get off without a sermon. The commissioners urged him to become a Christian. They also said: 'Our Queen hears that the Attah allows the sacrifice of human victims and wishes him to give up this custom, because it is contrary to the commandments of God.' The Attah promised to discontinue the sacrifices. The commissioners warned him: 'The Queen is very powerful; so much so, that the sun never sets on her dominions.' The Attah even agreed to sell a large tract of land 'to my sister the Queen' for the model farm, although land in the West African tribal system was communally owned and could not be sold. He had clearly decided to humour these strange visitors with their meaningless pieces of paper and their more substantial gifts. The Attah's last words were that he wanted to see the presents. Among them was a Bible in Arabic so that he might learn God's commandments. The treaty was drafted and signed in triplicate, the Attah making his mark in lieu of signing his name.

While the treaty-making was advancing briskly, the fever's rate of progress was even more rapid. Sentences like 'the fever was making fearful progress' punctuate the official narrative, and 'heat, dryness of the skin, and almost incessant vomiting became the most prominent symptoms'. By 17 September only six men aboard the *Soudan* were able to move. The total sick on the three ships increased to sixty, and there were seven dead. 'At night,' according to the narrative, 'nothing but muttering delirium or suppressed groans were heard on every side on board the vessels, affording a sad contrast to the placid character of the river.'

The commissioners imperturbably went about their business. Sunday service continued to be held aboard ship, with the melancholy sound of workmen nailing coffins for the men who had just died echoing in the background. Reaching the Niger–Benue confluence, they took every care to select the proper site for the model farm. The geologist made soil analyses and the botanist took samples of plant life. They finally fixed on a sixteen-mile-long tract along the Niger's right bank, which amounted to about a hundred square miles. A deed of cession was concluded between the commissioners and the Attah's ambassador for 700,000 cowries, or about £35 at the usual rate of a shilling for one thousand cowries. The cowries, which came from the Maldive Islands in the Indian Ocean, had been bought by the ton in London. The down payment of 160,000 cowries was produced in bags from the *Albert*'s hold, and in the damp heat of the lower Niger half-naked natives watched the white-uniformed Captain Trotter count them out in pint-pot measures. It was an historic occasion, the purchase of the first English settlement in the interior of Africa, and the first English foothold in Nigeria. It ranks with the purchase of Manhattan by the Dutch. The commissioners, attentive to the slightest legal detail, ceded the land to Mr Carr, the model farm's manager, for a nominal annual rent of a penny an acre, which was to be paid by the Model Farm Society of Mincing Lane, London. Mr Carr went ashore with his equipment and his pioneer farmers, who consisted of two Europeans, a gardener, a schoolmaster, and twenty-three Africans recruited in Freetown and Monrovia. An oil-press and a cotton-gin, the most ambitious of his implements, sank in the river as they were unloaded.

The ships were now ready to leave the model farm to its fate, but the fever had reached such proportions that it led to the unlikely spectacle of three English naval captains arguing about where their duty lay. Commander William Allen, who knew the river and its dangers, wanted all the ships to return to the relatively healthy climate of the open sea. Commander Bird Allen said the sick should be dispatched downriver aboard the *Soudan* and that the expedition should continue in conformity with the government's wishes. Captain Trotter said they had all been aware of the hazards when they started out, and that the objections he had heard did not seem to justify a retreat at so early a time, while there were still so many enjoying good health. As senior commissioner, he decided that the sick should be sent to the sea and that the two other ships would continue upriver. '*The Soudan,*' in the words of the narrative, 'got ready to receive her melancholy cargo.'

Since more cases were added to the sick list daily, William Allen urged Captain Trotter to reconsider. He pointed out that he was the only one with experience on the Niger, and said he considered it his duty to state the dangers of staying on the river. He argued that it would be prejudicial to their mission if they appeared before other native kings in a state of prostration. 'It was with much pain that Commander Allen felt compelled to differ in opinion from his colleagues.' the narrative said. 'He could not help anticipating the results which actually followed.' But Captain Trotter and Bird Allen were determined to go on. However, there were now so many sick that they decided that two ships would go back to the sea, and only the *Albert* would proceed on the mission. Mr Fishborne of the *Albert* was appointed captain of the *Soudan*, as the services of Commander Bird Allen as queen's commissioner could not be dispensed with, so Bird Allen went upriver with Captain Trotter aboard the *Albert*.

On 21 September 1841 the *Wilberforce* followed the *Soudan* down the Niger, its deck completely covered, fore and aft, on the port side and amidships, with hammocks and beds. The starboard side was kept clear for working the vessel. The men were protected from the sun by awnings and curtains. William Allen was so ill from fever and exhausted by 'the late animated discussions' that he could not receive his instructions in person from Captain Trotter. The river was high, and the floating hospital was carried swiftly along by the current. The narrative described the scene in true Victorian style:

> We proceeded through these narrow and winding reaches with feelings very different to those we experienced in ascending the river. Then the elasticity of health and hope gave to the scenery a colouring of exceeding loveliness. The very silence and solitude had a soothing influence which invited to meditation and pleasing anticipation for the future. Now it was the stillness of death – broken only by the strokes and echoes of our paddle-wheels and the melancholy song of our leadsmen, which seemed the knell and dirge of our dying comrades. The palm-trees, erst so graceful in their drooping leaves, were now gigantic hearse-like plumes.

More men aboard the *Soudan* and the *Wilberforce* died as they crossed 'the pestilential delta'. Added to the lack of proper medication was the uselessness of the ventilation apparatus, which restricted the flow of air in the crew's quarters instead of providing them with fresh air. The narrative politely said that it 'proved to be totally inefficient for the purpose intended by the talented contriver'. The large iron medicator aboard the *Wilberforce* was jettisoned. The two hospital ships put in at Fernando Po, where they saw the rotted hulks of Laird's ships.

Meanwhile, the *Albert* continued upriver with Captain Trotter and Commander Bird Allen. While still in the Attah of Idah's territory, Trotter stopped a large canoe carrying three slaves, 'resolved to show that the terms of the treaty were to be strictly enforced'. The slaves belonged to the son of a local chief, who said he was not aware that a treaty had been signed. Trotter insisted on freeing the slaves despite the chief's son's protest that he had lost eighty thousand cowries, and took them aboard the *Albert*, giving the two naked women English dresses and the man a sailor's frock. 'Their looks expressed a mixture of fear, amazement, and gratitude,' the narrative said. 'Kindness from their own species seemed new to them.' One of the women Trotter named Hannah Buxton, after the founder of the Society for the Extinction of the Slave Trade, and the man was named Albert after the prince consort. In each village they visited, the Reverend Schön explained the leading doctrines of the Christian religion to puzzled but interested audiences and promised that some of his countrymen would soon arrive 'to teach them better things'.

Bird Allen was by now so ill that on 3 October they had to turn back. They stopped at the Benue confluence to see how the model farm was doing and found that Mr Carr, Mr Kingdon the schoolmaster, and Mr Ansell the gardener were prostrate with fever. They took them aboard and left the farm in charge of a freed American slave from Liberia named Ralph Moore. Some progress had been made: eleven acres had been cleared, and the farmers were about to plant their first cotton crop. On 25 October, soon after the *Albert* had joined its sister ships in Fernando Po, Bird Allen died. 'He mingled his dust with others who like himself, had staked all in their desire to serve the land of the Negro,' said the narrative. The English cemetery at Fernando Po, where Richard Lander was buried, was filling up fast. Bird Allen was soon joined by Vogel the botanist, who had complained he did not have enough room aboard ship to store his specimens.

Mr Carr recovered and insisted on returning to the farm. He went up the Niger in native canoes and was never heard from again. Later reports said he had been captured in the delta, robbed, tied to a tree, and shot. The two surviving captains, William Allen and Trotter, felt it was their duty to make a second journey upriver. They were about to set out with the *Wilberforce* and the *Soudan* when government orders came to call off the mission. In the view of its sponsors, who had received a discouraging dispatch from Trotter, there had been enough casualties.

A junior officer, Lieutenant W. H. Webb, was placed in command of the *Wilberforce* and sent to fetch the survivors of the model farm. His trip to the Benue confluence and back took twenty-six days, during which two of the eight Europeans on board died. Webb found the model farm in a state of complete disorganization. Mr Carr was presumed dead and the *de facto* manager Ralph Moore had no authority. The clerk was selling stores for his own profit. The carpenter had built no houses, claiming he could find no wood. The settlers lived in slovenly mud huts, quarrelling among themselves and refusing to work. The first cotton crop had failed, probably because the seed had been damaged during the ocean voyage. The jungle had already reclaimed part of the cleared land. Webb decided that the farm should be abandoned. When he took a poll of the settlers, only nine wanted to remain. The noble experiment, intended as a refuge for slaves and a nucleus of Western civilization in the heart of Africa, ended after only a few months.

The best-intentioned and most carefully prepared of all Niger missions, fuelled by Victorian optimism and armed with Victorian morality, ended as a pathetic failure. The commissioners succeeded in delivering sanctimonious lectures to a number of African kinglets and signing a few meaningless treaties, but the cost was the death of one-third of the English crew, forty-nine of the 145 who had sailed from England in May 1841. All the science and wisdom and wealth of a superior society had been defeated by a tiny insect. The irony was that quinine was already known to be a cure for malaria. Forty years earlier,

Nelson in the Mediterranean had ordered the wooding and watering parties he sent to a small island off Sardinia to take Peruvian
bark twice a day. But there is often a lag between the discovery
of a cure and its adoption by the medical establishment. Naval
surgeons continued to view quinine with misgivings, and treated
fever with chloride of mercury, head-shaving, saline drinks,
cupping, calomel, and other specifics.

As a result of the expedition's failure, Buxton's Society for the
Extinction of the Slave Trade itself became extinct, and public
opinion in England turned against utopian schemes to make
Christian land-working gentlemen out of savages. Buxton died,
and his followers said that the shock of failure had killed him.
The government refrained from committing itself to any further
humanitarian projects in the African interior. The subject of the
Niger became taboo, and it was more than ten years before
another river mission was proposed. The mission's failure also
strengthened the belief of Liverpool merchants that the system
of coastal trade and African middlemen was the only sound one.
For the time being the Niger, having been found and navigated,
remained impenetrable.

In 1848 Captain Trotter, Commander William Allen, and the
medical officer T. R. H. Thomson published the official narrative
of the expedition. It was scornfully reviewed by Charles Dickens,
who considered the Victorian goal of civilizing the heathen
hypocritical cant. A few years later, Dickens wrote *Bleak House*,
one of whose characters, a middle-aged lady named Mrs Jellyby,
with eyes that seemed to be looking a long way off, had a philanthropic interest in a farm on the Niger called Borrioboola-Gha.
As Mrs Jellyby explained to a visitor, Esther Summerson:

'The African project at present employs my whole time. I am
happy to say it is advancing. We hope by this time next year to
have from 150 to 200 healthy families cultivating coffee and
educating the natives of Borrioboola-Gha on the left bank of the
Niger.'
I hinted at the climate . . .
'The finest climate in the world,' said Mrs Jellyby.
'Indeed, Ma'am?'
'Certainly, with precautions,' said Mrs Jellyby.
'You may go into Holborne without precautions, and be run
over. You may go into Holborne with precautions, and never
be run over. Just so with Africa.'

Eight

BARTH AND BAIKIE

In 1849 a disciple of Fowell Buxton named James Richardson approached the British government with a plan to send a mission overland from Tripoli into the African interior 'to help raise up degraded Africa to civilized Europe'. The mission would study ways of suppressing slavery and report to the government. Richardson had already travelled to Morocco and the Sahara, spreading the gospel of abolition. The Foreign Secretary at that time was Lord Palmerston, a dedicated friend of the anti-slavery movement. He was receptive to the plan. It had the advantage of avoiding the Niger, which had wiped out the two previous expeditions. It was a return to the longer but safer Tripoli route, already blazed by Clapperton. It was also a great deal less costly in both money and lives to send a few men by camel across the desert than to build and equip ships whose crews perished as soon as they reached the river.

Palmerston agreed to sponsor the mission on condition that it be joined by an experienced geographer who could chart the positions that were explored, for Richardson confessed a lack of 'a satisfactory education, more especially the ability of making astronomical observations'.

Germany at that time had the reputation for producing the best geographers, under Berlin University's Karl Ritter, the founder of modern geography. Through a German cartographer named August Petermann who worked at the London Observatory, Richardson got in touch with the Prussian ambassador to London, who passed on his request for 'a well-qualified scientific and literary man' to Ritter. The Berlin professor recommended one of his brightest former students, a young teacher named Heinrich Barth. The offer was probably the least generous ever accepted by an explorer – Barth could join the English mission provided he contributed £200 for his personal travelling expenses.

Barth left the classroom where he taught a little-attended course on 'the topography of some of the most renowned nations of antiquity', and became, in the words of another explorer,* 'perhaps the greatest traveller there has ever been in Africa'.

At the time when destiny, in the form of the British Foreign Office, tapped him on the shoulder, Barth was twenty-eight years old. He had been born in Hamburg, the third child of a Thuringian peasant who had prospered as a trader. His parents were strict Lutherans. Frail as a boy, he toughened his constitution with exercise and cold baths, and grew to a strong and healthy six feet. His early interests were antiquity and the Arab world, and he became an expert in both. He learned to speak fluent Arabic and took his degree in 1844 with an essay on the commercial history of the Corinthians. He then travelled for three years in Turkey and North Africa before returning to a teaching job in Berlin.

With Barth a new era of exploration opened. Sixty years before, the African Association had sent the American roustabout John Ledyard to look for the Niger. In this first, heroic period of African travel, the explorers had been chosen mainly for their willingness to take risks and for their physical stamina. They were resolute, courageous men, not scholars trained to gather and evaluate information, and their reports were patchy. Reared in the demanding school of German scholarship, Barth was the first successful learned explorer. Besides his erudition, he had the patience and cool judgment necessary for the compilation of facts in difficult surroundings. He had the reporter's eye for detail, and the scholar's passion for amassing data.

His achievement in the area of African discovery has not been equalled. He stayed longer in the field than any other explorer,

---

* Lord Rennell of Rodd, a recent president of the Royal Geographic Society, a Saharan explorer, and the author of a distinguished work on the Tuareg.

remaining five years without interruption in West Africa. During that time, he travelled more than ten thousand miles, reaching as far west as Timbuctu and as far east as the town of Masena, one hundred miles south-east of Lake Tchad. Much of this area was still blank on maps. Barth the geographer discovered and charted large sections of present-day Nigeria. He established that the Benue, the Niger's main tributary, was not linked to Lake Tchad. He was the first to note altitude differences in the Sahara, which had previously been shown on maps as a completely flat surface. Barth the surveyor was the first to chart the middle course of the Niger. Barth the historian listed the names of past rulers of African kingdoms, described methods of local government, and analyzed tax structures. Single-handed, he destroyed the myth that Africa was a dark continent living in savagery by showing that it had a highly involved history before the arrival of the white man. He gave a chronological list of Bornu kings from 850 to 1846. He found original Arabic source material proving that written historical sources existed for West Africa before the arrival of the Europeans. Barth the anthropologist gave an exhaustive analysis of every native custom from kinship structures to eating habits. Barth the philologist made vocabulary lists and described the Hausa language as 'the most beautiful, sonorous, rich and lively of all the languages of Negroland; but it is defective in verbal tenses'. He was the third nineteenth-century European to visit Timbuctu (after Gordon Laing and René Caillié), and stayed in the fabled city eight months, during which time he wrote its history, studied its mosques, and sketched its layout. He collected a mass of information so accurate that most of his findings still stand. No explorer before or since discovered more of Africa than this merciless fact-finder.

The name of this one-man orchestra of exploration should be as well-known as those of Livingstone, Mungo Park, and Captain Cook. Instead, he is the most neglected of the great explorers. His very erudition did him a disservice. The account of his trip was published in five volumes comprising 3500 pages of dry, dense information. His personal adventures, which rivalled those of Mungo Park and Dixon Denham, were buried amid treatises on annual rainfall and grain storage. The five portly volumes of Barth's *Travels in North and Central Africa* could not hope to have the popular success of Mungo Park's *Travels*. Barth lacked the light touch, introducing himself in his books as Heinrich Barth, Ph.D. Also, he was not an Englishman. In Germany he was compared to Herodotus, but in England he was ignored. Another contributing cause of his obscurity is that he survived his ordeal. It would have made a better story if he had died on the Niger, like Park and Lander. He is not even listed in certain well-known encyclopaedias.

Barth was recruited as a geographer to take part in a mission that was evangelical in its aim. Richardson the missionary was driven by his hatred of slavery, 'the most gigantic system of wickedness the world ever saw'. He had no interest in exploration, while Barth had no interest in conversion. Barth made it clear before they started out that his aim was to explore the middle Niger and Bornu. He recruited a young Prussian geologist named Adolf Overweg as his assistant. Overweg was a light-hearted youth who joined the mission out of love of adventure. When natives asked him for medical help, he treated them not according to their ailments but according to the day of the week, one day for calomel, another for magnesia, and so on. Barth the perfectionist was critical of Overweg, and said that his written reports were 'vague'.

The two Germans in the service of the British crown reached Tunis on 15 December 1849, and joined Richardson in Tripoli, in March 1850. There they were greeted by Frederick Warrington, the son of the famous Warrington who had helped so many other explorers over the Tripoli route, and who had succeeded his father as consul. Warrington helped them buy camels and supplies, and in June they were off across the sea of pebbles between Tripoli and Murzuk known as 'the fearful burning plain'. Their only startling item of equipment was a collapsible boat with which they intended to explore Lake Tchad and which was eventually given to the Sultan of Bornu as a gift from Queen Victoria. They experienced the same problems that had beset Clapperton and his colleagues a quarter of a century earlier. Nomads harassed and robbed them, and on several occasions threatened to kill them, even though they had adopted Arab dress. Barth called himself Abd el Kerim (the Servant of the Merciful) and was able to discourse fluently with the Arabs.

For Barth the worst moment of the crossing came in mid-July, when they approached the oasis of Ghat, about three hundred miles west of Murzuk. Barth left his guides and colleagues and wandered off alone to explore a mountain with a horseshoe-shaped crest. It was farther than he thought, and when he finally reached it he drank his small supply of water. Worried that the others would leave without him, he started back, taking a different route along a ravine. He soon realized he was lost, and fired his pistol to signal his colleagues. There was no reply. He stumbled on, out of water and exhausted, in the shadeless midday desert heat of July. A string of camels passed before his fevered eyes, then vanished. He climbed into a leafless ethel tree to rest, changing his position every few minutes to take advantage of the little shade afforded by the branches, and wondering how he could have strayed so far from his companions. As the day wore on, his thirst became unbearable. He knew he would perish if he did not have something to drink. He did the only thing there was left for him to do. He cut open a vein and drank his own blood, until he fainted 'and fell into a sort of delirium'. When he came to his senses, the sun had dropped behind the mountain. In the dim light, Barth saw something moving closer. This time it was no mirage, but a passing Tuareg on a camel. 'Aman, aman [water, water],' Barth cried, and in a few moments he felt his forehead sprinkled with the saving drops and broke out in an uninterrupted strain of 'praise Allahs'. The Tuareg took him back to his camp on his camel.

They reached the desert-fringe market town of Agades in time to join the annual salt caravan south, and Barth described this great spectacle as 'a whole nation in motion, going on its great errand of supplying the wants of other tribes, and bartering for what they stood in need of themselves. All the drums were beating, and one string of camels after the other marched up in martial order, led on by the most experienced or steadfast among the followers of each chief.'

Having crossed the desert, the three men separated on 10 January 1851. Richardson headed for Zinder, south of Agadir. Overweg left to explore the Hausa kingdom of Gobir, while Barth went south to Kano. They planned to rendezvous in April in the Bornu capital of Kukawa, on Lake Tchad. 'I now went on alone,' wrote Barth, 'but felt not at all depressed by solitude, as I had been accustomed from my youth to wander about by myself among strange people.' Barth had a feeling that he would not see Richardson again, for he was 'quite incapable of bearing the heat of the sun, and always carried an umbrella . . . there was some sinister foreboding in the circumstance that I did not feel sufficient confidence to entrust to his care a parcel for Europe . . . at the same moment of parting taking it myself to Kano.'

Barth was happy to be out of the desert and to be riding a horse instead of a camel, and he reached Kano in the best of spirits, even though he had almost no money left. He traded darning needles for food. He seems to have had a knack for getting on with Africans, who were kind to him even though they knew there was nothing to be gained. His easy friendliness was the best passport in West Africa. Wherever he went he was remembered with fondness. His secret was that he genuinely liked Africans. Barth was impressed by Kano, and predicted that its position between the desert and the sea would one day make it 'important even for the commercial world of Europe'.

Leaving Kano to make his April rendezvous with the others in Kukawa some 350 miles north-east, Barth entered the kingdom of Bornu on 24 March and came upon a richly-dressed man with an armed escort who asked him: 'Are you the Christian who is expected to arrive from Kano? Your fellow traveller died before reaching Kukawa and all his property was seized.'

'This sad intelligence deeply affected me,' wrote Barth, 'as it involved not only the life of an individual but the whole fate of the mission.' Richardson had died at the age of forty-five. He was too old and too florid for African travel. Alone among the anti-slavery leaders, he had not contented himself with writing pamphlets and making speeches, but had gone to the source of the evil, to help stamp it out. After visiting the village where Richardson was buried in a grove of fig trees, Barth went on to Kukawa. He saw the vizier, who gave him Richardson's journals. When Barth asked where the rest of Richardson's property was, he was told that his ornamental guns and pistols had been sold Like Clapperton before him in a similar situation, Barth reacted strongly to unfair treatment. 'I could not refrain from declaring,' he wrote, 'that if in truth they had behaved so unscrupulously with other people's property, I had nothing more to do with them.' Firmness had positive effects, and Barth was given good lodgings and even loaned money. Eventually, the vizier returned all Richardson's things, including the guns.

In May Overweg arrived, weak and ill. Barth set off alone once more to explore Lake Tchad and to reach the upper waters of the Benue, about four hundred miles due south of Kukawa. He reached the river on 18 June 1851, and established that its source was not Lake Tchad, which was perhaps the single most important geographical discovery he made. In a dispatch to Palmerston dated 20 May, he made a rare reference to his mission's supposed goal, the suppression of slavery, by expressing the conviction that 'along this natural highway European influence and commerce will penetrate into the very heart of the continent, and abolish slavery'. Palmerston, learning of Richardson's death in September 1851, wrote in the margin of a dispatch: 'I think that Mr Richardson's death ought not to make any difference in providing funds for the expedition. We do not want to save money by Richardson's death, but to obtain notwithstanding that misfortune the same information by means of the two that we expected from the three.'

His sojourn on the river had given Barth his first 'seasoning'. He was soon so weak from fever that he could scarcely stay on his horse, and decided to return to Kukawa. He kept up his health with coffee and a beverage of his own concoction made of tamarind water, an onion, a strong dose of black pepper, and a little honey. He called it 'the most useful medical drink in these countries'.

With Overweg's help, he quickly recovered, and the two men spent the rest of the year making short excursions in the Lake Tchad area. In 1852 Overweg was ill again, and Barth travelled alone, undergoing a variety of adventures with native chiefs. On one occasion he was put in irons and his luggage was seized. 'After all this trying treatment,' he wrote, 'I had still to hear a moral lecture given me by one of these half pagans, who exhorted me to bear my fate with patience, for all came from God.' Barth thus had first-hand experience of what it felt like to be a chained slave, and remained fettered four days until a friend secured his release. Another time he was accused of tampering with the weather. The natives believed that when he looked at clouds with a certain air of command, they passed by without raining. Barth explained that 'no man either by charm or by prayer was able

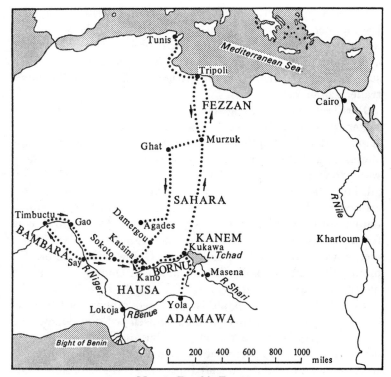

Map 6   Barth's Routes

either to prevent or to cause rain, but that God sent rain whenever and wherever it pleased him'. In Masena, on the river Shari,
about seventy miles south-west of Lake Tchad, he was suspected
of being a Turkish spy, because, his accuser said, only Turks
wore stockings. Barth was asked for his journal, and when he
showed it without hesitation he was set free. The most remarkable
thing is that throughout all these trials he never forgot to keep
up his journal, stocking it daily with a fresh supply of information.

In December 1851 he joined a caravan heading south into
Musgu country on a slave raid. He saw more than five hundred
slaves captured and was horrified when 'not less than 170 full-
grown men were mercilessly slaughtered in cold blood, the greater
part of them allowed to bleed to death, a leg having been severed
from the body'. He then saw the slavers separate families, which

was 'accompanied by the most heart-rending scenes, caused by the number of young children and even infants who were to be distributed, many of these poor creatures being mercilessly torn away from their mother'. He had at least fulfilled his mission's supposed aim to the extent of witnessing first-hand the slave-trader's practices.

Barth returned to Kukawa in August 1852 and found Overweg sicker than ever. Overweg thought an excursion would do him some good and in September they went on a shooting trip to the shores of Lake Tchad. While there Overweg waded into deep water to retrieve a bird he had shot and kept his wet clothes on all day. The next day he was too weak to eat, but stubbornly refused medicine. He had fits of delirium, 'muttering unintelligible words in which all the events of his life seemed to be confused, and rushed against the trees and into the fire, while four men scarcely were able to hold him'. Overweg died before the month was out, on Lake Tchad, much as Oudney had died a quarter of a century earlier.

In a letter written to an English geographer shortly after Overweg's death, Barth described himself as 'now lonely and companionless in these regions, . . . but nevertheless in good health and spirits . . . I am not a man who is afraid of death in such a cause . . . I tell you that I have full confidence in my safe return and in my being able to lay the proceedings of this expedition in an elaborated form before the public . . .'

Having explored as far east as he intended – he had made numerous excursions around Lake Tchad, to places no other European had ever visited – Barth now headed west towards Kano and the Niger. Reaching Katsina in January 1854, he found waiting for him a consignment of two boxes of sugar. Hidden under the sugar was $1000. In Sokoto he was welcomed by the son of Sultan Bello, who had mistreated Clapperton on his second expedition. He was shown Clapperton's house, and the new sultan apologized for his father's behaviour towards the dead explorer.

Barth reached the Niger in June 1853. 'We were now close to the Niger,' he wrote, 'and I was justified in indulging in the hope that I might the next day behold with my own eyes that great river of West Africa which has caused such intense curiosity in Europe, and the upper part of the large Eastern branch of which I had myself discovered.' On 20 June, 'elated with such feelings, I set out the next morning at an early hour, and after a march of a little less than two hours, through a rocky wilderness covered with dense bushes, I obtained the first sight of the river . . . I reached the place of embankment opposite the town of Say.' Forty-foot canoes took Barth and his party across the Niger. 'My camels, horses, people and luggage having crossed over without an accident,' he wrote, 'I myself followed about 1 p.m., filled with delight when floating on the waters of this celebrated stream the exploration of which had cost the sacrifice of so many noble lives.'

Timbuctu was Barth's destination, but instead of following the Niger upstream he set out with his camels and horses across the river's great bend. He disguised himself as a Tuareg, wearing an indigo face veil that stained his face. 'I thought it prudent,' he wrote, 'to conform to the innocent prejudices of the people around me, adopting a dress which is at once better adapted to the climate and more decorous in the eyes of the natives.' It was the rainy season, and he had to use rafts made from reeds to cross the swamped inner delta. His animals got stuck in bogs and his journals were soaked as he moved slowly from village to village, exchanging darning needles for supplies (a chicken cost a hundred cowries, equal to one needle). It rained so hard that some of his camels drowned.

Barth must have been a sharp trader, for when he reached a market town on a navigable branch of the Niger he hired a large dugout to take his entire party to Timbuctu for ten thousand cowries. The channels were obstructed with rank grass, so that the boat seemed to be gliding on a prairie covered with water-lilies. As he advanced, Barth wrote, 'the watercourse began to exhibit more and more the character of a noble river, bordered by strongly marked banks, clad with fine timber, chiefly tamarind and banana trees, and enlivened by cattle . . . we observed the first river-horses [hippos] we had as yet seen in the Niger, carrying their heads out of the water like two immense boxes.'

Barth arrived at Timbuctu's river-port of Kabara on 7 September 1853, and made a spectacular entrance into the city, spurring his horse to a gallop and waving his rifle, so that 'I was received with many salams'. He was forced to remain in Timbuctu eight months, and became a pawn in a struggle between two rival political factions. He was protected by the sheikh, Al-Bakai, who was involved in a running quarrel with a Fulani leader named Hammadi. Fortunately for Barth, the sheikh had enough of a following to defy Hammadi's order to have the Christian killed. Barth's stay in Timbuctu became a picaresque adventure full of plots and counter-plots, intrigues, imprisonment and release, armed bands prowling the city, and the constant risk of being kidnapped and killed. He spent much of the time confined to his house. He took the precaution of firing his six-barrelled pistol in front of his quarters, which convinced the townspeople that he possessed a veritable arsenal and probably had some bearing on his future safety.

Barth passed the time writing a history of the city and conducting theological discussions with the sheikh's younger brother, who tried to convert him to Islam, but could not shake Barth's stalwart Lutheran faith. Barth also occasionally saw the sheikh, a man of fifty, 'of almost European countenance'. 'Is it true,' the sheikh asked him, 'that the capital of the British empire contains 20 times 100,000 people?' The sheikh had heard this from his father, who had heard it from El Rais (the Major, as Gordon Laing had become known in Timbuctu).

When the Fulani patrols grew too insistent, the sheikh moved Barth to the desert camp where his troops were garrisoned. One day in the camp, a relative of the sheikh made the charge that Barth's only motive in visiting Timbuctu must be conquest. Barth indulged in one of his few flights of levity. 'I jestingly told them,' he wrote, 'that our government being informed that the natives of these tracts fed on sand and clay, had sent me out to discover how this was done, in order to provide, in a similar way, for the poor in our own country.'

Barth's prospects worsened when he heard on 17 March 1854 that the Fulani had sworn he would never again see the sun set over the town. He was again taken to the sheikh's camp, where he was insulted by an officer who spoke contemptuously of Christians, saying that 'they sit like women in the bottom of their steamboats and do nothing but eat raw eggs'. He was finally allowed to leave Timbuctu for good in May 1854. Barth got away just in time, for the French had begun their advance into southern Algeria, which made Europeans even less popular in Timbuctu. At the time he left, there was already talk of having him shot as a spy.

Following the Niger downriver, Barth reached the Tosaye gorges, 'that remarkable place where the noble Niger is compressed between steep banks to a breadth of no more than 150 yards, but of such a depth that the bottom has not been found by the natives'. Barth was heading back the way he had come, exhausted, penniless, and suffering from recurrent attacks of malaria. In England he had been given up for dead, for his letters from Timbuctu took eighteen months to reach Tripoli. He followed the Niger until Say and then headed north-east to Sokoto, where he learned that another explorer named Vogel had been sent to look for him. Dr Edward Vogel, an astronomer in the Bishop Observatory in Regent's Park, London, had been recruited in February 1853 to join Barth as 'an associate and scientific assistant' in charge of botanical and zoological research. Barth had also requested more barometers and thermometers, which were placed in Vogel's care. Once in Africa, however, Vogel's mission was to find Barth, and he set out with two English sappers and two interpreters.

Barth was on the road to Kukawa on 1 December 1854, when

> I saw advancing towards me a person of strange aspect – a young man of very fair complexion, dressed in a tobe like the one I wore myself, and accompanied by two or three blacks, likewise on horseback. One of them I recognized as my servant Madi, whom, when on setting out from Kukawa, I had left in the house as a guardian. As soon as he saw me he told the young man that I was Badul Kerim, in consequence of which Mr Vogel (for he it was) rushed forward, and, taken by surprise as both of us were, we gave each other a hearty reception from horseback . . . Not having the slightest notion that I was alive, and judging from its Arab address that the letter which I forwarded to him from Kano was a letter from an Arab, he had put it by without opening it, waiting till he might meet with a person who should be able to read it. In the midst of this inhospitable forest, we dismounted and sat down together on the ground; and my camels having arrived, I took out my small bag of provisions, and had some coffee boiled, so that we were quite at home.

Barth's meeting with Vogel is to Niger exploration what Stanley's meeting with Livingstone is to the saga of East African discovery. But the latter is world-famous while the former is practically unknown. To be sure, Vogel did not maintain Victorian decorum and say: 'Mr Barth, I presume?' Nor did

Vogel have Stanley's enterprise or reputation. Judging from the fact that he did not even suspect that the letter he had received could be from Barth, he appears to have taken a casual attitude towards his mission, and it was the blindest luck that made him run into the German explorer on a dirt trail in the middle of Africa. Still, Livingstone, when Stanley started looking for him, had been incommunicado no longer than Barth, who by this time had been in the African interior for five years. To emerge from Bornu, with its attendant dangers and miseries, into the arms of a man sent to find either him or his place of burial was the happy ending of a drama to which Barth's prose could not do justice. The news that Barth was alive and well was relayed to the British consul in Tripoli, who reported to London in March 1855 that 'the rumour of Dr Barth's death has most happily proved unfounded'.

Vogel was less lucky. After finding Barth, he explored Lake Tchad and the Benue. In January 1865 he visited Wadai, a remote kingdom to the east of Lake Tchad, and was murdered by the sultan. He may not have brought enough presents, or he may have been the victim of inexperience. No one knows. Attempts to learn more came to nothing, and his papers were never found. Of Vogel's party of five, only one of the sappers returned alive to England. The Earl of Clarendon, then Foreign Secretary, jotted in the margin of a Foreign Office report announcing the deaths: 'This is very melancholy.'

In May 1855 Barth started on the return journey across the Libyan desert, with considerable relief. 'I turned my back with great satisfaction,' he wrote, 'upon those countries where I had spent five full years in incessant toil and exercise.' Barth was without doubt the Niger explorer most popular with Africans. He respected the tradition of giving presents to local chiefs, and was never contemptuous of native customs. His scientific curiosity made him immune to prejudice. The Africans coined several affectionate nicknames for Barth, such as 'the man who spent a day in the unsafe wilderness', and 'the father of three', from his habit of wearing shoes over slippers and stockings. When the French Lieutenant Emile Hourst navigated from Timbuctu to the Niger delta in 1895, he pretended to be Barth's nephew, and by this stratagem, he said, 'I was able to emerge safely from every situation'.

Barth reached Tripoli on 28 August, stayed there four days, crossed to Malta on a Turkish steamer, and sent a telegram from Marseilles on 8 September. He was probably in London on the 16th, and was received by Lord Palmerston a few days later. His return was not noticed by the English press. There was nothing like the hue and cry made over other explorers. True, Barth had to compete for headlines with the Crimean War, Burton's search for the Nile, and Livingstone's discovery of the Victoria Falls. But there was more to it than that. Barth's mission was unpopular because he was German. While in Africa, he had been criticized for giving place names Teutonic spellings and for passing on information to his friend Petermann, who had it published in Germany first.

Barth suffered bitterly at being thus ignored. At a meeting in his honour in Berlin on 13 October 1855, he made the accusation that 'in England a few mean-minded individuals, seeking to exploit national enmity under the guise of scholarly questions, have given vent to their feelings in contemptible utterances against the leadership of an English expedition by a German'.

Barth nonetheless returned to England to write his books and attend to their publication. The Foreign Office gave him £2500 a year for five years, plus £2000 to defray publication costs. But his reputation declined further when he refused to dine with members of the Royal Geographic Society, which had awarded him its patron's medal, and failed to turn up at a scheduled lecture at the British Association for the Advancement of Science. 'Eager curiosity was baffled,' a newspaper wrote of this last incident. The English press accused Barth of having spent too much money. The Society for the Extinction of the Slave Trade attacked him for being involved in the slave trade and for bringing back two freed slaves as servants. Barth was so annoyed that he sent the servants back to Africa.

All was not gall, however, for Barth was showered with medals and awards, including an honorary degree from Oxford. He was given the Order of the Bath, a royal honour that no other explorer, not even Livingstone, had received. In December 1856 he met Livingstone, who gave him a copy of his *Missionary Travels and Researches in South Africa*, inscribed 'as a token of high regard and high appreciation of his services in opening Africa; by his friend and fellow labourer'.

But when the five volumes of his classic work had been published in 1857 and were received by the public with indifference, Barth returned to Germany, a permanently disappointed man, convinced that his achievement had been ignored because of his nationality and that the Nile explorers had grabbed the limelight at his expense. When the Order of the Bath was long in coming, he blamed 'a clique of jealous officials'.

Barth's difficult years in the wilderness seem to have aggravated an already stubborn and proud personality. As his anthologist, A. H. M. Kirk-Greene, put it: 'Continually forced to be on his guard against his environment and travelling companions, his innate distrust of mankind had grown to neurotic proportions, so that he suspected intrigues and calculated insults where none existed.'

In Germany, among his own people, Barth fared better. He was made president of the Geographical Society and professor-extraordinary at the University of Berlin. But his years in Africa had prematurely aged him. He died in 1865, at the age of forty-four, having become a misanthrope, cut off from society and living with his memories. As his brother-in-law wrote, 'His behaviour had taken on the serious, dignified, reserved, proud and almost arrogant quality of the Arab sons of the desert, with whom he had lived so long.'

When in 1852 the Foreign Office learned that Barth had charted the upper Benue and would remain several years on the middle Niger, it decided to send a ship to rendezvous with him on the river. Macgregor Laird, under contract to the Admiralty, built a 260-ton iron screw steamer rigged as a schooner, called the *Pleiad*. The command was given to John Beecroft, a Niger delta veteran who had been named consul of the Bight of Benin and Biafra in 1849. He was based on the British-held island of Fernando Po and had often sailed up the Niger. Beecroft, as England's man in the Bight, provided the same hospitality and assistance to explorers as Warrington in Tripoli. He seemed immune to fever, and claimed that he enjoyed the climate. The claim sounded like bravado when he died before the *Pleiad* reached Fernando Po.

Command then went to the expedition's medical adviser and naturalist, William Balfour Baikie, an Edinburgh-trained

Scottish doctor. Arriving to find Beecroft dead, Baikie wrote, in Victorian cadences, that 'his once iron frame sank under the combined inroads of climate and of disease, and he yielded up the vital spark in the land of his adoption'. Baikie is another unsung hero of African exploration. He was not an explorer in the strict sense, but he achieved something that required even greater courage: he remained in the African interior as a settler.

The *Pleiad*'s limited mission was to find Barth and conduct trade on the river. It was primarily a rescue ship. And yet it became the most successful Niger mission when, for the first time, Europeans spent months on the river without loss of life.

> The peculiar features of the expedition were [wrote Baikie], first, the employment of as few white men as possible; secondly, entering and ascending the rivers with rising waters, or during the rainy season; and lastly, it was anticipated that the use of quinine, as a prophylactic or preventive, would enable the Europeans to withstand the influence of the climate.

Thanks to his 'lastly', Baikie showed that there was a way to keep the delta from being the white man's grave, even though, ironically enough, he was to die of dysentery in Sierra Leone ten years later. And that way, which had been available for centuries, was the proper use of quinine. There would have been no colonization of Africa without quinine. The French in Algeria, like the English on the Niger, were decimated by malaria. And yet the cure had been known ever since, three centuries earlier, the Spanish conquistadors in Peru found natives chewing on the cinnamon-coloured bark of the cinchona tree to ward off fevers.

Cinchona bark was introduced to Europe in the seventeenth century, but its healing properties went unrecognized except by the Jesuit order, which gave it to its missionaries. It became known as 'Jesuit's bark', and the English, as good Protestants, wanted nothing to do with it. Cromwell died of malaria in 1658 because he refused to take it. Other cures, such as calomel and bleeding (cupping), became popular, at the expense of quinine. Thus the cure for one of the world's most widespread diseases remained unused because of prejudice and ignorance. An incalculable number of English sailors and explorers died on the Niger because they did not take it. On the island of Fernando Po, where John Beecroft died and where Richard Lander and many other victims of river expeditions were buried, one of the soldiers' daily duties was grave-digging. There were standing orders: 'Gang no. 1 to be employed digging graves as usual. Gang no. 2 making coffins until further notice.'

Mal-aria (bad air), or the ague, as it was then called, was believed to rise from stagnant waters or putrid exhalations of the earth. Even the great explorer Richard Burton, who served as consul in Fernando Po, and who had theories on everything, could offer no explanation for malaria, 'that mysterious agency, which, like the pestilence walking in darkness, ever hides its origin from the world and leaves us to grope for it in cosmical causes – vegetation, geology, geographical position, a rarefied atmosphere deficient in oxygen'.

Those who used the bark, however, appreciated its healing properties, and research went on to isolate its active ingredients. In 1820 two young French pharmacists, Letellier and Caventou, extracted quinine from the bark. Instead of taking out a patent, they gave their discovery to the world – but the world was slow to accept it. The use of quinine continued to be limited by its high cost, by the carelessness of sailors who forgot to take it, and by the ignorance of doctors who neglected to prescribe it.

In the 1830s, when the French expeditions in Algeria lost more men to malaria than in battle, a military surgeon named François Clément Maillot began using quinine with results startling enough to convince the worst sceptics. The use of quinine was the condition of French penetration of Algeria and eventually of the upper Niger, just as it was the condition of English penetration of the lower Niger.

It was not until 1897 that Sir Ronald Ross proved that female mosquitoes were the carriers of malaria. But long before the enemy was identified the harm it did could be treated. In mid-nineteenth-century England the advocates of quinine began to be heard. Alexander Bryson in 1847 presented the Admiralty with a 'Report on the Climate and Principal Diseases of the African Station'. He urged the regular use of quinine in wine, and wrote: 'It is firmly believed that although neither bark nor quinine has the power of preventing the germs of fever from lodging in the system, nevertheless they most decidedly have the power of preventing their development in pyrexial action.'

Baikie took Bryson's advice aboard the *Pleiad*, with such success that his mission was the turning point in Niger exploration. For the first time, a crew of English sailors went up the Niger and did not suffer a single casualty. As Baikie wrote in his narrative of the expedition:

> The great modern improvement is the discovery that quinine not only cures, but that it actually prevents, and that by taking this invaluable drug while in unhealthy localities, persons may escape totally unscathed . . . a person who has been using quinine as a prophylactic . . . will escape the fever much more easily, and have a milder and more manageable attack than another who has not been so employing it.

'I can affirm,' Baikie added, 'that after taking my morning dose (2–4 gr.) I felt fit for any kind of duty, all the languor of a close damp tropical night was dispelled, or in the evening after a hard day's work in the hot sun, nothing was so reviving or exhilarating than this invaluable drug . . . [other] drugs should be avoided as much as possible, especially calomel and other mercurials, which are not only unnecessary but have killed far more people than fever has.'

The *Pleiad*'s crew was made up of twelve Englishmen and fifty-four Africans. The idea was to let the Africans do the heavy work, and limit the white crew members to skilled and supervisory duties. Each crew member was given his twice-daily ration of quinine once the *Pleiad* reached the shores of West Africa in June 1854. Once on the Niger, Baikie stopped in villages to trade for ivory and sent out surveying parties to sound depths and inspect tributaries. After a month on the river, he reported that 'the health of all on board was perfect, and being quite clear of the swamps of the delta, we were in great hopes that this unlooked for exemption from disease might continue'. Soon, however, the second mate, Daniel John May, was felled by fever, 'but speedily recovered from his attack under the modern rational treatment'.

Baikie's voyage not only showed that Europeans could survive the African hinterland, it reawakened prospects of trade. His was the first mission to trade at a profit. In a single day, he purchased 620 pounds of ivory. He found 'numerous tribes, all endowed by nature, with what I may term "the commercial faculty".' The Niger, having outlived its villainous role as a reservoir of fatal miasmas, was once again described as 'a navigable highway, conducting us into the very heart of a large continent, and by means of its branches we are brought into immediate contact with many thousand miles of country'.

Baikie reached the Benue confluence and inspected the site of the abandoned model farm, which he considered badly chosen, as it bordered on a stretch of marshland. He went several hundred miles beyond the confluence, further than any European vessel had yet been up the Niger, but did not find Barth, who by this time had left Timbuctu and was on his way out of Africa via the Tripoli route. This was the only aspect of his mission in which Baikie did not succeed.

The *Pleiad* spent four months in all on the Niger, frequently running aground on sand bars. But the navigational problems were more than offset by the sensational news that the entire crew had survived. After so many disastrous missions, with the ships returning downriver laden with the dead and the dying, here at last was a voyage where all who had set out returned. The Victorian goals of ending slavery, bringing Christianity to the natives, and helping them prosper through trade, could once again be pursued. Thanks to Baikie, the Niger was tamed. It became an English river.

In England there was exultation at Baikie's success on the part of all those who had been connected with Niger exploration. The *Pleiad* returned in February 1855 with its full complement of men, having been away from England less than a year. Soon afterwards, Macgregor Laird wrote to the Foreign Secretary, the Earl of Clarendon:

> The plausible objection to exploring Africa – the risk of life – is answered: and the question now is, whether, after the lives of so many gallant men have been sacrificed during the first half-century in clearing that way, and that way now being proved to be safe and practicable, Her Majesty's government will, at an expense of a few thousands annually, complete the work of discovery in Central Africa, or allow that honour, which ought to belong to the British race, to be reaped by others.

With Laird and Baikie lobbying to follow up England's advantage on the Niger, the government slowly moved into action. In 1857 Laird obtained a contract from the Admiralty to send a steamer to the Niger for five years to carry passengers to and from Fernando Po. In this manner, without involving itself with unwanted permanent settlements, the government could maintain its footing in the interior and spur the decline of the slave trade.

That May the 77-ton steamer *Dayspring* sailed out of Liverpool under Baikie's command, with a cargo of goods and a crew of eleven, including the missionary Samuel Crowther, who intended to set up shop near the Benue confluence. Baikie's instructions were to establish trading stations on the Niger's banks. He left eight men in charge of a trading post in the delta which he called Lairdsport, and set up another post at the confluence which he called Lairdstown. The viability of these stations was based on one simple fact: the most important market city in West Africa, Kano, was thirty days from the Benue confluence and fourteen months from Tripoli. The English were beginning to reap the results of more than a century of Niger exploration.

The French at this time had their hands full settling Algeria. They were also established in Senegal, but malaria and commitments in North Africa kept them from venturing along the upper Niger. The great river, in the first years of West Africa's penetration by rival European powers, could rightly be called an English preserve. Once quinine made the river safe, England lost interest in the far longer and more difficult Tripoli route into the interior. The river route, apart from being quicker and easier, appealed to the world's mightiest naval power. This turned out to be an important factor in the eventual division of Africa.

The *Dayspring* spent three weeks at the confluence setting up the trading post and then headed upriver. On 7 October, while navigating past an island rock at Jebba, three hundred miles north of the confluence, the *Dayspring* foundered on a hidden boulder. Steamers up the Niger were rare, and the *Dayspring* was past repair. Baikie, his second-in-command Lieutenant J. H. Glover of the Admiralty's hydrographical department, a zoologist named John T. Dalton, the crew of eleven, and thirty-eight Krumen, were stranded on the Niger's east bank for one day less than a year, until a relief vessel came to retrieve them in October 1858. The one positive result of this enforced residence was that it showed that Europeans could stay in the interior without ill effect.

Lieutenant Glover, an enterprising young man, put the idle months to good use by surveying seven hundred miles of the lower Niger and venturing by canoe as far as the Bussa rapids where Mungo Park was killed. He found Park's nautical almanac, already mentioned by the Landers, and bought it from the chief. Another relic of Park's, a medal bearing the royal arms and the head of one of the Georges, which the chief wore as a ring, was not for sale.

Laird sent a paddle-steamer called the *Rainbow* to replace the *Dayspring*, in accordance with his Admiralty contract, and Baikie returned to the trading post at the Benue confluence, where he remained as consul for the rest of his life. Where the model farm had failed, Baikie succeeded. He founded a settlement that was the first permanent expression of British presence in the interior of West Africa. And he was its first English settler, the first of thousands of civil servants who governed what is today Nigeria.

Baikie stayed in Lairdstown, which he renamed Lokoja, for five years. The only other European was his friend John Dalton the zoologist. These two Conradian figures seem to have been obsessed with proving that an Englishman could live in the 'abominable fascination' of the African hinterland. Baikie did not, as his successors would, try to transplant England to Africa, with white suits, lawns, and cricket fields. He went native, and wore sandals and the long cotton shirt called a tobe. He had no tea or sugar. His luxuries were fish and palm oil, which he ate out of earthenware pots. He lived in a mud hut with a thatched roof and a hole to let smoke out. He took a black mistress, who gave birth to several half-caste offspring. He translated the Book of Genesis into Hausa, and wrote endless dispatches to the Foreign Office in his small, slanted, angular hand. He never complained, and in his first dispatch, dated 1 November 1859, he wrote: 'I would submit to any privation rather than give up what has cost us so much labour and what promises so well.' Baikie was a visionary, who saw his tiny enclave on the Niger as a starting point for a great imperial undertaking. He kept outlining his grandiose plans in his dispatches, which the Foreign Office ignored. The first dispatch signed 'Lokoja, confluence', was dated 10 October 1860. The nearest British settlement was Lagos, two weeks away. Baikie had a standing offer of a reward for the first native who brought the isolated post news that steamer smoke had been sighted. Lokoja still exists. It is a dismal Nigerian town, with a white shingle English church and a small, fenced-in cemetery filled with English tombstones. Baikie cleared a hundred acres, built houses, and drove himself to exhaustion working a fourteen-hour day. He wrote to a friend that he had had more than a hundred fever attacks.

He had settled in an area that still depended on the slave trade, and nearly every day he saw armadas of canoes carrying their manacled ebony cargos downriver, while at night the sky was red with the flames of villages burned during slave raids. Since Baikie gave refuge to slaves, he was not on friendly terms with the traders. And he could be cut off for months when Mr Laird's steamer was blocked by menacing natives on the banks or when the river was low. His situation made Baikie an advocate of gunboat diplomacy, and he wrote:

> Mr Laird was perfectly correct when he defined 'moral force in Africa' as meaning a 32-pounder with an English sailor standing behind it . . . It cannot be that such a worthless set of mere brutes, so few, too, in number, should continue, practically, to close the mouth of a large river flowing along half of a vast continent.

Having secured its first foothold, England was called upon to protect it with military power. Baikie asked for the regular visit of a properly armed vessel, which the Admiralty refused to give him, arguing that 'trade enforced by cannon shot will take no root'.

Things improved when Baikie made friends with the powerful Emir of Nupe, Masaba. Seeing that this strange and stubborn white man was there to stay, and realizing that Baikie's aim was to keep the peace, Masaba apparently decided to let him help govern his loose-knit states. The tiny English settlement slowly grew, and by 1863 there were two hundred natives under Baikie's care, either fugitive slaves or slaves he had bought with the proceeds of trade, at ten bags of cowries a head (about 12s 6d.). The Lokoja market was doing well. It was unlike any other African market in that it was closed on Sundays and bought slaves instead of selling them.

In the meantime Crowther developed his mission at the North

of the Benue, and in 1862 baptized his first native. It may well have been his efforts that were lampooned by Dickens in *Barnaby Rudge* when Mrs Vardon tells her daughter Polly about 'the voluntary sacrifices of missionaries in savage parts who live mainly upon salads'. In 1861 the Foreign Office, feeling that its limited aim of setting up inland trade stations had been more than achieved, decided to recall Baikie. The notice drafted in Whitehall took nearly a year to reach the consul in Lokoja. Baikie, determined to stay on at the settlement he had seen grow from nothing, disregarded the summons. He replied as tactfully as he could that 'I venture to defer my return', and outlined further plans for the future of Lokoja: 'What I look to are the securing for England of a commanding position in central Africa, and the necessity for making a commencement.' Baikie stayed on another three years, and saw trade prosper and the number of fugitive slaves grow. He got along well with the natives because he lived as they did, to the point of almost forgetting his native tongue, and he became known as 'the King of Lokoja'. The *Sunbeam*, the ship that brought Baikie the news of his recall, took aboard on its return passage the zoologist John Dalton, who was sick, and a few West African artifacts for the Commonwealth Exhibition of 1862.

Baikie's health too was broken, and in 1864 he was compelled to return to England. In October the paddle-steamer that came to fetch him dropped off his replacement, a Lieutenant Bourchier who was one of six consuls and vice-consuls who succeeded Baikie between 1864 and 1869, when the consulate was abandoned. Two of them are buried there. Baikie reached Sierra Leone in November, and wrote to Freetown to reserve space on the mailboat for England. He never took it. He died of dysentery in Sierra Leone. His journal, which was forwarded to England, was shown to Livingstone. He sent it to his assistant Dr Kirk, who returned it with a note saying:

We may conclude that poor Baikie was in a strange state of mind – no doubt being complicated with native women and a growing family of half-castes induced this . . . those who know what it is to be alone in savage parts will readily understand why Baikie's health failed, cut off as he was from the outer world and without the excitement of discovery and travel which we had during six years on the opposite coast.

Whatever his state of mind, Baikie was a pivotal figure of West African exploration. He had the tenacity to remain, and the vision to grasp that England's role was just beginning. He did nothing dramatic, but his quiet resolution won the admiration of those around him. And it was his proof that quinine could be used to prevent malaria that made the Niger route into the interior possible.

Queen Victoria wrote a personal letter to the Emir of Nupe informing him of Baikie's death. Stressing the slave question that had been uppermost in Baikie's mind, Queen Victoria wrote:

> We ask your Highness to use your great influence to put a stop to this traffic, and to prevent the wars that are undertaken in many cases for the sole purpose of procuring slaves to be sold for shipment overseas . . . We request you to accept our best wishes and so we recommend you to the protection of the Almighty. Given at our Court at Osborne the 20th July, 1865, in the 29th year of our reign. Your good friend, Victoria.

What more fitting tribute to Baikie could there have been than this equal-to-equal missive from the ruler of the world's most powerful nation to an African kinglet governing a few thousand naked subjects on the Niger's banks?

Nine

THE NIGER DIVIDED (I)

Until the middle of the nineteenth century, the English had the Niger to themselves. The Niger explorers were either English or, like Barth, in England's service. The campaign to suppress slavery, with its convenient combination of high morality and commercial profit, was a purely English affair. The sailors who died on the Niger because they did not take quinine, and those who survived because they did take quinine, were English sailors. The men who landed upriver with a Bible under one arm and a bolt of Manchester cloth under the other were English traders. The Niger was an English river in the sense that Englishmen had found it, mapped it, navigated it, and were determined to use it as a funnel to force civilization down the natives' throats.

England's interests were concentrated on the lower third of the river, the delta and the navigable stretch up to the Bussa rapids where Mungo Park had been killed. No English ship starting from the Bight could go beyond this point, or needed to, since palm oil was concentrated in the delta. Isolated explorers like Park, Gordon Laing, and Barth had seen the upper Niger and its important cities, Segou, Timbuctu, and Gao. But no explorer had ever reached the Niger's source, less than two hundred miles from the Atlantic, close to the border of British-occupied Sierra Leone. The English showed no interest in extending their influence to the upper Niger, and no missions were sent from Sierra Leone to explore the great river's headwaters.

Eventually another European power became interested in the upper Niger, and slowly extended its control down the river.

THE NIGER DIVIDED (I)

England's initial reluctance to own territory in the African interior turned into a race to limit the sphere of influence of the rival power, France. The struggle over the Niger, at first only dimly perceived and ending in direct confrontation, lasted for fifty years. More than any other single event, it embodied the scramble for Africa. Two styles of expansion and colonialism came face to face on the Niger's broad channel.

French ships had begun trading on the west coast of Africa in 1560, and the first permanent French counter had been built at the mouth of the Senegal river in 1638. The story of French forts on the Senegal coast was one of capture, loss, and recapture, in the context of international wars and negotiations. The forts were lost to England in one treaty and regained in another. Mainland France failed to support these far-flung outposts, which repeatedly found themselves bankrupt, with no funds to pay civil servants or soldiers. The different regimes that succeeded one another in France – the monarchy, the revolutionary government, the Napoleonic empire – did not provide the best circumstances for continuity in the administration of colonial outposts. France lost an empire in North America, but somehow hung on to its tiny West African posts. In the first half of the nineteenth century, a long list of naval officers governed the French station of St-Louis at the mouth of the Senegal river. They traded gum arabic on the coast and showed no interest in the interior.

Unlike England, France did not have an imperial vocation. Its arena had always been Europe. It was not interested in opening up new markets. Ever since Richelieu, it had kept colonies at a loss, as a prestige operation, to increase the king's grandeur. Occupied without enthusiasm, the colonies were abandoned without regret, like Canada, lost after a war with England, or Louisiana, sold to the Americans by Napoleon. Nor did France feel it had a mission to stamp out slavery, which was not permanently abolished in France until the 1848 revolution. French ships were among the worst offenders on the west coast, running the Blockade Squadron and carrying slaves to the Sugar Islands.

But in the case of England an imperial vocation did not mean indiscriminate expansion. England had India, and in the nineteenth century its eastern trade made West Africa an area of

241

peripheral interest. The policy of successive colonial secretaries was to avoid further involvement in the area. As late as 1881, the Colonial Secretary, Kimberley, told the Prime Minister, Gladstone: 'We have already quite enough territory on the West coast.' When a Niger protectorate was suggested, Kimberley replied: 'The coast is pestilential; the natives numerous and unmanageable. The result of a British occupation would be almost certainly wars with the natives, and heavy demands upon the British taxpayer.' The Niger was not worth the trouble. Civil servants in Whitehall were not eager to annex lands where they might be sent to die of fever. What British involvement there was in the area was not the result of a deliberate policy, but of reacting to circumstances.

Thus, neither France nor England had the remotest wish for territorial expansion in the Niger river area. In the case of both countries, the tail wagged the dog. A few determined individuals forced their respective governments into increasing involvement. The English were drawn into it, first because of abolition, then to protect inland traders, and finally to parry French expansion. England went from an absolute lack of interest in West Africa to the colonization of Nigeria. In 1806 the Colonial Office's total correspondence to West Africa was four letters to Goree, an island off the coast of Senegal. Fifty years later, Lagos was occupied, there was an English consul in Lokoja, and English gunboats policed the Niger. A hundred years later, there was a huge colony called Nigeria. British penetration was the work of explorers who found the way in, followed by private traders like Macgregor Laird, who did not wait for government protection to set up trading posts.

In the case of French expansion, it was not explorers or traders who led the way, but over-zealous soldiers who often exceeded their instructions. For more than forty years, West Africa was a private military fief where ambitious young French officers went to make names for themselves. Out of the army's unpopularity and discredit which resulted from Napoleon's defeat came this new breed of warrior princes, disdainful of civilian authority and of their own encrusted superiors. They sought fresh fields of endeavour far from weary Europe. They turned the upper Niger into a battlefield where, after performing heroic feats, they became the enlightened despots of native kingdoms. From 1852, when one officer, Faidherbe, arrived as governor of Senegal, to 1893, when another officer, Archinard, was replaced as governor by a civilian because of his high-handed ways, the Senegal and the upper Niger constituted a proving ground where French colonial soldiers waged constant warfare at the expense of peaceful commercial development.

Thus the conquest of the upper Niger was entirely due to ambitious field commanders testing their theories of pre-emptive attack, and the conquest of the lower Niger was due to English explorers, traders, and abolitionists. In both cases, the respective governments were dragged in to regulate a *de facto* situation of conquest. The French officer turned colonial expansion into an epic, the English trader turned it into a balance sheet. On the lower Niger the Union Jack followed commerce. On the upper Niger the Tricolor fluttered at the head of military columns.

The fact that the French waged a military campaign for half a century to secure control of the upper Niger was not only due to their thirst for battle, but also to political conditions in the area. The English on the lower Niger were able to operate with a minimum of military action because political power was fragmented among a large number of city-states. There was no central authority. British naval power on the Niger was sufficient to keep the peace.

The pattern of trade between delta states and Europeans had been set centuries before. There was a long tradition of profitable exchange. The delta states were like rival commercial firms, forming mergers with other firms, setting prices, watching the competition. But when the English traders moved inland after 1840, they violated the established pattern of free trade and tried, with the help of their government, to set up a monopoly situation. Once they had the run of the Niger, the big companies were no longer satisfied with the leisurely sandbeach policy of earlier years. They wanted to cut out the middlemen, bring down the price of palm oil, and increase profits.

There were three sets of middlemen between the naked African woman who boiled palm tree pulp and skimmed the oil as it rose to the surface, and the naked London woman who lathered Pear's soap on her white arms: the African organizers of the trade in the interior, the African merchants who bought oil in the interior and sold it on the coast, and the European traders who

THE STRONG BROWN GOD

bought the oil on the coast and carried it to England in their ships. The history of the delta in the second half of the nineteenth century can be summed up as a trade war designed to cut the African middlemen out of the palm oil business. Once the English companies succeeded in dealing directly with the producers in the interior, the coastal cities collapsed. Their only form of protest, harassment of the ships, was severely punished. In 1895 an armada of war canoes from the coastal city-state of Brass attacked the Royal Niger Company's headquarters at Akassa. British gunboats destroyed Brass in retaliation. The once prosperous city was reduced to subsistence fishing. Thus, on the lower Niger, the change in trade patterns led to the establishment of the English companies as the area's only real authority. As the city-states sank into squalor, the English filled the political vacuum.

On the upper Niger the situation was completely different. The French fought an uninterrupted fifty-year war of conquest against the standing armies of two powerful African empires. They laid siege to and captured the principal river cities. Each year, during the dry season, there was a four-month military campaign against African leaders who fought to maintain their territorial independence from European intruders. As they advanced from the Senegal to the Niger, the French entered the territory of an empire founded by a Moslem preacher called El Hadj Omar, which stretched from Timbuctu to the Niger source. From 1850 until 1890, when they took Segou, the French alternately fought and negotiated with El Hadj Omar, who was killed in 1864, and with his son Ahmadou.

While they were fighting El Hadj Omar in the east, another African leader named Samory was building up an empire to the south, starting from the area of the Niger source area in the Futa Jalon mountains. Samory waged a people's war against the French, raising militias and depending on surprise and ambush to make up for his lack of artillery. He was an early African nationalist, and kept the French at bay until his capture in 1898. Despite the contrast in local conditions and methods, the conclusion of the English trade war on the lower Niger and the French campaigns on the upper Niger would be the same: formal occupation and colonization.

*

The first of the French conquistadors was Louis Faidherbe, a military engineer who was appointed governor of Senegal in 1854, when he was only thirty-six. He stayed in the job until 1861 and was reappointed from 1863 to 1865. He thus had a total of nine years to transform Senegal from a collection of scattered trading counters into a powerful colony that would serve as a base for French expansion on the Niger. His instructions from the Navy Minister, Ducos, who was responsible for colonies, were 'to bring about the peaceful development of commercial interests'. But, added Ducos, he was also to show 'the people on the two banks [of the Senegal] that we are always ready to back up our authority with force each time it is questioned in the affairs of the river'. Peaceful commerce was soon forgotten as Faidherbe became involved in a long battle to pacify the Senegal. The development of commerce implied territorial expansion and conquest. Faidherbe was given a remarkably free hand by his minister. One reason why French colonial policy in West Africa advanced so much by fits and starts lies in the personalities of the colonial governors and their cabinet bosses in Paris. The combination of a weak governor and a cautious minister could paralyse colonial policy. A decisive minister who trusted his governor, on the other hand, could build an empire. Such was the case with Faidherbe, who began pacification operations a year after he was named, against Moors who levied tolls on the Senegal river. Extending French authority westwards, he built a fort at Medina in 1856, which gave him control over the navigable part of the river.

In April 1857 ten thousand of El Hadj Omar's warriors attacked the fort, which had a garrison of seven French and twenty-two native soldiers. The assault cost them three hundred dead and they pulled back and laid siege to the fort, where more than a thousand villagers had taken refuge. Munitions and food soon ran low. The river level was dropping, which meant that rescuers could not come by water. The commander, a mulatto named Paul Holle, was determined to blow the fort up rather than leave it to El Hadj Omar, whose troops were now dug in twenty-five yards from its walls. Holle's men were down to two cartridges each. Then on 15 July a rescue column commanded by Faidherbe crossed the Senegal and attacked El Hadj Omar's men from the rear, soon dispersing them. The fort's gates were opened and hundreds of famished natives ran out and began to devour grass and roots.

Faidherbe had won his first important battle and convinced the government in Paris that Senegal was not just a commercial counter but a genuine colony. Thus far, he had received the funds and equipment he needed. With each success, however, Faidherbe's vision became more grandiose, and in 1864 he proposed moving on from the Senegal to the upper Niger, and gaining a French foothold on that great avenue into the Sudanese hinterland. When he relayed these expansionist plans to the government of Napoleon III, they were met with misgivings. At the Second Empire court, he became known as 'the old mummy'. The minister Ducos, who had so staunchly supported him, replied with a list of arguments against extension of French influence on the Niger: the cost would be prohibitive, the posts would be forts rather than commercial centres, there would be serious supply problems for posts so far from the home base, the country was constantly perturbed by fanatical Moslem agitators. His main fear was that further expansion would lead to further warfare. Ducos added in his own hand that, despite his confidence in Faidherbe, 'you must understand how hard it is for me to approve of projects which could engage us in a policy where the slightest setback would force us to undertake serious expeditions'. Exhausted by malaria and rheumatism, Faidherbe left Senegal a year later, and the march on the Niger marked time for another fifteen years.

But Faidherbe, with characteristic independence of mind, had not waited upon Paris's approval before taking the first step in linking the Senegal with the upper Niger. In November 1863 he had sent a naval ensign named Mage and a doctor named Quintin on a two-man embassy to El Hadj Omar's capital of Segou. His instructions were brief: 'Leave as soon as you can, move as fast as you can, and try to reach the Niger.' The two men succeeded and spent twenty-seven months on its banks. They were impressed by Segou's fortified walls and eight wooden gates. El Hadj Omar was absent, but they were received by his son Ahmadou, who was about thirty, bronze-coloured, with a high forehead and a weak chin.

Mage and Quintin wanted to sign a treaty of peace and commerce with Ahmadou, but he kept them waiting endlessly, in virtual captivity. Whenever they asked to leave, he replied: 'Envoys must know how to wait.' In September 1864 Mage lost his temper and tried to leave Segou on a mule, but the gates were shut in his face. The two men stayed there a year more, venturing out from time to time to join Ahmadou in military expeditions against the Bambara, as an antidote to boredom. In February 1866 a treaty was finally signed assuring the passage of the French through El Hadj Omar's lands. El Hadj Omar had died by this time, but Ahmadou kept that fact to himself. Back in Paris in the autumn of 1866, Mage told the Navy Minister that the upper Senegal was not navigable and that it was pointless to build posts between the Senegal and the Niger. He was, however, in favour of French interventions on the Niger by keeping ships there.

Faidherbe's achievement was enormous. Faidherbe the realist forged from a few trading posts the colony of Senegal. He founded Dakar, created the Bank of Senegal, published a newspaper, and promoted groundnut exports. He created a school where the sons of native chiefs and notables could receive a French education, and learn about the Hundred Years War and the Carolingian kings. In 1861 it was renamed 'School of Sons of Chiefs and Interpreters'.

It was the first effort in a systematic French policy of forming native élites by teaching them the benefits of French civilization. One of the main benefits was the right to serve in the French army, and here again Faidherbe pioneered the way. His decree of 21 July 1857 said: 'There will be formed in the Senegal a corps of native infantry under the denomination of Tirailleurs Senegalais.' The native troops enlisted for two years and were paid fifty centimes a day. They were given a diet adapted to their customs and a uniform consisting of a white turban, blue jacket, ballooning blue pants, and a red belt. To naked natives pounding grain in the bush, all this seemed rather magnificent, and there were so many re-enlistments that the tirailleurs soon acquired the polish and discipline of a professional army.

But Faidherbe the visionary saw the possibility of a huge West African empire and was instrumental in persuading his government to change its colonial policy from commerce to conquest. Africa slowly began to be seen as a territorial annex increasing French power, rather than as a supplier of ivory and gum arabic.

Despite Faidherbe's great personal prestige, he frightened his superiors with his plan to march on the Niger. His ideas slept, while West Africa was forgotten in the European crisis that culminated in the Franco-Prussian war of 1870, and French defeat.

One antidote to that defeat was a renewed interest in colonies. France had lost Alsace-Lorraine but it could win new lands in West Africa. The humiliated French army could win a new reputation for itself on the upper Niger. After 1870 imperialism seemed to the French the only way of remaining a first-class power. Public opinion slowly shifted in favour of colonial expansion. France's growing empire was supported by nationalists who wanted, above all, vengeance on Germany. Men in the government like Jules Ferry, premier from 1880 to 1881, and again from 1883 to 1885, were ardent advocates of empire. Ferry was after all from Lorraine, born in St-Dié, and profoundly affected by the loss of his birthplace. His support of colonialism was not motivated by the possibility of trade, it was emotional, it was a way to make up for a loss, a way to prevent France's decline. Like the Victorian English, the French imperialists couched their expansion in terms of a civilizing mission. This was most clearly stated by Jules Ferry in a famous parliamentary debate on 28 July 1885 when he said: 'It must be openly admitted that superior races have a duty towards inferior races.'

'Oh! You dare to say that in a country where the rights of man were proclaimed?' a deputy named Jules Maigne replied. Another deputy, Monsieur de Guilloutet, said: 'It is the justification of slavery and the slave trade.'

Ferry stuck to his guns. 'I repeat,' he said, 'that superior races have a right, because they have a duty. It is their duty to civilize inferior races.'

In the Chamber of Deputies, a colonial lobby influenced the voters, kept up a press campaign, and promoted the idea that colonial expansion was healthy politically and economically. In 1883 a Colonial Department under its own under-secretary was set up, which became a full ministry in 1894. Its budget soared from 42 million francs in 1885 to 115 million in 1902. In the years between 1870 and 1900, France made a great financial and human effort to found an empire. Just as the English imperialists believed that profits and doing good went hand in hand, the French imperialists were sure of their moral mission, which at the same time wiped out the shame of the 1870 defeat. In 1900, the French Foreign Minister Delcassé told the Senate, in a burst of self-congratulation: 'I do not know whether colonial history can furnish any other example of such a prodigious and rapid expansion.'

Faidherbe's proposal for an advance on the Niger was resurrected in 1879 by a Ministry of Public Works engineer who published a brochure on the possibility of building a Senegal–Sudan railroad. This became part of a grandiose scheme to build a trans-Saharan railroad reaching Dakar. The Minister of Public Works, Monsieur de Freycinet, was an ardent supporter of this railway network through territories that France as yet knew nothing about, and sent exploratory missions along its proposed route.

One of the missions, led by a Colonel Flatters, entered Tuareg country in 1880 and was massacred when a treacherous guide led Flatters and his men into an ambush. There was such an outcry in the French press that plans for the trans-Saharan railroad were shelved and never revived. The other missions, however, had more positive results. The explorer Paul Soleillet, sent to Timbuctu in 1879, got as far as Segou, and described the upper Niger, rather extravagantly, as 'a country which, thanks to its fertility and the variety of its products, can be compared to the most opulent regions of India'. Soleillet spent nearly four months in Segou and was well treated by El Hadj Omar's son Ahmadou because he was a civilian. In the morning he acted as a doctor and in the afternoon he toured the countryside. He brought back stories of Ahmadou's brutality. When he took a village, it was said, he beheaded all the males over twelve years of age, determining their ages by measuring them with a rifle. He also found that the Bambara population of Segou was putting up considerable resistance to conversion to Islam. They were forcibly circumcized, but let their body hair grow as a sign of resistance. This was good news to the French, who in their conquest of Ahmadou's Islamic empire presented themselves as liberators of the oppressed Bambara.

On Soleillet's heels came a fire-eating officer of the Faidherbe variety, a brave but impulsive second-generation Frenchman named Joseph-Simon Gallieni. His father had left Italy after

the Austrian annexation of Milan to avoid serving in the Austrian
army, and had settled in France. He was naturalized French, and
became a career officer; his son followed in his footsteps. Gallieni
was a second lieutenant in the 1870 war and was taken prisoner.
The disintegration of the army at Sedan marked him: 'To escape
the depressing reminder of defeat.' he wrote, 'we had to divert
our efforts elsewhere. The colonies beckoned . . . for me, the
call came from Africa.' Captain Gallieni was put to work building
forts in Ahmadou's territory, where the French professed neutral-
ity. In March 1880 he was sent from Medina with 150 men and
300 donkeys to make the overland trek to the Niger and meet
Ahmadou in Segou. On the way he took advantage of tribal
quarrels to sign treaties with local chiefs. Ahmadou was furious
that the French were negotiating with tribes he considered
under his jurisdiction. He also guessed that the real purpose of
Gallieni's mission was to survey sites for forts. On 11 May, not
far from Bamako, Gallieni's column was ambushed. He lost
twenty killed and twenty wounded and most of his baggage. He
was the first French soldier to go into the bush with an escort
made up only of native troops, and was amazed by their loyalty
and courage. He could say without exaggeration that he owed
them his life. Gallieni had intended a show of force to persuade
Ahmadou to open the way to French occupation of the Niger.
Instead, he suffered a military defeat. He stubbornly continued,
but was stopped by Ahmadou's men in a village twenty miles
from Segou. There he and his men were held virtually captives
for four miserable months. They were sick with fever and out of
quinine. Finally, Ahmadou's negotiator arrived and told Gallieni:
'We like the French but do not trust them. They on the other
hand trust us but do not like us.' The negotiator also used the
British presence in Sierra Leone as a bargaining point. 'We do
not know the English,' he told Gallieni, 'and for sentimental
reasons we will always favour the French. But a babe who
cannot suck from his mother will suck from his grandmother.'

Gallieni had set out with the intention of dictating his terms
to Ahmadou: he wanted to occupy the Niger, build forts on it,
and police the river with gunboats; he wanted a French protectorate on the upper Niger in exchange for a pledge that the
French would never conquer Ahmadou's empire. But Gallieni
was in a weak bargaining position. All he obtained was the right

to establish commercial counters on the Niger. He promised he would build no fort on Ahmadou's territory. He also promised to send him the weapons he needed to defend himself against the French, four mountain guns and one thousand flintlocks, as well as an annual payment of 25,000 francs. Gallieni had reversed his position of trying to overthrow Ahmadou and instead agreed to arm him and recognize his claims as far as Timbuctu. Gallieni told his fellow officers he had no qualms about delivering the artillery, for the Africans would never learn how to use it. But his was hardly a diplomatic victory. The treaty he brought back did not mention a French protectorate, and the government in Paris refused to ratify it.

Soon after signing the treaty with Ahmadou Gallieni left West Africa and went on to a distinguished colonial career in Indo-China and Madagascar. He is remembered in both as the theorist of pacification. A military victory should be followed by an occupation of the terrain, the rallying of dissidents, the opening of markets and schools. Gallieni was the first to see that the soldiers' main task after conquest was government.

In September 1880 a ministerial decree put the upper Senegal military district under another fire-eater, Lieutenant Colonel Borgnis-Desbordes. An admirer of American 'go-ahead', he was convinced that total conquest was the only way to establish a French presence on the Niger. The excuse for his military campaigns was that he was surveying and clearing the route for the Niger–Senegal railroad. Each campaign was accompanied by a topographical mission. The three hundred mile-long railroad, from Kayes on the upper Senegal to Koulikoro, just above Bamako on the Niger, was completed in 1904. But when Borgnis-Desbordes left Africa in 1883, only ten miles of track had been laid.

It was Borgnis-Desbordes who established the pattern of a military campaign every dry season, so that for many years the upper Niger was in a state of permanent war interrupted by the rains. The principles of expansion were set. Gallieni's humiliating experience with Ahmadou determined his successors to rely on military might rather than negotiation. The railroad became a way of disguising the mounting costs of military expeditions. The moral justification for the campaigns was to free the oppressed tribes from what Gallieni called 'sanguinary potentates who loot and burn defenceless villages to procure prisoners they can sell'. In effect, the campaigns pitted black against black: the African chiefs' troops against French native troops. After centuries of being made slaves, the Europeans next forced the blacks into conscription to fight their own people.

Fighting, like work on the railroad, could only take place during the four to five months of the dry season, which helps explain how badly armed African leaders with ill-trained troops were able to hold off French forces for more than ten years. As soon as the rains fell, turning all paths to mud, French troops fell back to their nearest base and the Africans could disband and tend to their fields, while their military leaders had time to recruit new troops and find supplies and weapons. It was a West African version of the Truce of God, dictated by nature.

On his first campaign, in 1881, Borgnis-Desbordes took twenty officers, about four hundred men, and four mule-drawn cannons. It was nothing more than a punitive expedition: he destroyed some villages that had refused to negotiate with the French. The following year he made Bamako his objective, but a yellow fever epidemic prevented him from going in that direction. Instead, he decided to send a column against a new threat, the increasingly militant African leader Samory Touré, who had captured a market town on the Niger called Keniera. Samory, exulting over his victory, had demanded Borgnis-Desbordes's head and said he needed a few whites for toys for his wives.

From the moment Borgnis-Desbordes set out against Samory, the French conquest of the upper Niger became a two-front struggle, with Ahmadou to the east and Samory to the south. Samory was a remarkable man, who founded what was probably the best governed of all the nineteenth-century African empires. It had the main requirements of a modern state: central authority, a professional civil service, a loyal army. At its height it was the third largest West African empire, after the Sokoto Caliphate and Ahmadou's Niger bend empire. It ranged over much of present-day Guinea and Upper Volta. Samory, who called himself the Commander of the Faithful, united hundreds of unconnected towns and villages into a new Mali empire, using Islam as a bond of unity. He was himself a convert of modest origins. Born poor and self-educated, he respected scholars. He built schools in newly conquered villages, and used the army as an instrument of conversion and education.

Samory was a genuine African nationalist, who wanted to destroy tribalism by having men of different families and tribes work together at every level of government, and by opening promotion in the army to all. He divided his empire into ten provinces and 162 cantons of twenty villages each. Each canton was governed by a triumvirate consisting of an administrator, a military leader called a *sofa* and a religious leader called a *qadi*. He had 20,000 men under arms, 4000 of them with repeater rifles obtained from the British in Sierra Leone. He could also raise a people's militia of more than 100,000 men. Since he had no artillery, he avoided pitched battles, preferring ambushes, raids, and quick retreats. As he retreated over terrain he knew well, he practised the scorched earth policy, leaving the French a blackened and smoking country-side. Samory was clear from the start about French aims. Despite their offer of treaties, he knew they were out to conquer the upper Niger. He used Anglo-French rivalry to obtain help from the English, who gave him weapons and support. Hostilities with the French opened in 1882 and lasted, with interruptions, until Samory's capture in 1898.

In his first encounter in January 1882, Samory used his cavalry against the French, whose artillery broke the charge. Borgnis-Desbordes pursued him to the Niger market of Keniera, which Samory evacuated, leaving behind the heads of victims rotting on the ground. It was the first and last time Samory ever tried to win a pitched battle against the French. The following year, 1883, the French established themselves permanently on the Niger by taking Bamako. The French tactic in seizing fortified villages was always the same: artillery made a hole in the mud walls, troops poured in through the breach, and the village was taken in house-to-house fighting. Bamako fell in February. The French cremated their dead so that they would not be exhumed by the natives who used bones for amulets.

As Borgnis-Desbordes laid the cornerstone of the first French fort on the Niger he said: 'We will fire 11 cannon shots to salute the French colours, for the first time and for ever on the Niger's banks. The sound of our small cannon will not reach further than the mountains before us, and yet its echo will be heard far beyond the Senegal.' The echo that reached Paris said that 194 French soldiers had been killed in the campaign, and there was a flurry of anti-colonial feeling.

The French now had a supply base on the Niger and a port for their gunboats. Ahmadou moved his capital from Segou to the more remote Nioro. The French intended to control a large area with a few men, using forts, gunboats, and the railroad. Having captured Bamako, Borgnis-Desbordes had to consolidate his position. The further the French advanced the stiffer resistance grew. He had to send his men into battle in April, when it was so hot the barrels of their rifles burned to the touch. The soldiers grabbed the tails of their mules and let themselves be dragged along the paths. Borgnis-Desbordes received a letter from a chief named Mountaga, which said:

> To the uncircumcized son of the uncircumcized, colonel Desbordes, may God confound and cause you to perish with your partisans . . . none is so great an evildoer and traitor as you. You say you only want to make a commercial route. That is false, and contrary to good sense and reason. Your desire is to destroy the country, close the roads and make war on Believers . . . the day when we meet the birds in the sky will not have to hunt for food.

When he took command Borgnis-Desbordes told his men: 'We are not in the Sudan to speak but to act. We must reach the Niger and we will.' He attained his objective, but was exhausted in the process, and left Africa in 1883. He later fought in Indo-China and died in 1900 in Saigon. By this time, the French had recruited two hundred Chinese coolies to work on the Kayes–Bamako railroad, as well as Moroccans and blacks. They had to be protected from raids, and quarrelled among themselves. The French devised a novel form of punishment for troublemakers: they were tied to a tree at night with one arm free and a stick to fight off hyenas.

The annual campaigns succeeded one another like vintage years. There were great years and disappointing years. The campaign of 1884 was not a success. Samory took back some villages from the French. Parliamentary approval in Paris depended on military victories that the colonial lobby could publicize. But the combination of lack of results and the terrible climate made the whole venture unpopular. It seemed to be dragging on at great expense with no foreseeable result. Officers were reluctant to take command: they did not want to be remembered as having led the retreat from the upper Niger to the Senegal.

In 1885 Admiral Galibert, head of the West African desk, summoned two veteran officers of the Niger campaign, Archinard and Monteil, and asked for their advice. 'Gentlemen,' he began, 'I would like you to tell me very frankly. I have resolved to ask the Council of Ministers to abandon the Sudan . . . in the face of the hostile attitude of Parliament, I don't dare ask for the necessary credits for the pursuit of an undertaking which goes on and on without practical results.'

Monteil replied with a nineteenth-century version of the domino theory. If France gave up the upper Niger, he argued, its colony in Senegal would be threatened. The military situation would worsen rather than improve. More men and more money would be required to save Senegal without the Sudan than to finish what had been begun. Moreover, by leaving the Sudan France would be violating written treaties made with local chiefs. Archinard agreed, and said: 'The abandonment of the Sudan would be the start of a general revolt which would gravely compromise the security of our colony in the Senegal.' Before their eyes, Admiral Galibert tore up the speech proposing to give up the Sudan.

That winter the French scored a few victories over Samory, which led him to ask for a peace treaty. The French were glad to negotiate, for a treaty with Samory would give them a free hand against Ahmadou on the Niger. Negotiating with Samory proved to be time-consuming, and it was not until 1887 that a treaty was signed. A major named Peroz took a hundred men to Samory's capital, Bissandogou, near the present-day Guinean city of Kankan, not far from the Niger's source. Peroz had a letter from Samory as a passport through his dominions. The capital was a hill village with two streams running through it where Samory had built a palace and a mosque. Ivory trumpets announced Peroz's arrival, and his column was met by two hundred horsemen and five hundred foot soldiers wearing robes of flowing silk. Peroz had to listen to a two-hour welcome speech, followed by a parade of captive maidens carrying large copper tureens filled with food.

The next day Peroz was taken to meet Samory, who was reclining under a large awning, flanked by his chief adviser and his treasurer. He was a man of about forty, with a long thin nose and mobile eyes, a slight beard, and some kind of silver cosmetic around his eyes. He wore a black turban, Moorish boots, and a dark caftan. The only sign of his rank was a gold necklace. Behind him stood two men in red carrying silver axes, whose heads were covered with tiger skins. Samory invited Peroz to sit next to him and watch his cavalry. The horsemen galloped past, throwing their rifles in the air. There followed recitals, songs, and more welcome speeches, and Peroz was introduced to Samory's nineteen favourite wives, recumbent under the weight of their gold ornaments. After arduous negotiations, the treaty was signed on 25 March 1887. Under its vague terms, hostilities with the French were to cease, and Samory accepted the principle of a French protectorate on the left bank of the Niger.

Peroz left Samory's capital impressed by his army and by the court's savage customs. Among Samory's many wives, Peroz recounted, three had won the privilege of living in the palace. By one of these Samory had two pretty daughters, aged thirteen and fourteen. When he learned that they were flirting with a palace page, Samory had their hands chopped off, and then had them buried alive. 'Passing near this ignoble burial ground,' wrote Peroz, 'we saw between two huge stones, a tiny fist, clenched and bloody, its wrist circled by a gold bracelet.'

In 1888 Louis Archinard, already a veteran of several campaigns, was named commander of the upper Niger, or, as it was beginning to be called, the French Sudan. Archinard, the son of a Protestant schoolteacher, was a military engineer, a graduate of the École Polytechnique who had chosen the unpopular colonial artillery after graduating 137th in a class of 141. Thanks to this poor performance, he discovered his colonial vocation. In his five years of command, he destroyed Ahmadou's empire, resumed the war against Samory, and extended the French presence as far as Djenne. He was indefatigable. As a young captain, he was assigned to build a fort and wrote home: 'Nothing has ever interested me as much as the construction of this fort. I can think of nothing else. I dream about it at night. I wait for the day to come so I can start work.'

But Archinard's greatest triumph was not over African chiefs, but over the Colonial Department in Paris, whose support he fraudulently obtained. He interpreted silence as approval, and when there was any resistance to his campaign plans he sent forged reports of critical situations in order to get the go-ahead. For five years he conducted a private war, in defiance of his superiors and the French government. So long as he was successful there was hardly a murmur of protest, even though he systematically violated his instructions. When he was charged with deliberately failing to keep his superiors informed, he replied that he did not generally bother to report petty military incidents.

One of these petty incidents, which earned him a promotion to full colonel, was the capture of Ahmadou's 'impregnable bastion', Segou. Although Ahmadou had transferred his capital to Nioro, Segou remained the showpiece of his empire, where his treasure of 20 million francs was reputedly kept. It was surrounded by thick mud fortifications, and was said to be manned by élite troops who had sworn to die fighting rather than surrender. When Archinard asked for permission to march on the city, he received a vague wire from Paris that said: 'Do the best you can.' At the same time he sent Ahmadou cordial messages, pledged that their differences would never lead to war, and promised peace and friendship.

Archinard left the French fort of Medina on the upper Senegal in February 1890 with 742 men, 640 of them natives, and on 6 April reached a dune on the left bank of the Niger, across from Segou. He had more artillery than the French had ever used in Africa before. As soon as his column was spotted, the war-drum called Ahmadou's men to arms. It was an unequal contest. Archinard's cannon blew breaches in the walls and were out of range of Ahmadou's rifles. Segou was stormed without a single French casualty. By the time Archinard had crossed the Niger with his men, the do-or-die troops inside the fortress had fled, leaving only the women behind.

The fall of Segou had great propaganda value for the French. A haze of legend enveloped Segou, about the courage of its defenders and the size of Ahmadou's treasure, which turned out to be no more than 250,000 francs in gold and silver. Archinard named a puppet Bambara king and left a detachment of troops there. He did not even bother to justify the attack on the grounds of renewed aggression from Ahmadou. He felt that his mission of colonial conquest was its own justification. Now that the French controlled Segou and Bamako, they could begin to enforce freedom of navigation on the upper Niger. At the Paris Universal Exposition of 1889, one of the most popular exhibits was the 1400-pound gate, shot through with cannonballs, removed from one of the fortified cities captured by Archinard. The Sudan was becoming the French equivalent of the American West.

The following year Archinard marched on Nioro, about 350 miles north-west of Segou, and found it abandoned. The French now controlled the heart of Ahmadou's empire. Ahmadou, escaping with a few loyal men, had given up all idea of resistance. Exhausted, he fell from his horse and said: 'The French can kill me here if they want to. I'm not moving.' Ahmadou took refuge in the high sandstone cliffs of Bandiagara, with his few remaining supporters. Archinard did not bother to pursue him. His empire had collapsed, and he would never again be able to mount a counter-offensive against the French.

Having disposed of Ahmadou, Archinard moved against his other enemy in the south, Samory. In March 1891 his column crossed the Niger in dugouts. By this time Archinard had caught blackwater fever, and had to be carried on a stretcher, barely conscious. But he refused to interrupt the campaign, and made contact with Samory's troops on 8 April. He put them to flight and found modern Belgian repeater rifles abandoned in a ravine. The prisoners taken said Samory was not far off. Archinard reached Samory's capital of Bissandougou, where a few years earlier Major Peroz had signed a peace treaty, and destroyed it. He posted a garrison in nearby Kankan, but Samory and his men had dispersed. Archinard could not make them stand and fight, and as he pushed deeper into the interior his supply problems increased.

Troop movements for a large column in the Futa Jalon mountains involved countless difficulties. Archinard had 1000 soldiers, 144 of them Europeans, 2000 non-combatants, 350 pack animals, and four eighty-millimetre mountain guns. Native porters who carried fifty-pound loads on their heads escaped in the night, even though they were warned they would be shot if they were caught. Their scalps were worn to open sores like the sores on the backs of mules, they cut open their feet against stumps and rocks, and their faces were whipped by spiny branches. Archinard had received ministerial instructions from Paris forbidding him to requisition porters. But to go without porters would have meant giving up the campaign, so he relayed the instructions to his officers in the following form: 'Try to enlist volunteers.'

As they advanced along the Niger the French were continuously harassed by Samory's soldiers, who fired at them from the high grass on the river-bank. Samory had buglers who sounded the ceasefire to confuse the French. He was a natural guerrilla strategist with a good understanding of the terrain. He chose impassable rivers as lines of defence, avoided open ground, and moved swiftly from one position to the next. The European soldiers suffocated in the heat, were attacked by legions of flies and mosquitoes, and wondered what they were doing there. Samory had the added advantage of knowing that if he could hold off the French from December to March, when the first rains ended campaigning, he was safe for the rest of the year. The French claimed that Samory had English advisers in his ranks, along with troops from the native West India Regiment garrisoned in Sierra Leone. They did in fact take West India Regiment prisoners and found an ammunition box inscribed: Charles Garett, West African Company, Liverpool. Archinard described Samory as a bandit rather than a nationalist leader. 'Samory does not govern,' he wrote to the governor of Senegal in 1891, 'he represents no race or nation, he is content to destroy, exploit and depopulate for his personal profit.' Since Archinard disregarded the African leaders' valid claims to their lands, he might more properly have been termed the bandit. Trade was another victim of the constant warfare. While on the lower Niger English traders were making fortunes, the commercial results of twenty years of French presence on the upper Niger were negligible.

Archinard returned to France for a year of sick leave, and the campaign of 1892 was conducted by Lieutenant-Colonel Gustave Humbert, who wrote that 'Samory's troops fight like Europeans, with less discipline perhaps, but with much more determination'. The campaign was complicated by an outbreak of yellow fever, which took the lives of thirteen officers and sixty-seven men.

By this time Samory had an estimated eight thousand repeating rifles, obtained from the English, and the French made no headway.

Archinard was back in 1893, to wage his last campaign. Extending the French reach along the Niger, he marched in April on the merchant city of Djenne, which he thought could be taken without a struggle. He sent a delegation to the walls to negotiate surrender; but Djenne decided to fight. Archinard opened fire with his artillery and blew open one of the gates to the city. He shook his officers' hands before they took their three companies through the breach. The people of Djenne were heavily armed. Snipers fired at the French from the rooftops of its decorated houses. In the epic tradition of the West African campaigns, officers outdid one another in reckless *beau-geste*-style gallantry, charging at the head of their troops, regimental flag in hand. After some spirited street-fighting, the French flag was raised in the centre of the city. Houses were searched and weapons collected. The rich merchants of Djenne threw themselves at Archinard's feet and cried: 'Stop the fighting! Stop the tirailleurs! Everything is yours, we will do what you want!' Two officers and eleven soldiers had been killed, and there were sixty wounded.

But Archinard had assured the government that there would be no more military operations. When news of the casualties reached Paris, the Under-Secretary of State for the Colonies, Theophile Delcassé, summoned the veteran colonial officer Monteil and asked for explanations. 'There must be some military operations going on,' Monteil explained. 'If that is the case,' Delcassé replied, 'I will relieve Archinard of his command, for that would be a violation of his instructions, in which he agreed not to undertake any warlike action without the formal assent of the government.' Monteil persuaded Delcassé not to take any action against Archinard until he had received his full report. But when Archinard exceeded his budget by 700,000 francs, Delcassé lost his temper and had Archinard replaced by a civilian governor, in November 1893. Archinard was recalled, and his colonial career ended in disgrace. Forty years of military rule on the upper Niger ended with Delcassé's decision.

Archinard learned that he had been replaced in a newspaper article. He wrote to Delcassé:

I see from the evening papers that I have been relieved of my command before being able to send you my full report on the campaign. I am happy, as I give up my duties, to remember that at our last meeting, you honoured me by approving my conduct without restriction, and that you even had the kindness to add that you could always count on me. Despite the painful nature of my dismissal, these memories are too precious to prevent me from expressing my gratitude once again.

Adding a note of personal spite to Archinard's dismissal, Delcassé offered him the meaningless Cambodian decoration, 'Commander of the Dragon of Annam'. Archinard asked that it be given to one of his native officers. He then broke military tradition by turning over his correspondence with Delcassé to the *Figaro*. France talked of nothing else for a week. Soon the affair was forgotten and Archinard was named Inspector-General of Naval Artillery.

Now that a civilian governor had replaced Archinard, Paris hoped to implement a policy of peaceful commercial development on the upper Niger. But there were other headstrong officers who were not willing to let a civilian governor interfere with their dreams of conquest. The roaming and predatory Tuareg tribes in the Niger bend between Djenne and Timbuctu were their next target. Timbuctu, whose commerce depended on peace and open trade routes, had asked for French protection against the Tuaregs.

In December 1893 Lieutenant Boiteux, of the navy, who commanded the French flotilla on the Niger, left his base in Mopti and headed for Timbuctu against orders. Boiteux was acting in the name of inter-service rivalry. He felt that the army was hogging the action and wanted to show that the navy could also play a brilliant part in the conquest of the upper Niger.

In the wake of Boiteux's unscheduled departure, two military columns formed in Segou. One, under Lieutenant-Colonel Eugene Bonnier, the military commander of the French Sudan, was to reach Timbuctu in dugouts, on the river route. The other, travelling overland, was commanded by a forty-one-year-old major named Joseph Joffre. The future Marshal of France and commander-in-chief of French forces in the First World War had thus far not singled himself out, having remained a captain for thirteen years. Because he was an army engineer, he was sent to the upper Niger to supervise the construction of the railway. Instead, he won his first field promotion, against the Tuaregs.

Determined to be the first French officer to enter Timbuctu, Boiteux reached the river-port of Kabara, left his gunboat in the hands of his second-in-command, Ensign Aube, and made a triumphant entrance into the city. To pass the time, Aube went ashore with a French seaman and seventeen native crewmen, and attacked a party of Tuaregs. Their munitions exhausted, Aube and his landing party were massacred. Boiteux returned to find that his ensign had abandoned his boat and been killed in a meaningless raid.

Bonnier reached Kabara on 10 January 1894. He told Boiteux that he had acted with incredible rashness and lack of discipline, and that the massacre of Aube and his men ruined all chance of negotiation with the Tuaregs. Bonnier himself was by this time acting in defiance of orders, for three days out of Segou he had received a telegram from the civilian governor Grodet, ordering him to suspend operations. In true Archinard fashion, Bonnier replied that he was acting under instructions from Paris that gave him the right to resist aggression.

Lieutenant Boiteux took Bonnier's rebuke very badly, replying in an insolent tone, cursing and shouting that he had not been defeated, that on the contrary he had routed the enemy. Bonnier put him under arrest. Learning that the Tuaregs were massing near Goundam, a village on Joffre's overland route, Bonnier resolved to set out to help Joffre, and disperse the Tuaregs. He left on 12 January with 204 men, attacked a small group of Tuaregs, and took a few prisoners and about five hundred sheep. Grodet, furious at not receiving any reply to his telegrams, had relieved him of his command on 5 January.

Bonnier camped for the night in a small clearing, lit fires to keep away the bitter January cold, and posted sentinels on the crests of dunes. Bonnier shrugged off his guide's warning that they would be attacked during the night. In keeping with a peculiar French military custom, all the rifles were stacked in a row, one against the other. Dawn broke and a sentinel shouted 'aux armes'. Spears hissed through the camp, and soldiers numb from the cold stumbled in the half-light trying to reach their weapons as Tuareg horsemen charged, stampeding the bleating sheep before them. Those who did find their guns could not use

them because sand got into the breeches. The Tuaregs, bene-
fiting from total surprise against sleeping French troops in an
area they knew well, decimated their enemy. Native tirailleurs
fled through the desert. Bonnier was among the first killed. A
detachment later sent out to look for bodies found thirteen French
dead, and sixty-four of the 204 native soldiers. It was the worst
French defeat in thirty years of campaigning on the upper Niger.
The dead were cremated and their ashes were sent to Marseilles,
where a monument still stands to 'the conquerors of Timbuctu'.
Bonnier, the last military commander of the French Sudan, died
in an unheroic manner, fighting a Tuareg band armed only
with spears and swords, who showed that knowledge of the terrain and tactical skill could make up for lack of firepower. It may
have been the last battle where spears outfought rifles. Bonnier
died without knowing that he had been relieved of his command.

Meanwhile Joffre was progressing with difficulty over a dirt
track with 450 men and 200 horses. His mission, he later wrote,
was to 'declare our authority over the country and take possession of the part of the country populated by hostile tribes'.
The Niger was exceptionally high that year, swamping most of
the roads, and they had trouble finding supplies. As Joffre
advanced the Tuaregs harassed the column, capturing stragglers
and attacking at night. Scouts on camels on the crests of dunes
followed their movements. Joffre always pitched his camp in a
square with his back to the river, so that there were only three
exposed sides. He laid thorny branches on all three sides and
ordered frequent night patrols. Thanks to these precautions, he
escaped Bonnier's fate.

The first village that refused to place itself under Joffre's protection was Niafounke, about a hundred miles south-west of
Timbuctu, which he reached on 20 January. It was surrounded
by a moat of flooded river-water, and the horses sank in the mud
as they advanced. The infantry was able to get to within eight
hundred yards of the city, and saw four hundred warriors standing in line in front of its walls, with *griots* (native minstrels)
chanting battle songs to cheer them on. The warriors charged but
were stopped by the infantry's first volley. Joffre took the village
without a single casualty. Moving on, he took the village of
Goundam after a brief struggle, and entered Timbuctu on 12
February. He had covered 508 miles from Segou, largely over

swamped ground, in a month and a half, pacifying the area as he went. His total casualties were two soldiers who had died of illness. Using Timbuctu as a base, Joffre launched punitive actions against the Tuaregs, driving them away from their river bases and into the desert. He pursued the tribe that had killed Bonnier, killed about sixty of them, and recovered the guns they had taken from the French dead. By July he had the situation under control. All but four Tuareg tribes offered their submission, military posts were built at strategic points, and the sedentary population seemed glad to be protected from Tuareg raids. Joffre was promoted to Lieutenant-colonel.

After Joffre's success, orders arrived from the civilian governor to stop operations. A succession of military posts were built along the Niger, 250 miles downstream from Gao. The garrisons had standing orders not to venture further than half a day's journey from the river. In the face of French passiveness, the Tuaregs once again became rebellious, ambushing isolated French detachments and attacking unprotected villages. The French plan was to turn the Tuareg nomads into sedentary rural folk. But the desert men, who had lived for centuries from plunder and the sale of camels, would not change their ways. As one Tuareg told a French officer, 'see this hand, it knows only the hilt of my sword and the bridle of my horse'. But in the process of trying to domesticate the Tuaregs, the French gained control of two-thirds of the Niger.

Having pacified the Niger, they turned once more to their most durable enemy, Samory. In 1898 a French column led by Major de Lartigue headed due south 250 miles from Bamako to the town of Odienne. Learning from deserters that Samory had fled south-west, towards Liberia and the sea, de Lartigue started after him, even though the rainy season had begun. It was reported that Samory still had a standing army of one thousand horsemen armed with quick-action rifles and four thousand foot-soldiers. In September Major de Lartigue sent Captain Gouraud with two hundred men to try and head off Samory. Gouraud advanced through burning villages that stank from the rotting dead. He moved faster than Samory, who always travelled with a large civilian entourage. On the twenty-sixth a deserter told Gouraud that Samory was only half a day's march away. Two days later he caught up with stragglers, who told him that

Samory's morale was low. At dawn on the 29th, Gouraud attacked Samory's camp – he had orders to take the African chief alive. He and his men were concealed by the high grass until they reached a clearing from which rose the smoke of many fires. Samory was in front of his hut, reading the Koran. When he saw the turbans of the French tirailleurs he rose and tried to run for it, but was captured only a few miles from the safety of the Liberian border. Captain Gouraud also seized fifteen hundred rifles, ninety cases of ammunition, and Samory's personal treasure of gold and jewellery.

The French deported Samory to an island off Gabon, with four of his wives, and he died there of pneumonia two years later. On 13 October 1900 the Dakar newspaper editorialized: 'French West Africa is now freed of its irreconcilable enemy who for 15 years had sown terror from the banks of the Upper Senegal to the banks of the Volta.' With the capture of Samory the epic period of French colonialism on the upper Niger came to an end. In France schoolboys read illustrated books about his adventures, and his battles with Archinard became legend, like Sitting Bull and Custer. He is still remembered as the most difficult opponent France fought in its nineteenth-century colonial wars.

Even after civilian administrators had taken over from the officers, the French style of colonialism in West Africa was largely derived from the experience of conquest and military government. Administration on the upper Niger had been limited to providing logistic support for the armed columns chasing dissident African chiefs through the jungle. Commerce was forgotten in the rush to conquer and pacify. But because of the army's requirements, the officers were forced to adopt policies on questions such as education and slavery.

The same officers whose names were associated with the annual dry season campaigns were also the founders of schools, but their reasons for founding them were strictly military. There was a language problem between the French and the natives. The French needed interpreters on their campaigns. On one occasion Samory had repudiated a treaty because the French interpreter could not speak Mandingo properly. As the French advanced along the Niger, it became essential to train natives to speak French. The military became educators in order to pursue their conquests. The Colonial Minister in Paris encouraged this noble effort because it gave him an added argument in support of the controversial policy of conquest before Parliament. It was also convenient to employ French NCOs as teachers during the rainy season.

Thus the first schools were founded long before the area was pacified. In 1884 Borgnis-Desbordes started a school in a military post he had built three years earlier. The tradition was born of the soldier who had to fill in as teacher, doctor, and judge. By 1888 there were seven schools on the Senegal and upper Niger, with sergeants as headmasters. All the colonels who ruled the upper Niger with the absolute authority of Roman proconsuls recognized the need for schools, and all endorsed the doctrine that 'we do not have to instruct young blacks, we have to create Frenchmen'. Textbooks were written in France for young West Africans, informing them that 'my new fatherland, today, is France. I am French . . . when I am big, I will place the tricolor flag on top of my house every Sunday and I will tell everyone: Look at the fine flag'.

On the question of slavery, the army's policy was also dictated by its campaign requirements. On the Niger the only available beast of burden was man. The essential commodity on month-long campaigns over dirt paths through difficult terrain was porters, who were forcibly recruited and badly treated. It was impossible to treat them humanely, for if porters had carried the water and food they needed for the effort they were furnishing they could have carried little else. The French also had to assemble natives near their newly built military posts to grow enough food for their garrisons. They were able to solve both problems by founding 'freedom villages' for fugitive slaves, which were in fact refugee camps whose inmates performed forced labour for the French. The beauty of it was that these labour camps could be presented as a humanitarian effort to abolish slavery.

English involvement on the lower Niger had come out of a fierce moral determination to end slavery. The French, on the other hand, were indifferent to abolition and trade. Their occupation of the upper Niger had nothing to do with slavery and their attitude towards it developed out of the needs of conquest. During half a century of annual campaigns, the military adopted an anti-slavery posture mostly as a means of obtaining a steady supply of porters.

Slavery was not abolished in France until the 1848 revolution. But in Senegal, Faidherbe, although personally against slavery, took the position that it was part of the social order. The French attitude was based on tolerance of native customs. Fugitive slaves were sent back to their owners. From time to time someone in the French Parliament demanded that the 1848 emancipation proclamation be applied to West Africa, but to little avail. Officers in remote military posts found that the best way of forming alliances with local chiefs was to help them catch their fugitive slaves. No attempt was made to persuade the natives to change their ways. The English wanted to bring the natives round to Victorian standards of morality. The French believed that one had to take people as one found them.

In France the colonial lobby took up the defence of the military against abolitionist critics. A senator named Schoelcher said in 1880: 'We cannot impose our laws on them, we can no more ban slavery than we can ban polygamy, which is in their customs.' In 1893 Archinard sent a directive to his officers saying: 'Do not oppose the trade in captives, the moment for that has not come yet.' The military justified their position by holding that the cure was worse than the illness. To abolish slavery would lead to grave social disorders which would threaten France's presence in the area. Borgnis-Desbordes said in 1886 that the abolition of slavery would 'lead to a result which no one who knows the Sudan can deny: that we would have against us both the free men and the slaves'.

However, the military found a way of paying lip-service to abolition in the 'freedom villages'. The first were founded in the 1880s on French supply routes, and had between a hundred and four hundred inhabitants. They were often situated close to a river crossing used by troops, or near a well that had to be kept open, or a bridge that required protection. They were, in short, tailored to fit the needs of French troops, as a solution to logistic, strategic, and personnel problems.

The interesting thing is that although the villages were not founded because of any genuine interest in freeing slaves, the very fact that they existed compelled the French to adopt an anti-slavery stance. The villages, cynically built to meet the needs of the military, became real havens for escaped slaves. It came to be accepted that if a slave spent three months in a freedom village he could not be given back to his owner. He was even given a certificate of freedom, though this did not mean that he was free to leave the village, but that he must now submit to a new form of serfdom – to the French army – that was sometimes more inhuman than the slavery he had escaped.

In 1901 further progress was made when a civilian governor put an end to the three-month probation period. Now a slave was free as soon as he reached the village. By 1906 there were seventy-five freedom villages in the French Sudan, with a total population of fifteen thousand. They were artificial communities, mixing ethnic and tribal strains, populated with refugees, broken families, and prisoners of war. Those who could escaped from this new form of servitude. Those who remained were the sick, the elderly, and the helpless. They worked as porters or on the railroad, often in shameful conditions. In France the freedom villages were presented as the effort of an enlightened administration to put an end to slavery. Their real purpose was to provide a cheap and docile labour force in an area ravaged by war. The need for the villages vanished once the railway was built and the campaigns ended, and not a single village survived to become a permanent community. The inmates were finally freed and many of them settled in cities.

There had been one other effort to recruit manpower for the French: Faidherbe's creation of a native infantry corps in 1857. Here again the military set the long-term pattern of colonialism. In the Sudan, even after the era of military rule ended, the French were less interested in developing trade than in recruiting black troops to make up for the low population density of their own country. What Faidherbe said of the Senegal in the 1850s continued to be true of French West Africa right through the Second World War: 'Other colonies gave us products, this one gave us manpower.' After the freedom villages died out, the French intensified recruitment of black troops, who in peace time were assigned to public works projects and in wartime were sent to fight for the new fatherland they had read about in textbooks.

The black force's apostle was General Mangin, who had served as a young officer in the campaign against Samory. He was convinced that blacks made the best shock troops because they had a less developed central nervous system that allowed them to preserve their calm in the heat of battle. He also believed in the civilizing influence of war. The origin of social groups, he argued, was man's need to defend himself, and man's emergence from anarchy had come about through military leaders who became political leaders. Recruiting black troops could thus be seen as part of France's civilizing mission, it was a way of making Frenchmen out of savages. Afterwards, if they were still alive, they could become leaders in their own countries. On a more practical level, Mangin saw in black troops the only way France's forty million people could avoid defeat at the hands of seventy million Germans. Mangin lobbied for years until Parliament voted a law to incorporate black troops into the French army.

The French high command's disregard for human life during the First World War (in tactics once described as 'plugging empty shell-holes with live soldiers') may be in part attributed to the fact that influential generals like Mangin, Gallieni, and Joffre had undergone their combat training in the African bush. There they learned that the most plentiful and cheapest commodity in battle was human. When the First World War was declared, thousands of native sons of the upper Niger and the Senegal, hardly speaking a word of French, hardly knowing how to fire their weapons, accustomed to the bush and its sleepy ways, were shipped overnight to the freezing trenches of Verdun and the Somme. The cold did more damage than the Germans, and they had to be evacuated during the winter. By the time the armistice was signed, there were 134,000 black troops fighting in France, and a total of thirty thousand had died. The English, on the other hand, did not use African troops in European operations. The governor of Nigeria, Sir Frederick Lugard, sent three thousand Nigerians to reinforce the campaign against German East Africa, but he had misgivings even about this, and wrote: 'He (the black soldier) also knows how to kill white men, around whom he had been taught to weave a web of sanctity of life. He also knows how to handle bombs and Lewis guns and Maxims – and he has seen white men budge when he stood fast. And altogether, he has acquired much knowledge which he might put to an uncomfortable use someday.'

The French had no such qualms, and in 1919 applied

conscription to West Africa. African males at the age of nineteen had to report for three years' army service, whereas in metropolitan France service was eighteen months. Conscription created a class of Europeanized blacks who were cut off from their homes and traditions and yet not assimilated by the French.

Thus, on the upper Niger, a handful of ardent officers with large-scale plans won a colonial empire in spite of vacillating governments and fickle public opinion, which sometimes cheered them on and sometimes damned them. They realized Faidherbes's vision of giving geographical unity to France's scattered African possessions through control of the upper Niger. They did it for reasons that had nothing to do with trade or commercial gain – in fact they made trade impossible as they pacified the area with annual wars. They built schools, herded fugitive slaves into freedom villages, and recruited black troops for their own campaigns and later for France's European wars. After a fifty-year period of military rule, the French Sudan was handed over to civil servants, who received an already functioning colonial empire of three million square miles, eight times the size of France. It stretched from Dakar to Dahomey, from Timbuctu to Lake Tchad. Meanwhile, on the lower Niger, English traders were establishing a palm oil monopoly, moving further up the river, and finding that large-scale trading meant increasing involvement in local affairs, and rivalry with France. The English too would obtain a West African empire, not by conquest like the French, but grudgingly, in response to a set of circumstances brought about by commercial enterprise.

Ten

THE NIGER DIVIDED (II)

A<small>FTER</small> the consulate in Lokoja was closed in 1869, the only official British presence on the Niger was the annual gunboat that came upriver to shell villages that had harassed traders. English companies had succeeded in establishing trading stations above the delta and cutting the black middlemen out of the palm oil profits. But in so doing they had opened an era of anarchy. Their posts were attacked and their ships fired at. The Niger was a gauntlet of angry tribesmen that had to be run, for inland trade spelled the ruin of prosperous chiefs who had kept their tiny states going by means of brokerage commissions and 'comey', or dues on transiting ships.

By 1871 steamers from five companies travelled regularly from the delta as far north as Rabba, and the Niger's banks were dotted with small trading posts, manned by solitary young men consumed by fever and melancholy, who soon grew to hate the place, seeing in it none of the fascination that had inspired explorers. 'Of all beastly waters the Niger beats them all', one wrote. The traders negotiated with local chiefs for land rights, usually paying in cases of gin. A typical deed between a delta kinglet and a Liverpool company reads: 'If at any time the above named Company should wish to sell the within described piece of land, the aforesaid Company shall pay me or my successors five hundred cases of Gin V.H. or other goods to the same value and no further payment will be demanded hereafter.' Gin had apparently replaced the cowrie shell as legal tender.

In the absence of government support, the traders provided

for their own protection by fitting out armed canoes which were sent on punitive expeditions against hostile villages. At the same time, faced with constant disputes over money matters, they formed their own courts of arbitration in co-operation with local chiefs. The merchants of Bonny were the first to establish a so-called 'Court of Equity' in 1854. The court sat with the consent of Bonny's king, and the judges were the main black and white traders.

Ruling on cases such as non-payment of palm oil shipments and pilotage fees, the Court of Equity filled a real need and was adopted in other trading centres. By 1870 there were seven, and by 1872 the British consul for the Bight of Biafra had given them official status. Thus, owing to the litigation arising from trade and the enemies they had made by cutting out the middlemen, the merchants were forced to assume judicial and military powers similar to those that would have been set up by a colonial government.

Despite these efforts, trading ships continued to be attacked, and in 1871 one was destroyed by a sunken spike as it headed downriver. Hostile actions increased as the situation of the coastal cities that depended entirely on trade became more desperate. The King of Brass, Ockiah, took the unusual step in 1876 of writing to the Foreign Office to complain that English merchants had appropriated the palm oil trade and cut him out. 'It is very hard on us, in all the other rivers,' he said, '. . . the markets are secured to them, and why should a difference be made for this my river? We have no land where we can grow plantains or yams, if we cannot trade we must starve.'

The situation was irreversible. The traders, once established on the lower Niger, were not going to return to the coast and resume the system of African brokers. In 1871 the British government, looking for a way to help the traders without direct involvement or undue expense, hit on the idea of making an alliance with the Emir of Nupe, Masaba, who controlled an extensive tract on both banks of the Niger north of Lokoja. Masaba had been Baikie's friend and protector, and welcomed the extension of English influence so long as it did not encroach on his territory. As an ally of the English, trading his ivory and shea-butter against weapons and ammunition, he could increase his own power. A British envoy was sent to Masaba in 1871,

found him co-operative, and put English trade under his protection. The security of trade improved, but there was another
problem: competition among rival firms, which raised palm oil
prices and weakened the traders in their dealings with Africans.

Of the three main firms trading on the lower Niger, the smallest, Holland Jacques, ran into financial difficulties. Fresh capital
was needed, and the secretary, Captain Grove-Ross, appealed
to his son-in-law, John Senhouse Taubman. John Taubman had
a wild, headstrong younger brother named George Goldie
Taubman, who was looking for something to do and wanted to
leave England. The Taubman family bought out Holland
Jacques and put thirty-one-year-old George Goldie in charge. He
immediately went to Africa to see for himself why the company
was losing money. In this oblique manner, involving family
connections in a part of the world he knew nothing about, did
George Goldie Taubman meet his destiny.

Into the anarchic situation of rival firms fighting each other as
well as the natives stepped another of those providential men,
who was to carry out the next step in giving a reluctant England
a West African land empire. George Goldie Taubman accomplished a feat comparable to the conquest of British India, and
did it without bloodshed. He is as important a figure in African
history as Cecil Rhodes or Faidherbe. But he is far less known,
perhaps because he never had to win a war, more probably
because of his obsession with privacy. For after turning over to
England a territory seven times its own size, he burned his
papers, forbade a biography, and made his children vow never
to write anything about him.

Sir George Goldie, as he became known, dropping the
Germanic-sounding Taubman when he received his knighthood
in 1887, was the classic empire-builder, a man of great qualities
and great defects, ill at ease in his own country, requiring a
mission considerable enough to absorb his relentless energies
and fiery temperament.

Goldie was the youngest of four sons in a family of German
origin that settled on the Isle of Man in the eighteenth century
and made a fortune smuggling tea and wine into England. He so
effectively obliterated his past that the few scraps of biographical
information we have come from the one person who was able to
get him to talk about himself, a girl named Dorothy Wellesey,

who first met Goldie when she was ten and he was fifty-five – her stepfather Lord Scarborough had succeeded Goldie as head of his Niger Company.

In conversation with Dorothy Wellesey, Goldie described his un-Victorian youth, saying: 'I had the good fortune to lose both my parents before they could have any influence on me.' He was a brilliant but erratic student, and decided to go into the army engineers. But in those days, he recalled,

> I was like a gunpowder magazine. I was blind-drunk when I passed my final examination for the Engineers. Two years later a relation died, leaving me his fortune. I was so excited by the freedom this gave me that I bolted without sending in my papers, and leaving all my belongings behind. I went straight to Egypt. There I fell in love with an Arab girl. We lived in the desert for three years. Garden of Allah! She died of consumption. I came home to lead a life of idleness and dissipation.

Goldie's next escapade was to run away with the family governess, who 'compromised' him. They were married in 1871 in London's fashionable St Marylebone Church. He was a thorn in the side of Victorian society, boasting that he was an atheist, praising Ibsen and Wagner, arrogant and aggressive in a world of genteel conventions. At the same time he was imbued with the Victorian conviction that the people of West Africa, 'this lost thirtieth of the human race', could only progress if aided by the superior societies of Europe. He was also Victorian in his belief that material gain was civilizing. His temperament was not Victorian, and he was unsuited to the strait-laced climate of England at that time, but his ideas concerning Africa and empire were the typical products of a Victorian mind.

Although he went to West Africa to put a failing trading company on its feet, he later told Dorothy Wellesey that his real motive was patriotic.

> All achievements begin with a dream [he said]. My dream, as a child, was to colour the map red. In 1877 I left England (largely to escape from private entanglements) to explore the interior of Nigeria with my brother. He got fever badly when we were half-way up the river, and I had to bring him home. On the journey back I conceived the ambition of adding the region of the Niger to the British Empire.

Things cannot have been quite that simple. He must also have been drawn to Africa because of the demands of his nature. For he was uneasy in England, given to fits of depression, gauche in social situations, and lacking the warmth for emotional ties. He needed to throw himself into a great cause where he was the unchallenged leader.

Goldie arrived on the Niger, a fair, thin young man with piercing blue eyes, whom Dorothy Wellesey described as looking 'something between a vulture and a mummy'. He decided before leaving for Africa that the trouble with the Niger companies stemmed from commercial rivalry, and that salvation lay in association. It is a tribute to his strength of character and persuasiveness that a young man without previous experience in African trade was able to convince the hard-headed veterans of Niger trading stations to accept his proposals. The two most important companies, Miller Brothers and James Pinnock, merged with Goldie's Holland Jacques in 1879 to form the United African Company, which had a capital of £250,000. Each firm received a number of shares in the new company. They agreed to pool their resources, stop competing, and share the profits.

Goldie soon made the company a one-man show. He worked a sixteen-hour day, and expected others to do the same. He was bad-tempered and intolerant, and one of his subordinates was heard to grumble: 'Why do we suffer this man blindly, only to get hit?' To anyone who seemed tired or pessimistic, Goldie invariably advised: 'Seize the day, seize the day.' Back in England in 1880 to set up the new company's London offices, he interviewed an applicant for office boy and told him: 'We want a boy with his head screwed on right.' He insisted on his every order being carried out to the letter. A heavy cask arrived and the office boy told Goldie that he couldn't carry it to the first floor. Goldie shouted: 'Don't tell me that anything cannot be done. Go and do it.' He knew everyone's job better than they did, and was merciless with slackers.

The flaw in Goldie's united front on the Niger, however, was that once the new company had brought down the price of palm oil, new competitors were attracted. The French trading companies began to set up stations at some of the places where Goldie's company was already established, such as Abo,

Onitsha, and Egga. When the French firms prospered Goldie started a price war, and at the same time made offers to buy them out.

As Goldie later told a Reuters' correspondent in one of the only interviews he ever gave, his plans concerning the company had been 'played out like a game of chess'. He might succeed in buying out the French companies, but the problem would only recur, as English and foreign traders were drawn to easy profits on the Niger. Goldie realized that he had somehow to obtain a monopoly for his company.

Commerce was never pure. Governments supported their traders. French companies on the Niger meant an extension of French influence, and a base from which the French could eventually make territorial claims. Thus Goldie became much more than the director of a company that traded in palm oil in the African bush: he became the guardian of British interests on the lower Niger.

The French imitated Goldie's methods, buying land from local chiefs and signing treaties with them. They played on the dissatisfactions of coastal tribes like the Brass men to form alliances. By 1882 the Compagnie Française de l'Afrique Equatoriale had seventeen stations on the lower Niger. Directing French operations was a Corsican army major, Mattei, who was given the title of consular agent and made his headquarters in Brass. Recruited in Paris, Mattei was told by company directors: 'Your mission is more patriotic than commercial.' He roamed the Niger making treaties with chiefs.

Goldie decided that the only way to protect his company was to obtain a royal charter, which would give him the backing of the British government. Charters in previous centuries had protected the fur trade in Canada and the spice trade in the East Indies. But they were out of fashion. The last one granted, to the Hudson's Bay Company, had been abolished in 1869. Goldie proceeded cautiously. In 1882 he reorganized his company, under the name National African Company, with new by-laws empowering it to ask for a charter to exercise a trade monopoly on the Niger. Goldie realized the new company would have to win favour in business and government circles. By watering the stock, he increased the nominal capital to £1 million. He recruited peers and baronets for the board of directors. Lord

Aberdare, a personal friend of Gladstone and of the Foreign Secretary Lord Granville, became chairman of the board and invested £800 in the company. Goldie patiently built up connections which could help him involve the government in the affairs of his company. His influential directors became colonial lobbyists. In 1883 Lord Aberdare, sending his New Year's greetings to his friend Lord Granville, suggested negotiations with France on the Niger question.

It was slowly dawning on the English that Africa was becoming the stage for what one official called 'a very unpleasant state of things, each power grabbing what it can'. In 1883 the French grabbed Dahomey, driving a wedge between the two British colonies of Gold Coast and Lagos. French gunboats appeared on the Niger, and Mattei went two hundred miles north of the Benue confluence, signed a treaty with a chief, and hoisted the French flag. The French by that time claimed thirty-three stations on the Niger.

The head of the Consular and African Department, H. Percy Anderson, wrote in a memo in 1883: 'The French have a settled policy in Africa . . . and that policy is antagonistic to us. The progress of that policy is sometimes sluggish, sometimes feverish, but it never ceases.' In fact, French policy was more like the children's game of two steps forward one step back, depending on the minister in power.

The British government became concerned enough to establish a protectorate over the Niger delta in 1884, but the cabinet voted no funds to pay for its administration. Goldie had been asking that his chief agent on the Niger, David McIntosh, be given consular status, as his French rival Mattei had. The request was granted once the protectorate was set up. The government became obligated to the company, which agreed to let its employees perform consular duties. The decision to make McIntosh a vice-consul was a major victory for Goldie. The man who spoke for England on the Niger was one of his employees, empowered to make treaties in the name of the queen. Instead, he spent most of his time using his consular prestige to advance company aims.

The next threat to Goldie came when Bismarck invited the European powers to a conference in Berlin to order and regulate the partition of Africa. Bismarck was the perfect neutral host for such a conference, having declared that 'for Germany to acquire colonies would be like a poverty-stricken Polish noble-man providing himself with silks and sables when he needed shirts'. The conference was scheduled to start in November 1884. Goldie realized that if French traders were still on the Niger when the conference began, the European powers would set up some form of international control commission, which would ruin his plans for monopoly. England had to go to the conference able to demonstrate that the lower Niger was clearly in its sphere of influence. It was essential that Goldie buy out the French before the conference began. Circumstances were in his favour. The French company's only government protector, Gambetta, had died in 1882. Mattei complained that as consular agent he never received a single instruction. France had clearly lost interest in its stations on the lower Niger. The French traders' commercial position was not sound. Their capital was tied up in trading stations and ships. They had no liquid funds. Efforts to float shares failed. In 1883 two of their ships ran aground, a third one sank, and one of their stations burned down. Goldie waged a ruthless price war, telling McIntosh to cut prices by twenty-five per cent. The combination of bad luck, price cuts, and lack of support from the government, which was neglecting West Africa to pursue conquest in Indo-China, ruined the French companies. Two weeks before the Berlin Conference's inaugural meeting on 15 November 1884, Goldie bought out his chief French rival, the Compagnie Française de l'Afrique Equatoriale. Smaller French firms had been bought out earlier. Britain, worried that the Germans and French would charge them with ineffective occupation of the lower Niger, could now attend the conference with a strong hand.

The Berlin Conference was a solemn farce in which everybody but the people directly involved – the Africans – decided the fate of the continent. It achieved nothing except proclaiming the obvious: that European nations had imperial ambitions in Africa. Its resolutions were immediately broken. Its basic principle was that Africa should be divided among gentlemen, in an orderly manner, without the involvement of its inhabitants. A European state occupying the coast had a right to settle the interior, and could keep going inland until it met another European power.

When the question of the Niger came up, Britain insisted on her right to administer the area Goldie's company occupied, without the interference of an international commission. One of the behind-the-scenes advisers of the British delegation in Berlin was George Goldie. Bismarck supported the British position in return for Britain's recognition of the Belgian King Leopold's rights in the Corps.

The conference drafted a Niger Navigation Act full of noble but unenforceable decrees. It proclaimed complete freedom of navigation for the merchant ships of all nations. It barred special privileges for any company. It prohibited the payment of transit dues on the river. It ruled that the Niger would be neutral in time of war. But instead of being enforced by an international commission, the Niger Navigation Act was to be administered by England in the part of the Niger within its sphere of influence – the only part where trade was important. It was a triumph for British diplomacy and it ensured that every article in the Niger Navigation Act would soon be violated. If the passage of a foreign merchant ship was blocked by Goldie's company, its captain could appeal to the vice-consul, who was Goldie's employee.

England's new obligations under the Act meant that it had to establish some form of administration on the river to supervise free navigation and register complaints. Once again the English government bowed to Goldie by giving him the charter he had long requested. Once chartered, the company could discharge British responsibilities under the Act at no cost to the English taxpayer. The idea that some conflict of interest might arise between company policies and free navigation was not considered. After eighteen months of negotiations, the charter was granted and received the Great Seal of the Privy Council on 10 July 1886.

The company was called the Royal Niger Company, and had a distinctive motto and flag: a white ensign, bearing in the right-hand upper corner a circle, within which there was a Y-shaped figure, representing the Niger and the Benue, and the words Ars, Jus, Pax. In effect, the charter sanctioned Goldie's trade monopoly and gave him quasi-governmental powers. He was given the right to collect taxes to recover his expenses in administering the region. Thus the company became a two-headed animal, running a profit-making business on the one hand and an embryonic government on the other. The two heads constantly collaborated. The company's administrative powers helped it enforce a rigid trade monopoly, making life impossible for competitors. Its tax money was used to support its commercial policies. Who could distinguish, in many cases, between a commercial and an administrative expense? Troops sent to put down an uprising were paid for out of collected taxes, but keeping the natives orderly was also essential for the company's commercial operations. The board of directors was renamed the Council, and became the highest executive, legislative, and judiciary authority on the lower Niger. It could draft laws, arbitrate disputes, and make appointments. What was good for the Royal Niger Company was good for England.

Backed by the charter, the company launched a programme of expansion which laid the foundations for England's acquisition of Nigeria. Goldie's agents roamed the bush, their pockets filled with blank treaty forms. Local rulers signed with an 'X' after receiving a few presents, and the treaty was then registered before the consul, and ratified by the Foreign Office. The standard treaty, form number five, had as its first provision: 'We the undersigned, chiefs of ——, with the view to the bettering of conditions in our country and people, do this day cede to the Royal Niger Company, for ever, the whole of our territory extending from —— to ——.' The company concluded 250 such treaties, acquiring vast land tracts on the lower Niger, and using Lokoja as an advanced base for its expansion. The treaties completely violated local land laws, according to which the land belonged to the clan or tribe as a whole and could not be signed away without consultation. But from the company's point of view they were binding documents.

Lokoja, originally a few mud huts built by Baikie in 1860 at the Niger–Benue confluence, had by this time grown into a row of tin warehouses along the waterfront, with bungalows further back, and the cone-thatched cabins of the newly formed Royal Niger Constabulary. Samuel Crowther, now white-haired and dressed in a long black frock coat and trousers, preached in a mud and thatch church, still trying to convert the Moslem population and prevent the backsliding of the local clergy.

THE NIGER DIVIDED (II)

To discharge its administrative duties, the company set up a sort of capital at Asaba, 150 miles from the mouth of the Niger, with a supreme court, a central prison, and the main garrison for the five hundred-man constabulary. A senior judicial officer and a commandant of the constabulary were named. Company agents were empowered to judge civil and criminal cases. The senior judicial officer could sentence any foreigner to any term of imprisonment without right of appeal.

Administration went hand in hand with commerce. The company had about forty stations, directed by English or African agents. Stern-wheelers and launches thrashed up and down the Niger from station to station, collecting goods from corrugated iron sheds, not only palm oil but also ivory, shea-butter, potash, hides, tin, and gum. Purchases were based on the value of a 'head' of cowries, worth 1s 3d. A native brought in five shillings worth of palm oil, and the agent let him choose four 'heads' worth of Manchester goods: tobacco, salt, cloth, or trinkets.

When Liverpool traders formed an association to compete with the Royal Niger Company, Goldie fought back by banning the import of spirits. His own position was so strong by then that he did not have to rely on demon rum, and in any case there was no one to check how closely he enforced his own ban, which also allowed him to present himself as the champion of Victorian morality, while the Liverpool merchants were pictured as scoundrels trying to debauch the natives. Goldie quickly won the support of the missionaries. 'I cannot believe,' he wrote, 'that the conscience of Europe will long allow that the vast populous regions of tropical Africa should be used only as a cesspool for European alcohol.' Smuggling was severely punished: £100 fine and a month in jail for the first offence, £500, six months in jail, and the seizure of the ship and its cargo for the second.

Like Goldie, the company was secretive about its activities. Each official had to post a £1000 bond which he would forfeit if he gave information to the press or published a book or pamphlet. But the days when Baikie had gone native, wearing a tobe and siring half-caste children, had given way to a new policy of duplicating living conditions in England. In Old Calabar the company had a cricket field and a golf course, and there were social gatherings to which the ladies from the missions were

281

invited. Company agents dressed for dinner. The French Lieutenant Hourst, who took a gunboat down the Niger in 1896, while denouncing the company as a front for English imperialism, had to admit that it was a civilized front. 'The company,' he wrote, 'is but the screen behind which England hides herself . . . to the great detriment of the shareholders, the company tried to create an Empire . . . and is obliged to maintain a relatively large army.' In Lokoja Hourst was received by the commander-in-chief of the constabulary in conditions of surprising luxury. 'Music was playing as we were at breakfast,' he wrote, 'as if we were on board the admiral's flagship or at the Grand Hotel in Paris. Children played to us on the flute. We had printed menus, dainty salt cellars, caviar, whisky and soda, and good stout . . . Oh what a delight to eat a well-served meal on a tablecloth with fresh flowers.'

Company agents on the Niger were not only reasonably comfortable, they were all-powerful. The company, in violation of the Niger Navigation Act, drafted tariff regulations that made it difficult for non-company ships to trade on the river. On arrival in the delta ships had to be inspected and cleared at customs. They had to pay duty on their cargo and show invoices in English for all transactions, and could only trade at specified stations. Above Lokoja, there was a second inspection and a second round of duties. Every foreigner had to buy a licence to trade that cost £100. Non-company ships were thus tied up in expensive regulations and time-consuming red tape that practically guaranteed trading at a loss.

Goldie contended that he was not in violation of the Berlin agreement. The Act, he said, only mentioned navigation, not trade. Navigation meant moving on the river, which every ship was free to do. But if they landed they ceased to be navigators and became traders infringing on the company's domain. According to his reasoning, only ships in transit could claim free passage. The fact of the matter was that no steamship of the period could navigate the length of the lower Niger without having to put in for wood and provisions. The logical conclusion of Goldie's reasoning was that there was no such thing as navigation on the Niger.

Goldie's dictatorial control of river traffic was finally challenged by a German trader, Jacob Hoenigsberg. Even though he scrupulously complied with company regulations, Hoenigsberg was subjected to arbitrary interference. He was taking a cargo of salt to the Emir of Nupe in 1887 and had it cleared at the customs port of Akassa in the delta, paying the duty on the salt. Upriver he was stopped and ordered to obtain clearance again. Recognizing harassment when he saw it, Hoenigsberg abandoned his cargo and proceeded to Nupe, where he succeeded in setting the emir against the Niger company. The emir announced his independence of British rule and his advocacy of free trade.

Despite German government pressures, Goldie had Hoenigsberg arrested in January 1888 and brought to Asaba for trial. He was found guilty of attempting to promote strife and disorder, and deported. Germany, its feathers ruffled, pointed out that company regulations made a farce of free navigation on the Niger. Putting pressure on Westminster, Germany insisted that an English official be sent to investigate the company's rule. Lord Salisbury, the Prime Minister, who was fond of saying that Africa was the plague of Foreign Offices, agreed. The investigation was the first step in the takeover of the charter company by the British government, which slowly came to realize that the international complications created by Goldie's high-handed way of running things could only be met by an official British presence in the area.

Major Claude Maxwell Macdonald, a regular army officer with a long experience of Islamic Africa, who had served as military attaché in Cairo and consul in Zanzibar, was chosen to 'inquire into certain questions affecting Imperial and Colonial interests in the West Coast of Africa, and into the position of the Royal Niger Company'.

Macdonald was an industrious, fair-minded investigator, who drafted the first non-partisan reports on the company's rule. He made a first trip in the delta in March and April 1889, and a second trip upriver from July to October, and drafted a report on each trip. His goal, he said, was 'to make myself thoroughly acquainted with the wishes, feelings, and ideas of all classes of the community'. He travelled from village to village, talking to a cross-section of people, from company agents to rival traders, missionaries, and village notables. He conducted what was in fact a public opinion poll, asking each person whether they preferred a chartered company, a protectorate, or a colony. In contrast to the Berlin Conference, when Africa's destiny was decided without any say by its inhabitants, this may have been the first time that Africans were given the chance to decide what form of colonial government they wanted.

Macdonald pointed out the problem of separating company from government expenses. Was the company really spending what it claimed on administrative duties? Left to the judgment of company officials, the system could lead to all sorts of abuses. Macdonald recommended that Goldie make out a more detailed budget, with a sharper separation of the two kinds of expenses. For example, the company should explain when its ships were used on commercial business and when they were on official service. Macdonald's reports were turned over to the Foreign Office in 1890. Having found considerable opposition in the Oil Rivers region of the delta, to being placed under the charter, he recommended that the British government make the area a protectorate. As for the company, Macdonald did not question the principle of its monopoly but limited himself to suggesting minor reforms concerning customs duties, trade licences, and its budget.

A year later, Macdonald's report was acted on and he was appointed commissioner and consul-general of what would become known as the Niger Coast Protectorate. This was a major change in the British government's position. Until now, it had been content to let Goldie look after British interests on the Niger, largely because of Parliament's reluctance to earmark public funds for colonial ventures. Now it was facing the fact that government by delegation did not work. The situation was becoming too complicated to be left to the discretion of private merchants. The government now questioned Goldie's claim that he could manage the company's and the Africans' affairs with equal effectiveness. Having long been lulled by the convenience of its arrangement with the company to see only the advantages, the government, after Macdonald's reports, began to see the drawbacks. With the establishment of the Protectorate, two systems now functioned side by side on the lower Niger. Goldie would have to prove that his system worked best.

In 1890 France and England decided it was in their mutual interests to fix a north–south boundary starting from a point on the Niger to determine their spheres of influence. Before formal talks began, each side made extravagant claims concerning the area it controlled, in order to back up its demands at the negotiating table. In fact, by 1890 the French were not much further along the Niger than Segou, which Archinard had captured in 1889. They would not reach Timbuctu until 1894. The Royal Niger Company's northernmost station was at Egga, more than a hundred miles south of the Bussa rapids. Between the positions actually occupied by the French and the English lay a hundred-mile no-man's-land which each intended to divide at the expense of the other. The tactic was to claim to already have what one intended to get. Goldie proved to be the supreme player in this international poker game.

In January 1890 he sent an expedition to the King of Bussa and signed a treaty that gave the company full jurisdiction over foreigners coming through in exchange for an annual subsidy of fifty bags of cowries. Goldie also obtained rather dubious treaties with the Emir of Gandu and the Sultan of Sokoto. At the company's annual meeting in July, Lord Aberdare announced the new treaties and claimed they gave the company jurisdiction as far north as the Sahara. The French response was not long in coming. On 24 July the French ambassador to London, M. Waddington, called on the Prime Minister, Lord Salisbury (who acted as his own Foreign Minister), to ask that a line demarcating English and French spheres of influence on the Niger be drawn up. When a map was brought out, Lord Salisbury realized that Ambassador Waddington was so poorly prepared for the negotiations that he thought the dotted line representing Mungo Park's second trip down the Niger was the Royal Niger Company's boundary line. After several proposals and counterproposals, a line was finally agreed to, and a formal declaration was signed on 5 August 1890.

The agreement said:

Her Britannic Majesty's government recognizes the sphere of influence of France to the South of her Mediterranean possessions, up to a line from Say on the Niger to Burruwa on Lake Chad, drawn in such a manner as to comprise in the sphere of action of the Niger Company all that fairly belongs to the kingdom of Sokoto; the line to be determined by commissioners to be appointed.

Say, about forty miles south of the present-day capital of Niger, Niamey, was in the middle of the no-man's-land, roughly five hundred miles north of Bussa and five hundred miles south of Timbuctu. The 1500-mile-long line that was drawn in effect set the northern border of Nigeria. It was a victory for Goldie and British diplomacy, for the French recognized a British zone of influence far greater than the area the British effectively occupied, and also accepted England's questionable claims to the kingdom of Sokoto.

In a light-hearted speech at a Mansion House dinner on the day after the signing, Lord Salisbury said: 'We have been engaged in drawing lines upon maps where no white man's foot has ever trod; we have been giving away mountains and rivers and lakes to each other, only hindered by the small impediment that we never knew exactly where the mountains and rivers and lakes were.' In the House of Commons, Lord Salisbury said in reply to questions that the French had got mainly desert and that 'the Gallic rooster, who likes to scratch the earth, will wear down his claws, while the fertile region remains in our hands'. When imperialists charged him with having given away too much, he replied that he had given 'what agriculturalists would call "light" land'. Ambassador Waddington wrote to Lord Salisbury in hurt tones: 'No doubt the Sahara is not a garden, and contains, as you say, much "light" land; but your public reminder of the fact, was, you will allow, hardly necessary. You might as well have left us to find it out.'

In France, the Foreign Minister, Alexandre Ribot, faced an angry Chamber of Deputies on 4 November 1890.

> Our advance has been slower than the English advance [he explained]. We have reached Timbuctu but they have reached Say. They are strongly installed there, they have established their influence, and they aim to pursue their reconnaissance to the Niger bend . . . from where they can menace Timbuktoo . . . in this agreement, which you are criticizing so sharply, we have obtained that the English will not go beyond Say . . . you will ask – why did you not claim the flourishing cities of Sokoto? We could not do it because the English have already signed treaties with Sokoto.

Despite this explanation, there was an outcry in the French press and in the colonial lobby that France had been bilked.

The line agreed to, however, did not extend to lands on the Niger's right bank, which were still in principle there for the taking. Nor did the agreement alter the right to free navigation on the lower Niger. The French began a series of probes to test the effectiveness of the occupation in the British sphere of influence.

The first serious threat came from a private French colonial group which sent an African explorer, Lieutenant Mizon, to test freedom of navigation on the Niger. In October 1890 Mizon sailed up the Forcados river in the launch *René Caillié* with twenty-five armed men and a Hotchkiss cannon mounted on the bow. He did not stop to be cleared at the Royal Niger Company's custom post. On 15 October he was ambushed by natives on the river, and he and his interpreter were wounded. He found himself in the humiliating position of being towed to the company station of Akassa. There, the company's agent-general, Mr Flint, chided him for failing to obtain permission to enter Niger Company territory.

Flint told Mizon he could proceed up the Niger but not land on its banks, which was like telling him he could go swimming as long as he did not touch water. Mizon wired Paris for government support, and Flint, not forgetting his place as agent of a commercial company, charged him 1050.60 francs for the telegram. The French Foreign Ministry invoked the Niger Navigation Act to Lord Salisbury, describing Mizon's mission as 'purely scientific'. Goldie reluctantly had to let Mizon proceed on condition that he sign an agreement declaring his baggage and equipment in transit, and promising to observe the laws of the Niger territory, not to use his arms, and not to travel overland. Mizon signed, but by this time two months had passed, there was illness among the European members of his crew, and the waters of the Benue, which he hoped to explore, were too low to navigate. In France, there was indignation over Goldie's peremptory methods. Reaching Lokoja, Mizon had to wait until June 1891 for the Benue's waters to rise. He took advantage of the delay to have his steam launch looked at by the company mechanic, and he later claimed that the mechanic had sabotaged his engine. Mizon went three hundred miles up the Benue, as far as Yola, deep into the British sphere of influence. The Gallic rooster was not contenting itself with scratching the ground. Mizon stayed in

Yola five months and made friends with its emir, who allowed him to trade in the area. But Mizon did not sign a treaty, nor was he able to reach Lake Tchad and link up with French elements there.

In France, however, Mizon was welcomed in triumph, as if he had scored an important victory over the British. He was given the Legion of Honour and fêted at a ceremonial banquet attended by several cabinet ministers. Mizon was only too glad to play the role of the heroic explorer challenging perfidious Albion, and agreed to undertake a second voyage up the Niger. This time Mizon left in two steam launches, the *Mosca* and the *Sergent Malamine*, with a naval ensign, six other Europeans, and about a hundred armed native tirailleurs. Each launch was armed with a four-pound, quick-firing cannon. The French government again described the mission as 'essentially commercial and scientific'. The Foreign Office, hoping to avoid another diplomatic quarrel, told Goldie to give Mizon 'every facility'. Goldie told company officials to do no more for Mizon than was strictly necessary, and to use force against him only if he should violate company laws.

Mizon reached the mouth of the Niger in September 1892, stopped for clearance at Akassa, and proceeded upriver under the surveillance of an English launch. On the Benue, one of his launches ran aground in the territory of the Emir of Muri, who was hostile to the Niger Company. Mizon signed a treaty with the emir. What he had to do in return did not come out until May 1893, when the doctor of the Mizon mission, Henri Ward, returned to France because of illness and gave an interview to the newspaper *l'Intransigeant*. Ward was disgusted by what he had seen. Mizon, he said, was not the hero all France admired, but 'a vulgar careerist, without talent, without energy, who can only make his way by trickery'. To obtain a treaty from the Emir of Muri, Mizon had agreed to use his men and armaments on a slave-catching expedition. On Christmas Day 1892, Mizon had personally led an attack against a village, destroying its walls with his cannon and sending his tirailleurs to charge the defence-less villagers. There were 50 dead and 100 wounded, and 250 women and children were caught as slaves. In gratitude, the emir had given Mizon two girls aged twelve and thirteen. Ward added that the question asked of Stanley – 'How many niggers have you killed in Africa?' – could now also be put to Mizon.

Goldie had ample justification for sending an expedition out to arrest Mizon. He had waged war in an area under the British sphere of influence, sold arms to natives, and signed illegal treaties. He was in clear violation of his mission. Instead, Goldie patiently waited for the French government to recall Mizon – but that took time. Mizon meanwhile advanced to Yola, where he was able, thanks to gifts of weapons and silk, to sign a treaty with the emir on 25 August 1893. The Niger Company agent, William Wallace, arrived in Yola and demanded that Mizon pay duty on the goods he was carrying. Mizon refused, and Wallace, on 14 September, gave him twenty-four hours to comply or have his ships seized. Mizon replied that he would answer force with force, and sailed down the Benue in the launch *Mosca*, leaving the *Sergent Malamine* in Yola with eight tirailleurs and a French sergeant 'resident'. Wallace boarded the launch, arrested the French on board, and took it in tow. In Lokoja Mizon's ship was stopped and his ivory cargo seized. But Mizon was allowed to leave the Niger unmolested. In Paris he was again given a hero's welcome, and the imperialistic press managed to turn his misdeeds into a patriotic and high-minded crusade. Mizon went on to further exploration and died in the Indian Ocean in 1899.

Thanks to Mizon and other probing actions, the French were now gaining the distinct impression that the emperor had no clothes, that much of the territory south of the 1890 line had never seen an Englishman. Realizing what a mistake they had made in agreeing to cut themselves off from a lower Niger that was still ripe for the scramble, they began to look for ways to circumvent the agreement. After Mizon, their policy shifted. Instead of basing their claims on treaties, which the British could usually match, they began to occupy territories where there was no British presence. Also, by 1894 the French had established their first colony with an outlet on the Gulf of Guinea, Dahomey, a sixty-mile-wide band between German Togo and English Lagos. Dahomey provided an excellent base for sorties into the unoccupied hinterland of the lower Niger, saving the French months of difficult overland travel from the Saharan fringe.

The French, animated by the grand design of connected colonies from the Mediterranean to the Gulf of Guinea, wanted an open corridor that would link Dahomey with the rest of French West Africa, as well as access to the navigable Niger below the Bussa rapids. The obvious solution was to occupy the little-known kingdom of Borgu, south-west of Bussa and directly north of Dahomey. Since it lay on the Niger's right bank, it had not been included in the 1890 agreement. Moreover, Goldie had neglected to sign treaties with any of Borgu's rulers. Borgu could thus be said to belong to whoever occupied it first. This in any case was what the French intended to prove.

Anticipating their intentions, Goldie decided to send a mission into Borgu ahead of his French rivals. For this important task he picked a professional soldier who had already made his name in the pacification of Uganda, where he had ousted a pro-French faction to win the day for British interests – Frederick Lugard. The Borgu mission was Lugard's introduction to West Africa, where he would eventually make his name as the first governor of Nigeria and the apostle of indirect rule. Lugard was one of those remarkable Englishmen whose career was synonymous with the word empire. The eldest son of a Madras chaplain, his life could be summed up by listing the place names where he had served: Afghanistan, Burma, Uganda. His place in history, however, was earned as a man of peace, for it was he who created Nigeria out of the commercial company left by George Goldie.

Lugard became an employee of the Royal Niger Company, at £1000 a year. Like other employees he had to pledge secrecy and promise not to write anything about the company. Goldie advised him to proceed to Borgu with a small force. 'Presents and soft words,' he said, 'are more effective with these West African rulers than a force, sufficient to arouse alarm but not strong enough to overawe. Besides, we want treaties and not conquest.' Lugard's instructions were to 'zig-zag a good deal, so as to run networks of treaties across and between the few treaties obtained by the French'. The French, however, were bent on effective occupation as well as treaty-signing. Captain Decoeur was named head of the French mission to Borgu and told to occupy the places he visited. He left Marseilles on 24 July 1894, bound for Dahomey, from which he would recruit his troops and travel overland to Borgu. Lugard left Liverpool four days later.

The little-known, unexplored, and dirt-poor kingdom of Borgu had become the prize in a contest between France and England. The newspaper *Politique Coloniale* wrote that it was 'a veritable steeplechase . . . to gain that part of the buckle of the Niger which impinges on the lower river'. It was more like blind man's buff than a steeplechase, since neither Decoeur nor Lugard had the remotest idea where the Borgu capital of Nikki was situated. Decoeur had a head start and a shorter distance to travel, but Lugard had an advantage in being able to take the river route as far as Jebba. All that was known concerning Borgu was that its warlike people used poison arrows and had a superstitious fear of white men, and that its illiterate kings were under the influences of Moslem holy men.

Lugard reached Jebba by steamer in early September and got together forty raw Hausa recruits, forty donkeys, and 320 porters. It was the middle of the rainy season, and he continued overland to Bussa in driving rain. Progress was slow; it took eight hours to cross a single stream. The high wet grass soaked the sacks of hay used as saddles for the donkeys and doubled their weight. The frustrations of command in West Africa came home to Lugard, who wrote: 'To describe the difficulty of getting savages to grasp one's intention and assist with any semblance of sense, especially when one is ignorant of their language, is a task beyond the ability of my pen.' Reaching Bussa on 16 September 1894, Lugard met the king and wrote in his diary how much he disliked the company policy of 'abasement before these petty African chieflets'.

Lugard was hoping that Decoeur, who had a four hundred mile trek through jungle and savannah between Porto Novo and Borgu, would wait until the rains stopped. But Decoeur was just as determined as Lugard to win the 'steeplechase', and set off across the rain forest of lower Dahomey with 290 armed men. Spurred by the dismaying vision of Decoeur arriving in Nikki ahead of him, Lugard drove on his unmanageable crowd of porters, his donkeys 'as useless in the rain as brown paper', and his officers sick with fever. To keep his men marching, Lugard imposed a strict standard of discipline. A Nupe porter who dropped his load was given thirty lashes. 'As much as I abhor flogging,' Lugard wrote, 'if it has to be done I mean it to be done in earnest –

thirty lashes laid on so that each one leaves its mark for a week or more.' He was even harder on himself than on others. When he was feverish, 'ten grains of Antifyring and thirteen miles marching in a blazing sun, in a perfect bath of perspiration, put me right'.

Lugard reached the Borgu principality of Kiama on 15 October and signed a treaty with the king. He did not know that the people of Borgu believed the written word had magic powers, and that signing one's name was considered dangerous. Thus, the King of Kiama signed not his name but the name of one of his Moslem clerks. In Nikki, the Borgu capital which Lugard reached on 5 November, he was again duped by the natives. He had the satisfaction of seeing that Decoeur had not arrived, he had won the steeplechase. But a messenger met him outside Nikki, told him the king could not see him, and then spat into a bamboo container around his neck to protect himself from contact with the white men. The king was old and blind, Lugard was told, and the real power lay with his Moslem adviser, the Liman. Lugard gave the Liman presents and blank treaty form number twelve (for Moslems). On 10 November the treaty was signed, but the name of a king six years dead was used. Lugard, however, left Nikki confident that he had succeeded in his mission. 'I sincerely and earnestly hope,' he wrote, 'that after the treaties that I have made, which are thorough and not a farce, that the Company will never "swap" or abandon Borgu to France but get it included in the British Empire eventually.'

Five days after Lugard's departure from Nikki, Captain Decoeur trudged into the village with his tirailleurs and learned that he had come in second. This only made him more determined to sign a better treaty than Lugard's. His large force of soldiers was sufficient persuasion to make the King of Nikki sign a treaty placing himself 'under the exclusive Protectorate of France', on 26 November. With Decoeur's arrival in Borgu, the scramble on the lower Niger began.

Meanwhile, Lugard was ambushed in Borgu country on his way back to Jebba, on 17 November. Bowmen crawling through the high wet grass fired at his column at close range. The Hausas responded with wild firing, as dangerous to each other as to the enemy. Lugard was struck in the head by a poison arrow that pierced his pith helmet. A Hausa pulled at the arrow, but it was so firmly lodged that he had to brace his foot against Lugard's head for leverage. 'The only casualty in the fighting line was myself,' Lugard wrote, 'an arrow having penetrated deep in my skull. I ate indiscriminately all kinds of native concoctions said to be antidotes against the poison . . . the result proved satisfactory.' Lugard was back in Jebba on 13 January 1895, and from there returned to England, where he would remain until his services were again required on the Niger two years later. The first heat of the steeplechase had gone to England. But the French now knew that much of the area claimed by the Royal Niger Company was unoccupied, and initiated a policy of pinpricks, of missions and raids aimed at planting the Tricolor on the lower Niger.

In November 1894 Major Toutée and four other Frenchmen took the overland route from Dahomey and reached the Niger in February 1895. Toutée was travelling as a private navigator but began behaving like a political agent as soon as he was on the lower Niger, making treaties right and left, even in places like Kiama where Lugard had preceded him. The treaties contained clauses for occupation, building forts, and stationing garrisons in the area. Toutée built a fort across the river from a village called Bajibo in Nupe country, below the Bussa rapids, on the right bank of the Niger. It was called Fort d'Arenberg, in honour of the prince who supported the colonial party in Paris. Toutée was only twenty-five miles north of Jebba, which he visited in a dugout, finding a Royal Niger Company trading post directed by an unfriendly African named Wilhelm, who traded English goods against shea-butter, rice, and rubber.

As he navigated the Niger, Toutée expected to find the English well established above Bussa, but saw not a single Englishman in Bussa itself, and signed a treaty with its king. He wrote to his superiors that the French had been made fools of in the 1890 agreement. But his garrison in Fort d'Arenberg soon made itself unpopular by looting and interfering in local affairs, and the chiefs began to regret the days of Royal Niger Company control. Realizing that it would be dangerous for him to remain, Toutée asked to be evacuated downriver. This time, he found the company agents most helpful. In Jebba Wilhelm gave him a turkey and some canned milk. The brief French toe-hold on the

Niger was removed when Fort d'Arenberg was evacuated in September 1895 and subsequently taken over by the Royal Niger Company, which renamed it Fort Goldie.

By 1890 the Niger Company had set up more than a hundred trading posts on the lower Niger, and employed about fifteen hundred men. In 1892 Lord Salisbury could flatter himself that Goldie had succeeded in occupying the lower Niger 'without the expenditure of imperial funds, or the sacrifice of the life of a single British soldier'. In 1894 Henry Dobinson, archdeacon of the Niger, wrote: 'It certainly is an inspiration in this rather forlorn and desolate land to see in every river and settlement the brave old Union Jack floating in the breeze. Our countrymen are wonderfully energetic and pushing.'

The company's problems in the north stemmed from its inadequate presence. In the south, however, the company was so ever-present that no one else could trade on the Niger. Its monopoly was so rigidly enforced that some of the delta city-states were pushed into open hostilities because they were deprived of their livelihood. In 1893, after a long trade war, Goldie had bought out the Liverpool merchants'interests on the Niger. They had to restrict their trading to the Oil Rivers. After that, Goldie had a virtual one hundred per cent monopoly. He was the only trader on the lower Niger and the Benue.

The situation became critical for the delta city-states. Since 1891 the lower Niger had been divided into two areas – a Niger Coast Protectorate under Consul-General Sir Claude Macdonald, comprising the Oil Rivers area, and the company territory under royal charter on the lower Niger. Inhabitants of the delta city-states, which were part of the protectorate, were treated as foreigners when they entered Goldie's domain. A trader from Brass, who entered company territory to exchange his goods for palm oil, needed a licence to trade that cost £50 a year, plus £10 for every station traded at, plus another £100 if he intended to trade in spirits, without which trade in the delta had become impossible. On top of that, he had to pay duties on whatever goods he brought in and out. These fees and duties made legitimate trade impossible to the natives of the delta.

The only way the city-states could keep trading was to

smuggle canoes full of palm oil past Goldie's customs posts at night. The people of Brass, a large island at the mouth of the Nun river, were particularly active in this way. Goldie severely repressed the Brass smugglers, sinking their canoes when they were caught. Resentment at company arrogance grew in Brass. Brass had a legitimate complaint. Its villages were built on mangrove swamps that could produce next to no food. Its livelihood had always been based on trade, first the slave trade, then palm oil. It had converted from one to the other after repeated guarantees from the English that there would be no loss in the volume of trade.

The Landers, visiting Brass in 1823, had written: 'Of all the wretched, filthy, and contemptible places in this world of ours, none can present to the eye of a stranger so miserable an appearance, or can offer such disgusting and loathsome sights, as this abominable Brass town.' Reached through a forest of mangroves, it was built on marshy ground on the edge of a lagoon. At low tide the lagoon was a smooth, stinking surface of black mud. 'Even in the hands of an active, industrious race,' wrote the Landers, the soil 'would offer almost insuperable obstacles to general cultivation; but with its present possessors the mangrove itself can never be extirpated, and the country will, it is likely enough, maintain its present appearance till the end of time.'

Having been pushed out of their share of the palm oil trade by Goldie, the people of Brass were reduced to misery. Their chiefs were humiliated and angered by the company's harsh measures. This was no longer trade, but a monopoly situation that implied military superiority and the subjugation of dissident populations. As further reprisal for the smuggling, the company seized canoes bringing food to Brass. On one occasion the wife of a prominent Brassman was raped by a company clerk aboard one of the hulks used as depot. Pushed to the wall, the chiefs of Brass appealed to Macdonald, saying that 'the ill-treatment of the Niger company is very bad. They said that the Brassmen should eat dust. According to their saying we see truly that we eat the dust.'

By the end of 1894 the company blockade on the Niger had cut smuggling down to a trickle. In Brass a newly elected king called Koko convinced his people that taking up arms was the only way they could regain their trading rights and their honour. As Koko and the chiefs later wrote to Macdonald: 'If we Brass people die through hunger we had rather go to them [Goldie's company] and die on their swords.' Koko had a courageous but suicidal plan for attacking the company headquarters at Akassa, about twenty miles west of Brass, and consisting of thirty-five acres of wharves, customs houses, and repair shops. His ragtail army of badly armed men in war canoes was ready to take on the Royal Niger Company, which had a well-armed constabulary of several thousand men and was backed by British naval power.

Koko was counting on one surprise attack, so that the company too would eat dust. In January 1895 over a thousand warriors, practically the entire male population of Brass, moved silently in war canoes down creeks overhung with mangrove branches, towards Akassa. In the lead canoe stood King Koko, in battle-dress, his body rubbed with chalk, monkey skulls hanging from his waist. Koko was hoping for total surprise, but someone in Brass had warned the British. Mr Harrison, the acting vice-consul, who lived with the traders in a special part of town, had received a letter on the eve of the attack saying: 'Brass people leaving tomorrow at noon to destroy Niger company's factories and lives at Akassa on Tuesday morning. Be sure you send at once to stop them. AN OBSERVER.' Anderson at once advised the agent-general in Akassa, Joseph Flint, who refused to take the warning seriously. There was no constabulary in Akassa, and none was asked for. No defence measures were taken in the port.

The Brass war canoes came into Akassa on 29 January, in the pre-dawn darkness, under a heavy mist. Twenty-four African employees were slaughtered in their huts as they slept. Flint and his European colleagues were saved by the arrival of a mail steamer which distracted the Brassmen long enough for them to flee in a launch. In a fury of vengeance, the Brassmen went through Akassa with hammers and crowbars, West African Luddites destroying the machinery and engines of the hated steamships. They looted the warehouses and took sixty prisoners. The heads of the natives killed in the attack were taken back to Brass as trophies. About forty of the prisoners were eaten during a victory celebration; natives painted white danced as they held pieces of their victims. Several Christian chiefs of Brass refused to join in and spirited their captives to safety. Goldie was shocked. 'We always looked on Akassa as being as safe as Piccadilly,' he said.

Oddly enough, when news of the attack reached England there was considerable public sympathy for the Brassmen. It was felt that they must have had real grievances to be pushed into such a desperate act. For the first time the British government did not fully support Goldie. Macdonald's reports gave the Brassmen's side of the story, explaining that Goldie had caused their poverty and provoked their attack. Macdonald even explained away the cannibalism as 'a form of sacrifice which their forefathers have practised from time immemorial'.

A half-hearted punitive expedition was sent to Brass in February. The chiefs were asked to surrender their war canoes, weapons, and loot, and to accept a fine. They replied that they had nothing against the queen but would continue to oppose the Niger Company until they had their share of trade. The chief naval officer in the Bight, Admiral Sir Frederick Bedford, took a small fleet to Brass and gave King Koko an ultimatum to comply with the terms. When Koko asked for more time while secretly blockading the river, the British attacked Brass and burned several villages. The Brassmen were, however, allowed to keep their weapons. Goldie insisted that they surrender their guns. Macdonald wired the Foreign Secretary, Lord Kimberley:

> People of Brass understand thoroughly reparation has been and is being made for past offences; cannons, canoes, plunder and prisoners have been surrendered, and the chiefs who took part in the atrocities fined; towns are destroyed, trade almost ruined, women and children starving in the bush; hundreds have been killed; smallpox has been raging; the rainy season is beginning. I have seen all this and visited the towns destroyed. I most strongly deprecate further punishment in the name of humanity, and request a settlement of the question.

The Foreign Office decided to send a special commissioner, Sir John Kirk, to investigate the Brass situation. Kirk arrived in June, and the chiefs of Brass sent a letter to the Prince of Wales thanking him for the investigation and explaining that it was their

> grievances and sufferances here under the Royal Niger Company, which have driven us to take the laws into our own hands by way of revenge in looting the Company's factories at Akassa and

attacking its officials for which we are now very very sorry indeed, particularly in the killing and eating of parts of its employees . . . we now throw ourselves entirely at the mercy of the good old queen, knowing her to be a most kind, tender-hearted, and sympathetic old mother.

Sir John Kirk's report recommended giving the Brassmen duty-free access to the Niger. Kirk acknowledged that 'the rules in force are practically prohibitive to native trade, and the Brassmen are right in saying that this is so. They are for all intents and purposes excluded from the Niger if they are to respect these regulations.'

The same month the Brassmen sent their letter to the Prince of Wales, the Conservatives came back to power in England, with Lord Salisbury as Prime Minister and, for the first time, a devoted imperialist as Colonial Secretary – Joseph Chamberlain. From the moment he came to power, Chamberlain was determined to replace Goldie's company with direct British administration on the Niger. He was convinced that a private company could no longer cope with the growing international complications. He wanted England to take over the territory carved out by Goldie, and was not afraid of a direct confrontation with the French. With Chamberlain, British policy came full circle from the time when West Africa was considered a place to stay out of at all costs. Since Chamberlain was planning to replace Goldie, he shelved Kirk's report, which was concerned with reforming the Royal Niger Company. Thus the Brassmen, despite their plea to the Prince of Wales, continued to be excluded from trade. Goldie, however, was working himself out of a job.

Government intervention did not come for five more years, during which Goldie continued to run the company as a one-man show. During that period he had to face crisis after crisis. No sooner had the French challenge been met in the north than the Brassmen attacked in the south. No sooner had Brass been 'pacified' than the Anglo-French conference on the Niger resumed in Paris, in January 1896. Experts on both sides who had never seen the Niger argued for days over unfamiliar place names, and invoked treaties with native chiefs who did not have the remotest idea of what was in them. The talks were broken off in May when the English said they could not give the French access to the navigable Niger. No sooner had the conference been called off than a new threat to Goldie arose in the Moslem dominions of Nupe and Ilorin.

Nupe and Ilorin were powerful emirates above Lokoja, the first straddling the Niger, the second further to the west. Goldie had managed to remain on amicable terms with the emirs, but in 1896 points of friction arose. The Emir of Ilorin attacked a detachment of Lagos constabulary which he felt had occupied part of his territory. Chamberlain, always quick to take up the gauntlet, told Goldie to mount a campaign against Ilorin. At the same time Goldie was having trouble from Nupe, which was carrying out slave raids in company territory, and which had captured a patrol of forty-five constables in June 1896. Goldie resolved to march on Nupe in the autumn, as soon as the river was high, and then to take Ilorin.

In London Goldie supervised every detail of the campaign's preparation. He bought the first machine guns, Gatling guns, and had one brought to his London office, and sighted it across the Thames. He stirred up public opinion in his favour by presenting the forthcoming campaign as a crusade to suppress slave-trading in the two emirates. Both Nupe and Ilorin had standing armies. Nupe could raise between ten and thirty thousand men, armed with rifles, and much of its army was cavalry.

Goldie knew he would be badly outnumbered, but relied on technological superiority. He used canned foods for supplies, surrounded his camp with wire at night to trip up enemy cavalry, took along incendiary shells to set fire to thatch roofs, and bought electric searchlights and Maxim guns that could be carried in parts by porters. The period of peaceful trade was over. Like the French on the upper Niger, the British were being drawn into a large-scale military campaign.

The march on Nupe started from the company station at Lokoja on 6 January 1897. There were 513 African soldiers, 30 British officers, and about 900 porters, under the nominal command of Major Arnold. But Goldie also went along, as eager as a young officer on his first campaign, wondering how his Maxims and seven cannon would do against the Nupe cavalry. He was fifty, but he said the excitement made him feel like a twenty-year-old.

The Nupe capital of Bida, about a hundred miles north of

Lokoja, was reached on 26 January. In front of the city's fortified walls were massed thousands of Nupe horsemen in high-peaked saddles with huge brass and iron stirrups, their white robes ruffling in the wind, waving swords and spears, to the sound of small drums and deep horns. They charged Goldie's column, which broke and retreated to its camp on the far side of a ravine. There they fought off the Nupe horsemen, and their cannon inflicted heavy casualties on the massed cavalry. During the night, the twelve-pound Whitworth gun arrived and was fired at Bida, using compass bearings. The next morning, Goldie's troops advanced again, using the square formation and meeting the cavalry charges with co-ordinated volleys and rapid fire from the Maxim guns. When they got to 2500 yards from the city walls they were within artillery range. Shell after shell poured into the city, indicating their course with plumes of white smoke. The Nupe army scattered when they saw Bida on fire, but snipers in the bushes continued to harass the British flanks, and Goldie's manservant fell at his side, mortally wounded. His total dead were one officer and seven men. Modern armaments had carried the day. In Hilaire Belloc's words:

> *Whatever happens we have got*
> *The Maxim gun and they have not.*

Goldie marched into Bida, having won the most important battle ever waged on the lower Niger. It was important for two reasons: first, it put an end to the slave trade in the area, which Goldie had previously been forced to condone to remain on good terms with the emir. Goldie, convinced that it was the main cause of African 'backwardness', was now able to abolish the legal status of slavery in all the company's possessions. Second, it was the first application of indirect rule. Since Goldie did not have the personnel or resources to govern Nupe directly, he appointed a new emir who signed a treaty recognizing that Nupe was under the control of the company. The treaty said that 'the Emir Mohammed will govern the rest of Nupe (with the exception of a three-mile zone on the Niger's banks) but will conform to such directions in respect of his government as the representatives of the Company may give him from time to time'.

Indirect rule in what would one day be Nigeria did not arise from any theory of colonial government, but as a practical necessity dictated by the means Goldie had at hand. But it was in Goldie's nature to make of necessity a principle and in 1898 he became the first theorist of indirect rule, explaining why it was preferable:

> Even an imperfect and tyrannical native administration, if its extreme excesses were controlled by European supervision, would be, in the early stages, productive of far less discomfort to its subjects than well-intentioned but ill-directed efforts of European magistrates, often young and headstrong, and not invariably gifted with sympathy and introspective powers. If the welfare of the native races is to be considered, if dangerous revolts are to be obviated, the general policy of ruling on African principles through native rulers must be followed for the present.

After Bida, the capture of Ilorin was an anti-climax. Goldie's column surrounded the city on 16 February, and Ilorin was shelled to rubble. Again Goldie signed a treaty with the emir, who agreed, among other things, 'to take every step in his power to prevent the further introduction of gin and rum into his country from Lagos, and to destroy all the gin and the rum that may be found in his country'.

The Nupe and Ilorin victories were the high point of Goldie's career in West Africa. He was in theory merely the head of a private company that traded in palm oil for the benefit of its stockholders. Yet in that capacity he had led a military campaign against two powerful African leaders and conquered them. The Royal Niger Company flag flew from the fugitive emir's palace in Bida. The results of the campaign and its low cost of £25,000 were duly reported at the company council in London, in a burst of self-congratulation:

> If the magnitude of the results achieved, the powerful forces overcome, and the difficulties of carrying on war from a base itself 300 miles from the sea in an unhealthy Equatorial region, are taken into consideration, it may be confidently said that the Niger Sudan campaign has proved the least costly military operation of its kind in modern times.

But the campaigns were also Goldie's swan song, for as he took Nupe and Ilorin the French, moving in when his hands were tied, occupied Bussa. Lieutenant Bretonnet, who had accompanied

Mizon on his expedition, was in Bussa at the same time that
Goldie was taking Ilorin and wrote to Goldie that 'I have taken
possession in the name of the French Republic and I occupy
effectively the territory of Bussa'. Bretonnet called himself the
'French Resident of the Middle Niger', an area which he said he
was planning to administer. The French occupation of Bussa
eventually brought France and England to the brink of war on
the Niger and destroyed Goldie's charter company. It was a test
case of whether effective occupation superseded treaty rights.
Bussa was not the unexplored Borgu, it was a station on the
Niger which Goldie's company had claimed since 1885. Occupying Bussa was striking at the heart of the company's claims. In
this direct confrontation with a foreign power, it became appa-
rent that a private company could no longer be left to handle the
interests of England or cause the commitment of government
troops.

Goldie had brilliantly employed the refurbished seventeenth-
century device of the chartered company to annex great blocks
of West Africa for Britain. The Royal Niger Company had done
a heroic job of keeping poachers off its grounds, but between
challenging Nupe and challenging France there was some difference in scale.

As Margery Perham so nicely summed it up in her biography
of Lugard, the European nations in Africa at this time

> were not unlike a lot of greedy, quarrelsome children in a school
> playground; none quite big enough to dominate all the others,
> kicking and then making up to each other, sulking, coaxing, tell-
> ing each other secrets and then 'splitting', combining for a
> moment and then breaking up. Britain was the rather aloof child
> in the corner, a little superior, unwilling to join wholeheartedly in
> the rough games, and yet warily watching lest too many of these
> quarrelling schoolmates combined against her.

On the Niger, however, Britain became less and less the aloof
child in the corner, and was increasingly obliged to join in the
rough games.

When the Portuguese discovered Benin in 1485, it was a prosperous little kingdom with an intelligent, civilized people,
whose bronze 'lost wax' statues are still considered the highest

achievements of African art. The Oba, or king, was a member of an old and uninterrupted dynasty. He lived in an impressive palace, surrounded by courtiers, priests, and wives. His subjects accepted him as ruler by divine right, and the sole arbiter of life and death. To exercise this power, and to placate supernatural forces, the Oba conducted human sacrifices during elaborate court ceremonies, such as the royal coral beads feast.

The Benin capital, Benin City, was more of a real city than other West African communities, with the exception of the great cities on the Niger bend, Djenne and Timbuctu. It was encircled by a high ochre wall and a broad ditch six miles in circumference. Around the Oba's palace were a council hall, shrines, workshops, walled quadrangles containing the altars of past kings, and a dormitory for the Oba's wives. Early visitors lauded the excellent reception Benin gave white men. A seventeenth-century trader, James Barbot, wrote that 'Europeans are so much honoured and respected at Benin that the natives give them the emphatic title of . . . children of God'.

Benin's fortunes increased with the growth of the slave trade, and its influence extended beyond its borders. But when the English moved in and fought the slavers Benin began its slow decline. The Oba, in retaliation to English policies, closed his country to trade. Isolated in the delta, cut off from trade, in thrall to its king and priests, the Benin people fell into degradation, multiplying tortures and human sacrifices to please the gods and improve their fortunes. Few Englishmen had ever been to Benin City. But in 1892 a consul managed to sign a treaty with the Oba placing the country under British protection and abolishing the slave trade and human sacrifice. The Oba, however, could not remain in power if he respected the treaty. He resisted further offers to open trade.

Benin was outside Goldie's domain; it was under the jurisdiction of the Niger Coast Protectorate. Putting pressure on Benin, protectorate officials encouraged non-Benin traders not to pay Benin customs, cutting off one of the little kingdom's last remaining sources of income. The Oba stubbornly refused to give in. Benin appeared to the British as an enclave of dissidence and barbarism in the delta protectorate, where elsewhere the palm oil trade was thriving and slavery and human sacrifices were being stamped out. In December 1896 the acting consul-general,

James Phillips, sent a message to the Oba saying that he would like to visit him to discuss the opening of trade and the abolition of human sacrifice.

Without waiting for an answer, Phillips mounted his expedition. To prove his peaceful intentions, he did not take a military escort, but invited other protectorate officials and several members of trading companies. To add a colourful note, he took along the protectorate force's drum and fife band. English and native veterans of the delta advised Phillips against going. A native chief dropped on his knees and pleaded with him. But Phillips was ready, with 240 carriers and nine other Englishmen, whom Captain Alan Boisragon, of the protectorate constabulary, described in polo terms as 'men hard to hustle off the ball'.

While preparing for departure in Sapele, a delta village forty miles south of Benin City, in December 1896, Phillips received a message from Oba Ovonramnen, thirty-fifth of his line, explaining that he was in the midst of observing an annual ceremony called the *Ague*, celebrating his father's death, and during which he could not be seen by strangers. He asked Phillips to delay his visit. A messenger was sent with Phillips's reply:

> The acting consul-general received the king's message and was pleased to hear that his friend, the king of Benin, had been gratified with the present sent up to him. As he accepted this present it proved that the king was the white man's friend and he [Phillips] was now coming to visit the king with nine other white men and was bringing a much larger present. He regretted he could not wait two months, as the king suggested, but he had so much work to do in other parts of the protectorate that he was obliged to come up now.

Before leaving, the ten white men – Phillips, two constabulary officers, four protectorate officials, and three trading company agents – learned the Benin form of greeting: one made three circles with the closed right hand, while the left hand was held open with the thumb pointing upwards. Then one rubbed the two open palms together and nodded slowly, saying: 'Adoo, adoo.'

Phillips decided to send back the drum and fife corps, whose uniforms might have cast doubts over the mission's peaceful intentions, and left Sapele on 2 January 1897. They boarded the steam launches *Daisy* and *Primrose* and went west on the Benin river to Gwatto creek, where they disembarked and began the twenty-eight miles overland to Benin City. The carriers followed the launches in canoes.

Phillips decided the order of march, with himself in the lead, flanked by a guide and an interpreter, who were dressed in what looked like cycling outfits, knickers, stockings, and tennis shoes. Phillips's orderly, wearing a blue uniform, carried the consul-general's flag, a blue ensign with the protectorate crest in the corner. He was followed by the other white members, and the long line of native carriers. Phillips told the officers they could carry revolvers so long as they did not show them. Captain Boisragon and Major Copland-Crawford, the two constabulary officers, had removed their coats because of the damp heat and left their revolvers in their locked boxes.

Their overland trek began on 4 January, over a smooth, level path, cleared of creepers, with bush on both sides. The members of the mission were in high spirits. They promised that they would celebrate Copland-Crawford's birthday on 6 January, and observed that it would be the first time such a large party of white men had ever drunk Her Majesty's health in Benin City.

The first Benin men they met seemed glad to see them, and gave them 'the freedom of the country' by washing their boots. Another messenger was sent to the Oba with a lamp, a bottle of gin, a piece of cloth, and a malacca walking stick. By 3 p.m. they were half-way to Benin City, with only fourteen miles to go. One of the protectorate officials, Mr Locke, had stopped to tie a bootlace, when a volley of gunfire rang out from the bush. They thought it was a fusillade in their honour until they saw the porters scatter. Captain Boisragon doubled back to find his revolver, but Phillips, standing in the middle of the path in his pith helmet, called out: 'No revolvers, gentlemen.'

Looking for his box, Boisragon saw six carriers lying in the road. Their heads had been cut off with machetes. 'Impossible as it sounds,' he wrote, 'one poor chap was sitting on the ground straight up, but with no head.'

Phillips, standing conspicuously at the head of the column, was killed almost at once. Major Copland-Crawford went towards the warriors, making the Benin salutation. 'I can see the dear old man now,' wrote Boisragon, 'standing some way in the bush, nodding his head like an old Chinese Mandarin, rubbing his hands slowly up and down.'

The sound of a big drum came from the distance, and the interpreter clapped his hands to his ears and said: 'My God, the war drums.' A native fired point blank at Boisragon, who was hit in the right arm. 'The force of the blow was so great,' he wrote, 'that it knocked me over like a shot rabbit.' When he got back to the others only Locke was still alive, although he had been hit four times.

Locke and Boisragon escaped into the bush, scrambling on their hands and knees through brambles with barbs like fish-hooks. The Benin warriors were too busy quarrelling over the loot to pursue them. They hid until nightfall and the next day looked for Gwatto creek. For five days they lived on plantains and dew from leaves. Boisragon's wound was gory and fly-infested. 'My arm had begun to go bad,' he wrote, 'and smelled so much that it made Locke very nearly sick, and forced him to get away from me as far as he could, and made me wish I could do the same.'

When they reached the creek, friendly villagers took them in hand and got them past Benin patrols by hiding them under mats in their canoes. Rounding a bend in the creek, they came upon a protectorate launch, and soon their rescue was being toasted with champagne.

The massacre of an unarmed British column on a peaceful mission required an immediate reprisal. Less than a month later, ten ships steamed up the Benin river, carrying a force of twelve hundred men under the command of Lieutenant-Colonel Hamilton. On 4 February Rear Admiral Rawson and Consul-General Moore inspected the troops in Sapele. An advance column of seven hundred men began the northward march to Benin City, on a path so narrow that a man could touch the bush with outstretched arms. They marched under huge cotton trees whose splayed roots straddled the path, and tangles of orchid-studded creepers. There was an overpowering smell of decay, and the danger of malaria and cholera. The men wore medicinal 'cholera belts'. They fired precautionary volleys ahead of them and put a Maxim gun up front when they saw that the Benin warriors always attacked the head of the column rather than its centre, where they would have done greater harm.

THE NIGER DIVIDED (II)

Even though they were marching through the maze of water-ways that is the Niger delta, there was a water shortage. The attacking force was cut to five hundred men, which marched on Benin City with two days' water rations. They fought off ambushes, and white casualties were buried where they lay, their tombstones just names carved on trees. The long column, expanding and tightening like a concertina, advanced along the trail. On 17 February, one day's march from Benin City, they saw their first human sacrifice, a gagged and mutilated young woman lying on the grass next to a goat with broken knees. Commander R. H. Bacon, one of the officers in the advance column, asked the guide what it meant and was told it was to prevent the white men from coming any further. When they came upon a second sacrifice, one of the soldiers said: 'It is just about time someone did visit this place.'

The next day they came upon a stockade with a cannon from the days of the Portuguese. They were now within artillery range of Benin City, and poured shells inside the walls. People in the city later said: 'There was not a white man in sight. Yet here were two messages from the sky. Truly the white men are gods.'

As they approached Benin City they were fired upon by warriors hiding in tree platforms. One thousand yards from the walls, a group of warriors made a stand but dispersed after a skirmish, some of them up trees. The Benin capital was captured on 18 February 1897, six weeks after the massacre. The total casualties were three officers, ten seamen, and four Africans killed.

The Oba and his entourage had fled when the shelling began, and the British forces set about systematically destroying the city. As Commander Bacon wrote: 'We wanted to teach them a lesson of respect for the poor fellows they had murdered and the White Queen they had insulted.' Benin City was a large rambling town, divided by a broad avenue, with houses of red mud thatched with palm leaves. Near the Oba's palace there was a palaver house, a large oblong building with a roof of galvanized iron, and doors covered with stamped brass, and the sculpture of a huge brown serpent fixed to the wall. Further on were store-houses full of the cheap finery the traders used to decorate the natives, absurd satin umbrellas, glass walking sticks, and comic opera gold-braided uniforms.

307

Then came the juju compounds, grassy enclosures surrounded by high walls, with an altar at one end where sacrifices were performed. On the raised altars stood carved ivory tusks on top of antique bronze heads. In front of each bronze and ivory god there was a small mound on which the victim's severed head was placed. The altars were drenched in blood and the grass in the compound seemed to have been watered with blood. 'No white man's internal economy could stand the smells,' wrote Bacon, 'the whole town seemed one huge pest-house.'

To Victorian English officers, Benin must have presented a scene of pagan depravity beyond imagination. Captain Boisragon described

> altars covered with streams of dried human blood . . . huge pits, forty to fifty feet deep, filled with human bodies dead and decaying, and a few wretched captives rescued alive . . . everywhere sacrificial trees on which were the corpses of the latest victims . . . on the principal sacrificial tree, facing the main gate of the King's Compound, there were two crucified bodies, and 43 more in various stages of decomposition. On another tree a wretched woman was found crucified, whilst at its foot were four more decapitated bodies. To the westward of the king's house was a large open space, about 300 yards in length, simply covered with the remains of some hundreds of human sacrifices in all stages of decomposition.

Decaying bodies were not all that the British found, however. Bacon wrote that 'buried in the dirt of ages, in one house, were several hundred unique bronze plaques, suggestive of almost Egyptian design, of really superb casting . . . in one well forty-one tusks were discovered. Of other ivory work, some bracelets suggestive of Chinese work and two magnificent leopards were the chief articles of note. Bronze groups of idols and two beautifully-worked stools were also found'.

On one hand fanatical cruelty and killing, on the other the greatest treasure of African art ever discovered. The combination was baffling, and the English did not linger to ponder its meaning. They left a destroyed city after three days, taking with them 2500 bronzes and ivory sculptures. 'Goodbye Benin,' Bacon wrote, 'your character must indeed be bad if the longing of 700 men to see you is in three days changed to a fervent desire never to look upon your red walls again.'

The Oba was pursued and captured. After a judicial hearing he was deported to Calabar, where he died in 1914. Other chiefs directly responsible for the massacre were captured and executed. After deporting Oba Ovonramnen, the British were forced to rule the kingdom, for by Benin law a new Oba could not be crowned while the old one still lived. As Consul-General Moore wrote, the British expedition had freed the Benin population from 'a most appalling yoke of pagan Ju-Juism, which deadened every feeling of right and crushed out all desire for improvement . . . I suppose that no worse state ever existed in any country or at any time'.

Like the French, who occupied Timbuctu after Colonel Bonnier's column was massacred by the Tuaregs, the British were pushed into direct rule of a delta state by an ambush. It was the only way they could put an end to the native practices they could not abide, human sacrifices, cannibalism, and slave-raiding. The same year and the same month, February 1897, and almost on the same day, the British task force in the delta took Benin City and George Goldie captured Ilorin. But Goldie now had to face a direct French threat in Lieutenant Bretonnet's occupation of Bussa.

This threat was too serious to be settled at the local level by Goldie, by sending out a punitive expedition against the French. It was a conflict between French and British colonial policy. The French, pushed by a vigorous Foreign Minister, Gabriel Hanotaux, held that on the Niger 'possession was title'. The Royal Niger Company continued to argue that title belonged to whoever could claim priority of treaty, whether the area was occupied or not. But British rights seemed increasingly theoretical in the face of an effective French presence on the Niger.

For the first time the Niger question took priority in French and English foreign ministries. The possibility that France and England might go to war over the issue was expressed. The initiative passed from Goldie to the Colonial Secretary, Joseph Chamberlain, who embodied a new age of aggressive imperial expansion which would lead England to Fashoda and the Boer War. Chamberlain had been named Colonial Secretary in 1895 and held the post during eight critical years. He was the first Colonial Secretary to realize that formal state control was needed in West Africa, because the traders, instead of guaranteeing peace, were contributing to unrest. He was also a devout believer in the British imperial mission, peppering his speeches with statements like 'the British race is the greatest of governing races that this world has ever known' and 'we are predestined by our defects as well as by our virtues, to spread over the habitable globe'. From the start, Chamberlain took a hard line. 'My own idea,' he wrote, 'was that the only hope of a peaceful arrangement was to convince the French, from the first, that they had tried our patience too far and that they must give way or take the consequences.'

Chamberlain stopped relying on treaty rights as Goldie had done and decided to meet occupation with occupation. He developed what he called a 'chess-board policy', which meant that everywhere the French built a post the British would move in next to them, until the Niger region looked like a chessboard covered with French and British squares. Unlike his predecessors, who had been satisfied with letting Goldie run things, Chamberlain was ready to spend money and commit troops to defend British interests on the Niger. He decided to create a West African Frontier Force to police the chessboard.

For the first time since Goldie had been granted his charter, what was good for the Royal Niger Company was no longer good for the British government. The government wanted to keep the French out of the area, even if it meant fighting. Goldie's main interest was to control river navigation for commercial reasons. The Niger Company had pioneered imperial aims by staking out territory that no one claimed. Now that there were rival claims, imperial and commercial aims diverged. Goldie was in favour of retrenchment around the Niger to protect trade, while Chamberlain was intent on not giving up any territory to France, and said he would hold on to the Niger 'even at the cost of war'.

Chamberlain was a stockholder in the Royal Niger Company, and a long-time sympathizer with its objectives, but when the two men met on 27 May 1897 Goldie managed to alienate the Colonial Secretary. He refused to assist imperial troops with company funds unless he was guaranteed that the company would retain its charter. Goldie's position was based on the feeling that if the charter was going to be revoked there was no

point in spending company money. He held that the charter
company was not responsible for defending itself against the
aggression of foreign powers. But by refusing to support the
frontier force, Goldie sawed off the branch he was sitting on,
and ensured the revocation of his charter. For, if the government
had to pay the entire cost of the frontier force, it felt it might as
well take over the territory and obtain some revenue from its
administration to offset costs.

Patience and understanding of someone else's point of view
were not among Chamberlain's virtues, and on 19 September he
wrote to the Under-Secretary of State for the Colonies, Lord
Selborne: 'If this is his [Goldie's] view, our best course will be to
expropriate him lock, stock, and barrel, paying the capital value
of his property but allowing nothing for goodwill on future profits, since these are altogether dependent on the expenditure we
are to make.'

On the Niger, the French Tricolor flew in an increasing
number of places, and in Paris in August 1897 the Niger Commission reconvened. Neither side would bend from its basic
position. The British wanted evacuation of the French, and the
French insisted on a corridor from Dahomey to the Niger, one
hundred miles long and thirty miles wide.

Chamberlain chose Lugard to head the frontier force, because
of his successful race to Borgu in 1890 and his friendship with
Goldie, who was still a formidable power in the area. Lugard
was summoned to the big room of the Colonial Office, with its
globes and maps and fireplace, on 12 November 1897. He
found Chamberlain's haughty, monocled countenance rather
awesome. 'When he screwed his eye-glass,' Lugard wrote, 'you felt
as if you were going to be sifted to the marrow.' Chamberlain
was abrupt and domineering. Their conversation, reconstructed
from Lugard's private diaries, went as follows:

'When will you be ready to go?'

'Whenever I am ordered.'

'You had better go at once. Nothing will be done until you get
out.'

'Certainly. But I hardly yet know what I am to do.'

Chamberlain explained his chessboard policy. Lugard was to
occupy the country where the French held posts and infiltrate the
country around them. Lugard should never fire the first shot,

'but if through them a collision should occur, *tant mieux*, and we can go for them'.

Lugard, although opposed to the chessboard policy, said nothing, but 'as J.C. went on, I purposely showed in my face and manner my strong dissent – as he became domineering, I grew very obstinate and reserved'.

Reginald Antrobus, head of the African section, came in and said that Goldie continued to make difficulties over the frontier force. Chamberlain was furious. 'Goldie is always changing and I never know where he is,' he said. 'He had agreed definitely [to support the force] and even made other proposals regarding his own future which I am prepared to consider. Well, anyway, you will have 300 of their men.'

'I have had a note from Sir George,' Lugard said, 'who says he is probably resigning the governorship.'

'If the Niger Company do not help, it will be the worse for them,' Chamberlain fumed. 'Anyhow, we have all their resources. You are to raise a small West African army to go anywhere in Africa and do anything.'

'Such a force would not be available for eight months or a year; until then it would be only an armed rabble.'

'I don't expect you to do anything for a long time,' Chamberlain said, contradicting his earlier statement that he wanted Lugard to get going at once. 'You are to advise the government of all the requirements of such a force. Expense is no object – plenty of guns and everything. Two gun-boats will be there practically under your orders. Where will you have your head-quarters, I wonder?'

'Lokoja,' Lugard replied, for he wanted complete independence from the protectorate and from the Royal Niger Company.

Lord Selborne, the Under-Secretary of State for the Colonies, who was also present, had noticed Lugard's disapproving expression, and suggested he speak his piece about negotiations with the French. Lugard asked Chamberlain if he could speak frankly and was told he could.

'Then send an ultimatum to Paris,' Lugard said, 'saying that unless they withdraw from Bussa, about which, unlike the rest of Borgu, there can be no dispute, there will be a collision. Then advance, occupying the banks of the Niger, without going inland, since the river is the strategic base. Give Hanotaux a sop by the cession, as suggested by Goldie, of the Sokoto empire North of latitude 12 . . .'

Lugard's position was a faithful echo of the Royal Niger Company's policy of retrenchment around the Niger and giving up large tracts of land to the French. Chamberlain was made even angrier by Lugard's incursion into foreign policy and swore that he 'would never be a party to giving up our country in order to get what is already ours'. Lugard, feeling he could not implement a policy with which he was in total disagreement, decided to resign. It was Goldie, who wanted a frontier force commander who agreed with him rather than with Chamberlain, who persuaded him to remain. Lugard, with his usual zeal, threw himself into the recruitment of two battalions of twelve hundred men each, commanded by British army officers and NCOs. He supervised every detail, down to the tin-tacks.

Goldie was given assurances that he would be paid back for any money the company spent supporting the frontier force, and agreed to co-operate, even though he knew the company's days were numbered, for the Treasury was already studying the terms of reimbursement for its takeover.

On 27 January 1898 Lugard again went to Downing Street to see Chamberlain, who, aware of their differing views, asked outright: 'Are you prepared to undertake this task? Or must I find another man?'

'If you desire me to go, Mr Chamberlain,' Lugard replied, 'I go. But the policy is, in my opinion, wrong and it is impracticable.'

'I cannot send a man to carry out a policy in which he does not concur,' Chamberlain said. 'Let me hear your objections. I conclude they are military ones.'

But after Lugard had repeated his position, Chamberlain said: 'Well, I would like you to go, Lugard.' Thus Chamberlain sent a man to West Africa whom he knew disagreed totally with his instructions, which were to push into Borgu wherever the French were and disrupt their lines of communication.

Lugard arrived in Lokoja on 16 April 1898, with the rank of brigadier-general. He hoped that Goldie would succeed in upsetting the chessboard policy, 'for otherwise I am in the dilemma of having to carry it out, mad and impossible as it is'. In Paris the negotiations were deadlocked. The French press was up in arms over Lugard's appointment, which was described as symbolizing 'the fierce and grasping spirit of perfidious Albion'. Hanotaux warned that with French and British posts side by side, 'the hot temper of any individual officer may precipitate a war'. The men in the posts were cut off from regular communications with their superiors, and did not receive day-to-day instructions. There had already been incidents. In February, in a village called Boria, French Senegalese troops had ordered British Hausa troops to pull down the Union Jack. The Hausas stood fast, and no shots were exchanged. But if Chamberlain's instructions to occupy posts near the French and cut off their lines of communication were carried out, war would be hard to avoid.

The Anglo-French conflict on the Niger turned into a flag-hoisting war. James Willcocks, who had been Lugard's second-in-command on the first Borgu expedition, was sent forth to occupy posts near the French, hoist the Union Jack, and consider those places British territory. He left Lokoja on 24 April. An outbreak of hostilities would only be prevented if both sides kept their tempers when provoked.

In the heart of the Borgu, Willcocks raised the flag at a village two miles from Kiama, about fifty miles west of Bussa. On 5 May a French NCO with twelve Senegalese arrived and asked to see Willcocks. They saluted each other and each other's flags with rather forced courtesy. The NCO accused Willcocks of having invaded a French-occupied territory, and said: 'You have insulted our flag. The history of Borgu shows how England has over-ridden all treaties.'

'The history of Borgu,' Willcocks replied, 'has surely yet to be written.' The discussion remained even-tempered, and eventually the French NCO left. Willcocks continued on his semi-comic, semi-dramatic mission of finding out where the French flag flew while trying to keep the bullets from flying. Once he and his men approached a French post in pouring rain. They had no food and could not light a fire to boil water. The French corporal who commanded the post first protested at their presence and then gave them food and water.

Still exploring the area around Kiama, Willcocks reached a British village called Betikuta and found the French installed 400 yards away. He sent a message to the French resident at Kiama that unless the Tricolor near Betikuta was removed he would hoist the Union Jack 400 yards away from Kiama. The French, always strong on rhetoric, replied that Willcocks's 'evil deeds will raise a cry of horror throughout the land'. Willcocks was sure that this was the show-down, and that this game of 'capture the flag' in the African bush would precipitate a war between England and France. Preparing for the worst, he built a palisade and a trench two miles from Kiama and raised the Union Jack.

The obscure village of Betikuta was on the front pages of newspapers in Paris and London. Despite the clamour in the press, foreign offices remained calm, and stuck to the policy that local colonial interests should be subordinated to general Anglo-French relations. No one really wanted to go to war over Borgu. Lord Salisbury, the Prime Minister, wrote that he would not go to war 'for the sake of a malarious African desert'. In Paris, thanks partly to the presence in Borgu of Lugard's frontier force, the Niger Commission was anxious to reach an agreement. The British, who were at that time also racing the French on the upper Nile, were eager to settle before they took Khartoum, for, as Salisbury wrote to Chamberlain, 'we shall get nothing out of the French Assembly after that event'. The British ambassador to France, Sir Edmund Monson, did everything he could to reach a settlement. He saw the Niger question as an easily removed thorn in the side of Anglo-French relations.

On 30 May 1898 Willcocks sent Major Arnold with a company of infantry to plant the flag before Kiama, and prepared a reserve force should Arnold be opposed. 'I have seldom spent a more anxious hour', he later confessed. A French officer advanced towards Arnold and his men, made a formal protest, and said he would offer no resistance. Two hours later a French messenger arrived at Kiama to say that the signature of a Niger Convention in Paris was imminent.

On 7 June Lugard wired Chamberlain that there was a grave danger that fighting would break out. By this time Chamberlain had grudgingly swung round to Salisbury's less belligerent views. 'We are now,' he had written to Salisbury on 3 June, 'giving them [the French] what they asked for – they ought to be content. It is more than I am – except that I am glad to meet your wishes.' In this newly conciliatory frame of mind, Chamberlain replied to Lugard that he should avoid a collision at all costs. The agreement in Paris was days away, despite long French harangues about the mercenary quality of British involvement and rhetorical contrasts between the money-grubbing merchants of the Niger Company and the selfless Frenchmen whose only object was to spread civilization. The French public, however, was by now absorbed by the Dreyfus case, and had lost interest in the Niger.

On 14 June 1898 the Niger Convention was signed, providing a happy, bloodless ending to twenty years of Anglo-French rivalry on the Niger. No French or English soldier was called upon to 'die for Betikuta'. The agreement can be credited to Chamberlain's initial stubbornness, Lugard's soldierly reflex in carrying out a policy with which he disagreed, Salisbury's determination not to fight for Borgu, and Hanotaux's equal reluctance to start a war on the Niger. The French gave up their claim to a corridor from Dahomey to the lower Niger, and evacuated their posts on the river well above Bussa. Britain kept its hold on the lower Niger and Sokoto. The French were able to join their West African holdings, from Algeria on the Mediterranean to Dahomey on the Gulf of Guinea, and from Mauretania to the Congo. They later grouped these holdings into two vast federations, Afrique Occidentale Française in 1904, and Afrique Equatoriale Française in 1910. Two-thirds of the Niger flowed through French territory. England agreed to lease to France, for thirty years, two plots of land on the lower Niger, to be used as trade warehouses. In effect, the 1898 convention established the broad outline of modern Nigeria's borders. Nikki, the capital of Borgu that Lugard had reached before the French in the 'steeplechase' of 1890, was lost to England and became a part of French Dahomey.

Boundary commissions were set up to trace borders that were the result of a compromise between the territorial demands of two European nations. They completely ignored ethnic and geographic factors. Tribes with identical pasts and cultures would soon find themselves under different laws and learning different languages, although the signers of the Convention in their wisdom included the following article:

It is understood that if the inhabitants living near the frontier thus determined should express the wish to cross the frontier in order to settle in the French possessions, or, inversely in the

British possessions, no obstacles will be placed in the way of their so doing, and they shall be granted the necessary time to allow them to gather in all standing crops, and generally to remove all the property of which they are the legitimate owners.

On 14 March 1900 the British commissioner John Irvine Lang met the French commissioner Major Georges Toutée in Dahomey, and they began tracing the border, using the primitive method of marking trees along an arbitrary line, taking advantage of natural boundaries like rivers whenever they could. On the trees were chiselled a rudimentary 'F' or 'E'. The markers were placed at five hundred yard intervals 'to impress the minds of the natives with the existence of a real frontier between the territories of the two European nations'. The boundary-tracing uprooted thousands of Africans, who left their homes in order to be on the same side of the border as the rest of their tribe.

The Royal Niger Company had played no significant part in the Niger Convention of 1898. Goldie had been overtaken by events, and it was only a matter of time before the charter was revoked. Now that borders were being traced, they had to be protected, and the territory within them administered by direct imperial control. The Royal Niger Company had outlived its use. Goldie, resigned to the company's fate, ran operations on a shoe-string, like a man who has sold a house and refuses to keep up maintenance on it even though he continues to occupy it.

The terms of transfer were worked out between the company and the Treasury. The company gave up its administrative powers, treaties, land and mineral rights, war materials, steamers and stores, and kept its plant, stations, and wharves. The total compensation amounted to £865,000, divided as follows: £300,000 covering the company's public debt, incurred as a result of the cost of administration; £300,000 in compensation for the expense of developing the territory; £150,000 for land and mineral rights; and £115,000 for company assets, buildings, ships, and other material.

Goldie did not feel this was an unduly generous settlement, and the Royal Niger Company council appealed to its shareholders' patriotism in a letter announcing the transfer and advising them that they should be content with the knowledge that they have 'added to Her Majesty's Empire a vast and populous province, including the most valuable section of tropical Africa, which would otherwise have been partitioned between foreign powers'.

As a large sum of public money was involved, the agreement had to be passed by both houses of Parliament. At about the time the Bill was coming up for debate, Goldie gave his only recorded interview, to Reuters, on 5 July 1899. Asked whether the government had made a good deal, he replied: 'Very much so, as a pecuniary transaction; for the empire is buying for a mess of pottage a great province, which has cost 20 years of arduous labour to build up, and for which either Germany, or France, or both, would have paid a very different sum.' Asked whether the company had made a good deal, Goldie replied with a story about a stagecoach passenger who had been robbed but was told he should consider himself lucky that he had been left his clothes. Concerning his personal feelings, Goldie admitted there was 'some slight wrench' in giving up his 'almost uncontrolled powers', and added, in terms couched in Victorian morality: 'There is also some pleasure at having realised what, in 1877, was only a conception, subject to risks of failure. Today Great Britain is about to take up and carry on our work, which, while giving peace and freedom to the millions of Nigeria, will add not inconsiderably to the well-being of the millions of our own island.'

Goldie wanted to get across that his real purpose had not been commercial but imperial. 'If we had had a little less ill luck throughout,' he told the Reuters correspondent, 'we should have extended British influence over double our present area, and should, in extent of territory, have rivalled British India. Not that the loss is very greatly to be regretted, for England has, in Nigeria, even as now limited, the most populous and valuable area of tropical Africa.' Goldie was then asked: 'Have you carried out all that you intended?' He replied: 'By no means!'

Chamberlain, who held £3000 worth of company shares, was reluctant to discuss the Bill in Parliament, but on 19 July 1899 he said in a brief speech: 'I do not think that even as a pecuniary bargain this country will have any reason to regret the change they are asked to assent to.' There were some MPs who thought the government was paying Goldie too much, and who pointed to discrepancies in the valuation of company property. But on

27 July, after a tame debate, the Bill passed the House of Commons, 181 to 18. It had no trouble in the House of Lords, where Salisbury paid tribute to 'the adventurers and patriots to whose efforts the preparation of this territory [for Imperial rule] is due'. The British government had bought an empire for less than a million pounds.

Goldie's bitterness at being ousted from Nigeria made the rest of his life a gloomy anti-climax. Privately, he complained that 'an imperial administration may steal a horse while a chartered company may not look over a hedge'. Chamberlain asked him to be governor of the new colony, but he refused, saying it was 'very mechanical' work. There was a move to call Nigeria 'Goldesia', as Rhodesia had been named after Cecil Rhodes, but Goldie would have none of it. Goldie was fifty-three when the charter was revoked. He might have embarked upon a second career of distinguished service, but he was a weary and disappointed man, who said, like Othello: 'I have done the state some service, and they know it. No more of that.' At the same time, he was too proud to accept appointments which did not give him the uncontrolled power he had enjoyed on the Niger. He was the sort of man who, like Milton's Satan, preferred to reign in hell than serve in heaven.

Goldie sold out his interest in the company, which continued to trade on the Niger and in 1920 was bought out by Lever Brothers. In 1904 he wrote to a friend that he no longer took 'a special interest in West Africa'. But he continued to be fascinated by great rivers, the highways of empire. At one time Brazil asked him to administer the upper Amazon, but he would not work for a foreign power. He became interested in China, and in 1900, on his first holiday in twenty years, set out to travel along the Yangtze. But he arrived in the midst of the Boxer Rebellion, and in the face of anti-European feeling was forced to turn back. His mind was filled with great ventures, but he never found another Niger. For the rest of his life he was out of the limelight, forced into an early retirement that must have been particularly galling for a man of his vigour and experience. He brushed aside the offers that came his way, such as the governorship of an Australian province.

Later he accepted odd jobs, drew up a plan for self-government in Rhodesia, was placed on two royal commissions, and became an alderman on the London County Council. It was better than running a golf course, as other men who had governed great colonial provinces returned to do. He became interested in the American race problem, and urged the United States government to deport its entire black population to Africa without delay. He worked out a detailed plan covering the cost and logistics of such a repatriation.

He developed a mania about publicity. He made his children promise never to write anything about him. 'All that I wish to be recorded of myself,' he said, 'can be read under the articles headed "Nigeria" and "Goldie" in the Encyclopedia Britannica. If you break this promise to me, I swear I will rise and haunt you.' Worse, he destroyed all his personal papers and the company records, which summed up the life of an institution that had played a decisive part in African history. Part of Goldie's action was due to a genuine distaste for self-congratulation.

> *L'oeuvre c'est tout* [he wrote], *l'homme c'est rien*. We (not I) bring up our children to think that fame, position, recognition by the public are proper objects of ambition. I loathed them all . . . real happiness is only found in doing good work, in however small (or great) a sphere. Having all my life regarded self-advertisers from Caesar to Napoleon as the worst enemies of human progress, I cannot in my old age forswear my principles, and join the army of notoriety hunters.

But another part was the *auto-da-fé* of an embittered man, who felt that his achievements had not been acknowledged. His pride turned inward and became self-destructive, and he condemned himself to historical obscurity.

In his early seventies Goldie's health failed. He had emphysema, in which air enters the tissues around the lungs. He could hardly walk or talk, and compared himself to a trout gasping in a fisherman's basket. He spent his time reading and reliving the past. On 20 August 1925, at the age of seventy-nine, he died in a small hotel room in Piccadilly. Over his grave in Brompton Cemetery stands a granite cross that says: 'Sir George Taubman Goldie, founder of Nigeria.' Dorothy Wellesley described it as

> a closed-in place, a cross, herded in with his fellows: in death, as in life, the least spectacular of men. A grave more unsuitable it is impossible to imagine. "Consistent to the end," I thought,

remembering the grave of Cecil Rhodes among the boulders of the veldt, and those of many nonentities who lie in Westminster Abbey, and St Pauls. In Brompton Cemetery are no great spaces, no rivermouth, no wind from the sea.

Since Goldie did not want to be governor of the newly formed Protectorate of Northern Nigeria, the job went to his old friend Lugard, who was back in Lokoja on 31 December 1899. The next morning, 1 January 1900, troops of the West African Frontier Force and the Royal Niger Constabulary drew up in a hollow square on the Lokoja parade ground, a space cleared out of the bush not far from the 'Y' where the Benue joins the Niger. At 7 a.m., in the chill morning air, Lugard and his civil aide walked from his riverside bungalow up the laterite road to the parade ground. In one corner of the parade ground the Royal Niger Company flag flew from a tall staff. Standing under the flag, Lugard read the queen's proclamation. The company flag was hauled down, and the Union Jack was run up. The batteries flanking the troops fired a 31-gun salute as an African military band struck up 'God Save the Queen'. The troops gave three cheers for their new sovereign. Lugard read the royal warrant of appointment for the British officers and NCOs. The troops marched round the parade ground, and Lugard complimented them on their appearance. The queen's proclamation was read in Hausa, Yoruba, and Nupe. The constabulary were told they were now part of the imperial forces. With that, the powers of the Royal Niger Company were turned over to the British crown, which acquired an area of close to half a million square miles. Two new provinces, Northern and Southern Nigeria, were incorporated by the Order in Council of the queen into the British empire. After the explorers and the traders, the age of civil servants had dawned.

That evening at dinner with Lokoja's entire British population of fifty persons, Lugard in his toasts remembered the Niger Company's early days, when it had fought off the French and hostile tribes with hardly any support from the government. Goldie had won for England a vast area, despite indifference at home, and created a situation where 'an Englishman's word is regarded as a thing that is never broken. An ignorant savage will accept a piece of paper on which is written he knows not what, secure in the certainty that this just demand will be honoured on presentation.'

As Margery Perham, Lugard's biographer, writes: 'The speeches were over, the flag was up, and the next morning Lugard sat down in his makeshift office and faced the cold realities of his assignment.' Lugard was to remain in Nigeria another eighteen years, first as high commissioner of Northern Nigeria, then as governor of all of Nigeria after the northern and southern parts were amalgamated in 1914.

For Goldie indirect rule had been a practical necessity. Lugard made it a principle of government.

> In the earlier stage of British rule [he wrote], it is desirable to retain the native authority and to work through and by the native emirs. At the same time it is feasible by degrees to bring them gradually in approximation with our ideas of justice and humanity . . . in pursuance with the above general principles the chief civil officers of the provinces are to be called Residents, which implies one who carries on diplomatic relations rather than Commissioners or Administrators.

On the upper Niger, the French overthrew and replaced native chiefs and tried to govern their West African territories in the same way that they governed Brittany or the Auvergne. The policy of direct rule had its roots in the historical formation of France. The great task begun by the Capetians and continued through eight hundred years of monarchy was to impose political and cultural uniformity on the welter of languages, customs, and feudal privileges that was provincial France. There was something deep in the French historical experience that led colonial administrators to pursue centralization as far afield as Africa. The English experience with the Scots and the Irish was quite different; they were never fully assimilated, and the Irish home rule question has not been solved to this day.

The French mission of centralization was continued after the revolution by every subsequent regime, but to it was now grafted the republican ideology that all men are created equal before the law. The rights of man were applied to French West Africa along with direct rule. The French policy was called 'assimilation', and was enshrined in the resolution of the Colonial Congress of 1889: 'All the efforts of colonization must tend to propagate among the natives our language, our methods of work, and gradually the spirit of our civilization.'

Thus the aims of France and England once they began ruling West Africa were quite different. The English believed they were a race endowed, like the Romans, with a genius for government, and that they had a vocation to guide colonized people towards self-government. They always maintained that their presence was temporary and that once they had formed native élites they would leave. The French believed they were a race like the Greeks, with a gift for transmitting the highest form of civilization, and that every African native was a potential Frenchman. They disregarded local customs, traditions, and social organizations, and imposed the *Code civil* and the lessons of French history textbooks. It never occurred to them that the Africans might be attached to their own form of civilization.

In practice, both direct and indirect rule were imperfectly applied, and both carried within them the seeds of contradiction. Lugard seemed on solid ground when he said that 'an arbitrary and despotic rule, which takes no account of native customs, traditions, and prejudices, is not suited to the successful development of an infant civilization, nor, in my view, is it in accordance with the spirit of British colonialism'.

The system of indirect rule worked well in Northern Nigeria, where powerful emirs had been ruling for centuries. British officials there practised a policy of deliberate self-effacement. There were native courts with native judges. The people paid taxes directly to the emirs, and the English collected half the proceeds to cover the costs of administration. Native treasurers were responsible for their own budgets. But even in the north, indirect rule had its limits. Certain local practices, such as mutilation for the punishment of crimes, in keeping with Koranic law, could not be tolerated. Lugard instituted flogging as a swift and relatively humane form of punishment. The flogger was restrained by having to keep cowrie shells in his armpit.

But in Southern Nigeria, with its hundreds of rain forest and delta tribes, political authority was hopelessly fragmented. Lugard approached the problem as he had in the north, combing the delta for men he could install as the southern equivalent of emirs. He never grasped the complex nature of tribal power, based on pressure groups, family ties, and layers of authority that provided checks and balances against one another. He imposed on the south a system that had worked in the special conditions of the north. In the Niger delta indirect rule meant having to accept cannibalism, twin-murder, and the poison ordeal. It meant supporting local rulers like the king or Alafin of Oyo, who when he took power entered the palace through a doorway newly cut into the wall, stepped over the blood of a sacrificed couple, and retired into his inner sanctum to eat his predecessor's heart.

Indirect rule in the south did not succeed in ordering the maze of tribal interests. It entrenched local chiefs and kept tribal rivalries alive. In the long run, the legacy of indirect rule to an independent Nigeria might be said to have contributed to the Biafran war. The existence of still powerful tribal chiefs created a permanent crisis that led to army intervention, rebellion, and secession.

The French, on the other hand, reduced the power of local chiefs. Symbols of traditional rank and other privileges were done away with. As Ken Post has written in *The New States of West Africa*, the French legacy 'was rather one of greatly centralized decision-making and administration, and of the supremacy of the executive over all other branches of government. Thus the institutions and values to hand were usually much more suitable instruments for the political élites than those at the disposal of their English-speaking counterparts.' The paradox is that indirect rule, working within the framework of existing native traditions, provided a less serviceable model for independent African nations than the steamroller of direct rule, which sought to abolish traditional elements of authority.

Direct rule was of course more flexible than it sounds. The Napoleonic Code was curiously adaptable to local custom. It was possible, for instance, by applying the logic of the Code, to conclude that cannibalism was not a crime. Where was the crime in eating a native who had died a natural death, before he was buried? His remains had not been sold, there had been no murder, no grave-robbing, no illegal trade. In many instances, the French were able to reconcile local practices with Western logic.

Sometimes there were cases that even the Code could not handle. A mysterious death in a village was attributed by rumour to an old sorceress. The French arrived with a doctor and a jurist. The doctor performed an autopsy and found no trace of poison. Rumour persisted and threatened to disturb public order if the guilty party was not arrested. The sorceress was questioned. Far from denying it, she cheerfully admitted casting an evil spell over the deceased. The jurist threw up his hands: 'Here was a village that wanted to punish the accused for a crime impossible to prove, and here was the accused confessing that crime, which to our Western minds could not have been committed: Where was the Code in all this?' The woman was let off.

The natives were just as baffled by the French as the French were by the natives. They could not understand why the *Code civil* provided that a man could be found guilty and then freed because of an irregularity in his trial. In one instance, a native truck driver was arrested eleven times for traffic violations. The twelfth time he was given a prison term for causing an accident in which several passengers were hurt. The sentence was voided because he had not been charged with two separate offences, violating a traffic regulation, and causing damage to his passengers. He was freed, and wondered at the strangeness of French justice.

The French soon found that the policy of assimilation was impossible to carry out. To make Frenchmen out of twenty million Africans proved as difficult as finding emirs in the Niger delta was for the British. It did not take long for assimilation to develop into the acceptance that Africans were culturally separate and impossible to assimilate, which had been the British view from the start. The French proclaimed the equality of Africans, while in fact the vast majority of Africans were denied the rights of French citizens. The colonial governors might be imbued with the rights of man, but their rule was nonetheless paternalistic and authoritarian. Natives could be jailed five days without a trial. They were second-class citizens. Legislation was by decree. The natives had no say in making their own laws. Education was focused on training clerks and subalterns. Thus the civilizing mission of the French, faced with the reality of West Africa, led to a régime of juridical inequality in a French republic founded on the rights of man. Like the English, the French acted in contradiction of their own policy.

The natives were finally given citizenship rights in 1946, after contributing their manpower reserves to two European wars. A French writer described the dream come true:

> West Africa is a French land, its inhabitants are as French as those of Romorantin or Pézenas . . . they may not dress like the people of Provence or eat like Bretons or get married like Lyonnais. But does that prevent them from being French? Is it wrong that there should be this diversity and that we are not all made according to the same model?

No British imperialist could have made such a statement. The English remained aloof from colonized people. They did not intermarry and breed a generation of half-castes. They did not want to turn the natives into Englishmen, for they did not believe such a transformation was possible. They saw their mission as essentially moral, to direct and guide inferior peoples for their own good. As Arthur Conan Doyle wrote:

> The running of a tropical colony is, of all tests, the most searching as to the development of the nation that attempts it. To see helpless people and not oppress them, to see great wealth and not confiscate it, to have absolute power and not abuse it, to raise the natives instead of sinking yourself, these are the supreme trials of a nation's spirit.

In England much more than in France an entire culture encouraged the imperial mission. Darwin taught natural selection and the survival of the fittest. Kipling was imperialism's poet laureate. Public schools stressed the values that made empire-builders: strength of will, firmness of character, fortitude, a sense of duty, and the stoic imperturbability best expressed in the famous exchange at Waterloo: Uxbridge – by God, I've lost my leg. Wellington – so you have. England, much more than France, was shaped by its imperial attitudes. Imperialism was a deep urge of the English collective psyche, the desire of an insular people for a larger life. It also allowed the English to demonstrate the fact of their inherent superiority. Cecil Rhodes put it most candidly: 'We happen to be the best people in the world, with the highest ideals of decency and justice and liberty and peace, and the more of the world we inhabit, the better it is for humanity.'

THE NIGER DIVIDED (II)

Viewed with hindsight, the imperial ideologies of England and France were necessary to justify the unprovoked invasion of a weaker people, the illegal occupation of their lands, and their economic and human exploitation. The myth was that the English and the French were settling Africa for the satisfaction of making the world a better place, which had the added benefit of proving to themselves their own moral excellence. Empires existed for the advantage of backward races and as evidence of superior peoples' virtues. The fact that empire was essential for France and England if they were to retain their rank as first-class powers was lost in the chorus of self-praise. Heightened rivalries between European powers in Africa had caused the scramble. Men like Chamberlain were willing to go to war over a few square miles of West African bush. Territorial expansion in Africa was proof of great power status in Europe.

By 1900 the Niger was permanently divided between two European nations who both claimed that imperialism was a noble and disinterested cause. They ruled the Niger until 1960, by which time Nigeria and all the French West African colonies had become independent. After this brief colonial interlude the river was returned to its first settlers, who used the borders drawn up by the European boundary commissions to mark out their own nations. And so the cycle closed, which had begun with the trials of a handful of explorers in an undiscovered land.

EPILOGUE

WEST AFRICA is so fixed in its ways that when I spent three months there in 1972, following the Niger's course from its source to its mouth, I had, two centuries later, experiences identical to Mungo Park's. Unpleasant as some of them were, they did give me a bond with the explorers I was writing about. I had done more than read their journals. I had covered the ground they had covered. Some of the things that had happened to them had happened to me. I could not know them physically but I could feel what they had felt. In this way I experienced what D. H. Lawrence called 'the spirit of place'.

On the ferry that crosses the Niger at Gao, my fellow passengers marvelled at my compass, checking the needle's direction against the position of the sun and praising the white man's magic. In Gao I washed my hair with scented soap and was walking down the street on my way to the police commissariat when I was attacked by a swarm of bees. They smelled the soap in my hair and mistook me for a flower. I fled, my hands shielding my face, but the bees followed, a thick and noisy halo that swirled about my head. I ran into the commissariat, and I have never seen a place empty so fast. The uniformed policemen climbed out of windows and hid in closets. I jumped under a desk, where the bees could not follow. When they returned, the police kindly spent twenty minutes extracting bee stings from my neck and head. When they told me that bee stings could be fatal, I remembered that the swarm which had attacked Park's expedition had killed seven donkeys.

EPILOGUE

In Mopti I was arrested, for reasons that remain obscure, by an over-zealous policeman. I think he objected to my entering a mosque with a loaf of bread under my arm. It soon became clear that the charges would be dropped if his palm was crossed with silver. That had not changed since Park's day: the natives still saw the white man as a heaven-sent opportunity for profit. Local potentates still had to be placated with offerings. In some places cowrie shells were still used as legal tender, but I was able to get by with coins and notes.

Like Park I was the victim of rapaciousness, and like him also the beneficiary of unexpected kindnesses. One evening in the bush outside Segou I ran over a guinea hen and was wondering how to cook it. A native appeared out of the darkness, gathered wood, made a fire, skinned the guinea hen, roasted it on a forked stick, and left as silently as he had arrived, refusing offers to share it.

In Timbuctu I was laid low for a week by a mysterious fever. As I roamed the silent dusty streets of that depressing town in the evening coolness, I decided that Africa defeats us all and that I should cut short my trip. Then I met a French drop-out who had been in West Africa eighteen months. He had reversed the colonial image of the superior, wealthy white man. He was poor, and begged from the blacks, as Park had been forced to do. In Abidjan a colonial settler had told him, shocked: 'I have been in West Africa thirty years and this is the first time I have ever seen a white man beg.' Meeting the drop-out made me resolve to go on.

If I had decided to leave, I could have flown out of Timbuctu. There are daily flights. Certain things along the Niger have not changed, but the river flows in historical time, and now planes are reflected in its water alongside dugouts. The river's physical appearance also changes, and in the early 1970s, after years of subnormal rainfall, it dropped to its lowest level in this century. In summers, normally the rainy season, it was carrying one quarter of its pre-drought flow. South of Gao, in the Niger bend, normally a deep navigable channel, giraffes were seen crossing the river. Timbuctu's river port of Kabara was dry; houseboats were grounded on the dusty, fissure-streaked river-bed. The pasture land of the inner delta pushed forth tufts of dry yellow grass. Cattle lay fallen like empty water-skins. In the drought that struck the countries on the Sahara's southern rim, the Niger became an inadequate rampart against the encroachment of the desert, which is advancing at the rate of several miles a year, turning rangeland to sand. Travelling down the Niger in that period of drought made me realize that rivers too are mortal.

The other great change on the Niger today is technology. In its Nigerian third, Old Bussa, where in 1806 Park was ambushed and drowned in the rapids, has vanished. In its place rises the Kainji dam, the fourth largest in Africa. Visitors can stand on top of the Kainji dam and see, on one side, a vast artificial lake that supplies Nigeria with tons of fish, and on the other 280,000 cubic feet of water per second roaring down from the dam's crest to be converted into electricity, for nine of Nigeria's twelve states, by whirring orange turbines. Somewhere beneath this man-made waterfall lie Mungo Park's bones.

Another facet of technology was evident in the Niger delta, which became for a time an enclave called Biafra. The road to Port Harcourt was littered with pieces of wrecked planes. During the war the road was used as an airstrip. The doors of native huts were decorated with post-industrial good-luck charms, bits of plane fuselage. The city of Onitsha, like Dresden after the Second World War, was bombed to rubble. It once boasted the largest covered market in West Africa.

In the wake of war the crime rate rose to the point that public executions took place, reminding one that it was not so long ago that Niger delta tribes like the Benin conducted large-scale ritual killings. A public execution in Port Harcourt in the summer of 1972 was held in the sports stadium. Newspaper announcements urged the population to attend. Beer was sold to the spectators. Six young thieves were tied to empty oil drums. They made brief statements of repentance over the loudspeaker system. The firing squad jogged onto the field and lined up. Blindfolds were applied, rifles were fired, and bodies went limp. The spectacle was strongly ritualistic.

When I reached the end of the Niger's course, coming out of the obscurity of the mangrove swamp into the brilliant light of the sea, I also came to one of the causes of the Biafran war, the channels dotted with the metal towers of the wells that pump up Nigeria's main source of revenue. In the former slave counters

EPILOGUE

of Brass and Bonny now stand the oil refineries and the gleaming steel cylinders of the 'tank farms', closed off by high metal fences. Giant tankers lie offshore waiting for the oil to be pumped into their holds. The Niger has been consistent in its role as provider. Its wealth has always been there, like the river itself, waiting to be discovered.

BIBLIOGRAPHY

Chapter one: The Niger Sought

Proceedings of the African Association, London, 1810.
Records of the African Association, London, 1964.
Sir Joseph Banks, by H. C. Cameron, London, 1952.
The Earth's Grandest Rivers, by Ferdinand C. Lane, New York, 1949.
Rivers and their Mysteries, by A. Hyatt Verrill, New York, 1922.
Mission du transatlantique, par le Capitaine Cortier: rapport geologique et hydrologique, par M. R. Chudeau, Paris, 1925.
The Penetration of Africa, by Robin Hallett, London, 1965.
The Niger Explored, by E. W. Bovill, London, 1968.
The Search for the Niger, by Christopher Lloyd, London, 1973.

Chapter two: The Niger Described

The description of the river is based on my travels from the Niger's source to its mouth, during three months in 1972.
    Other works consulted:
Les Sorkos (Bozos), by Z. Ligers, Paris, 1964.
Le Niger en kayak, by Henri Lhote, Paris, 1943.
In the Niger Country, by Harold Bindloss, London, 1950.
Etude da'ménagement du fleuve Niger, by O. Gautier, Paris, 1969.
Sociétés d'Initiation Bambara, by D. Zahan, Paris, 1960.
La Religion et la magie Songhai, by Jean Rouch, Paris, 1960.
Le Moyen Niger et sa boucle, by Gaston Mourgues, Paris, 1933.

BIBLIOGRAPHY

Le Niger en pirogue, by Jean Rouch, Paris, 1954.
Histoire des Bambara, by L. Tauxier, Paris, 1936.
Histoire des Peulhs, by L. Tauxier, Paris, 1934.
Quelques aspects de la magie africaine, by H. Labouret, Paris, 1950.
Du Niger au Golfe de Guinée, by G. L. Binger, Paris, 1892.
Le Niger, by E. Bèrc de Rivières, Paris, 1953.
Segou, vieille capitale, by A. Bime, Paris, 1952.
Essais sur la religion Bambara, by G. Dieterlen, Paris, 1951.
Organization sociale des Dogon, by D. Paulme, Paris, 1940.
Noirs et blancs en Afrique, by D. Westermann, Paris, 1937.
Living Races of the Sahara Desert, by L. Cabot Briggs, Cambridge, 1958.
Travels in West Africa, by Major W. Gray, London, 1825.
Le Niger, by F. de Lanoye, Paris, 1858.
Les Peulhs, by J. de Crozals, 1883.
Djenne, by Charles Monteil, Paris, 1932.
Sahara and Soudan, by G. Nachtigal, Paris, 1881.
The Negroes of Africa, by M. Delafosse, Paris, 1936.
People of the Veil, by F. R. Rodd, London, 1926.
Vision d'Afrique, by Louis Proust, Paris, 1924.
Le Plateau Central Nigerien, by L. Desplagnes, Paris, 1906.
Haut–Senegal–Niger, by M. Delafosse, Paris, 1912.
Voyages aux rives du Niger, by L. Jacolliot, Paris, 1878.
The Primitive City of Timbuktoo, by Horace Miner, London, 1955.
West African Religion, by G. Parrinder, London, 1949.
The Saga of the Niger, by R. Owen, London, 1961.

Chapter three : The Niger Reached

Europeans in West Africa, Hakluyt Society, London, 1941.
La Découverte de l'Afrique au moyen age, by Charles de la Roncière, Paris, 1925.
Description de l'Afrique septentrionale, by El Bekri, translation by Macguckin de Slane, Paris, 1859.
Travels in Africa and Asia, by Ibn Batuta, London, 1929.
Voyages, by Cadamosto, Hakluyt Society, London, 1937.

History and Description of Africa, by Leo Africanus, Hakluyt Society, London, 1896.

Tarikh es Sudan, by Abderrahman-Essadi, translation by Houdas, Paris, 1898.

Tarikh el Fettach, by Mahmoud Kati, translation by Houdas, Paris, 1913.

Navigations médiévales, by R. Mauny, Lisbon, 1960.

The Age of Reconnaissance, by J. H. Parry, New York, 1963.

Tableau géographique de l'ouest africain au moyen age, by R. Mauny, Dakar, 1961.

The Golden Trade of the Moors, by E. W. Bovill, London, 1968.

Relation d'un voyage du Touat, Charles de la Roncière, Paris, 1919.

L'Islam dans l'AOF, by A. Gouilly, Paris, 1952.

The Immense Journey, by Loren Eisely, New York, 1970.

Les Empires du Mali, by Charles Monteil, Paris, 1968.

Lost Cities of Africa, by Basil Davidson, New York, 1959.

Britain, Sahara, and Western Sudan, by A. Adu Boahen, London, 1964.

Caravans of the Old Sahara, by E. W. Bovill, London, 1933.

African Glory; the Story of Vanished Negro Civilizations, by John C. de Graft-Johnson, New York, 1955.

L'Empire de Gao, by Jean Boulnois, Paris, 1954.

Islam in West Africa, by J. Spencer Trimingham, Oxford, 1959.

European Beginnings in West Africa, by J. W. Blake, London, 1937.

Conquest of the Western Soudan, by A. S. Kanya-Forstner, London, 1969.

A Thousand Years of West African History, by Ian Espie, London, 1965.

Maps and their Makers, by G. R. Crone, London, 1953.

The Geography of Claudius Ptolemy, by E. L. Stevenson, New York, 1932.

L'Europe découvre l'Afrique, Hubert Deschamps, Paris, 1965.

Histoire des explorations, Hubert Deschamps, Paris, 1967.

Missions to the Niger, Hakluyt Society (4 vols), London, 1956.

European Beginnings in West Africa, J. W. Blake, London, 1937.

BIBLIOGRAPHY

Chapter four: The Niger Explored

Records of the African Association, London, 1964.
Missions to the Niger, Hakluyt Society (4 vols), London, 1966.
The Discovery of the World, Albert Bettex, London, 1960.
West African Explorers, by C. Howard and J. Plumb, London, 1951.
Proceedings of the African Association, vols I and II, London, 1810.
The Social Life of Scotland in the 18th Century, by Henry Grey Graham, London, 1932.
View of the British Empire, especially of Scotland, by J. Knox, London, 1785.
Travels, by Mungo Park, London, 1954.
Mission to the Interior of Africa, by Mungo Park, London, 1815.
Mungo Park and the Niger, by Joseph Thomson, London, 1890.
Mungo Park, by W. H. Hewitt, London, 1923.
'The Death of Mungo Park at Bussa', by K. Lupton, *Nigeria Magazine*, Lagos, 1962.
The Banks Letters, edited by Warren R. Dawson, London, 1958.
Autobiography of Sir John Barrow, London, 1847.
Journal of Friedrich Hornemann's Travels, Hakluyt Society, London, 1964.

Chapter five: The Tripoli Route

Missions to the Niger, Hakluyt Society (4 vols), London, 1966.
Travels, by Captain G. F. Lyon, London, 1821.
Travels and Discoveries, by Oudney, Clapperton, and Denham, London, 1826.
Travels through Central Africa to Timbuktoo, by René Caillié, Paris, 1830.
Le Major A. Gordon Laing, by A. Bonnel de Mézières, Paris, 1912.
Travels in the Timanee, by Major A. G. Laing, London, 1825.
The Great Sahara, by James Wellard, London, 1964.
A Biographical Memoir of Clapperton, Oudney, and Laing, by T. Nelson, London, 1830.

Travels in the Great Desert of Sahara, by James Richardson, London, 1848.

The Barbary Regencies, by Lord Robert Grosvenor, London, 1830.

Letters to Richard Tully, London, 1957.

Annales tripolitaines, by L. C. Féraud, Paris, 1927.

Barbary Legend, by G. Fisher, London, 1957.

The Colonial Office in the Early 19th Century, by D. M. Young, London, 1961.

Chapter six: The Niger Conquered

Records of Captain Clapperton's Last Expedition, by Richard Lander, London, 1830.

Journal of a Second Expedition in the Interior of Africa, by the late Commander Clapperton, Philadelphia, 1829.

The Niger Journal of Richard and John Lander, edited by Robin Hallett, London, 1965.

'The Niger, the Manservant, and the Printer', by Morchard Bishop, *Cornhill Magazine*, No. 997, London, 1953.

The Travels of Richard and John Lander, by Robert Muish, London, 1837.

The Navy and the Slave Trade, by C. Lloyd, London, 1949.

Chapter seven: Traders and Missionaries

Narrative of an Expedition into the Interior of Africa by the River Niger (1832–1834), by MacGregor Laird and R. A. M. Oldfield, London, 1837.

A Narrative of the Expedition to the Niger River in 1841, by W. Allen and T. R. H. Thomson, London, 1848.

Trotter's Expedition to the River Niger, London, 1968.

Africa and the Victorians, by R. Robinson and J. Gallagher, London, 1961.

Borioboola-Gha, by H. J. Pedroza, Abadam, 1960.

Trade and Politics in the Niger Delta, by K. Onwuka Dike, Oxford, 1956.

The African Slave Trade and its Remedy, by T. Fowell Buxton, London, 1840.

BIBLIOGRAPHY

Medical History of the Expedition to the Niger, by J. O. Mac-
William, London, 1843.
Medicine and the Royal Navy, by C. Lloyd and J. L. S. Coulter,
London, 1961.

Chapter eight: Barth and Baikie

Travels and Discoveries in North and Central Africa, by Heinrich
Barth, London, 1858.
Africa and its Explorers, edited by Robert I. Rotberg, Harvard,
1970.
Britain, the Sahara, and the Western Soudan, by O. A. Boahen,
London, 1964.
*Narrative of an Exploring Voyage up the Rivers Kwora and Binue
in 1854*, London, 1856.
Voyage of the Dayspring, by A. C. G. Hastings, London, 1926.
The Fever Tree, by Duran-Reynals, Paris, 1960.

Chapter nine: The Niger Divided (I)

Les Pionniers du Soudan, by Jacques Meniaud, Paris, 1931.
Voyage à Segou, by Paul Soleillet, Paris, 1887.
Le Commerce dans le Golfe de Guinée, by Bernard Schnapper,
Paris, 1961.
Figures des conquestes coloniales, by E. F. Gautier, Paris,
1931.
Méthodes et doctrines coloniales de la France, by H. Deschamps,
Paris, 1960.
Le Partage de l'Afrique noire, by H. Brunschwig, Paris, 1961.
Mission au Niger, by General Gallieni, Paris, 1890.
Lettres du Soudan, by Charles Mangin, Paris, 1895.
Histoire de l'Afrique occidentale, by P. Chailley, Paris, 1935.
Faidherbe, by G. Hardy, Paris, 1938.
Deux missions françaises chez les Tuaregs, by F. Bernard, Paris,
1896.
L'Occupation de Tombouctou, by G. Bonnier, Paris, 1926.
Récits de la campagne du Niger, by E. Peroz, Paris, 1894.
Archinard et le Soudan, by E. Requin, Paris, 1921.

Instructions générales données de 1763 at 1870 aux gouverneurs et ordonnances des établissements français en Afrique occidentale, by Christian Schefer, Paris, 1927.

Prelude to the Partition of Africa, by John D. Hargreaves, New York, 1963.

The French in West Africa, by Alexander S. Kanya-Foster, Cambridge, 1965.

From French West Africa to Mali Federation, by William J. Foltz, New Haven, 1965.

Les Sénégalais au service de la France, by C. Duboc, Paris, 1939.

Histoire des colonies françaises, by G. Hanotaux, Paris, 1931.

La Force Noire, by General Mangin, Paris, 1910.

Samory le sanglant, by C. Duboc, Paris, 1937.

Les Villages de liberté en Afrique noire française, by Denise Bouche, Paris, 1968.

Mercenaires noirs, by Abdoulaye Ly, Paris, 1957.

The Colonial Office in the 19th Century, by D. M. Young, London, 1961.

Chapter ten: The Niger Divided (II)

French Enterprise in West Africa, by Lieutenant Hourst, Paris, 1896.

Service Africain, by Robert Delavignette, Paris, 1946.

The Benin Massacre, by Captain Boisragon, London, 1897.

The City of Blood, by R. H. Bacon, London, 1897.

A Short History of Benin, by J. U. Egharevba, London, 1963.

Trade and Politics in the Niger Delta, by K. Onwuka Dike, London, 1956.

La France et l'Angleterre, by Jean Darcy, Paris, 1904.

Sir George Goldie, by J. E. Flint, London, 1960.

Sir George Goldie, by Dorothy Wellesey, London, 1934.

Dahomey, Niger, Tuareg, by Major Toutée, Paris, 1897.

Le Niger, by Captain L'Enfant, Paris, 1903.

'England and France on the Niger, the race for Borgu', by F. D. Lugard, *Nineteenth Century,* XXXVII, 1895.

The Map of Africa by Treaty, by E. Hertslet, London, 1909.

Histoire des colonies françaises, by G. Hanotaux, Paris, 1923.

Lugard, the Years of Adventure, by M. Perham, London, 1956.

The Story of Nigeria, by Michael Crowder, London, 1967.

BIBLIOGRAPHY

The History of Nigeria, by Sir Alan Burns, London, 1969.

British Enterprise in Nigeria, by A. N. Cook, London, 1943.

Up the Niger, by A. F. M. Ferryman, London, 1892.

Campaigning on the Upper Niger, by C. F. S. Vandeleur, London, 1898.

Nigeria under British Rule, by M. M. Geary, London, 1927.

The Vision and the Need, by R. Faber, London, 1963.

The Wheel of Empire, by A. Sandison, London, 1964.

The Character of British Imperialism, by V. Harlow, London, 1965.

The Economic Revolution in British West Africa, by Allan McPhee, London, 1926.

Le Partage de l'Afrique, by G. Hanotaux, Paris, 1904.

The Life of Joseph Chamberlain, by J. L. Garvin, London, 1934.

The Life of Robert, Marquis of Salisbury, by G. Cecil, London, 1932.

History of French Colonial Policy, by S. H. Roberts, London, 1929.

INDEX

INDEX

Baikie, Dr W. B., 230–1, 232–4, 235–9, 272

al-Bakai, Sheikh, of Timbuctu, 226

Bamako, 29, 79, 95, 250, 252; French take, 253, 254

Bambara people, 40, 76, 77, 247, 249

Bambuk kingdom, Houghton in, 67, 68

Bandinel, J., Foreign Office clerk, 139, 141

Bani R., tributary of Niger, 32

Banks, Sir J., of African Association, 18, 19, 65, 103; and Houghton, 66, 67; imperialist speech by, 81–2; and Ledyard, 20–1; and Park, 68, 80

Barbot, J., trader, on Benin, 303

Barca Gana, general under el Kanemi, 125

Barrow, Sir J., of African Association and Admiralty, 104, 105, 106, 114, 127, 176–7; on Landers, 190

Barth, Heinrich, 32, 99, 102, 217–30

Bathurst, Lord, Colonial Secretary, 133, 135, 136, 137; on Barrow, 104; instructions given to explorers by, 110, 116, 124, 158

Beaufoy, H., of African Association, 18, 19, 21, 23

Bedford, Admiral Sir F., commanding in Bight of Benin, 297

Beecroft, Capt. J., consul, 230

bees, kill donkeys and horse, 92, 328

Bello, Sultan of Sokoto, 121; and Clapperton, 127, 128–9, 158–9, 161, 167–8, 169, 170; and Laing, 147–8; and Lander, 173; son of, and Barth, 224

Belloc, Hilaire, quoted, 300

Benin, Bight of: consul of, 230; mouth of Niger in, 131, 138, 176

Benin, kingdom and city of, 53, 58–9, 303; attacks Phillips's expedition, 304–6; reprisals on, 306–9

Benincasa, Grazioso, cartographer, 56

Benue R., tributary of Niger, 34, 184, 222; French on, 287

Berlin Conference (1884), 277–9

Betikuta, Anglo-French confrontation at, 314–15

Biafran war, 324, 330

Bida, Nupe capital: taken by Goldie, 300

Bismarck, O. von, 277–8, 279

Bissandogou, Samory's capital, 255, 258

Blockade Squadron of Royal Navy, 160, 173, 194, 203, 241

Blumenbach, J. F., ethnologist, 82

Boisragon, Capt. of Niger Constabulary, 304, 305–6, 308

Boiteux, Lieut., commanding French flotilla on Niger, 261, 262

Bonaparte, Napoleon, 84, 86

Bondou, King of, 67, 73–4

Bongola, freed slave with Laing, 144, 149, 150–1, 152

Bonnel de Mézières, A., investigates killing of Laing, 151, 154

Bonnier, Lt-Col., commander in French Sudan, 261, 262, 263

Bonny, delta port, 194, 272

Borgnis-Desbordes, Lt-Col., campaigns of, 251, 252, 253–4, 266, 267

Borgu kingdom: French and British competition for, 290–3, 313

Bornu kingdom, 106, 107, 114, 115, 121, 134; list of kings of, 218; at war with Sokoto, 167, 168, 169, 170

boundary commissions, 316–17

Bourchier, Lieut., consul at Lokoja, 238

Boy, King of Brass, 186–9, 197

Bozo people, Niger fishermen of Egyptian origin, 30–1, 36

Brass, coastal city-state, 186, 194, 244; Ockiah, King of, 272; people of, attack Akassa, 244, 295–6

Bretonnet, Lieut., occupies Bussa, 301–2, 309

INDEX

INDEX

INDEX

Galam, on Senegal R., 61

Galibert, Admiral, of French Colonial Office, 255

Galliéni, General J. S., campaigns of, 249–51, 269

Gama, Vasco da, 60

Gambia R., 61, 66, 92

game park, on Niger, 34

Gandu, Goldie obtains treaty with Emir of, 285

Gao, on Niger, 34, 48, 99; ferry at, 328

Garama, Roman remains at, 117

George IV, 114, 129, 134, 169

Ghadames, desert city, 141, 142

Ghana empire, 46

Ghat, oasis of, 118

Gibbon, Edward, reads al-Idrisi, 43–4

gin, as currency, 271

Glover, Lieut. J., with Baikie, 101, 235, 236

Gobir, Hausa, kingdom, 220

gold, West African, 46, 48, 50, 52, 59–60, 67

Goldie, Sir George (Taubman), 273–5; on the Niger, 275–85; and the French, 287, 288, 289, 290, 294; campaigns against Nupe and Ilorin, 299–302, 309; and delta states, 297; government and, 298, 310–11, 312, 313, 317, 318, 319–22

Gomes, Fernao, Portuguese merchant and explorer, 57–8

Goree Island, 66, 89, 90, 242

Gouraud, Capt., defeats Samory, 264–5

Granville, Lord, Foreign Secretary, 277

Gray, Capt. W., with Colonial Office expedition, 104

Grodet, French governor, 262

groundnuts, trade in, 247

gums, trade in, 241, 281

gunboats on Niger: British, 271, 312; French, 254, 277, 282

el Hadj Omar, 244, 245, 247

Hamilton, Lt-Col., commands expedition against Benin, 306

Hammadi, Fulani leader, 226

Hanotaux, Gabriel, French Foreign Minister, 309, 312, 314, 316, 327

Hausa language, 218, 236

Hausa troops, with British, 291, 292, 314

Hawkins, Sir John, 61

Henry the Navigator, Prince of Portugal, 52, 54

Herodotus, on Africa, 42, 45

Hesiod, quoted, 26

hippopotamus, 31, 33, 99, 183, 225; tame, 50

Hobart, Lord, Colonial Secretary, 88

Hoenigsberg, J., German trader: R. Niger Co. and, 282–3

Holland Jacques, trading firm, 273, 275

Holle, Paul, defender of Medina, 245

Horace, on Africa, 37

Hornemann, Friedrich, 82–7, 102

Houghton, Daniel, 66–7, 68, 102

Hourst, Lieut. E., voyages down Niger, 228, 282

Houtson, trader, as guide to Clapperton, 163, 165

human sacrifice, 59, 174–5, 204, 210; in Benin, 303, 307, 308

Humbert, Lt-Col. G., commander against Samory, 259

Ibn Batuta, traveller, 49

Ibn Khaldoun, historian, 44, 46

Ibo people, 185; Obi of, 186, 197–8, 208–9

Ibo town, 197, 208

Idah, on Niger, 198, 199, 200, 209; Attah of, 209–10

al-Idrisi, geographer, 43, 48, 49

Ilorin emirate, Goldie defeats, 299, 301

imperialism, 81–2, 104, 167, 326; accidental, 195; French, 248–9

imprisonment of explorers: Barth, 222; Lander, 186–7; Park, 75

In Salah (Algeria), 142, 143

indirect rule, 290, 300–1; Lugard's principle of, 322, 323

Isaaco, guide to Park, 92, 94, 97, 98

345

INDEX

INDEX

Timbuctu, 33–4, 48, 50–1, 140; Barth in, 218, 225–6; Caillié in, 156–7; French in, 263, 288, 329; Laing in, 146–9; requests French protection against Tuaregs, 261

tin: mining for, 38; trade in, 281

Tirailleurs Sénégalais, 247, 314

Toole, E., assistant to Denham, 132

Tosaye gorges, 34, 227

Toutée, Maj. G., 293: boundary commissioner, 317

trade with West Africa, 192–3

trading posts, 195, 238, 271

treaties with African chiefs, 203, 204–5, 208, 209; of French, 250, 288, 289, 290, 292, 293; of trading firms, 271, 280, 290, 292

tribal society, 40, 323–4

Tripoli, 106–8, 153

Tristo, Nuno, Portuguese explorer, 57

Trotter, Capt. D. H., with Buxton's expedition, 206, 207, 208, 212, 213, 214, 215

Tuareg people, 33, 34, 36, 51, 112; Ajjer, at Ghat oasis, 118; Ahagger, attack Laing, 144; defeat Bonnier's party, 262–3; French actions against, 264; massacre Flatters' party, 249; and Park, 97, 99: as pirates on Niger, 156: plunder caravans, 141, 143: rescue Barth, 220; Timbuctu asks for French protection against, 261

Tuckey, Capt. J. K., leads Admiralty-sponsored expedition, 104–5

Turner, General, on Laing, 137

Tyrwhitt, J., vice-consul at Kakawa, 132–3

United African Company, 275

Victoria, Queen, 239

Vogel, botanist, 207, 214

Vogel, Dr Edward, astronomer, 227–8

Voltaire, on Scotland, 70

Waddington, M., French ambassador in London, 285, 286

Wallace, W., agent of R. Niger Co., 289

Walli, King of, 73

Ward, Dr Henri, with Mizon, 288

Warrington, Emma, married to Laing, 138–9, 140; second marriage and death of, 154

Warrington, Frederick, consul in Tripoli, 219

Warrington, Hanmer, consul in Tripoli, 107, 108–11, 114, 116, 118, 119, 124, 132, 133, 138, 140, 152–4

Webb, Lieut. W. H., fetches survivors of model farm, 214

Wellesey, Dorothy, on Goldie, 273–5, 320–1

West African Frontier Force, 321

West India Regiment: men from, with Samory, 259

West Indies, slave trade to, 61, 159, 241

Whydah, port, 158, 163

Wilberforce, William, 159

Willcocks, J., with Lugard, 314, 315

Windham, Richard, at Benin, 59

women, African: explorers and, 165–6, 173, 236

Wood, Thomas, son-in-law of Warrington, 154

Yauri, 99, 100, 101, 165: Lander in, 182; Sultan of, 181

yellow fever, 202, 252, 259

Yola, on Benue R., 287, 288, 289

Yoruba people, 164, 173

Zaria, Emir of, 173

Zuma, rich widow, 166, 180–1

Zurara, chronicler, 53

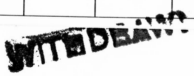